ESTHER IN ANCIENT JEWISH THOUGHT

The book of Esther was a conscious reaction to much of the conventional wisdom of its day, challenging beliefs regarding the Jerusalem Temple, the land of Israel, Jewish law, and even God. Aaron Koller identifies Esther as primarily a political work, and shows that early reactions ranged from ignoring the book to "rewriting" Esther in order to correct its perceived flaws. But few biblical books have been read in such different ways, and the vast quantity of Esther-interpretation in rabbinic literature indicates a conscious effort by the Rabbis to present Esther as a story of faith and traditionalism, and bring it into the fold of the grand biblical narrative. Koller situates Esther, and its many interpretations, within the intellectual and political contexts of Ancient Judaism, and discusses its controversial themes. His innovative line of inquiry will be of great interest to students and scholars of Bible and Jewish studies.

AARON KOLLER is Associate Professor of Near Eastern and Jewish Studies at Yeshiva University. He is the author of *The Semantic Field of Cutting Tools in Biblical Hebrew* (2012).

ESTHER IN
ANCIENT JEWISH THOUGHT

AARON KOLLER

CAMBRIDGE
UNIVERSITY PRESS

CAMBRIDGE
UNIVERSITY PRESS

University Printing House, Cambridge CB2 8BS, United Kingdom

Published in the United States of America by Cambridge University Press, New York

Cambridge University Press is part of the University of Cambridge.

It furthers the University's mission by disseminating knowledge in the pursuit of education, learning, and research at the highest international levels of excellence.

www.cambridge.org
Information on this title: www.cambridge.org/9781107048355

First published 2014

Printed in the United Kingdom by CPI Group Ltd, Croydon CR0 4YY

A catalogue record for this publication is available from the British Library

Library of Congress Cataloguing in Publication data
Koller, Aaron J., 1978–
Esther in ancient Jewish thought / Aaron Koller.
pages cm
Includes bibliographical references and index.
ISBN 978-1-107-04835-5
1. Esther, Queen of Persia.   2. Bible. Esther – Criticism, interpretation, etc.,
Jewish.   3. Rabbinical literature – History and criticism.   I. Title.
BS580.E8K65   2014
222′.90609–dc23
2013032790

ISBN 978-1-107-04835-5 Hardback

Contents

Figure

Tables

Acknowledgments

It gives me much pride to be able to say that this book emerged directly from teaching an undergraduate class on the book of Esther. In the context of preparing that class, certain patterns in the early reception history of Esther began to seem clear to me. After the semester, I wrote what I thought would be a short paper showing that the reactions to Esther in Hellenistic and Roman times were overwhelmingly negative.

Moshe Bernstein, my first teacher in the intellectual history of that era, was kind enough to read that paper. Besides his usual detailed critical comments, he made the suggestion to unpack some of the inordinately dense footnotes I had included, include all the rabbinic material I repeatedly had written that space precluded treatment of, and see if there wasn't a book here. It took a few more years of research and thinking, but I hope the present work justifies his intuition. At a much later stage, Moshe read a complete draft of the book, saving me from numerous errors, adding some of his own insights, and generally improving the book.

Three talented undergraduate students later contributed their time and energies to improving the book: Mark Glass, Jina Davidovich, and Emmanuel Sanders all reviewed parts of the manuscript, checked the original texts, and made numerous suggestions, large and small, which improved the finished product. Two other students, Tuvia Tendler and Yosef Kornbluth, caught typographical and other errors, and contributed to a better final product.

I am fortunate to work in an institution that has, perhaps, the best Jewish Studies faculty in North America, and a stellar faculty in other departments, as well. My colleagues, especially in fields close to my own, have always been founts of information, inspiration, and suggestions, and their own fascinating work ensures that our intellectual lives are rich and always exciting. I do not consider myself to be an expert on the Second Temple period in Jewish history, and I would have been even more reluctant than I am to write about that field were it not for the support and criticisms of colleagues. Three colleagues – who happen also to be good friends – provided feedback and encouragement: Ari Mermelstein and Joseph Angel, from within Yeshiva University, and Michael Tzvi Novick, whom we'd like to claim (we did, after all, study ancient Hebrew phonetics together in a seminar at Yeshiva University many years ago), but who more properly belongs to Notre Dame. Without these readers, the book would be a far inferior work to what it is now.

Among my senior colleagues, Larry Schiffman was very helpful in navigating the pragmatics of publishing this book. Barry Eichler, my mentor in two different schools and dean of Yeshiva College for the past four years, has been a source of guidance and support in countless ways. Richie Steiner tolerated my excursion into this field, and has patiently encouraged me to now get back to "real" work.

I was fortunate that Eric Schmidt of the University of California Press read a draft of this book with interest and appreciation. A long preliminary conversation with Eric led me to restructure the book in ways which – once he pointed them out – seemed intuitive and which have greatly improved the presentation, and also gave me an appreciation for what a good editor can do for a book. At Cambridge University Press, Laura Morris was just such an editor, and was kind and encouraging in addition. Anna Lowe shepherded the book through its final stages with skill.

In a more personal vein, my parents have helped and supported me in the obvious ways in which parents do such things, even from a distance, even when their children are to some extent grown up – with love, links, and cookies. Beyond such treasured tokens, though, they have served for me as models as Jews who have lived in multiple worlds, grappling with the advantages of diaspora and the pull of the homeland. As much as this book is meaningful, I hope it is meaningful to them. My in-laws, from much closer proximity, have helped out in all sorts of ways, emotional and practical. We are very lucky that our lives and interests are so intertwined and overlapping, and this makes everything more enjoyable and more rewarding.

Dalya and Shachar have always been willing interlocutors in my thinking about Esther, and it is through them that the relevance and potential power of ancient texts becomes clear to me. The story of Esther is one of many stories that we have shared, and I hope we have many more to share in the coming years. Finally, my wife Shira, my one true queen, has lived through the process of reading and writing about Esther for years. Perhaps she is just relieved that this book is about something other than tools, but her genuine passion for the subject matter, her clear thinking, and her guidance have refined the analyses offered here. More significantly, a story about a woman who knows how to deploy her sparkling personality, dazzling interpersonal skills, penetrating intellect, and profound beauty in the service of the greater good can only be about Shira. It is to her, with love, that this is dedicated.

Abbreviations

AB	Anchor Bible
ABD	David Noel Freedman, *Anchor Bible Dictionary* (New York: Doubleday, 1992)
ANRW	*Aufstieg und Niedergang der römischen Welt*
AT	Alpha Text
BN	*Biblische Notizen*
BZAW	Beihefte zur Zeitschrift für die alttestamentliche Wissenschaft
CBQ	*Catholic Biblical Quarterly*
CBQMS	Catholic Biblical Quarterly Monograph Series
CEJL	Commentaries on Early Jewish Literature
Cowley	A. E. Cowley, *Aramaic Papyri of the Fifth Century* B.C. (Oxford University Press, 1923)
CRINT	Compendia rerum Iudaicarum ad Novum Testamentum
DSD	*Dead Sea Discoveries*
HAR	*Hebrew Annual Review*
HSS	Harvard Semitic Studies
HTR	*Harvard Theological Review*
HUCA	*Hebrew Union College Annual*
JAJ	*Journal of Ancient Judaism*
JANES	*Journal of the Ancient Near Eastern Society*
JAOS	*Journal of the American Oriental Society*
JBL	*Journal of Biblical Literature*
JJS	*Journal of Jewish Studies*
JNES	*Journal of Near Eastern Studies*
JPS	Jewish Publication Society
JQR	*Jewish Quarterly Review*
JRS	*Journal of Roman Studies*
JSIJ	*Jewish Studies: An Internet Journal*

JSJ	*Journal for the Study of Judaism*
JSOT	*Journal for the Study of the Old Testament*
JSP	*Journal for the Study of the Pseudepigrapha*
JSQ	*Jewish Studies Quarterly*
JTS	*Journal of Theological Studies*
LXX	Septuagint
MMT	Miqṣat Maʿasē ha-Torah
MT	Masoretic Text
PAAJR	*Proceedings of the American Academy for Jewish Research*
RB	*Revue Biblique*
REJ	*Revue des Études Juives*
SBL	Society of Biblical Literature
SBLDS	Society of Biblical Literature Dissertation Series
STDJ	Studies on the Texts of the Desert of Judah
TAD	Ada Yardeni and Bezalel Porten, *Textbook of Aramaic Documents from Ancient Egypt* (Winona Lake, IN: distributed by Eisenbrauns, 1986)
TSAJ	Texte und Studien zum antiken Judentum
VT	*Vetus Testamentum*
ZAW	*Zeitschrift für die alttestamentliche Wissenschaft*

Introduction

Few biblical books are at the same time as familiar as Esther and have been read in such thoroughly different ways. The aim of this book is to recover how the book of Esther was read by its first readers, and perhaps even how it was intended by its author, by situating it within Jewish thought regarding the Persian Empire. Seeing the contours of the thought current prior to the writing of Esther allows us to see how the book reacts to those ideas. Tracing the contours of this thought in the centuries following the writing of Esther allows us to understand the ancient reactions to the book. The basic thesis of the present book is that Esther, first and foremost, is a work of politics. The author peopled his narrative with historical personages, and deployed sophisticated literary techniques and structures, but these are not utilized for their own sake. Instead, they are pressed into service to tell a story which explores diaspora life and personal identity.

Midway through the Persian Empire, Jews throughout the realm were engaged in introspection and debate regarding their own position in the world in which they found themselves. To what extent had the world changed? Were the Persians just another foreign overlord, like the Assyrians and Babylonians before them, or did the stability of the Persian Empire reflect a new world order? Could one still hope for Jewish autonomy in one's own land, or were such notions relics of a past era? How did one define what it meant to be a good Jew in such conditions, and had the very terms of that question been altered by life in unending exile? On these and other questions central to Jewish identity and existence, Esther staked out provocative and daring positions.

The conceptual heart of the present book is Part 3, Chapters 9 through 12, which chronicles early reactions to the book of Esther from Hellenistic and Roman times. These reactions are generally oblique. To find them, a wide range of Jewish texts in Greek, Hebrew, and Aramaic, all of which have something to say about the book of Esther, are surveyed. In some cases, such as the Additions to Esther, the relationship to the book is explicit; in other cases, such as the story of Judith, the Genesis Apocryphon from Qumran, and a tale about Alexander Janneus preserved in later sources, the relationship is implicit. I argue that all of the sources from this period reflect a negative attitude toward the book of Esther.

The most notable counter-example to this generalization is a later source: the synagogue paintings at Dura Europos, which include the story of Esther, front and center in the Jews' house of worship. This source, from third-century Syria, is both later than the other sources discussed and the only evidence of the attitude toward Esther current among Jews in the eastern Diaspora. Both of these distinctions make a difference.

It is argued that a negative attitude toward Esther was the prevalent one in Palestine throughout the time of the Second Temple, but that contemporary diaspora Jews may have thought about the book very differently. As time went on, however, attitudes within Jewish society changed, reflecting developments within Jewish political thought, itself reflecting to a large extent the dynamics of actual politics. Many of the reasons that Palestinian Jews had to condemn the book vanished by the end of the first century CE. As a result of long processes, and especially of the trauma of the destruction of the Temple, the formerly stark divisions between "homeland" and "diaspora" dissipated, and Esther became a book beloved by Jews everywhere.

The claim that Jews in Second Temple times overwhelmingly denounced, disparaged, or disregarded Esther leads naturally to two further avenues of inquiry. The first is to explore whether the ideologically opposition evoked by the book was expected by the author of Esther. I contend, in the first two parts of the book, that the provocation represented by Esther was entirely deliberate. Part 1, consisting of Chapters 1 through 4, sets the stage by attempting to reconstruct the contours of "conventional wisdom" regarding issues of Jewish political thought and identity in early Second Temple times. Drawing on the various biblical books from the sixth and fifth centuries – from the time of the Neo-Babylonian and Persian Empires – I trace the expectations, beliefs, and opinions which seem to have been widespread, especially on issues of politics, religion, and identity.

On a long list of issues, the author of Esther opposes the conventional wisdom. Part 2, Chapters 5 through 8, attempts to establish just what the book of Esther asserts, politically and ideologically. It seems clear, on close inspection, that the author denies the expectations of a second exodus which will bring an end to the exile; he denies the relevance of the Davidic dynasty; he denies the centrality of Jerusalem and of the province of Judea. The king of Persia, far from being God's emissary, is depicted in starkly negative terms, and the law of the land is absurd. All of this opposed, in dramatic fashion, much of what the other Jewish texts of the era propound. It can be concluded that this opposition was intentional, and was likely the original purpose of the book's composition.

Once it is argued that the book of Esther intentionally entered the political arena, the negative reactions to the book traced in Part 3 of this book turn out to be unsurprising, and in fact predictable. Whereas Esther champions a hero who intermarried and lives her life in the Persian palace, many of the Jews in Palestine would have reviled such a character. She would have been condemned for compromising her religion and culture, and the fact that she used her status to save her kinsmen would not persuade these readers otherwise. Surely if she had stood her ground and refused to enter into such a compromised position – perhaps even at the cost of her own life – God would have effected a miraculous salvation for his people.

While the first area of research took the reactions to Esther and looked backward in time, to investigate the motivations for the book to begin with, the second avenue opened is the later history of the book's interpretation. In particular, the rabbinic reactions to the book of Esther can now be seen in a richer and more complex context. There is more explicit treatment of Esther within the corpus of rabbinic literature than of any other biblical book except for Genesis. Many studies have illuminated individual details of the Rabbis' treatment of the book. Part 4 of this book, consisting of Chapters 13 through 15, attempts to sift and organize dozens of individual comments in order to see the patterns in the rabbinic approaches to Esther as a whole.

The Rabbis were faced with all of the same problems with the book that their counterparts faced in Hellenistic and Roman times. They had an additional handicap, however, in that the book was already by their time canonical, and therefore neither suppression nor heavy-handed editing was a viable option for them in dealing with the book. Instead, they turn to interpretation to bring Esther in line with conventional biblical and rabbinic thinking. Drawing on other biblical texts, such as Daniel, much of Esther is re-read in insightful and far-reaching ways.

The investigation carried out here surveys the rabbinic texts as a whole, but also searches for differing attitudes toward Esther within these sprawling corpora. Part 3 helps elucidate the findings here, as well, since on the whole, few consistent differences are found between earlier and later rabbinic sources, or between sources of Palestinian and Babylonian provenance. There are a number of specific motifs whose origins can be isolated, but the general themes appear to be common throughout rabbinic literature.

In the Rabbis' hands, Esther observes the laws of kashrut, Shabbat, and menstrual purity. The Jews were punished for their failure to scrupulously observe many of the laws, but the piety of Mordecai and Esther moved God and others in heaven to mobilize on the Jews' behalf. Esther enabled the reconstruction of the Second Temple. Xerxes took his place in the long list of foreign kings who believed themselves to be more powerful than God; like his royal predecessors, Xerxes was brought low by the biblical story as read by the Rabbis. He is depicted as a pale image of Solomon, much as his palace is depicted as a pale image of the Temple in Jerusalem, and Susa itself is depicted as a pale image of Jerusalem.

All of this is part of a large-scale and sustained effort on the part of the Rabbis to rid Esther of the parts of the story which are troubling or challenging, and to transform the story into a conventional biblical story. Elements strikingly absent from the biblical book itself, such as sin and punishment, Jewish law, prayer, providence, and, most importantly, God, are reintroduced into the story. Through these techniques, Esther has been converted into an eloquent statement of orthodox theology, rather than the trenchant and penetrating challenge to the conventional wisdom it once was.

PART I

The provocation
Conventional wisdom in early Second Temple Judaism

CHAPTER I

Setting the stage
The theological challenge of political stability

1. Introduction

As the Persian Empire entered its second century of rule, the Jews of Persia struggled with difficult questions regarding their own identities and their positions within Persian and Jewish societies. Since Cyrus had brought the Babylonian Empire under Persian control in 539, and in one fell swoop gained control over nearly all the lands in which Jews were resident, Jews had the option of moving "back" to Jerusalem and its environs, to the Persian province of Yehud.[1] Some, indeed, had taken the opportunity, and since the late sixth century BCE there had been a community in Jerusalem, centered on the Second Temple. For many of the Jews, however, the idea of moving "back" seemed artificial. They, after all, had never seen Yehud, or any land other than where they lived now. Their ancestors had been exiled from that land in the early sixth century, through a series of events that left an indelible imprint on their national and political consciousness. This was family lore, though, not a central part of their identity.[2]

---

[1] The degree to which Cyrus supported the return of the Jews to Yehud, as opposed to simply allowing it, is debated: the book of Ezra claims that those returning received imperial financial support for the construction of a temple, but some modern scholars are skeptical. See, for example, Amélie Kuhrt, "The Cyrus Cylinder and Achaemenid Imperial Policy," *JSOT* 25 (1983), 83–97, and the discussion in Lester L. Grabbe, "Biblical Historiography in the Persian Period: Or, How the Jews Took Over the Empire," in Steven W. Holloway (ed.), *Orientalism, Assyriology and the Bible*, Hebrew Bible Monographs 10 (Sheffield Phoenix Press, 2006), 400–14.

[2] The terminological conundrum regarding the "Jews" is now a well-studied question. Cynthia Baker, "A 'Jew' by Any Other Name?," *JAJ* 2 (2011), 153–80 provides a thorough and insightful discussion of the major contemporary scholarly views (Cohen, Blenkinsopp, Mason, and Brettler). I refer to these people as "Jews" throughout, in a manner that accords with Brettler's arguments. This would also be acceptable to Blenkinsopp, since the discussion here relates to the Persian period and not earlier. See Marc Zvi Brettler, "Judaism in the Hebrew Bible? The Transition from Ancient Israelite Religion to Judaism," *CBQ* 61 (1999), 429–47, and Joseph Blenkinsopp, *Judaism, the First Phase: The Place of Ezra and Nehemiah in the Origins of Judaism* (Grand Rapids, MI: Eerdmans, 2009). For a more fundamental defense of the translation of *yehudim* of Esther as "Jews," see Anne-Marie Wetter, "How Jewish is

It was now more than a century after Cyrus. Not a person alive remembered a time when the Persians were not in control. As this reality became less traumatic and more "normal," the theological challenge it presented became more difficult. In centuries past, prophets had foretold an exile, and so the idea of life outside of a national homeland did not present much in the way of theological problems. Of course, exile had been predicted as a punishment, and so the experience provoked much soul-searching and self-interrogation. "What had we done wrong?" asked the Jews. "Has God forsaken us? Are we no longer His chosen people?"[3] These questions swirled as the Jews became accustomed to living as a minority, alongside other minorities, in the midst of a great empire. The great prophets Jeremiah and Ezekiel had provided intellectual and theological responses to these questions.[4] Other Israelites, their voices preserved in psalms and laments, provided other responses, less abstract and more experiential.

Jews made their peace with the changed reality. They worked hard to forge an identity in exile that would allow them both to thrive in their wider societies and to retain their loyalties as Jews.[5] Some lived in voluntarily segregated areas, such as the town of al-Yahūdu, "the town of the Judeans," near Nippur.[6] Most, however, tried to manage multiple loyalties, and as a

Esther? Or: How is Esther Jewish? Tracing Ethnic and Religious Identity in a Diaspora Narrative," *ZAW* 123 (2011), 596–603, and see also Moshe Bar-Asher, "Il y avait à Suse un homme juif – איש יהודי היה בשושן הבירה," *REJ* 161 (2002), 227–31.

[3] The responses to these questions were most thoroughly studied by Dalit Rom-Shiloni, אלהים בעידן של חורבן וגלויות: תיאולוגיה תנ"כית (Jerusalem: Magnes, 2009).

[4] See the studies of Dalit Rom-Shiloni for insightful analysis of the prophetic and other responses: "Ezekiel as the Voice of the Exiles and Constructor of Exilic Ideology," *HUCA* 76 (2005), 1–45; "Deuteronomic Concepts of Exile Interpreted in Jeremiah and Ezekiel," in Chaim Cohen, Victor Hurowitz, Avi Hurvitz, Yochanan Muffs, Baruch Schwartz, and Jeffrey Tigay (eds.), *Birkat Shalom: Studies in the Bible, Ancient Near Eastern Literature, and Postbiblical Judaism Presented to Shalom M. Paul on the Occasion of his Seventieth Birthday* (Winona Lake, IN: Eisenbrauns, 2008), 101–23. See also William M. Schniedewind, "'Are We His People or Not?' Biblical Interpretation during Crisis," *Biblica*, 76 (1995), 540–50, on the responses found in some of the psalms.

[5] For discussions of how the Judeans preserved their identity/identities in the eastern Diaspora, see Israel Eph'al, "The Western Minorities in Babylonia in the 6th–5th Centuries BC: Maintenance and Cohesion," *Orientalia*, 47 (1978), 74–90, and Bustenay Oded, "The Judean Exiles in Babylonia: Survival Strategy of an Ethnic Minority," in Menahem Mor, Jack Pastor, Israel Ronen, and Yakov Ashenazi (eds.), *For Uriel: Studies in the History of Israel in Antiquity Presented to Professor Uriel Rappaport* (Jerusalem: Zalman Shazar Center for Jewish History, 2005), 53*–76*.

[6] F. Joannès and André Lemaire, "Trois tablettes cunéiformes à onomastique ouest-sémitique (collection Sh. Moussaïeff) (Pls. I–II)," *Transeuphratène*, 17 (1999), 17–34; Ran Zadok, *The Earliest Diaspora: Israelites and Judeans in Pre-Hellenistic Mesopotamia*, Publications of the Diaspora Research Institute 151 (Tel Aviv: Diaspora Research Institute of Tel Aviv University, 2002), 33–35; Laurie Pearce, "New Evidence for Judaeans in Babylonia," in Oded Lipschits and Manfred Oeming (eds.), *Judah and the Judaeans in the Persian Period* (Winona Lake, IN: Eisenbrauns, 2006), 399–411; W. G. Lambert, "A Document from a Community of Exiles in Babylonia," in Meir Lubetski (ed.), *New Seals and Inscriptions: Hebrew, Idumean, and Cuneiform* (Sheffield: Phoenix, 2007), 201–05.

community, the Jews were successful at this. Jews occupied positions in the bureaucracy, usually lowly ones, but occasionally rising to impressive heights.[7] These very efforts, which made life in the Diaspora less challenging, caused the theological challenge to grow. It dawned on people slowly, until it became a roaring undercurrent of Jewish thought. The prophets of centuries past had always promised that exile would be a temporary state of affairs. The Jews would be punished, the conquering nation would exhaust its power, and then the new world order would crumble. Seventy years, Jeremiah had said. Others spoke in less specific terms. No one had spoken of exile as an irrevocably changed reality.

2. Hopes for a second exodus

The prophets had even spoken of a second exodus from Babylonia; indeed, "the idea is a common one in the literature of the period."[8] Interestingly, this was a reversal of the use to which the Exodus had been put in previous decades. Both Jeremiah and Ezekiel had utilized the imagery of the Exodus with a vicious twist. Jeremiah prophesied: "I shall fight with you, [says the Lord,] with an outstretched hand and a strong arm, and with fury and wrath, and with great anger, and I shall strike (*ve-hikkēti*) the inhabitants of this city [Jerusalem] – human and animal! They shall die in a great plague."[9] Equally ominously, Ezekiel foretold: "I will take you out (*ve-hotzēti*) of [Jerusalem] and put you into the hands of strangers, and I will execute judgments (*shefātīm*) on you."[10] Jeremiah was clearly playing on the Exodus narrative: in Egypt, too, God said, "I will strike (*ve-hikkēti*) all the firstborns in the land of Egypt, from human to animal," and of course, there, too, a plague (*dever*) had struck.[11] Ezekiel, as well, had Exodus on his mind: two of his terms, "I will take you out" and "judgments" are particularly

[7] Daniel L. Smith-Christopher, "Prayers and Dreams: Power and Diaspora Identities in the Social Setting of the Daniel Tales," in John J. Collins and Peter W. Flint (eds.), *The Book of Daniel: Composition and Reception, VT* Suppl. 83.1 (Leiden: Brill, 2001), 278.

[8] Sara Japhet, "People and Land in the Restoration Period," in Georg Strecker (ed.), *Das Land Israel in biblischer Zeit* (Göttingen: Vandenhoeck & Ruprecht, 1983), 03–125, reprinted in her *From the Rivers of Babylon to the Highlands of Judah: Collected Studies on the Restoration Period* (Winona Lake, IN: Eisenbrauns, 2006), 112. See also the discussion and references in Rom-Shiloni, "Deuteronomic Concepts of Exile Interpreted in Jeremiah and Ezekiel," 118.

[9] Jeremiah 21:5–6. [10] Ezekiel 11:9.

[11] For these elements, see Exodus 12:12 and 9:1–7. Dalit Rom-Shiloni, "Facing Destruction and Exile: Inner-Biblical Exegesis in Jeremiah and Ezekiel," *ZAW* 117 (2005), 189–205, esp. 192–94, sensitively analyzes the dynamics of this reuse of the Exodus vocabulary.

reminiscent of the earlier narrative.[12] For example, in Egypt God had said, "I will take you out from under the burdens of Egypt; I will save you from their labor; I will redeem you with an outstretched arm and with great judgments."[13]

The shocking detail in these prophecies, of course, was who was targeted in them. In the Exodus narratives, the object of the "judgments" is the Egyptians, and the Israelites are to be removed *from* Egypt to march *to* Israel and Jerusalem. In Ezekiel, the reverse is foretold: Israel themselves will be subjected to the judgments, and they were be removed *from* Jerusalem.

The prophets who worked after the exile, on the other hand, reversed this motif once again, and began to speak of a second exodus much more similar to the original one. This re-reversal occurs within Ezekiel himself. Once the Jews are in exile, he foretells another, more dramatic enactment of the Exodus:

> Therefore say to the House of Israel, "Thus said the Lord God: Will you defile yourselves in the path of your ancestors, and whore after their detestations? . . . As I live – declares the Lord God – I will reign over you with a strong hand, with an outstretched arm, with outpoured fury! I will take you out of the nations, and gather you from the lands in which you are scattered, with a strong hand, with an outstretched arm, with outpoured fury. I will bring you to the desert of the nations, and there I will enter into judgment with you, face to face. *Just as I entered into judgment with your ancestors in the desert of the land of Egypt*, so will I enter into judgment with you!" – thus speaks the Lord God. "I will pass you under the staff and I will bring you under the bond of the covenant; I will remove the rebels and sinners against me from among you: I will take them out from the land in which they are dwelling, but they will not arrive at the land of Israel, and you will know that I am the Lord . . . when I take you out from the nations and gather you from the lands in which you are scattered, and I will be sanctified there in the eyes of the nations. You will know that I am the Lord when I bring you to the land of Israel, to the land which I swore to give to your ancestors."[14]

---

[12] For "I will/did take out," see also Exodus 7:5; 12:17; 29:46; 32:11; and of course the Decalogue (Exodus 20), "I am the Lord God who *took you out* of the land of Egypt . . ." For "judgments," see also 12:12..

[13] Exodus 6:6; cf. also 7:4 See the discussion in Michael Fishbane, *Biblical Interpretation in Ancient Israel* (Oxford University Press, 1985), 366–67, and Rom-Shiloni, "Facing Destruction and Exile," 202. Another reference to the Exodus early in Ezekiel may be the "mark" (*tāw*) on the foreheads of those to be saved in Ezekiel 9:4–6; see the suggestive remarks of R. David Qimḥi *ad loc.*, as well as the highly relevant Samaritan practice described in Bernard M. Levinson, *Deuteronomy and the Hermeneutics of Legal Innovation* (New York and Oxford: Oxford University Press, 1997), 58 n. 15, and the Greek evidence discussed in John W. Olley, "Ezekiel LXX and Exodus Comparisons," *VT* 59 (2009), 116–19.

[14] Ezekiel 20:30–42. Parts of this passage are closely paralleled in Psalm 106:26–27. For comments on this relationship and its implications, see Tzvi Novick, "Law and Loss: Response to Catastrophe in Numbers 15," *HTR* 101 (2008), 10.

The underlined phrases are again strikingly reminiscent of passages from the Exodus narrative. In case the allusions were lost on any particularly obtuse readers, Ezekiel makes the referent clear: "Just as I entered into judgment with your ancestors in the desert of the land of Egypt . . ." The allusions cluster around a particular passage in Exodus.[15] One verse from this passage has already been mentioned, but the wider context can now be cited in full:

> God spoke to Moses and said to him, "I am the Lord. I appeared to Abraham, to Isaac, and to Jacob as El Shaddai, but with my name YHWH I did not become known to them. I also established My covenant with them, to give them the land of Canaan, the land in which they have dwelled, where they sojourned, and I have now heard the groaning of the Israelites, whom the Egyptians are enslaving, and I have remembered My covenant. Therefore say to the Israelites: "I am the Lord! I will take you out from under the burdens of Egypt; I will save you from their labor; I will redeem you with an outstretched arm and with great judgments. I will take you to be my people, and I will be your God. You shall know that I am the Lord, your God, who brings you out from under the forced labors of the Egyptians. I will bring you to the land which I swore to give to your ancestors – to Abraham, to Isaac, and to Jacob – and I will give it to you as a heritage; I am the Lord."

The reference to the "outstretched arm" (*zerōaʿ netūyāh*) particularly binds these two texts; the phrase occurs only in this passage in Exodus and in later biblical references to the Exodus.[16] The "outstretched arm" has been coupled with a phrase which is common in the Exodus narrative: "a strong arm."[17] To these has now been added also "poured-out wrath" (*ḥēmāh*

---

[15] Exodus 6:2–8. The close connection was observed by Johan Lust, "Exodus 6,2–8 and Ezekiel," in Marc Vervenne (eds.), *Studies in the Book of Exodus: Redaction, Reception, Interpretation* (Leuven: Leuven University Press and Peeters, 1996), 209–24, who drew the conclusion that Exodus 6:2–8 was based on Ezekiel; for the opposite (and far more compelling) view, that Ezekiel 20 draws heavily on Exodus 6, see Risa Levitt Kohn, *A New Heart and a New Soul: Ezekiel, the Exile and the Torah, JSOT* Suppl. 358 (London: Sheffield Academic, 2002), 98–103; Rom-Shiloni, "Ezekiel as the Voice of the Exiles and Constructor of Exilic Ideology," 13' and Rebecca G. S. Idestrom, "Echoes of the Book of Exodus in Ezekiel," *JSOT* 33 (2009), 489–510.

[16] Besides our example, it also appears in Deuteronomy 4:34 ("Or, has any god tried to go and take for himself one nation from within another, through wonders and signs and marvels, through war, and through a mighty hand and an outstretched arm, and through awesome power, like all that the Lord your God did for you in Egypt, before your eyes?"); 2 Kings 17:36 ("the Lord, who brought you out of the land of Egypt with great power and with an outstretched arm"); Psalm 136:12 ("He took Israel out from among them . . . with a mighty hand and an outstretched arm"); see also Acts 13:17. The single exception is Jeremiah 32:17, which uses this phraseology in reference to the Creation. For a wider-ranging discussion of the components יד חזקה and זרוע נטויה, see Karen Martens, "'With a Strong Hand and an Outstretched Arm': The Meaning of the Expression ביד חזקה ובזרוע נטויה," *Scandinavian Journal of the Old Testament*, 15 (2001), 123–41.

[17] For יד חזקה in Exodus, see 3:19; 6:1; 13:9; 32:11.

shefukhāh), and the triad has been used to dramatically reverse the vision of the Exodus, since the three are now directed at Israel rather than at the Egyptians.[18] The goal is the same, however: that Israel should know "that I am the Lord."

Creative use of the Exodus was made also by other contemporary writers.[19] Notable is the allusions to the Exodus in the work of the sixth-century prophet known as Second Isaiah. In the collection in Isaiah 40–55, the return from the Babylonian exile is foretold in language and imagery drawn from earlier periods of Israelite history. Dramatic examples are provided by two brief passages.[20]

> Thus said the Lord, who makes a road in the sea and a path in the mighty waters, who removes chariots and horses, mighty and strong together: they lay down; they will rise no more; they were extinguished, snuffed out like flax.[21]
>
> Awake, awake, garb yourself in strength, O arm of the Lord! Awake as in days of old, generations long gone. Was it not You who hacked Rahab into pieces, who pierced the Dragon? Was it not You who dried up the sea, the waters of the Great Deep, who made the depths of the sea a path for redeemed ones to pass through? So let those liberated by the Lord return, and come to Zion with shouting, eternal joy on their head. Let them attain happiness and joy, since agony and groaning have fled.[22]

Both passages refer to the crossing of the Reed Sea. The second passage, from Isaiah 51, is remarkable for combining mythological themes (hacking Rahab, piercing the Dragon) with historical references (making a path in the sea for the "redeemed" to pass through).[23] The pivot on which this connection hinges is "drying the sea," which is a reference both to primordial battles against the sea, and to historical events of the Exodus.

---

[18] The reversal extends to the details. "The land where they dwelled" in Exodus refers to Canaan itself, where Abraham, Isaac, and Jacob had dwelled and to where their descendants would now "return"; in Ezekiel "the land where they dwelled" refers to the exilic lands where the Israelites are now, and from where they may or may not ever make it back to Canaan.

[19] For one example, and some discussion of the general phenomenon, see Adele Berlin, "The Message of Psalm 114," in Chaim Cohen, Victor Avigdor Hurowtiz, Avi Hurvitz, Yochanan Muffs, Baruch J. Schwartz, and Jeffrey H. Tigay (eds.), *Birkat Shalom: Studies in the Bible, Ancient Near Eastern Literature, and Postbiblical Judaism Presented to Shalom M. Paul on the Occasion of his Seventieth Birthday* (Winona Lake, IN: Eisenbrauns, 2008), 358–62; my thanks to Joseph Angel for this reference.

[20] For discussion, see Baruch J. Schwartz, "Ezekiel's Dim View of Israel's Restoration," in Maragaret S. Odell and John T. Strong (eds.), *The Book of Ezekiel: Theological and Anthropological Perspectives*, SBL Symposium Series 9 (Atlanta: SBL, 2000), 51–52.

[21] Isaiah 43:16–17.   [22] Isaiah 51:9–11.

[23] For an insightful study of this passage, see Jeremy M. Hutton, "Isaiah 51:9–11 and the Rhetorical Appropriation and Subversion of Hostile Theologies," *JBL* 126 (2007), 271–303.

More than that, though: this passage combines the imagery of the Exodus with the imagery of a pilgrimage to the Temple in Jerusalem.[24] It seems that through the centuries when the First Temple stood, the idea of Exodus – with people streaming to the land of Israel – became conflated with the idea of pilgrimage – with people streaming from all over the land to Jerusalem. Thus the prophet foretells a return not just to Yehud, but specifically to Zion, to Jerusalem.[25]

Elsewhere the prophet foretells that the details of the return to Zion from Babylon will be as miraculous as the sojourn in the desert of Egypt was:

> Go out of Babylon, flee from the Chaldeans! Tell it with loud shouting, make it known; bring it out to the ends of the land, say: "The Lord has redeemed His servant Jacob!" They have not thirsted in the dry places: He brought water for them from a rock, made it flow for them; he cleaved a rock and water gushed.[26]

But the prophet also makes it clear that this will be no mere repeat performance. The Second Exodus will surpass the first one, as described in the passage immediately following one discussed above: "Do not recall the earlier events, and do not contemplate what happened long ago. Look, I am doing something new, it will happen now, and you will know it: I will make a road in the desert and rivers in the wilderness."[27] Now it is true, as one might object, that this is not *very* different from the original exodus, although a river in the desert may be more impressive than a mere stream flowing from a rock.[28] But God insists that indeed, the Second Exodus will be preferable in other ways as well: "For you will not depart in haste (*be-ḥippazōn*), and you will not leave in flight, for the Lord will walk in front of you and the God of Israel will be your rear guard (*me'assēf*)."[29]

This is clearly intended as an improvement over the exodus from Egypt; in that case, Deuteronomy 16:3 reports, everything was done in haste ("for you left the land of Egypt in haste [*be-ḥippāzōn*]"). Furthermore, the promise that God himself will walk both in front of and behind the Israelites is a marked improvement over the Egyptian Exodus, in which

---

[24] Melody D. Knowles, "Pilgrimage Imagery in the Returns in Ezra," *JBL* 123 (2004), 57–74.

[25] This differs somewhat from the analysis of Knowles, *ibid.*, esp. p. 62; she emphasizes the *difference* between Exodus imagery and pilgrimage imagery, despite drawing attention to the passages in which these images are combined. The different emphases of our analyses have implications regarding the interpretation of Exodus imagery in Ezra; see below.

[26] Isaiah 48:20–21.   [27] Isaiah 43:18–19.

[28] And therefore I am not inclined to emend the MT in line with 1QIsaᵃ, which reads "paths" in place of "rivers": then there is no difference at all!

[29] Isaiah 52:12.

Israel was apparently led by a rotating team of God's messengers: "The Lord was walking in front of them, in a pillar of cloud by day to guide them on the path, and in a pillar of fire at night to illuminate for them, so they could travel day and night."[30]

Besides the use of Exodus-inspired imagery, late sixth-century Israelite prophets were clearly also inspired by the very idea of a mass exodus. Early in the Persian period, the hope among some was for a migration of the Israelite population en masse, not only from Mesopotamia but from wherever they might be, to Israel. For example, Zechariah foretells:"Thus said the Lord of Hosts: I will save my people from the land of the east and the land of the setting sun, and I will bring them that they may dwell within Jerusalem, and they will be my people and I will be their God, with truth and justice."[31] There is an allusion here to the passage in Exodus already cited ("I will take you to be my people, and I will be your God . . . I will bring you . . ."), which is not surprising to find given the passage's popularity in Zechariah's century. But the use to which it is put is interesting: the Exodus is the model for a future mass exodus, in which all of Israel will return to their native land. Indeed, Zechariah had certainly expected a mass return to the land of Israel as a prerequisite to the reconstruction of the Temple in Jerusalem: "Distant ones will arrive, and take part in the building of the Temple of the Lord, and then you will know that the Lord of Hosts has sent me to you."[32] For him, the division of the nation was anomalous and surely temporary; the future, no doubt, would be different.[33]

Despite all the differences between the visions of Ezekiel, Second Isaiah, and Zechariah, however, all the voices from the past spoke as one in assuring the Jews in Persia that their exilic existence was temporary.[34] Their very lives, however, screamed that the opposite was true. The Persians ruled, from south of even Egypt in the southwest, through Yehud and Syria,

---

[30] Exodus 13:21; see also 14:19. That the prophecies of Second Isaiah were meant to foretell a future Exodus that would surpass even the first one was perceived by a midrash (Exodus Rabbah §19): "God said to them: in this world, when the Israelites ate the *pesaḥ* in Egypt, they ate it in haste, as it says, 'This is how you shall eat it . . . [in haste]' (Exodus 12:11), as in 'for you left the land of Egypt in haste' (Deuteronomy 16:3). But in the future, 'For you will not depart in haste, and you will not leave in flight' (Isaiah 52:12) . . . In the past, I and my entourage used to walk in front of you, as it says, 'The Lord was walking in front of them by day. . .' (Exodus 13:21), but in the future I myself, as it says, 'for the Lord will walk in front of you and the God of Israel will be your rear guard'" (Isaiah 52:12)."
[31] Zechariah 8:7–8.
[32] Zechariah 6:15. See Peter R. Bedford, "Diaspora: Homeland Relations in Ezra-Nehemiah," *VT* 52 (2002), 162; Oded, "The Judean Exiles in Babylonia," 69*.
[33] John Kessler, "Diaspora and Homeland in the Early Achaemenid Period: Community, Geography and Demography in Zechariah 1–8," in Jon L. Berquist (ed.), *Approaching Yehud: New Approaches to the Study of the Persian Period*, Semeia Studies 50 (Atlanta: SBL, 2007), 137–66, esp. 153 and 162.
[34] See further *ibid.*, 147–65.

Mesopotamia, the Persian heartland. Their power stretched even further west, through the rugged mountains of Afghanistan, and further east, to legendary African lands of jungles and precious minerals and spices. Militarily, the Persians reached even beyond those expansive borders, warring with the Greek city states, but it was as a machine of peaceful bureaucracy that the Persians were most renowned. Everywhere they controlled, roads were built, laws enacted, and edicts proclaimed. The king sent officials to all reaches of the empire to standardize the legal proceedings and ensure that all residents of the Persian Empire were under his control. A communication system the likes of which had never been seen united the vast empire, so that from a throne room in Persia, the king could rapidly communicate with his subjects throughout the realm, from southeastern Asia through northeastern Africa.[35] The sight of the royal horses, bearing riders with official dispatches, was a common one along the main roads. Communications were conducted in Aramaic, and throughout the empire this was the language of the educated elites.

All of this filled Persian subjects with pride, and with a sense that this was simply the way the world would forever be. There was no end in sight, no reason to think that the empire would crumble. It was true, the people could remind themselves, that the Assyrians had risen to great power, and then fallen hard; the Babylonians, too, had controlled a great empire and then virtually disappeared as a political force. But the Persians had already ruled for twice as long as the Assyrians, and three times as long as the Babylonians, ever had. And while the Assyrians and Babylonians had expanded by force, fighting their way to their heights and then all the way to their demises, the Persians excelled at peaceful governance. Their empire did not depend on constant warfare. It was a smoothly integrated, highly efficient system, which – as far as anyone could tell – could simply go on for ever.

What had happened to the prophets' promises? What had happened to the hopes for the future, to the Second Exodus, to the return to ancestral lands and political autonomy? What had happened to God?

3. Reevaluating past and present

Those Jews who had returned from Babylonia to Jerusalem had waited for a sign that God was indeed with them. None was forthcoming. Despite the promises of the prophets, despite the expectations and high hopes, the

---

[35] See Pierre Briant, *From Cyrus to Alexander: A History of the Persian Empire* (Winona Lake, IN: Eisenbrauns, 2002), 357–77.

return to Yehud was underwhelming. The community that found itself in Jerusalem a decade into Persian reign, in 530, was small and impoverished. The economy was in tatters, and even subsistence farming was not succeeding. The community managed to survive from year to year, but they waited still for developments that would vindicate their decision to come to Yehud. They lacked political power and economic success, and pined for overt religious exoneration. Where were the miracles of the "Second Exodus"? Why were there no plagues, no splitting of the sea, no fire and brimstone, no mass return? Where, again, was God?

They had arrived with the intention of building a Temple to God, but were no longer sure that God wanted them to do so.[36] The indecisiveness of the people was exacerbated by the opposition of their neighbors to their construction project. Led by Governor Tattenai, the Persian official in charge of the area including Yehud, the returning Jews were met with resistance and opposition when they attempted to build the Jerusalem Temple.[37] The combination of internal skepticism and external opposition was enough to put the construction project on hold indefinitely – or at least until God made it clear that this was something he was actually interested in.

In 516, the prophet Haggai argued that God was waiting for the people of Jerusalem to make the first move.[38] He was holding back rain, according to Haggai, because he was awaiting the construction of his Temple. The people had argued that they could not build a Temple until they were assured of God's presence among them, but Haggai quoted God: "I *am* with you!"[39] The evidence would be the *result* of the Temple-building, not its prerequisite.

---

[36] In an insightful paper, Israel Eph'al argued that the major question for Jews was whether the exile had a set time at which it was set to end, or whether the end time was flexible and dependent on actions on the ground. See Eph'al, "לקביעת זמנה של הגאולה בתקופת שיבת ציון," *Tarbiz*, 76 (2007), 5–16.

[37] Ezra 5:3 – 6:13. Because Haggai and Zechariah discuss only internal strife, while Ezra and Nehemiah discuss only external conflicts, some modern scholars are skeptical of this historicity of the account here. Peter Ross Bedford, *Temple Restoration in Early Achaemenid Judah* (Leiden: Brill, 2001), 32–33, argues that Ezra is late, unreliable, and tendentious, and that history must be written on the basis of Haggai and Zechariah; see also Lisbeth S. Fried, "The House of God Who Dwells in Jerusalem," *JAOS* 126 (2006), 94–95. On the other hand, Elie Assis, "To Build or Not to Build? A Dispute Between Haggai and his People (Hag 1)," *ZAW* 119 (2007), 515, argues that both accounts are accurate, and that it is only a matter of focus which divides the accounts.

[38] Fried argues that the Temple project was begun during the reign of Cyrus, and that what Haggai was talking about was not the *beginning* of the construction, but the *completion*. The structure was there, but it needed to be paneled. See Fried, "The House of God Who Dwells in Jerusalem," 94–95.

[39] Haggai 1:13. For this understanding of the dispute between Haggai and the Jerusalemites, see especially Assis, "To Build or Not to Build," 514–27. For additional facets (or alternative interpretations) of the Jews' delay in building the Temple, see John Kessler, "Building the Second Temple:

That fall, the Temple was duly built and dedicated. No miracles accompanied the dedication of the Temple, and those who remembered the Temple of Solomon actually cried when they saw the new one.[40] It paled in comparison, lacking the splendor that had so filled the Jews' ancestors with pride. Haggai knew that some of the people actually claimed that the Temple was "nothingness"[41] – what was it worth, after all? But he promised that history would bear out the wisdom of their investment, and that this second Temple would in some way surpass the first.

The aspirations of the community of builders were not that it should be their temple alone, but that it should serve as a focal point for Jews throughout the empire and the world. With the Temple functioning, God could again reign over all of Israel together.[42] Although the significance of the new Temple may have been cosmically of great consequence, the city of Jerusalem continued to struggle economically and politically. As a later writer put it: "the city shall be rebuilt, with piazza and moat, but distressed by the times."[43] For the residents of Yehud, Jerusalem was not merely a symbol, but the ideological, political, and geographic center of their lives. Towns in Yehud clustered around Jerusalem, and the fate of Jerusalem was seen as emblematic of the fate of the community as a whole.

Half a century later, signs of divine providence were still lacking. So where was God? Among the Jews who moved back to Yehud, the outlines of an answer began to emerge. They posited that the Persians were in control only nominally, as agents of God helping the Jews reinstate their covenantal destiny in the land. The Persian kings were actually God's way of working things out. Had not the prophet explained that Cyrus was "God's anointed one" (*mashiah*)?[44] Had God not moved his spirit to allow the Jews to return to their lands and rebuild their Temple? Was this not enough to make it

Questions of Time, Text, and History in Haggai 1.1–15," *JSOT* 27 (2002), 243–56, Hayim Tadmor, "'The Appointed Time has not yet Arrived': The Historical Background of Haggai 1:2," in Robert Chazan, William W. Hallo, and Lawrence H. Schiffman (eds.), *Ki Baruch Hu: Ancient Near Eastern, Biblical, and Judaic Studies in Honor of Baruch A. Levine* (Winona Lake, IN: Eisenbrauns, 1999), 401–08, and Eph'al, "לקביעת זמנה של הגאולה."

[40] Ezra 3:12. See Elie Assis, "A Disputed Temple (Haggai 2,1–9)," *ZAW* 120 (2008), 582–96.
[41] Haggai 2:3: "Is it not like nothingness (*ayin*) in your eyes?"
[42] Bedford, *Temple Restoration*, 263–64. [43] Daniel 9:25.
[44] The significance of this epithet in the context of Second Isaiah and of the sixth century has been thoroughly studied by Lisbeth S. Fried, "Cyrus the Messiah? The Historical Background to Isaiah 45:1," *HTR* 95 (2002), 373–93. Fried "suggest[s] ... that the Deutero-Isaianic writer wrote as a contemporary of Cyrus, and that he wrote to legitimize him as the Davidic monarch, heir to the Davidic throne. The line of the Achaemenid kings would now take the place of the Davidides" (*ibid.*, 374). Fried's discussion is wide-ranging and sophisticated, but presents no arguments which necessitate the conclusion that the "anointedness" of Cyrus is as significant as she claims – only a framework within which the bestowal of such status could be understood, if it were in fact bestowed. It still seems preferable to me to presume the claim to be less grand: the prophet claims that Cyrus was

clear that God was behind all this? True, there had been no grand miracles, no miraculous conquests. True, the Temple built was not nearly as grand as the one constructed by Solomon; not only did it lack the ornateness, but even some of the sacred vessels were missing. But it was a Temple nonetheless, and it functioned; it demonstrated that God had orchestrated the Jews' return to Jerusalem, and that he had met them there.

Indeed, by the fifth century it was clear that Zechariah's vision was not going to come true. Some, no doubt, concluded that the prophecies of redemption had been nullified, or, worse, falsified. Others more stubbornly held out hope. Some did not give up hopes of a second exodus, and saw one, writ small, in events of the middle of the century.

anointed by God to take over the world and support the rebuilding of the Temple, much as the priests of Marduk in Babylon saw the hand of Marduk at work in the successes of Cyrus. See also Manfred Oeming, "'See, We Are Serving Today' (Nehemiah 9:36): Nehemiah 9 as a Theological Interpretation of the Persian Period," in Oded Lipschits and Manfred Oeming (eds.), *Judah and the Judaeans in the Persian Period* (Winona Lake, IN: Eisenbrauns, 2006), 571.

CHAPTER 2

The movement of Ezra and Nehemiah

1. The movement of Ezra and Nehemiah

In the 450s and 440s the Jews in the east saw two of their rising stars move west.[1] Ezra, a skillful bureaucrat with a strong sense of nationalism alongside a set of skills that enabled him to assert himself among the Persians, was sent to Yehud by the Persian court.[2] His job there was to codify the Jewish laws in a way which would allow them to be used by the Persians to govern the Jews.[3] For Ezra, this was a perfect job. He was able to serve the Persians by asserting and emphasizing Jewish difference.[4] He spent his time in Jerusalem ensuring that the Jews were living by their laws, and emphasizing the differences between the community within Jerusalem – which he defined as the "members of the exilic community" – and others.

Not all of his contemporaries were convinced that such harsh divisions were valuable or necessary. Some pointed to strands of tradition that seemed to allow for neighboring people to become part of the community by marrying in, and for cooperation with neighbors on matters of politics.

---

[1] For the westward orientation of the Jewish leaders of the Persian period who are preserved in the biblical canon, see Elsie R. Stern, "Esther and the Politics of Diaspora," *JQR* 100 (2010), 42.

[2] For a discussion of the dynamics of the royal decree and Ezra's mandate, see Kyong-Jin Lee, *The Authority and Authorization of Torah in the Persian Period*, Contributions to Biblical Exegesis and Theology (Leuven: Peeters, 2011), 213–53.

[3] See esp. Richard C. Steiner, "The *mbqr* at Qumran, the *Episkopos* in the Athenian Empire, and the Meaning of *lbqr'* in Ezra 7:14: On the Relation of Ezra's Mission to the Persian Legal Project," *JBL* 120 (2001), 623–46. Gary N. Knoppers, "Beyond Jerusalem and Judah: The Mission of Ezra in the Province of Transeuphrates," *Eretz-Israel*, 29 (2009), 78–87, argues that the mandate to Ezra in 7:25–26 gives him authority over all the competing YHWHistic groups in the southern Levant, outside of Yehud (Idumea, Transjordan, Samaria), and makes his version of the religion the official one.

[4] Jon L. Berquist, *Judaism in Persia's Shadow: A Social and Historical Approach* (Minneapolis: Fortress, 1995), 10 and *passim*; Peter Frei, "Persian Imperial Authorization: A Summary," in J. W. Watts (ed.), *Persia and Torah: The Theory of Imperial Authorization of the Pentateuch*, SBL Symposium Series 17 (Atlanta: SBL, 2001), 5–40, and, with more nuanced historical analysis, Steiner, "The *mbqr* at Qumran," 623–46.

Still, Ezra succeeded in shifting the terms of the communal discourse. He was prepared to abandon dreams of mass returns to Yehud.[5] Permission to migrate had been granted eighty years earlier, and clearly the restoration of the entire nation, as the earlier texts had described, was not going to take place. On his arrival he worked hard to re-orient the Jerusalem community in their attitudes toward the Diaspora communities. They were no longer to be viewed merely as potential compatriots in Yehud, and not to be belittled for that reason, either. Ezra looked to the east and saw sources of support. It was there that his own attitudes had been forged, and there that his beliefs about Jewish identity and Persian irrelevance had been strengthened.[6]

This was not an abandonment of the dream of an exodus, though. On the contrary, Ezra – or the chronicler of his journey to Yehud, and specifically to Jerusalem – drew on exodus motifs in describing the voyage.[7] According to some observers, "Ezra's march to Jerusalem was a cultic procession which Ezra understood as a second exodus and a partial fulfillment of prophetic expectations."[8] The most striking detail was certainly the date of Ezra's march: he and those accompanying him began their journey, leaving the Ahawa River, on the 12th day of Nisan. He may have intended to leave earlier, but paused at the Ahawa River to await Levites. Although these were not technically necessary for his purposes, since (as he knew) there were Levites in Jerusalem already, he seemed to be modeling his procession on that of the Israelites in the wilderness, and for this purpose Levites were required.[9] Indeed, Ezra (or the chronicler of his voyage) claimed explicitly that his journey was chaperoned by "the arm of the Lord,"[10] which had been so significant in the Exodus. This fulfilled the promises made by the sixth-century prophets of the Return.

[5] See Yonina Dor, האומנם גורשו 'הנשים הנכריות'? שאלת ההיבדלות בימי שיבת ציון (Jerusalem: Magnes, 2006), 32–33, for discussion.

[6] Bedford, "Diaspora: Homeland Relations." Bustenay Oded, "Exile–Homeland Relations during the Exilic Period and Restoration," in Michael Heltzer and Meir Malul (eds.), Tᵉshûrôt LaAvishur: Studies in the Bible and the Ancient Near East, in Hebrew and Semitic Languages: Festschrift Presented to Prof. Yitzhak Avishur on the Occasion of his 65th Birthday (Tel Aviv and Jaffa: Archaeological Center Publications, 2004), 153*–160*, esp. 157*, rejects Bedford's views.

[7] On the mythology of Ezra's return, see Bob Becking, "'We All Returned as One!' Critical Notes on the Myth of the Mass Return," in Oded Lipschits and Manfred Oeming (eds.), Judah and the Judaeans in the Persian Period (Winona Lake, IN: Eisenbrauns, 2006), 3–18.

[8] Klaus Koch, "Ezra and the Origins of Judaism," Journal of Semitic Studies, 19 (1974), 173–97; the quoted line is Koch's "first thesis," defended ibid., 184–89.

[9] Ibid., 187.

[10] Ezra 7:6, 28; in 8:22, 31 the expression "the arm of our God" appears, as well. See Koch, "Ezra and the Origins of Judaism," 187 with n. 2, 188.

Of course, there were numerous differences between Ezra's return and the Exodus,[11] but already in the previous century Israelite writers had conflated images of the Exodus with images of the pilgrimage to Jerusalem,[12] and Ezra's narrative continues this practice. Rather than head for "the Land," as those leaving Egypt did, Ezra's mission proceeds toward Jerusalem.[13] The journey itself is described as an *ăliyyā*, a "going up," from the verbal root consistently used to describe pilgrimages to Jerusalem.[14] The images of exodus and pilgrimage have been seamlessly blended in the narratives of Ezra.

The use of these motifs made powerful statements about the community being forged by Ezra. "The community has been reborn specifically as a *worshiping* community, a community that places Jerusalem and its temple at the center of its worship life."[15] There may also have been – as there invariably are – political overtones to the invocation of the Exodus motifs: just as in the original Exodus, here, too, the returnees see the land as theirs to be taken.[16]

The returnees of Ezra's time also saw God's hand in the actions of the Persian kings.[17] Even the law of the Torah was now authorized by the king, and its legitimacy now derived from it being sanctioned by the Persian imperial powers. "Ezra and Nehemiah represent Persian imperial law and Judean law under Persian domination as collaborations among the king, God, and Jewish agents."[18] The opening chapters of the book of Ezra may be read as making just this claim: those returning with Ezra were supported by God and king. To put it differently, they were supported by the king, who was in turn supported by God.[19] This ideology matched the Persian claims: the Persian kings claimed divine support for their actions, as well.[20]

---

[11] An additional point in the Ezra narrative which has been claimed to be based on the Exodus story is the "gold and silver" brought with the returnees. The differences here far outweigh the similarities, however; see Knowles, "Pilgrimage Imagery in the Returns in Ezra," 57–60.

[12] See above, Chapter 1, n. 25.

[13] For example, 1:3–4 and 1:11; see Knowles, "Pilgrimage Imagery in the Returns in Ezra," 66–67.

[14] *Ibid.*, 67–68 and 71.   [15] *Ibid.*, 73.

[16] This is explored well by P. Abadie, "Le livre d'Esdras: Un midrash de l'Exode?," *Transeuphratène*, 14 (1998), 19–31. In answer to his own question, Abadie says that the book is *not* a midrash in the technical sense, but is something similar. See also, along similar lines (but with a more critical bent), Robert P. Carroll, "The Myth of the Empty Land," *Semeia*, 59 (1992), 79–93.

[17] According to Oeming, "'See, We Are Serving Today' (Nehemiah 9:36)," 571–88, this is the view presented in Nehemiah 9:36–37, as well.

[18] Stern, "Esther and the Politics of Diaspora," 34.

[19] Bob Becking, "Continuity and Community: The Belief System of the Book of Ezra," in Bob Becking and M. C. A. Korpel (eds.), *The Crisis of the Israelite Religious Traditions in Exilic and Post-Exilic Times*, Oudtestementliche Studien 42 (Leiden: Brill, 1999), 256–75; Becking, "'We All Returned as One!,'" 13.

[20] See my paper "Negotiating Empire: Living Jewishly under the Achaemenids in Persia and Palestine," in Daniel Tsadik (ed.), *Israel and Iran: From Cyrus the Great to the Islamic Republic* (Leiden: Brill, forthcoming), and see further below, pp. 43–44.

Thus God was seen to be operating, and even fulfilling the promises of a second exodus, without a mass national migration to the land of Israel. Things were happening on a smaller scale than might have been expected, but they were happening. The Exodus was fulfilled in the migration of a small minority.[21] The Temple had been constructed without fanfare, through internal and external opposition. The resulting building was far less impressive than the First Temple had been, and all signs of miracles were lacking. But this was enough for the Jews of Yehud. The necessary conclusion was that God had changed his modes of operation. He now worked through political forces, and did not intervene in nature or alter the fabric of Creation itself. But he could be seen in the workings of everyday life, if one looked from the right angle.

Some of the Jews who lived in Persia and in Mesopotamia did not think this was all quite right. None of the prophets had foretold that the Jews would return in a trickle, of their own initiative, and construct an unimpressive Temple. No one had told them to expect that the Jews would return to their own land without the governing power's collapse. Did it even count as "returning" if all that it entailed was moving from one Persian province to another, without even leaving the empire?

Some of these Jews felt that their choice to remain in the center of the empire was justified. If God had not ushered them back to Yehud in grand fashion, it meant that they were to stay where they were. Was this because God was yet planning something grander? Perhaps. But perhaps it was because the plans had changed and power had shifted. No longer was political autonomy on a small scale the central goal of a people. Was there any value in living on a small parcel of land, far from the halls of power, where one could be autonomous – in a sense – but essentially powerless? The world just seemed too large for that now. Maybe it would be preferable to live a life of political dependency as part of the great empire. One sacrificed the dream of autonomy, but hadn't the past few centuries shown that this dream was a mirage anyway? Living as part of the empire opened up all sorts of possibilities.

A few years later, another leader of the Persian Jewish community left the community and relocated to Yehud. Nehemiah, a Jew who had risen to the highest echelons of domestic politics in Susa, persuaded the king to send him to Jerusalem as governor. No longer would the Jews in the capital have a defender on the inside; henceforth Nehemiah would be working for the

---

[21] On the influxes of Jews from the east to Jerusalem and Judea, see (despite his misguided polemical thrust), Becking, "'We All Returned as One!,'" 8–12.

Jerusalemites alone, not the Jewish community as a whole. What did Nehemiah's contemporaries, left back in Susa, think of the move? Presumably for many in the community it was a tough loss. One of their own, a success story, who had risen to a position of influence from where he could affect the status of his brethren, had thrown it all away. Technically he might have gotten a promotion, from a domestic position in the palace to a post governing Yehud. But everyone knew that governing a far-flung province meant no influence back in the central government. Nehemiah might be in charge in Yehud, but this was small consolation for the Jews in the empire more broadly.

Ezra and Nehemiah both argued hard for the centrality of Jerusalem. This was not so much an argument about reality as an argument for ideology: Jerusalem *should be* the center of the Jewish world. In reality, Jerusalem was unimpressive in the Persian period, and the rhetoric of centrality was therefore all the more necessary, to compensate. But compensate they did, substituting rhetoric and politics for monumental architecture and political power.[22]

In this case, too, the Jews of Yehud could claim Persian imperial ideology as support for their positions. Cyrus appears to have desired to create a province of Yehud around a strong city of Jerusalem, as part of a long-term strategy designed to allow him easy access to Egypt.[23] The Egyptian ambitions of the Achaemenids were fulfilled before Jerusalem was rebuilt, however.

The major project undertaken by Nehemiah was the construction of a wall around Jerusalem.[24] As Nehemiah tells the story, this was a project

---

[22] Melody D. Knowles, "Pilgrimage to Jerusalem in the Persian Period," in Jon L. Berquist (ed.), *Approaching Yehud: New Approaches to the Study of the Persian Period* (Leiden: Brill, 2008), 7–24; Melody D. Knowles, *Centrality Practiced: Jerusalem in the Religious Practice of Yehud and the Diaspora during the Persian Period*, Archaeology and Biblical Studies 16 (Atlanta: SBL, 2006), 77–103. Similarly, Jacob L. Wright, *Rebuilding Identity: The Nehemiah-Memoir and its Earliest Readers*, BZAW 348 (Berlin: De Gruyter, 2004), 85 and 92 argues, that Jerusalem was not the center of the empire in any sense, but that it was the ideological center in the consciousness of Judean leaders there.

[23] Briant, *From Cyrus to Alexander*, 43–50; see the discussion in Ziony Zevit, "Is there an Archaeological Case for Phantom Settlements in the Persian Period?," *Palestine Exploration Quarterly*, 141 (2009), 124–37, esp. 133–34.

[24] See the correlations between the textual description and the archaeological remains in Hanan Eshel, "ירושלים בימי שלטון פרס: מתאר העיר והרקע ההיסטורי," in Shmuel Ahituv and Amihai Mazar (eds.), *The History of Jerusalem: The Biblical Period* (Jerusalem: Yad Yitzhak Ben-Zvi, 2000), 327–43. Eilat Mazar has argued that further sections of this wall were excavated in excavations directed by her: "The Wall that Nehemiah Built," *Biblical Archaeology Review*, 35.2 (2009), 24–33, 66, and see also Gabriel Barkay, "מבט נוסף על ירושלים בימי נחמיה," חידושים בארכיאולוגיה של ירושלים וסביבותיה, 2 (2008), 47–54, who accepts Mazar's identification. For a contrasting view, see Israel Finkelstein, "Persian Period

undertaken with the approval of the Persian monarch,[25] but the symbolism was lost on no one.[26] The neighboring communities, led by the governor of Samaria to the north, protested immediately. The Yehudim, the residents of Yehud, were creating a *de facto* autonomous realm, insulated not only from their immediate neighbors, but from Persian society in general. Official protests were filed with the Persian authorities, in which the seditious history of Jerusalem was paired with the obvious desire of Ezra and Nehemiah to create barriers between their community and the rest of the world. Would the Persians really allow this? After a bureaucratic investigation of the history of the case and the relevant data, the government decided that, indeed, construction could proceed.[27] With the initiative of Nehemiah, Cyrus' original plan was brought to fruition. With the construction of a wall, a real independent city was created once again; "the outcome served pragmatic interests of both the Persians and the people of Yehud."[28]

Within the Jewish world, too, the actions of Ezra and Nehemiah provoked a vociferous response. Just a few decades earlier, some had foreseen the Temple as a unifying force, not only for Jews all over, but for everyone who desired to worship God. Drawing on a prophecy of Isaiah's from more than two centuries earlier, one prophet had described the Temple as a "house of prayer for all nations."[29] The prophet did *not* claim that foreigners were like Israel in God's eyes; he went further than that. God is more pluralistic: "my house welcomes all peoples."[30]

Jerusalem and Yehud: A Rejoinder," *Journal of Hebrew Scriptures*, 9 (2009), www.jhsonline.org/Articles/article_126.pdf (accessed January, 2010), who dates the wall (and the account in Nehemiah 3) to the Hasmonean period.

[25] In chapter 2, Nehemiah reports that he asked the king's permission to travel to Jerusalem to "build it," and when he arrived, immediately set to work constructing the wall. See the analysis of Nehemiah 3 by Mordechai Cogan, "Raising the Walls of Jerusalem (Nehemiah 3:1–32): The View from Dur-Sharrukin," *Israel Exploration Journal*, 56 (2006), 84–95, who argues that chapter 3 originated as a report on the construction project to be filed with the king.

[26] Oeming, "'See, We Are Serving Today' (Nehemiah 9:36)," 582–83.

[27] For the bureaucratic processes involved, see Richard C. Steiner, "Bishlam's Archival Search Report in Nehemiah's Archive: Multiple Introductions and Reverse Chronological Order as Clues to the Origin of the Aramaic Letters in Ezra 4–6," *JBL* 125 (2006), 641–85.

[28] Zevit, "Is there an Archaeological Case for Phantom Settlements in the Persian Period?," 134.

[29] Isaiah 56:7. The view of Steven Tuell – that Isaiah 56 is a conscious response to Ezekiel 44, and that the בני נכר are the group on which the author of the text is part – is difficult to accept, and the parallels are uncompelling, although the contrasting ideologies really do exist in the texts. Cf. Steven S. Tuell, "The Priesthood of the 'Foreigner': Evidence of Competing Polities in Ezekiel 44:1–14 and Isaiah 56:1–8," in John T. Strong and Steven S. Tuell (eds.), *Constituting the Community: Studies on the Polity of Ancient Israel in Honor of S. Dean McBride Jr.* (Winona Lake, IN: Eisenbrauns, 2005), 183–204.

[30] See the discussion of this passage by Moshe Greenberg, "A House of Prayer for All Peoples," in Alviero Niccacci (ed.), *Jerusalem – House of Prayer for All Peoples in the Three Monotheistic Religions* (Jerusalem: Franciscan Printing Press, 2001), 31–37 (quotation from p. 34).

Ezra and Nehemiah were moving the Temple community in precisely the opposite direction. Even those worshiping the same God were barred from entry into their society; a combination of genealogy and biography was necessary to gain recognition from the new authorities in Jerusalem. Barriers – legal, physical, and social – were erected and strengthened at every turn, and exclusivity was the mode of operation in Jerusalem now.[31] This was not a simple vision to impose, and there was a long-running dispute between Nehemiah's separatist party and the "assimilationist party," which included "the gentry (not the plebeians) who intermarried with the leading families of neighboring territories."[32]

The returnees imposed their ideas of separation, in part, by de-legitimizing the community in Judea when they arrived. Competing narratives circulated about the origins of these people, who were mostly subsistence farmers and were overawed by the arrival of the thousands of Jews from Babylonia bearing gold and silver vessels.[33] Some of the returnees dismissed them as foreigners who had usurped Israelite land in the absence of any Israelites; other narratives claimed that they were introduced to the land by the Assyrians centuries ago as part of the Assyrian policy of cross-exiling peoples. What was a given was that these were not people with an equal claim to be God's chosen people, as the Jews in Babylonia and in Yehud had.[34]

Ezra took guidance from no one outside of Jerusalem, and fought with less hard-line elements within Jerusalem, as well. Rejecting all cooperation, Ezra insisted that his community would consist of only pure-blooded Jews who had been to exile and returned. He was willing to cut all ties to his neighbors in Yehud. For support, he argued that the residents of Yehud should look not around their own homes, but to the east, to the Jews yet in the Diaspora. Ezra took pains to emphasize the ties that bound the Jews who had returned to Yehud to those still in Diaspora, and these inevitably had to come at the expense of their ties to the other people living nearby.

Ezra and Nehemiah were far more successful at establishing strong borders around their community than at integrating the community from

---

[31] For a discussion of the various lines of evidence and ideology converging on "separation" as the ideology of Ezra and Nehemiah, see David Janzen, *Witch Hunts, Purity, and Social Boundaries: The Expulsion of the Foreign Women in Ezra 9–10, JSOT* Suppl. 350 (Sheffield Academic, 2002), 87–105.

[32] See Morton Smith, *Palestinian Parties and Politics that Shaped the Old Testament* (New York: Columbia University Press, 1971), 155.

[33] Carroll, "The Myth of the Empty Land," 81.

[34] For discussion of the relevant biblical texts, see Mordecai Cogan, "For We, Like You, Worship Your God: Three Biblical Portrayals of Samaritan Origins," *VT* 38 (1988), 286–92.

within.[35] Dissent and disagreement proliferated, and neither leader was inclined to countenance discord. Their method rather was to quash other voices. Eventually Ezra laid the blame for the discontentment at the feet of the most vulnerable sub-group within the community: the women who had married in. Of varying origins but (presumably) devoted to their husbands and their new community, these women nonetheless became the targets of Ezra's most vociferous campaign. Uncompromising in his attitudes and his tactics, Ezra forced the men of Jerusalem to divorce these wives and expel the children they had borne.

This had economic implications,[36] but these were almost certainly secondary in Ezra's mind.[37] His goals, rather, were social and religious. It seemed essential to him to keep outsiders outside the community, for in his mind the community in Jerusalem was still an exilic community, still under constant existential threat. Having suffered the trauma of the loss of autonomy, Ezra responded by building walls and emphasizing difference.[38] Otherwise, he reasoned, all would be lost. Long had they waited for redemption, but none was forthcoming. To Ezra's mind, Persian rule was

---

[35] For this point and its explanatory power, see Janzen, *Witch Hunts, Purity, and Social Boundaries*.

[36] Cf., e.g., Kenneth Hoglund, "The Achaemenid Context," in Philip R. Davies (ed.), *Second Temple Studies 1: Persian Period*, JSOT Suppl. 117 (Sheffield Academic, 1991), 54–72, at 67–68. Sara Japhet, "גירוש הנשים הנכריות (עזרא ט'-י'): המסגרת המשפטית התקדימים וההשלכות על קביעת הזהות היהודית" in Moshe Bar-Asher, Noah Hakham, and Yosef Ofer (eds.), *Teshurah le-Amos: Asupat Meḥḳarim be-farshanut ha-miḳra mugeshet le-Amos Hakham* (Alon Shvut: Tevunot, 2007), 379–401, also argues that the tactic was legal and the implications economic. Tamara Cohn Eskenazi, "The Missions of Ezra and Nehemiah," in Oded Lipschits and Manfred Oeming (eds.), *Judah and the Judaeans in the Persian Period* (Winona Lake, IN: Eisenbrauns, 2006), 509–29, argues from the vocabulary used that ownership of the land was the issue foremost in Ezra's mind. Ina Willi-Plein, "Problems of Intermarriage in Postexilic Times," in Moshe Bar-Asher, Dalit Rom-Shiloni, Emanuel Tov, and Nili Wazana (eds.), *Shai le-Sara Japhet: Studies in the Bible, its Exegesis and its Language* (Jerusalem: Bialik, 2007), 177–89, argues that Nehemiah was not interested in intermarriage as a religious issue, but as a sociolinguistic problem. On the other hand, Ida Fröhlich, "'Mamzer' in Qumran Texts: The Problem of Mixed Marriages from Ezra's Time – Law, Literature and Practice," *Transeuphratène*, 29 (2005), 103–15, argues that the prohibition against intermarriage was based on the concept of *kil'ayim* (illicit mixtures). For discussion of modern scholarly views, see David Janzen, "Scholars, Witches, Ideologues, and What the Text Said: Ezra 9–10 and its Interpretation," in Jon L. Berquist (ed.), *Approaching Yehud: New Approaches to the Study of the Persian Period*, Semeia Studies 50 (Atlanta: SBL, 2007), 49–69; Dor, 'האומנם גורשו הנשים הנכריות?', 104–50.

[37] Daniel L. Smith-Christopher, "The Politics of Ezra: Sociological Indicators of Postexilic Judaean Society," in Philip R. Davies (ed.), *Second Temple Studies 1: Persian Period*, JSOT Suppl. 117 (Sheffield Academic, 1991), 73–97.

[38] See Hagith Zlotnick-Sivan, "The Silent Women of Yehud: Notes on Ezra 9–10," *JJS* 51 (2000), 3–18, who notes that "Ezra-Nehemiah appears to be fundamentally concerned with issues of identity and boundaries" (p. 3). Zlotnick-Sivan argues that in fact the prescribed divorces never took place, but that the real point was the ceremony of communal affirmation anyway (p. 13); this position is argued more strongly by Dor, 'האומנם גורשו הנשים הנכריות?', for whom the ceremonial statement made by the community that in principle they would like to separate from foreign women was itself significant from an anthropological perspective.

just an extension of Babylonian domination; the Jews were still "slaves in their own land."[39] For people who believe that their community and everything they hold dear are under siege and threat of annihilation, erecting barriers as powerful as possible seems like the only reasonable response.[40] Intermarriage not only directly brought outsiders in, but also stripped Ezra's community of its uniqueness within the sprawling behemoth of the Persian Empire: if the Jerusalem community mixed with its neighbors, they were becoming just another group of Persian citizens.[41]

Again, Ezra's and Nehemiah's actions provoked anger from their ideological foes. The end of Ezra's career is not recorded, and some have claimed that he was summarily recalled to Persia by the authorities, after leading Jewish families in Yehud complained about the havoc this outsider was wreaking within their own families.[42] There certainly were heated disagreements about these policies, even within families. A certain Yehiel and his five brothers all appear in the list of men who had to expel their wives, but Yehiel's son Shecaniah was the leader of those agitating for action. The youth, with their greater passion and energy, were on Ezra's side, and carried the day.[43] The elders, though, were not enthralled with this new zealousness.

Some of the texts produced in Yehud in the following decades included responses to the hard-line views of Ezra and Nehemiah. Accounts of the past became a microcosm of arguments about the present. Nehemiah, for example, referred to Solomon as an example of the dangers of "foreign wives":

> Did not King Solomon of Israel sin on account of such women? Among the many nations there was no king like him, and he was beloved by his God,

---

[39] Nehemiah 9:36–37. For the foregoing, see esp. Daniel L. Smith-Christopher, "Reassessing the Historical and Sociological Impact of the Babylonian Exile (597/587–539 BCE)," in James M. Scott (ed.), *Exile: Old Testament, Jewish, and Christian Conceptions, JSJ* Suppl. 56; (Leiden: Brill, 1997), 22–23.

[40] Smith-Christopher, "Reassessing the Historical and Sociological Impact," 36, reporting that when Native Americans or Aboriginal Australians read the narratives of Ezra, they identify with him and his tactics.

[41] Daniel L. Smith-Christopher, "The Mixed Marriage Crisis in Ezra 9–10 and Nehemiah 13: A Study of the Sociology of Post-Exilic Judaean Community," in Tamara C. Eskenazi and Kent H. Richards (eds.), *Second Temple Studies 2: Temple Community in the Persian Period, JSOT* Suppl. 175 (Sheffield Academic, 1994), 243–95.

[42] Smith, *Palestinian Parties and Politics*, 121–22; cf. also Mary Douglas, "Responding to Ezra: The Priests and the Foreign Wives," *Biblical Interpretation*, 10 (2002), 1–23. Douglas claims that Leviticus and Numbers were compiled and published in response to Ezra, to demonstrate that there is nothing impure about intermarriage; this is precisely the opposite of the argument mounted by Smith, *Palestinian Parties and Politics*, 173–74, according to whom Nehemiah 10 is a conservative protest against the relatively liberal law of intermarriage in the Pentateuch.

[43] See Ezra 10:2 and 10:26, and Douglas, "Responding to Ezra," 13–14.

and God made him king over all Israel; nevertheless, foreign women caused even him to sin. Shall we then listen to you and do all this great evil and act treacherously against our God by marrying foreign women?[44]

In this interpretation of Solomon's sins, Nehemiah was following the earlier book of Kings.[45] Not too long after Nehemiah, the book of Chronicles rewrote much of earlier Israelite history on the basis of Kings, but the author of this book chose to excise all criticisms of Solomon's foreign wives.[46] In fact, Chronicles accepts marriages between Israelites and others as part of life, including a number of such exogamous pairings in the genealogy of Judah himself.[47] The author of Chronicles seems to be trying to undercut the claims made by Ezra and Nehemiah for the importance of genetic purity: not so, says Chronicles, and it never has been so.

One of the more fascinating arguments mounted by Nehemiah against these marriages was a sociolinguistic one: "I saw the *yehudim*, who brought in Ashdodite, Ammonite, and Moabite women, and their children – half spoke Ashdodite and were not able to speak Judahite – and so on, the language of each people. I contested with them and degraded them, and struck some of those men."[48] This may have struck many observers as odd: after all, Nehemiah himself spoke Persian and Aramaic before he spoke Hebrew. Typically the language of the home did follow the man of the house, but was Nehemiah really prepared to wade into the domestic situations negotiated by various married couples? That seemed to many to be crossing the line, and turning the personal into the political.[49]

---

[44] Nehemiah 13:26–27.

[45] For analyses of the criticism of Solomon in Kings, see Shaye J. D. Cohen, "Solomon and the Daughter of Pharaoh: Intermarriage, Conversion, and the Impurity of Women," *JANES* 16–17 (1984–85), 23–37, and Marvin A. Sweeney, "The Critique of Solomon in the Josianic Edition of the Deuteronomistic History," *JBL* 114 (1995), 607–22.

[46] Armin Lange, "The Significance of the Pre-Maccabean Literature from the Qumran Library for the Understanding of the Hebrew Bible: Intermarriage in Ezra/Nehemiah – Satan in 1 Chr 21:1 – the Date of Psalm 119," in André Lemaire (ed.), *Congress Volume Ljubljana 2007*, VT Suppl. 133 (Leiden: Brill, 2010), 180–82.

[47] Gary N. Knoppers, "Intermarriage, Social Complexity, and Ethnic Diversity in the Genealogy of Judah," *JBL* 120 (2001), 19–23 and 29–30.

[48] Nehemiah 13:23–25.

[49] For some insightful comments on Nehemiah 13 from a sociolinguistic perspective, see Katherine E. Southwood, "'And They Could Not Understand Jewish Speech': Language, Ethnicity, and Nehemiah's Intermarriage Crisis," *JTS* 62 (2011), 1–19, and Gerald A. Klingbeil, "'Not So Happily Ever After ...': Cross-Cultural Marriages in the Time of Ezra-Nehemiah," *Maarav*, 14 (2007), 64–66. Klingbeil points to Psalm 45:11 as attesting to an earlier cultural ideal: women abandon their cultural heritages for the sake of that of their husbands. Jon L. Berquist, "Constructions of Identity in Postcolonial Yehud," in Oded Lipschits and Manfred Oeming (eds.), *Judah and Judeans in the Persian Period* (Winona Lake, IN: Eisenbrauns, 2006), 64, notes the irony of a concern for linguistic purity appearing in a bilingual book.

Back in the Persian heartland, reaction to the reforms of Ezra and Nehemiah was presumably ambivalent. Many in the east supported Ezra, especially since he drew his legitimacy from the exilic community. The vigorous defense of Jewish identity was also appreciated by many, who feared that as time went on and lines were blurred, Judaism itself might be lost. His strong-arm tactics likely attracted much criticism, although defenders claimed that there was no alternative given the circumstances.

Certainly Ezra was wise enough never to criticize those who had remained in the east, and thus did not alienate this important source of support.[50] Jerusalem was a pilgrimage center and might perhaps serve as an anchor of religious life, but never was it claimed that those not in Yehud were delegitimized.[51] Indeed, Ezra uses "Israel" as a way of indicating his "acceptance of the international nature of the Judean people." All who venerate the Temple in Jerusalem and look to the leadership in Jerusalem as the leadership of this new international community are *yehudim*. But that was not to imply that it made no difference whether one lived in Yehud itself or supported it from afar. "Judaism has become an international religion, but the religious practices of the 'children of the exile,' who live in different international settings, are not and cannot be completely identical."[52] Indeed, Ezra's identification of "Israel" with the exile was seen by all as "a privileging of the Diaspora in the continuing history of the Judean people." According to Ezra, those who had returned and now lived in their ancestral land were still identified primarily on the basis of their experience in the Diaspora.[53]

2. Reactions in the Diaspora, from the right and from the left

Some Jews in the Diaspora, however, reacted negatively to some of the tenets of Ezra's platform. While he aimed to strengthen Jewishness by utilizing Persian power, and seemed to see political authority as merely a way of achieving religious goals, others argued that simply being a loyal Jew,

---

[50] Shemaryahu Talmon, "שיבת ציון – השלכותיה לעתיד," *Cathedra*, 4 (1977), 26–30, esp. 29–30.

[51] John Kessler, "The Diaspora in Zechariah 1–8 and Ezra-Nehemiah: The Role of History, Social Location, and Tradition in the Formulation of Identity," in Gary N. Knoppers and Kenneth A. Ristau (eds.), *Community Identity in Judean Historiography: Biblical and Comparative Perspectives* (Winona Lake, IN: Eisenbrauns, 2009), 135–37 and 144–45.

[52] Gary N. Knoppers, "Ethnicity, Genealogy, Geography, and Change: The Judean Community of Babylon and Jerusalem in the Story of Ezra," in Gary N. Knoppers and Kenneth A. Ristau (eds.), *Community Identity in Judean Historiography: Biblical and Comparative Perspectives* (Winona Lake, IN: Eisenbrauns, 2009), 170.

[53] *Ibid.*, 168.

without political involvement, was the best way to achieve success in Persian terms. These people told stories about Jews who had bravely stood up to the authorities, and had even narrowly escaped death as the price for their insurrection. According to the stories, God would protect those who remained loyal to their religion at all costs. Characters such as Daniel, Hananiah, Mishael, and Azariah were said to have survived harrowing experiences in order to prove their faithfulness. These stories claimed that if one was loyal as a Jew, worldly success would follow: Daniel became the chief interpreter of the court; Hananiah, Mishael, and Azariah were all appointed to high-ranking positions of governance.[54]

In sum, these stories aimed for a complex message, a corrective to the simplistic position asserted by Ezra.[55] Being a Jew and being a Persian are both valuable. These stories were not sanguine about retaining dual loyalties. When these values conflict, the choice must be clear: first and foremost, loyalty must be to one's Jewish identity. God will then ensure survival and even success. Paradoxically, for these Jews success was measured in foreign terms: God would reward loyal Jews by securing promotions for them in the *foreign* courts.

These notions, especially in the aggregate, no doubt offended other Jews in the eastern Diaspora. Little can be said about the communities or the intellectual circles in which different ideas traveled, but there were clearly some Jews who did not accept the conventional wisdom sketched until this point. Rather than speculate regarding who these Jews were or where they lived and worked, we will allow a single fictional Jew named Marduka to stand in for this collective.[56] (Thus, "Marduka (fictional character)" here can be seen as simply a stand-in for the clumsy locution "the anonymous author of the book of Esther.")

Marduka may have lived in Susa toward the end of the fifth century and into the fourth century BCE, and was acutely aware of the fact that his name could be traced back to the name of the Babylonian god Marduk. Nevertheless, he treasured his Jewish identity, although he mostly wore it privately. Externally, he was entirely Persian. His loyalties were first and

---

[54] For a fuller discussion of the image of the Diaspora in Daniel, see Sharon Pace, "Diaspora Dangers, Diaspora Dreams," in Peter W. Flint, Emanuel Tov, and James C. VanderKam (eds.), *Studies in the Hebrew Bible, Qumran, and the Septuagint Presented to Eugene Ulrich*, VT Suppl. 102 (Leiden: Brill, 2006), 21–59, and see below.

[55] See Smith-Christopher, "Prayers and Dreams," 266–90.

[56] For the name Marduka in the period under discussion, see the references in Carey A. Moore, "Archaeology and the Book of Esther," *Biblical Archaeologist*, 38 (1975), 74. But whereas Moore uses this personal name as evidence for a historical Mordecai, I am simply referring to it as a name that existed in the Persian period.

foremost to the empire, which, he believed, was the sole protectorate of the Jews – and all other loyal people.

Inwardly Marduka was intensely Jewish, with deeply held beliefs about the Jewish people and Jewish texts and history. He was well educated, and made sure to read the old Israelite texts carefully. He was well acquainted with the lore of times past, with the stories of the Patriarchs, of the Exodus, and of the early monarchies of Saul and David. He reveled in the tales of their successes, and lamented the decline of the monarchy and the fall of Jerusalem. He thought it foolish to spend too much time worrying about the past, however. What's done is done, Marduka would often say, to himself and anyone else who would listen. This infuriated some of his friends, who would insist that what's done had to be undone, and point to Nehemiah as their exemplar.

Sometimes the question was put explicitly: who was the better Jew? Was it the Jew who stayed in Susa to advocate on behalf of his people, working behind the scenes to ensure that the Jews throughout the empire could enjoy the freedoms and rights they took for granted? Or was it the Jew who trekked back to Jerusalem, sacrificing the luxuries of a court life for the hardship of life in a western province, but getting his hands dirty with the work of rebuilding the Jewish community around Jerusalem?

Marduka was sure that it was better to stay where the power was, to use that power for the greatest good. He was also vehemently opposed to the stories about Daniel and his friends; these he found to be not just misguided, but actually dangerous. He became furious when some well-intentioned friends entertained his children with variations on the story of Daniel in the lions' den. "Do you want my children to believe that God will protect them from lions if they are foolish enough to get tossed into the den?" he asked. He feared that children growing up on these stories – and even adults who did not think hard enough about them – might be led to believe absurdities. They might rely on miraculous experience to protect them from the empire. Far wiser, he knew, was not to cross the empire in the first place. He had seen a number of colleagues who thought they could fight the bureaucracy, and not one of them had garnered a promotion as a result. Not one of them was alive.

This was not to say that the Persians were vicious, or even unkind. Marduka couldn't help but think that they were actually fair. Loyalty was demanded, that was true, but that did not seem unreasonable. If you played by their rules, life under the Persians was good. It was stable, safe, and secure; good jobs, even government jobs, were available to be had.

All of this did gnaw at him, though, for religious reasons. What had happened to God? In all the stories he knew from the past, God played a central role. He communicated, he orchestrated, he castigated, he defended, he triumphed. Most importantly, he *acted*. But where was he now? It seemed that he was simply no longer needed; the world was running well in his absence, thanks to the one who now called himself the "King of Kings" – the Persian monarch. Was this really the new reality? Had the God of Israel ceded control of the world to the king of Persia? It seemed like an absurd conclusion to come to, but it also seemed like an unavoidable one.

Finally Marduka decided to tell a story that would explain his thinking. He knew his views were not the conventional wisdom on many issues, but they seemed so obvious to him. The first decision he made was to write in Hebrew. Not all the Jews in his community could read, let alone write, Hebrew, but his own education had been quite strong, and he was confident that he could write a whole story in Hebrew. He savored the idea, too. Some had taken to calling Hebrew "Yehudite,"[57] or, in other words, the language spoken by the people of Yehud.[58] Others called it "the language of the sanctuary" (*leshon ha-qodesh*).[59] Marduka could add this to the list of things that bothered him. Hebrew was not the language of the sanctuary, or the language of the residents of Yehud; it was the language of the Jews!

In the exile in Babylonia and Persia, the Jews spoke Aramaic, at home and in their interactions with their neighbors. The Babylonians had a proud linguistic heritage, and never failed to remind anyone who would listen that the greatest literature in the world was in *their* language, Akkadian. The famed laws of Hammurabi were still being studied and copied, and the epic story of Gilgamesh's quest for immortality was still told reverently two millennia after Gilgamesh's death. By the time the Jews arrived in Babylonia, however, Aramaic had become the language of commerce, politics, and even law.[60] For the Jews this was fortunate, since many already spoke Aramaic, and the rest picked it up rather quickly.

---

[57] Nehemiah 13:24.
[58] This usage goes back at least to the eighth century BCE, when it presumably distinguished "Judean" from "Israelite" Hebrew; see 2 Kings 18:26–28 = Isaiah 36:11–13.
[59] For some discussion of the term, see Esther Eshel and Michael E. Stone, "לשון הקודש באחרית הימים לאור קטע מקומראן," *Tarbiz*, 62 (1993), 169–77, and Seth Schwartz, "Language, Power and Identity in Ancient Palestine," *Past & Present*, 148 (1995), 3–47.
[60] See Hayim Tadmor, "The Aramaization of Assyria: Aspects of Western Impact," in H.-J. Nissen and J. Renger (eds.), *Mesopotamien und seine Nachbarn: Politische und kulturelle Wechselbeziehungen im alten Vorderasien vom 4. bis 1. Jt. v. Chr.* (Berlin: Dietrich Reimer, 1987), 449–70, and Hayim Tadmor, "On the Role of Aramaic in the Assyrian Empire," in Masao Mori,

Many – Marduka wished he could say all, but lamentably that was not true – many of the Jews made sure to teach their sons Hebrew, as well. Hebrew was taught as a language of prayer and as a sacred language of texts encountered by every Jewish school child in the Diaspora.[61] The community worked hard to preserve their identity, and studying the Hebrew language and Hebrew texts was one of their primary means of doing so.

It was thus maddening for Marduka, and other Jews in the eastern Diaspora, to learn that back in the west, the Jews in Jerusalem were claiming the Hebrew language as their exclusive inheritance. This was symptomatic, Marduka felt, of a larger trend. Those over in Yehud had been arrogating the position of the "legitimate" Jews for themselves, but this was something that Marduka's story would contest at every turn. His choice of language excited him, because "the use of Hebrew allowed one to assert one's Jewishness simply by speaking."[62]

In formulating his ideology, it seemed to Marduka that the ideology against which he was railing was in fact a composite. There was a linguistic component – the view that Hebrew was *leshon ha-qodesh*; there was a geographic component – the view that Jewish life should be centered in Jerusalem; there was an ethnic component – the view that the leaders of the Jews, even now, ought to be from the House of David; there was a genealogical component – the view that Jews had to be pure-blooded and separate themselves from their neighbors; there was a historiosophical component – the view that the ideal future would be the mass return of all Jews to Israel, as had happened in the time of the Exodus; there was a political component – the view that the Persian bureaucracy was acting out God's will on the earth. This complex of beliefs, what he began to think of

---

Hideo Ogawa, Mamoru Yoshikawa (eds.), *Near Eastern Studies Dedicated to H.I.H. Prince Takahito Mikasa on the Occasion of his Seventy-Fifth Birthday* (Wiesbaden: O. Harrassowitz, 1991), 419–35.

[61] This sounds like a modern arrangement, but it should be emphasized that the study of Hebrew was assuredly alive and well in the Persian Diaspora, at least among some elements of the Jewish population. Although much of the literature produced there was in Aramaic – such as Daniel 2–7 and some of the texts discovered among the Dead Sea Scrolls, but clearly much older (on this, see my paper "Jewish Aramaic Literature of Achaemenid Times," presented at the SBL annual meeting in San Francisco in November 2011) – there is also the evidence of texts such as Ezra-Nehemiah and others composed in Hebrew. The precise dynamics of this Hebrew education are not known, of course. Cf. Oded, "The Judean Exiles in Babylonia," 68*, and Joachim Schaper, "Hebrew and its Study in the Persian Period," in William Horbury (ed.), *Hebrew Study from Ezra to Ben-Yehuda* (Edinburgh: T. & T. Clark, 1999), 15–26.

[62] Mark W. Hamilton, "Who Was a Jew? Jewish Ethnicity during the Persian Period," *Restoration Quarterly*, 37 (1995), 102–17 (quotation from p. 114). This is contra Stern, "Esther and the Politics of Diaspora," 25–53, who argues on the basis of the use of Hebrew that the book was composed in Palestine. For some discussion of the use of Hebrew in Persian period Yehud, see Schaper, "Hebrew and its Study in the Persian Period," 15–26, which focuses on what can be inferred about the study of Hebrew, but not on the literature we actually have in Hebrew.

as the Hebrew-Jerusalem-David-endogamy-Exodus-God complex, was not articulated by all, or even by most, contemporary writers with whom Marduka was familiar. But the more he listened to his contemporaries, the more he realized that it was this complex that constituted the position that most of his colleagues took for granted. And so he undertook to dismantle this complex, one element at a time.

CHAPTER 3

Authoring/editing

Joseph, Daniel, and God

1. The composition of the book

A common modern view of the book of Esther holds that the book as we have it in the Masoretic Text (MT) was not composed *de novo*, but represents instead an edited version of an earlier story. That story is preserved in some Greek manuscripts of Esther, which have an edition of the book known as the Alpha Text. This Alpha Text (or AT) is itself not just a translation of the purported earlier version, but has been supplemented with other narrative pieces which will be discussed below (pp. 113–23). When these supplementary sections and other signs of later editing are stripped away, we are not left with a translation of the Hebrew text of Esther known to us, however, but instead we find a story which shares the same broad narrative outline, but differs from Hebrew Esther in important ways.[1]

---

[1] For the view that the AT represents a translation of a pre-MT version of Esther, see C. C. Torrey, "The Older Book of Esther," *HTR* 37 (1944), 1–40 *passim*, esp. 14–15; David J. A. Clines, *The Esther Scroll: The Story of the Story, JSOT* Suppl. 30 (Sheffield: JSOT, 1984), 75–114; Michael V. Fox, *The Redaction of the Books of Esther: On Reading Composite Texts*, SBL Monograph Series 40 (Atlanta: Scholars, 1991); and Michael V. Fox, *Character and Ideology in the Book of Esther*, 2nd edn. (Grand Rapids, MI: Eerdmans, 2001), 254–73; the arguments of Clines and Fox are accepted and developed by, e.g., Frederic W. Bush, *Ruth, Esther*, Word Biblical Commentaries 9 (Waco, TX: Word, 1996), 282–92, and Jon Levenson, *Esther: A Commentary*, Old Testament Library (Louisville and London: Westminster John Knox, 1997), 33; according to Linda Day (*Three Faces of a Queen: Characterization in the Books of Esther, JSOT* Suppl. 186 [Sheffield: JSOT Press, 1995], 18), the scholarly consensus is to accept the view of Clines and Fox. Not everyone has accepted this view, though (thus raising the question of what makes a "scholarly consensus"); according to Emanuel Tov, Kristen De Troyer, and Tricia M. Aven, the AT is a revision of the LXX; see Tov, "The Lucianic Text of the Canonical and the Apocryphal Sections of Esther: A Rewritten Biblical Book," *Textus*, 10 (1982), 1–25, revised in Tov, *The Greek and Hebrew Bible: Collected Essays on the Septuagint, VT* Suppl. 72 (Leiden: Brill, 1999), vol. 1, 535–48; De Troyer, *The End of the Alpha Text of Esther: Translation and Narrative Technique in MT 8:1–17, LXX 8:1–17, and AT 7:14–41*, tr. Brian Doyle, Septuagint and Cognate Studies Series 48 (Atlanta: SBL, 2000); De Troyer, "The Letter of the King and the Letter of Mordecai," *Textus*, 21 (2002), 175–207; Aven, *Three Versions of Esther: Their Relationship to Anti-Semitic and Feminist Critique of the Story* (forthcoming). Aven dates the AT to precisely 38–41 CE. On the basis of this general approach, Joshua E. Burns, "The Special Purim and the Reception of the Book of Esther in the Hellenistic and Early

The story tells of a Jewish man in Susa, who raised his orphaned cousin, Esther, who later becomes queen. Despite her upbringing, she eases into life in the palace, to the point that her connection to her cousin, and to the Jewish people, is uncertain.[2] When an adversary threatens to annihilate the Jews, she has to be persuaded by Mordecai to intervene: "Do not refuse to enter the king's presence and charm him – for my sake and the people's, remembering the days of your humble station when you were brought up by me ... Therefore, call upon God and speak on our behalf to the king, and deliver us from death!"[3] Esther does act, and when she reveals the plot to the king, and after the king discovers Haman's conflict with Mordecai as well, he reacts with incredulity at Haman's foolishness (8:14): "Did he intend to hang even Mordecai, who saved me from the hand of the eunuchs? Did he not know that Esther is of his ancestral race?!"

This tale drew on earlier stories, of course. At some level, the story of Mordecai and Esther seems to have been based on the Babylonian creation myth, known as *Enūma ēlish* (literally, "when on high" – the opening words of the text). In that story, too, there is a hero, Marduk, whose ethnic group (in this case, the gods) faces the mortal threat of annihilation (at the hands of Tiamat). Prior to any direct encounter, Marduk sends intermediaries, the Annunaki, to try to intervene, much as Mordecai sends Esther to intervene. Marduk kills Tiamat, Qingu, and the eleven monsters created by them, much as the Jews kill Haman and his ten sons (and his wife Zeresh?). As a result of the victory, Marduk becomes leader of the gods, endowed with new powers, much as Mordecai becomes vizier of the empire after his victory, also endowed with new powers. At the same time, the Annunaki

Roman Eras," *JSJ* 37 (2006), 22, argued that "it seems clear that AT Esther represents another attempt to recontextualize the book's message for the benefit of a Hellenized, or perhaps Romanized, Jewish audience." A slightly different view was argued by André Lacocque, according to whom the AT was "meant for a non-Jewish audience" ("The Different Versions of Esther," *Biblical Interpretation*, 7 [1999], 321). In my view, the arguments presented by De Troyer for the late date of the AT are not compelling. For one more view – that the AT is a pre-LXX translation of the MT – see Karen H. Jobes, *The Alpha-Text of Esther: Its Character and Relationship to the Masoretic Text*, SBL Dissertation Series 153 (Atlanta: Scholars, 1996). See also Lisbeth S. Fried, "Towards the *Ur*-Text of Esther," *JSOT* 88 (2000), 49–57, whose final argument against the view of Fox et al. is that it is unlikely that the redactor of MT would remove references to God (see also Lacocque, "The Different Versions of Esther," 320), but see below.

[2] This is a major theme of the discussion in Martien A. Halvorson-Taylor, "Secrets and Lies: Secrecy Notices (Esther 2:10, 20) and Diasporic Identity in the Book of Esther," *JBL* 131 (2012), 467–485; see esp. p. 482.

[3] AT of Esther 5:4. There is no agreed numbering of the passages in the AT; the translation and reference here and below are from Clines, *The Esther Scroll*, 227; see also the translation by Karen Jobes in Albert Pietersma and Benjamin G. Wright (eds.), *A New English Translation of the Septuagint and the Other Greek Translations Traditionally Included under that Title* (New York: Oxford University Press, 2007), 431.

celebrate: "they rejoiced and they were glad; they brought him gifts and presents." The Jews, too, celebrate with "a day of feasting and happiness" and "the sending of portions to one another." Both stories also feature banquets as the setting of important moments, and other linguistic and ideological parallels which link the two.[4]

This story was not about any festival; there is no concluding etiology justifying Purim at the end.[5] In fact, the story does not easily reduce to being *about* anything at all. It is a charming tale, "the story of a conflict between two courtiers which precipitates a threat to the Jewish people."[6] Along the way, the story touches on issues of piety, assimiliation, and loyalty, but it draws no certain conclusions, and makes no emphatic claims.

2. Modeling heroes

Marduka took this tale and adapted it.[7] It cannot be said with certainty when the book of Esther, as we have it, was composed, but a date in the latter half of the Persian period, in the early fourth century BCE, accounts well for all the data.[8] The author probably lived in, or in the vicinity of, Susa itself. To situate his story, he harks back to an earlier, more glorious time of

---

[4] The connection between Esther and *Enūma elish* is discussed most fully by Adam Silverstein, "The Book of Esther and the *Enūma elish*," *Bulletin of the School of Oriental and African Studies*, 69 (2006), 209–23. Silverstein takes the MT as his point of departure, so includes some parallels, not as strong as those discussed here, which are found only in the MT and not in the Proto-AT. If those parallels are judged to be compelling, one would have to stipulate that the author/editor who transformed the Proto-AT story into the story found in the MT was further influenced by the *Enūma elish* tale.

[5] See Fox, *The Redaction of the Books of Esther*, 119 and 125. Stephanie Dalley argued that Esther was composed in seventh-century Assyria; a key part of her argument is the word, *pûr*, meaning "lottery," which is an Assyrian word that contrasts with Babylonian *isqû* "lottery." See Dalley, *Esther's Revenge at Susa: From Sennacherib to Ahasuerus* (Oxford University Press, 2007). This is a provocative but very problematic book; see my review in *Review of Biblical Literature*, www.bookreviews.org/pdf/6731_7297.pdf (accessed June 19, 2013). In the AT, however, the notice about the *pûr* is missing from 3:7 (see Halvorson-Taylor, "Secrets and Lies," 474 n. 25, for the significance of this), adding a further complication to Dalley's hypothesis. (I did not realize this when I wrote the review just mentioned.)

[6] Clines, *The Esther Scroll*, 78.

[7] It is possible that the author of the MT Esther did not work directly on the Proto-AT, but that the works should instead be seen as two versions of a shared proto-text. This is the argument of Fox, *The Redactions of the Books of Esther*, e.g., the diagram on p. 9. Fox admits that this is not certain, however, and he "speak[s] of proto-AT as the background of the MT Esther; this is shorthand for speaking of proto-Esther as attested in the proto-AT" (*ibid.*, 97). I will follow this practice, as well, if only as a heuristic model.

[8] The language is obviously Late Biblical Hebrew (see the data in Ronald L. Bergey, "Late Linguistic Features in Esther," *JQR* 75 [1984], 66–78), but it goes beyond that, showing closer affinities to Mishnaic Hebrew than any other book. For a good study of such features, see Harald Martin Wahl, "Die Sprache des hebräischen Esterbuches, mit Anmerkungen zu seinem historischen und traditions-geschichtlichen Referenzrahmen," *Zeitschrift für Althebraistik*, 12 (1999), 21–47. Still, it is impossible

Persian history: "It was in the days of Xerxes – the Xerxes who ruled from India to Nubia, 127 provinces." His readers would have known of a different Xerxes (II), who reigned for less than two months (in 424 BCE). They also may have known that the Persians lost control over Egypt in 399, and thus looked back to the era of Xerxes I as the high-water mark of Persian territorial control.

The author began by complicating the heroes somewhat. The literary Mordecai lived in the Persian city of Susa, and had lived there his whole life, but a notice was added in the new story about his family's origins: he was now a descendant of a certain "Kish, who had been carried into exile from Jerusalem by Nebuchadnezzar king of Babylon, among those taken captive with Jehoiachin king of Judah."[9] Thus, his diaspora identity became an explicit part of his biography. Mordecai was also further developed in the MT version: "he becomes not only the savior of the people but also their spiritual leader."[10]

Mordecai's cousin, who possessed very little biography in the AT version of the story, was also complicated somewhat: she was given a Hebrew name, Hadassah, in addition to her name Esther, from the Persian word for "star."[11] Her personality, too, is more developed in the MT version of the story, in which she grows from a "malleable, nervous little beauty" to a courageous leader who takes initiatives and achieves great dignity.[12]

---

simply to line up the late biblical books in chronological order, given the geographic variation; we have no knowledge of what the Hebrew written by Jews in the eastern Diaspora looked like, and how it differed from the Hebrew utilized in Palestine, so the linguistic analysis cannot help us narrow the date down further. For other, literary considerations, see Sara R. Johnson, "Novelistic Elements in Esther: Persian or Hellenistic, Jewish or Greek?" *CBQ* 67 (2005), 571–89, with many further references to earlier scholarship on the dating of the book. A recent thorough discussion of the issue by Aven, *Three Versions of Esther*, chapter 1, arrives at a date of 400 BCE.

[9] For more on this introduction, see below, pp. 45–53.

[10] Fox, *The Redaction of the Books of Esther*, 122.

[11] The etymology of Esther as deriving from the Persian word for "star" is found already in the Babylonian Talmud (Megillah 13a), where it is quoted in the name of R. Nehemiah: "Hadassah was her name, and why was she called 'Esther'? Because the nations of the world called her that after 'Istehar' [Venus, the morning star]." It is found also in the two rabbinic Targumim to Esther and other rabbinic texts; see further Eliezer Segal, *The Babylonian Esther Midrash: A Critical Commentary*, 3 vols., Brown Judaic Studies 291–93 (Atlanta: Scholars, 1994), vol. II, 44–45. The medieval Arabic-speaking Jewish commentators also knew this etymology; Tanhum ha-Yerushalmi, for example, writes, "It is said moreover, that, 'Esther' is taken from the name of the Morning Star, which in Persian is אסתהר, though the ה was elided and it became אסתר" (Michael G. Wechsler, *Strangers in the Land: The Judaeo-Arabic Exegesis of Tanhum ha-Yerushalmi on the Books of Ruth and Esther* [Jerusalem: Magnes, 2010], 219, and see there, n. 115, for further references). For the etymology, see Ran Zadok, "Notes on Esther," *ZAW* 98 (1986), 107. For a different recent suggestion, see David Testen, "Semitic Terms for 'Myrtle': A Study in Covert Cognates," *JNES* 57 (1998), 281 n. 2.

[12] Fox, *The Redactions of the Books of Esther*, 122–23.

Marduka also added a patronym to Esther: whereas in the AT, she was just Esther (AT 2:7), he added "daughter of Avihayil."[13] This identification means that she has an explicit father, with a Jewish name, through whom her ethnic identity may be visible; this identifying marker is deployed later in the story, as well, as an effective way of reminding the reader of Esther's complicated identity.[14] Whereas "in the AT, her nationality, status, and other family connections are unexplored," and "her relationship to Mordecai appears to be the focus,"[15] in the new story, it was specifically the issues of identity, and the complexity of diaspora identity personified by Esther, that were the focus.

Marduka thought that the dual names were particularly poignant and significant, as they reminded him of the biblical Joseph. The connection to Joseph began to look even larger in Marduka's mind as he went on. After all, Joseph, too, was a Jew in a foreign court. Not only had Joseph not flaunted his Jewish identity, but he had actively hidden it from his own brothers. Some in the court had used his ethnicity to try to keep him down, belittling him as a "Hebrew kid" (Genesis 41:12). Later he was stripped of his "Hebrewness," and rose to great power in his new persona as an Egyptian. With an Egyptian name, an Egyptian wife, and an Egyptian accent, Joseph, now in the guise of Tsafenath Paneah, was a wonderful role model for Marduka/Mordecai.[16]

Even better, Joseph had used his deep acculturation to save the Jews. Arguing for assimilation was not Marduka's goal; he wanted to show that acting that part of the dominant culture would actually be better for the Jews in the long run. This was not because he thought God would miraculously step in, as the stories of Daniel claimed, but because from the inside the bureaucracy could be used as a tool to help. But one had to be inside to use it. Joseph had understood that: he did not want to be ruler because the power was intoxicating, but because the power could be beneficial. "It is Joseph's Otherness as an Egyptian official that makes him most valuable in the eyes of the Israelites. Yet his Otherness is only apparent, for deep down, Joseph is still his father's son and the brother of his brothers."[17] Wasn't that what Marduka had been trying to argue?

The use of Joseph had another advantage. Marduka well knew that some of his colleagues in the Jewish community had modeled their heroes after

---

[13] Halvorson-Taylor, "Secrets and Lies," 477–78.   [14] See below, pp. 74–78.

[15] Halvorson-Taylor, "Secrets and Lies," 478 n. 37; see also p. 482.

[16] See esp. Carolyn B. Sharp, *Irony and Meaning in the Hebrew Bible*, Indiana Studies in Biblical Literature (Bloomington: Indiana University Press, 2009), 55–60, and at length below.

[17] Sharp, *Irony and Meaning in the Hebrew Bible*, 59.

Joseph, as well, but had insisted on improving on the prototype. There was one particular story that came to mind in this regard, a story of a Jew, Daniel, in the court of a foreign king, making a name for himself by interpreting dreams.[18] This, like the story of Joseph, was a tale of a king who had a dream and sought help from his wise men regarding it. The king's reaction was described in the same way as Pharaoh's reaction had been (*va-tippā'em rūḥŏ*[19]), and in both cases the professional wise men proved unable to help with the dream. In both stories a royal official informs the king of the Israelite who can do better than the professionals, and in both the Israelite is explicitly identified as an exile, a "Hebrew lad" or a "Judean exile." In both stories the Jewish "lad" claims that God has sent the dream and its interpretation, and that history itself is dictated by God. Both dreams turn out to be symbolic, referring to the future. And in both cases the Israelite interpreter is rewarded with great political power.[20]

This was quite a brilliant use of allusions, Marduka thought. What he found maddening was that the storyteller actually made his hero *superior* to Joseph.[21] This was true first with regard to his interpretive powers: while Joseph merely interpreted the dreams Pharaoh told him about, Daniel had first to divine what the dream was, since Nebuchadnezzar refused to share it.[22] But the superiority of Daniel was also emphasized with regard to his

---

[18] This story reaches us as chapter 2 in Daniel.   [19] Genesis 41:8; Daniel 2:1 and 2:3.

[20] For full discussions of the parallels, see Robert Gnuse, "The Jewish Dream Interpreter in a Foreign Court: The Recurring Use of a Theme in Jewish Literature," *JSP* 7 (1990), 40–42, and Matthew Rindge, "Jewish Identity under Foreign Rule: Daniel 2 as a Reconfiguration of Genesis 41," *JBL* 129 (2010), 85–104. See also Stefan Beyerle, "Joseph and Daniel: Two Fathers in the Court of a Foreign King," in Friedemann W. Golka and Wolfgang Weiß (eds.), *Joseph: Bibel und Literatur: Symposion Helsinki/Lathi 1999*, Oldenburgische Beiträge zu Jüdischen Studien 6 (Bibliotheks- und Informationssystem der Universität Oldenburg, 2000), 60–63.

[21] This was perceived by the political scientist Aaron Wildavsky, *Assimilation versus Separation: Joseph the Administrator and the Politics of Administration in Biblical Israel* (New Brunswick and London: Transaction, 1993), 126–29, who sums up the literary relationship by referring to the song from "Annie Get your Gun": "Anything you can do I can do better." Indeed, Wildavsky's compelling argument is that Genesis itself means to hold up Joseph as an example *not* to be followed; his character – administrating from within the system with calculated efficiency but no heart – is meant to be contrasted with that of Moses, who perceives the immorality of the system and breaks free. See also the sensitive review by Leon Kass in *Commentary*, 96.3 (September, 1993), 58–61. For a critical discussion of Wildavsky's approach to Joseph, and a broader discussion of the differing twentieth-century Jewish approaches to Joseph, focused on the question of how much assimilation or acculturation is acceptable, see the penetrating essay of Pierre Birnbaum, "Exile, Assimilation, and Identity: From Moses to Joseph," in Elisheva Carlebach, John M. Efron, and David M. Myers (eds.), *Jewish History and Jewish Memory: Essays in Honor of Yosef Hayim Yerushalmi* (Hanover and London: Brandeis University Press and the University Press of New England, 1998), 259–65.

[22] On the similarities between the stories with regard to the interpretation of dreams, and the point that Daniel is depicted as superior to Joseph in this regard, see also Nili Shupak, "A Fresh Look at the Dreams of the Officials and of Pharaoh in the Story of Joseph (Genesis 40–41) in the Light of Egyptian Dreams," *JANES* 30 (2006), 103–38, esp. 104–05.

piety. Joseph had merely sufficed with saying "the power is not in me: God will respond regarding the fate of Pharaoh."[23] Daniel beseeched God for wisdom, and, when it was granted, embarked on a long prayer of thanks and praise to God.[24]

Marduka could not be sure, of course, of the intentions of those who put the story together in just this way. But he could not help but think that the story was meant to correct the story of Joseph. Clearly those who told the story of Daniel did not think that Joseph was an appropriate role model. Joseph, after all, was completely assimilated. He spoke Egyptian and married an Egyptian, and gave his sons names which expressed his gratitude to God for helping him to *forget* his past and thrive in his new land.[25] Certainly, Joseph should not be *emulated*. The Jews should be advocating more connectedness, and more piety! This, in any event, was how the story of Daniel-the-dream-interpreter looked to Marduka. Joseph was a hero, to Marduka's mind, but this story cast aspersions on his place in the Jewish memory.

3. Control of the world: God or king?

As Marduka began to write, a number of points became clear to him. The king was crucial; he was all-powerful. Marduka knew well the power of the king. But he also knew well that the bureaucracy functioned no matter who was at the controls, and that the king could not be relied on to guide the empire with wisdom or ethics. This was one more issue about which he wanted to contest the claims of some of his contemporaries.[26]

---

[23] Genesis 41:16. For discussion, see Miriam Sherman, "Do Not Interpretations Belong to God? A Narrative Assessment of Genesis 40 as it Elucidates the Persona of Joseph," in *Milk and Honey: Essays on Ancient Israel and the Bible in Appreciation of the Judaic Studies Program at the University of California, San Diego* (Winona Lake, IN: Eisenbrauns, 2007), 44–45.

[24] Daniel 2:18 and 2:20–23. According to many scholars, these passages are a later addition to the story in Daniel 2. For a detailed argument to this effect, more precise than previous attempts, see Michael Segal, "From Joseph to Daniel: The Literary Development of the Narrative in Daniel 2," *VT* 59 (2009), 123–49. Segal contends that 2:15–24a were added by the author of Daniel 7. More important to my mind is the ideological value of the addition: whereas in the story as it originally stood, Daniel was compared to Joseph, the additional verses make Daniel religiously superior to Joseph. It should be noted that if Segal is correct, a fourth-century author would not have known Daniel 2 in its current form, and could therefore not have responded to it. I am unconvinced by the dating of the addition, however; the connection to Daniel 7, while undoubtedly real, does not necessitate Daniel 7 in its current form, with the little horn. If Segal is correct, however, the details of the presentation above – but not the central theses – will have to be modified.

[25] Genesis 41:51–52. See further below, Chapter 7.

[26] For a fuller discussion of this issue, see Koller, "Negotiating Empire."

Many of the Jews who had returned to Yehud, and in particular those associated with the Ezra-Nehemiah movement, argued that there was a confluence of wills between the human monarchs and God.[27] It was true that this type of thinking had roots in earlier Israelite thought; a century earlier, Jeremiah had conceived of the Babylonians as the arm of God (see especially Jeremiah 25 and 27),[28] and a century before that, Isaiah claimed that Assyria was the rod of God's wrath.[29] In the Persian period, this view became very popular. It is clearly expressed in the discussion of the Temple in Ezra and Nehemiah: according to these books, the Temple was built at the behest of God, through Persian imperial decree and with Persian financial support.[30] It was the view of the prophet who called Cyrus "[God's] appointed one."[31] Ezra and Nehemiah went out of their way to remind everyone, at every opportunity, that the *Temple of the Lord* had been built at the behest of the Persian king, and even with Persian imperial support. And indeed, in one passage, the claim is even made that the exiles claimed to be the only ones authorized to build the Temple, "just as King Cyrus, king of Persia, commanded us"![32] No one was quite sure whether the latter claim was true, but it made its point very strikingly: the Persian king was a servant of God.[33]

---

[27] Sara Japhet, "Sheshbazzar and Zerubbabel against the Background of the Historical and Religious Rendencies of Ezra-Nehemiah:Part 1," *ZAW* 94 (1982), 66–98, reprinted in and cited from Japhet, *From the Rivers of Babylon to the Highlands of Judah: Collected Studies on the Restoration Period* (Winona Lake, IN: Eisenbrauns, 2006), 53–84, at 59; see also Wright, *Rebuilding Identity*, 83. André LaCocque, *Esther Regina: A Bakhtinian Reading*, Rethinking Theory (Evanston, IL: Northwestern University Press, 2008), 36, also emphasizes the blurred lines between God and the king in the narratives about Persia.

[28] On this motif in Jeremiah 27–29 in particular, and the question of the relationship of these chapters to the rest of the book of Jeremiah on the one hand and to Daniel on the other, see Paul-Alain Beaulieu, "The Babylonian Background of the Motif of the Fiery Furnace in Daniel 3," *JBL* 128 (2009), 273–90, esp. 288–90.

[29] See esp. Baruch A. Levine, "הוי, אשור שבט אפי" (ישׁ' י:טוֹ) – אמונת הייחוד המקראית באספקלריה מדינית-בינלאומית," *Eretz Israel*, 27 (2003), 136–42; Levine, "Assyrian Ideology and Israelite Monotheism," *Iraq*, 67 (2005), 411–27.

[30] This point is made by many; see e.g. Japhet, "Sheshbazzar and Zerubbabel," and David L. Petersen, "The Temple in Persian Period Prophetic Texts," in Philip R. Davies (ed.), *Second Temple Studies 1: Persian Period, JSOT* Suppl. 117 (Sheffield Academic, 1991), 131–32.

[31] For the significance of this text in this regard I am indebted to Ari Mermelstein. Joseph Angel pointed out that Chronicles, too, takes this approach to history; the very last chapter in the book asserts that both the exile at the hands of Nebuchadnezzar and the restoration ordered by Cyrus were performed in fulfillment of the will of God.

[32] This is Ezra 4:5, discussed in this regard by Hamilton, "Who Was a Jew?," 113–14.

[33] Petersen, "The Temple in Persian Period Prophetic Texts," emphasizes that the claim that the Temple was built at the request of God, through Persian decree and with Persian financial support, shows the author of Ezra-Nehemiah purposefully creating a picture that emphasizes the unifying power of the Temple (see esp. pp. 131–32), especially since the claims may not be true.

The stories circulating about Daniel drew more complex pictures of the relationship between the power of the Persians and God than the simplistic equation claimed by Ezra and Nehemiah's followers. Marduka found these stories troubling, as well. This issue was broached in the first lines of the story about Daniel's relocation to exile. The story claimed that God handed victory, including some of the Temple vessels, to Nebuchadnezzar; thus the king, powerful as he might appear, was reduced to being a puppet of God.[34]

On the other hand, the stories were vicious in their satirization of the foreign kings. Over and over the stories told of kings being reduced to powerless chumps in the face of God. One story told that Nebuchadnezzar himself was made less than human as punishment for not recognizing God (Daniel 4). Multiple stories reported that when God and the king clashed, the king had no chance of imposing his will: in Daniel 3, Hananiah, Mishael, and Azariah are tossed into a fiery furnace for their failure to bow down to Nebuchadnezzar's idol, but are protected by an angelic figure, and in Daniel 6, Daniel himself is cast into a den of lions for praying to God and thus violating a decree that Darius the Mede was tricked into making; he, too, is protected by an angel. Still other stories claimed that the kings of the great empires were at God's mercy but could not even understand God's messages without the help of Jewish interpreters:[35] in Daniel 2, Nebuchadnezzar dreams of a statue with component parts, representing the four great empires of the world, and in Daniel 5, Belshazzar sees incomprehensible writing on the wall, and both the dream and the writing are deciphered only by Daniel.[36] The kings in these stories are "inept and occasionally ridiculous."[37]

Clearly the kings in these stories are not evil.[38] But Marduka found the implication of the stories absurd all the same. These texts all claim that the immense royal power is actually subject to the will of God. One can

---

[34] See Daniel 1:1–2.

[35] See Athalya Brenner, "Who's Afraid of Feminist Criticism? Who's Afraid of Biblical Humour? The Case of the Obtuse Foreign Ruler in the Hebrew Bible," *JSOT* 63 (1994), 42 and 48–51, on the kings in Daniel (esp. Belshazzar).

[36] According to Segal, "From Joseph to Daniel," 143–44 n. 51, only Nabonidus and Daniel could *see* the writing on the wall in chapter 5, while no one else could see anything at all.

[37] Erich Gruen, "Persia through the Jewish Looking Glass," in Tessa Rajak, Sarah Pearce, James Aitken, and Jennifer Dines (eds.), *Jewish Perspectives on Hellenistic Rulers* (Berkeley: University of California Press, 2007), 53–75 (quotation from p. 69). See also Erich Gruen, *Diaspora: Jews amidst Greeks and Romans* (Cambridge, MA: Harvard University Press, 2002), 135–212.

[38] For a more nuanced discussion of the image of the empire in the book of Daniel, see Pace, "Diaspora Dangers, Diaspora Dreams." She concludes: "The author thus presents a nuanced examination of foreign laws that can be kept and foreign laws that should be abhorred ... Even a sympathetic king, such as Darius (Daniel 6) may not be able to protect the community against those who hate and fear them – how much more so a king who despises them" (58–59).

conclude, therefore, that if the king is successfully wielding his power, it is at the pleasure of God that he does so.

Marduka knew that the view of the king as God's actor on earth was precisely what the Persian kings themselves argued.[39] The difference was only with regard to which deity was the power behind the throne: Darius claimed (in his inscription at Behistun) that his actions were authorized by Ahuramazda, whereas Ezra and the others claimed that it was the God of Israel who controls even foreign kings. The Jews thus subverted and co-opted the Persian ideology, but the Jewish historiosophy reflected here agreed that the king's actions are the means by which the divine will is executed in the world.

This was what did not sit right with Marduka. Could the king of Persia really be God's emissary on earth? The king of Persia, he knew, was an unreliable and unpredictable, power-hungry leader, who made decisions on the basis of political calculations and personal opportunities. Was this the way God wanted the world to be run? Marduka could not accept such a view. It was therefore critical for him to show in his story that the king was not someone who could be trusted. He was not an evil person, by no means an enemy of the Jew, but he acted in his own best interests and in the best interests of his own dynasty or those closest to him, not in the best interests of God's people. Marduka's story therefore would be radical: it would contain no mention of God.[40]

He decided to set his story a few generations back, under the now-legendary king Xerxes I. No one could doubt the power of the empire under Xerxes. His reach was immense, and he had even invaded Greece and defeated the Spartans. If ever a king could have appeared to have the power of God on his side, it was Xerxes I. (More recently there had been another king Xerxes, but his power paled in comparison to that of the first one.) So the story began, "It was in the days of Xerxes, the Xerxes who ruled over 127 provinces, from India to Nubia."

---

[39] See James Bowitck, "Characters in Stone: Royal Ideology and Yehudite Identity in the Behistun Inscription and the Book of Haggai," in Gary N. Knoppers and Kenneth A. Ristau (eds.), *Community Identity in Judean Historiography: Biblical and Comparative Perspectives* (Winona Lake, IN: Eisenbrauns, 2009), 106–07.

[40] In the AT, God is mentioned fairly regularly. If those notices are original, we have to conclude that the author of the MT version removed them. I do not find this far-fetched at all, since the non-mention of God plays a critical role in the story (see below, pp. 96–103). However, the later Greek translation of Esther also contains references to God, in precisely the same places. Rather than posit that the names were removed and then restored, therefore, it is also possible to suggest that the names of God were introduced, secondarily, into the AT, along with the Additions, under the influence of the LXX version. See also below, Chapter 9, n. 57.

CHAPTER 4

Identity of a hero
Mordecai the yehudi, scion of the House of Saul

1. Fronting identity: who is a *yehudi*?

When it came to introducing his main Jewish characters, Marduka chose to begin, "There was a *yehudi* in the fortress Susa, named Mordecai..." This was appropriately subversive, on several fronts. First, the term for "fortress," *bīrāh*, had recently been co-opted by some of his co-religionists to refer to the Temple in Jerusalem.[1] This may have been the result of a shift of the status of Jerusalem in the fifth century: it became the capital of the province of Yehud, replacing Mizpah. Its fortifications had been restored, and *bīrāh* (literally "fortified town, citadel") was now appropriate.[2] But this introduction asserted as explicitly as possible that the *real*, relevant *bīrāh* was not Jerusalem, but Susa.[3]

Marduka delighted not only in the Babylonian name borne by his hero, but in assigning him a politically resonant gentilic, as well. He well knew that in the past, *yehudi* had meant "of the tribe of Judah." Even in the not-too-distant past this had been true, and Jeremiah had used the term in what seemed like a natural extension of its original sense: a *yehudi* was one who lived in Judea, even if ethnically he or she belonged to the tribe of Benjamin or another tribe.[4] But more recently the reference of the term had been much contested.

---

[1] 1 Chronicles 29:1, 19 in which David prays that his son Solomon has the strength to built the *bīrāh* which he has prepared.

[2] On the term *bīrāh*, see André Lemaire and Hélène Lozachmeur, "Bīrāh/Birtā' en Araméen," *Syria*, 64 (1987), 261–66. On the status of Jerusalem at this time, see Oded Lipschits, "Achaemenid Imperial Policy, Settlement Processes in Palestine, and the Status of Jerusalem in the Middle of the Fifth Century B.C.E.," in Oded Lipschits, and Manfred Oeming (eds.), *Judah and the Judaeans in the Persian Period* (Winona Lake, IN: Eisenbrauns, 2006), 34–40.

[3] For the archaeology of Susa, including comments regarding the geography within the book of Esther, see Jean Perrot, "'Shoshan ha-Birah,'" *Eretz Israel*, 20 (1989), 155*–160*.

[4] See, e.g., Jeremiah 40:11–12, and also 43:9; 44:1; 52:28. Some comments on the use of *yehudi* before and after the destruction of the First Temple can be found in Brettler, "Judaism in the Hebrew Bible?," 429–30.

The politicization of the terminology began in the late sixth century, when some Jews returned to Jerusalem. Zechariah had begun using *yehudi* to refer to a subset of the Jews. In a striking passage, Zechariah had written:

> Thus said the Lord of Hosts: Whole peoples and the residents of many cities are still to come! The residents of one will go and say to the residents of another: "Let us go and request the favor of the Lord and to seek the Lord of Hosts – I will go, too!" The many peoples and the great nations will come to seek the Lord of Hosts in Jerusalem and to request the favor of the Lord. Thus said the Lord of Hosts: In those days, ten men will grab, from languages of all the nations, they will grab the cloak corner of a Jew (*ish yehudi*) and say, "Let us go with you, for we have heard that God is with you!"[5]

The prophet here uses imagery partly drawn from the eighth century prophets Isaiah and Micah.[6] Those prophets had foreseen many nations streaming to Jerusalem, which in the vision had become a beacon of justice and righteousness to the world. Zechariah here adapts that picture to what he hopes will be the new reality. In particular, it can no longer be taken for granted that the Judeans are already in Jerusalem; now they have to make the pilgrimage, as well. Whereas Isaiah and Micah assumed that the Judeans would be worshiping God in Jerusalem, and foresaw other nations of the world joining in, Zechariah adds that those other nations will be guided on their way by Jews (*yehudi*) who will themselves stream to Jerusalem from various parts of the world to join in the worship of God there.[7] The other nations ("peoples," "residents of many cities," "many peoples," "great nations," "languages of all the nations")[8] will grasp the hem of a *yehudi* and hitch a ride to Jerusalem in order to pay homage to the God of Israel.[9]

---

[5] Zechariah 8:20–22.

[6] See Isaiah 2:2–4 = Micah 4:1–4, and see the differing analyses of this relationship of Dominic Rudman, "Zechariah 8:20–22 & Isaiah 2:2–4/Micah 4:23: A Study in Intertextuality," *BN* 107–08 (2001), 50–54, and Elie Assis, "Zechariah 8 and its Allusions to Jeremiah 30–33 and Deutero-Isaiah," *Journal of Hebrew Scriptures*, 11.1 (2011), 11–12 and 20.

[7] For the motivations of the Jews in Zechariah 8:23, see Kessler, "Diaspora and Homeland in the Early Achaemenid Period," 154 and n. 56.

[8] Contra E. Lipiński, "Recherches sur le livre de Zacharie," *VT* 20 (1970), 43–46, who takes these expressions to refer to Diaspora Jews who sympathize with the Yehud community.

[9] The "grasping of the hem" is now a well-studied practice, which features prominently in the description of the Samalian king Panammuwa in Herbert Donner and Wolfgang Röllig, *Kanaanäische und aramäische Inschriften*, 5th edn. (Wiesbaden: Harrassowitz, 2002), no. 215, line 11 (פי אחז בכנף מארה מלך אשור). As Shalom Paul writes, all relevant texts should be interpreted "not merely as submission but an act of declaring allegiance to the god whose hem of the garment is being grasped" – and the expression is therefore quite appropriate in the context of the non-Jews joining the *yehudim* on their way to worship the God of Israel in Jerusalem. See Shalom M. Paul, "Gleanings from the Biblical and Talmudic Lexica in Light of Akkadian," in Marc Brettler and Michael Fishbane (eds.),

Thus the *ish yehudi* in Zechariah's vision is most naturally understood to be the Diaspora Jew on his way to Jerusalem to join the community in Yehud in worshiping God there. Zechariah's use of *yehudi* is political and deliberately inclusive, therefore. Some of his contemporaries restricted the term to citizens of Yehud, but he expanded the definition to include co-religionists in other regions – as long as they accepted not only the legitimacy but the centrality of the community of Yehud.[10]

If Zechariah began the process of politicizing the terminology, the provocateurs were again the Ezra-Nehemiah group. In official Persian bureaucratic terminology, a *yehudi* was a resident of Yehud or a descendant of the people exiled from the territory now known as Yehud.[11] Ezra and Nehemiah, however, deployed the term *yehudi* shrewdly. Sometimes they used the term to refer to residents of Yehud: "When Sanballat heard that we were rebuilding the wall, he got angry and very mad, and he mocked the Judeans (*yehudim*). He said to his brothers and the Samarian nobles: 'What are the miserable Judeans (*yehudim*) doing?!'"[12] But Nehemiah also uses "the Judeans" to refer to some elite stratum within Judean society.[13] In particular, he uses the term to refer to "the socially and economically superior stratum of Babylonian immigrants."[14]

Minhah le-Nahum: Biblical and Other Studies Presented to Nahum M. Sarna, JSOT Suppl. 154 (Sheffield: JSOT Press, 1993), 242–56, reprinted in and cited from his *Divrei Shalom: Collected Studies of Shalom M. Paul on the Bible and the Ancient Near East, 1967–2005*, Culture and History of the Ancient Near East 23 (Leiden: Brill, 2005), 182–86. The idiom is found in Ugaritic (Edward L. Greenstein, "'To Grasp the Hem' in Ugaritic Literature," *VT* 32 [1982], 217–18) and in Akkadian, as well (Ronald A. Brauner, "'To Grasp the Hem' and 1 Samuel 15:27," *JANES* 6 [1974], 35–38). In *ibid.*, 38 n. 11, Brauner cites Zechariah 8:23, and notes that the *'iš yehudi* here is designated the superior one by virtue of having his hem seized. See also Hayim Tawil, "Hebrew בְּגַד קְצָר = Akkadian *qāta napāṣu*: A Term of Non-Allegiance," *JAOS* 122 (2002), 80–81.

[10] Kessler, "Diaspora and Homeland in the Early Achaemenid Period," esp. 162, argues that Zechariah, as opposed to many of his contemporaries, "is painfully aware of the existential reality of a depopulated Yehud and an extensive diaspora" and that "such a perspective stands in significant tension with other contemporary and near-contemporary sources." The understanding of *yehudi* relied on above is essentially that of Carol L. Meyers and Eric M. Meyers, *Haggai, Zechariah 1–8*, AB 25B (Garden City, NY: Doubleday, 1987), 441. For further discussion (and a different view) regarding the meaning of *yehudi* in the Zechariah passage, see Kessler, "Diaspora and Homeland in the Early Achaemenid Period," 151 with n. 44.

[11] Cf. the Aramaic attestations in Ezra 4:12, 4:23, 5:1, and 6:7. The first attestation is in a letter written by the "men of the province of Beyond the River," complaining that the *yehudim* who had returned to Jerusalem were building the walls. The second, third, and fourth examples are related to the first, and refer to the same group of people.

[12] Nehemiah 3:33–34. See also Nehemiah 1:2 and 4:6.

[13] Smith, *Palestinian Parties and Politics*, 152 and 264 n. 17; Japhet, "Sheshbazzar and Zerubbabel," 73 n. 48.

[14] Joseph Blenkinsopp, "Temple and Society in Achaemenid Judah," in Philip R. Davies (ed.), *Second Temple Studies 1: Persian Period, JSOT* Suppl. 117 (Sheffield Academic, 1991), 47.

There was resistance to such usage, however. The Israelite community in the southern Egyptian garrison of Elephantine called themselves *yehudim* (in the Aramaic determined plural form, *yehudayya*); in a letter addressed to the leadership of Jerusalem,[15] they identify themselves as, "your servant Yedaniah and his entourage, the priests of YHW, and all the *yehudayya*, freemen of Elephantine."[16] The modern editor of that letter, Sir Arthur Cowley, observed that *yehudi* is used here to mean "an ordinary member of the community who is not a priest [*kohen*] or an intellectual leader [*hakham*]."[17] Interestingly, in the first draft of this letter, they had addressed it to "the nobles of the *yehudayya*." The writers may have realized, however, that they were thus playing into the hands of the Jerusalemite leadership, by ceding to them the designation *yehudi*. So in the final draft, they addressed it to "the noblemen of Yehud."[18] Not entirely surprisingly, the Jerusalem leadership never responded to the request from Elephantine.[19] Three years later, another similar plea was issued, but this time the addressees were made to Bagohi, along with Delaya and Shemaya, sons of Sanballat, governor of Samaria.[20]

The only other Persian period text which uses *yehudi* as an ethnic term rather than as a geographic or political term is the book of Esther. Here the

[15] They were writing to request help with the reconstruction of their temple, which had been destroyed by their neighbors. The help of the leadership in Yehud or Samaria was needed either because it had legal jurisdiction or because it had influence with the imperial government; for discussion see Bedford, *Temple Restoration*, 144 n. 127.

[16] Quoted from *TAD*, vol. A, 4.8 (= Cowley 31), lines 21–22. The terms יהודין and יהודיא appear elsewhere in *TAD*, vol. A, 4.3.12 and 4.1.1, 10, and יהודי in appears in vol. B, 2.2.3, 2.9.2, 3; 3.1.3; 3.6.2; 3.13.2; see Knowles, *Centrality Practiced*, 9 n. 24, and Wright, *Rebuilding Identity*, 157 n. 95.

[17] A. E. Cowley, *Aramaic Papyri of the Fifth Century* B.C. (Oxford University Press, 1923), 117.

[18] Compare *TAD*, vol. A, 4.7 (= Cowley 30), lines 17–19, with *TAD*, vol. A, 4.8 (= Cowley 31), lines 18–20. Bezalel Porten, "The Revised Draft of the Letter of Jedaniah to Bagavahya (*TAD*, vol. A, 4.8 = Cowley 31)," in Meir Lubetski, Claire Gottlieb, and Sharon Keller (eds.), *Boundaries of the Ancient World: A Tribute to Cyrus H. Gordon*, *JSOT* Suppl. 273 (Sheffield Academic Press, 1998), 235, notes that the expression "nobles of Yehud" is the usual one, pointing to Jeremiah 27.20; 39.6; Nehemiah 6:17; 13:17. See also Knowles, *Centrality Practiced*, 41 n. 52, who observes the change from *yehudayya* to *yehud*.

[19] *TAD*, vol. A, 4.8 (= Cowley 31), line 18; see Smith, *Palestinian Parties and Politics*, 171–72. Indeed, even later in Ptolemaic Egypt *yehudi* was a term that denoted an individual originally from Yehud, and had no religious meaning. Evidence for this comes from legal documents. All "Hellenes" (i.e., non-Egyptians) had to give their name, patronym, and geographic origin. Sylvie Honigman, "The Birth of a Diaspora: The Emergence of a Jewish Self-Definition in Ptolemaic Egypt in the Light of Onomastics," in Shaye J. D. Cohen and Ernest S. Frerichs (eds.), *Diasporas in Antiquity,*; Brown Judaic Studies 288 (Atlanta: Scholars, 1993), 94–95, has observed that common examples of this last category were *Ioudaioi* (Judeans), *Thraikes* (Thracians), and *Krētoi* (Cretans). Since the question was the individual's place of origin, the use of *Ioudaioi* reveals that this was, in fact, a spatial term and not one of religious identity. (For the changed reality in Roman Egypt, see *ibid.*, 95–99.)

[20] *TAD*, vol. A, 4.9; see Bezalel Porten, *Archives from Elephantine: The Life of an Ancient Jewish Military Colony* (Berkeley: University of California Press, 1968), 289.

usage is pervasive.[21] This is, of course, no accident, and it is not a neutral development within Hebrew.[22] (In fact, in later Hebrew the word for "Jew" is not *yehudi* at all, but *yisra'el!*)[23] It is, rather, the result of the conscious decision on the part of Marduka to subvert current usage. Much like his decision to use the Hebrew language to assert his identity as a full-blooded Jew, his decision to introduce his hero as a *yehudi* is designed to assert that those in Jerusalem do not have a monopoly on the term, much less the concept.[24]

In other words, it is not true, asserts Marduka through his choice of terms, that the only legitimate Jewish authority is to be found in Jerusalem and its environs. It is not true that the true *yehudi* is the one who lives in Yehud. Instead, a *yehudi* can be four generations removed from Jerusalem, for affiliation is not dependent on geographical location.

2. Introducing Mordecai: noble as Saul

In introducing his first main characters, Marduka made two further decisions. First, he made Mordecai and Esther Benjaminites; second, he associated them with the elites who had been exiled in 597 along with Jehoiachin. The linkage with Benjamin was an overtly political statement. Dreams of a Davidic restoration circulated widely in the early days of the Second Temple.[25] Drawing on prophecies from as long ago as the days of Amos and Micah, and as recent as Ezekiel in the early days of Babylonian

---

[21] Blenkinsopp, *Judaism, the First Phase*, 19–28.

[22] For a useful study of the term, see Herbert Schmid, "Die 'Juden' im Alten Testament," in Brigitta Benzing, Otto Böcher, and Günter Maye (eds.), *Wort und Wirklichkeit: Studien zur Afrikanistik und Orientalistik. Eugen Ludwig Rapp zum 70. Geburtstag*, vol. 1: *Geschichte und Religionswissenschaft – Bibliographie* (Meisenheim am Glan: Anton Hain, 1976), 17–29. Schmid sees the forty-one (!) occurrences of *yehudi* in Esther 3–10 as the first ethnic uses of the term, and argues that the rise of the term "Jew" was a result of the fact that in the Diaspora, "the relationship to God and to the land of the fathers was lost." Therefore, the connection must be through "direct ethnic descent" and "the indirect effect of the Torah as constitutive of 'the Jews'" (*ibid.*, 27–28). Schmid relates this also to the occurrences in Daniel 3:8, 10, but those men are literally Judeans according to the narrative, having themselves been exiled from Judea (1:6). See also Bar-Asher, "Il y avait à Suse un homme juif," 227–31.

[23] This was noted (for other reasons), by Brettler, "Judaism in the Hebrew Bible?," 444–45, and Baker, "A 'Jew' by Any Other Name?," 169 n. 72.

[24] This is pushed even slightly further by Anselm C. Hagedorn, "The Absent Presence: Cultural Responses to Persian Presence in the Eastern Mediterranean," in Oded Lipschits and Gary N. Knoppers (eds.), *Judah and the Judeans in the Achaemenid Period: Negotiating Identity in an International Context* (Winona Lake, IN: Eisenbrauns, 2011), 52; Hagedorn sees in Esther the notion that "religion as an ethnic marker does not matter anymore."

[25] A thorough survey of the texts is available in W. H. Rose, *Zemah and Zerubbabel: Messianic Expectations in the Early Postexilic Period*, JSOT Suppl. 304 (Sheffield Academic, 2000).

domination, visions had circulated of a restored monarchy, with a descendant of David on the throne.[26] Zechariah in particular had accentuated this theme of the Restoration.[27] In Zechariah's thinking, the construction of the Temple, for which Zerubbabel was responsible, emphasized the connections between this figure and David, who had wanted to build a temple but never succeeded.[28]

Zechariah's contemporary Haggai even went so far as to reverse an earlier prophecy of Jeremiah. Whereas that great prophet had promised that "even if Coniah [= Jehoiachin] were the signet ring on my right hand, I would tear you off and give you to those who seek your life," Haggai had God say, "I will take you, Zerubbabel my servant, son of Shealtiel, and make you like a signet ring."[29] With this verbal refashioning – in fact, rejection – of Jeremiah's prophecy, Haggai gave voice to the perception that the reality was that the Davidic dynasty was on the rise and would once again reign in Jerusalem.[30]

---

[26] For a concise statement of these prophetic traditions, see Anthony R. Petterson, *Behold your King: The Hope for the House of David in the Book of Zechariah*, Library of Hebrew Bible/Old Testament Studies 513 (New York and London: T. & T. Clark, 2009), 147–48. According to Assis ("Zechariah 8 and its Allusions," 16–19), Zechariah tones down his rhetoric about the Davidic dynasty as time goes on and Zerubbabel passes from the scene, so that in Zechariah 8, which according to Assis is later than 1–7, the idea of the restoration of the dynasty is lacking altogether.

[27] Many scholars have seen this to be a particular theme of Zechariah 9–14 (esp. 12–13), and the precise contours of the visions of David contained in these chapters have been extensively discussed; see the detailed and perceptive analysis of Carol L. Meyers and Eric Meyers, "The Future Fortunes of the House of David: The Evidence of Second Zechariah," in Astrid B. Beck, Andrew H. Bartelt, Paul R. Raabe, and Chris A. Franke (eds.), *Fortunate the Eyes that See: Essays in Honor of David Noel Freedman in Celebration of his Seventieth Birthday* (Grand Rapids, MI: Eerdmans, 1995), 207–22. One of the major arguments of Petterson, *Behold your King*, is that there is continuity between Zechariah 1–8 and 9–14 in this regard – so much continuity, in fact, that the whole book may be profitably read as the work of a single author.

[28] Petterson, *Behold your King*, 247–48.

[29] See Jeremiah 22:24–25 and Haggai 2:23; the connection is drawn, and analyzed, by Petterson, *Behold your King*, 63–65.

[30] Some have argued that there were those in the Persian period who argued for Benjaminite leadership, and thus revived Saul as a model, and that tensions between Judah and Benjamin actually ran high in the Persian period. See for this, with discussion of Esther in this regard, Yairah Amit, "The Saul Polemic in the Persian Period," in Oded Lipschits and Manfred Oeming (eds.), *Judah and the Judeans in the Persian Period* (Winona Lake, IN: Eisenbrauns, 2011), 647–61. For a fuller argument for a Davidic–Saulide rivalry in the Persian Period, with suggestions for specific backgrounds to the rivalry, see Diana V. Edelman, "Did Saulide–Davidic Rivalry Resurface in Early Persian Yehud?" in J. Andrew Dearman and M. Patrick Graham (eds.), *The Land that I Will Show You: Essays on the History and Archaeology of the Ancient Near East in Honour of J. Maxwell Miller*, JSOT Suppl. 343 (Sheffield Academic Press, 2001), 69–91, and see the discussion with critical comments of Joseph Blenkinsopp, "Benjamin Traditions Read in the Early Persian Period," in J. Andrew Dearman and M. Patrick Graham (eds.), *Judah and the Judeans in the Persian Period* (Winona Lake, IN: Eisenbrauns, 2011), 629–45. I am suggesting something different: the author of Esther utilized Saul as a model not because he was seriously advocating Benjaminite leadership – he would have opposed that as much as he opposed Davidic leadership, if it was centered in Jerusalem! – but as an anti-David.

The heroes of this story would thus be anti-heroes in some contemporary eyes. Marduka knew well that proponents of the Davidides could easily point out that Saul, the original Israelite king from Benjamin, had been a fatally flawed character. In formulating his hero, therefore, Marduka would make sure that they – and in particular, Esther – corrected all of the flaws inherent in her predecessor.

To make sure there was no doubt about these allusions, or as to where the political sympathies of the story lay, the name of the grandfather of Mordecai and Esther, Shimʿi, was mentioned.[31] The last famous Shimʿi was the one who walked alongside David in his hour of greatest despondence – when his son Absalom rebelled against him and he had to flee Jerusalem, his own capital city – and verbally abused him. Now another Benjaminite, a descendant of another Shimʿi, would be the hero of the story.

Besides ineluctably conjuring anti-Davidic sentiments, the story of Saul had an additional facet that was attractive to Marduka: the Saulides, the one family in Benjamin ever to hold political power, had lost it centuries ago. This rang appropriate to Marduka's ears. The Benjaminites might have lost power half a millennium earlier, but hadn't all Jews lost political power again in the previous century? There could be no forgetting this, in Marduka's mind. The Jews lived in exile; they were an exilic people. Whether they lived in Persia or Yehud, they were in exile. This is as if to say: "To be a Jew, after 587 BCE, is always to have been unhomed. Jewish identity in Esther is always already dispersed, displaced."[32]

To return to the way Marduka formulated the heroes' introduction, we can now note that it was designed to sound familiar to his readers: "There was a man, a *yehudi*, who lived in the fortress of Susa,[33] whose name was Mordecai, son of Yair, son of Shimei, son of Kish, a Benjaminite, who was exiled from Jerusalem with the exile which was exiled together with Jeconiah, king of Judah, which was exiled by Nebuchadnezzar, king of Babylon" (Esther 2:5–6). Surely no one would miss the allusion to the

---

[31] Timothy Beal, *The Book of Hiding: Gender, Ethnicity, Annihilation, and Esther* (London and New York: Routledge, 1997), 33.

[32] *Ibid.*, 33.

[33] For the syntax of 2:5 and its possible diachronic significance, cf. Job 1:1, and see Avi Hurvitz, "The Date of the Prose-Tale of Job Linguistically Reconsidered," *HTR* 67 (1974), 28–30, and cf. also 2 Samuel 12:1, and the discussions of Rezetko, "Dating Biblical Hebrew: Evidence from Samuel-Kings and Chronicles," in Ian Young (ed.), *Biblical Hebrew: Studies in Chronology and Typology* (London: T. & T. Clark International, 2003), 215–50, at 236–37, Ian Young, "Is the Prose Tale of Job in Late Biblical Hebrew?" *VT* 59 (2009), 606–29, at 617–18, and the further references in each.

introduction of Saul: "There was a man from Benjamin whose name was Kish, son of Abiel, son of Zeror, son of Bekorath, son of Aphiah, son of a Benjaminite."[34] This introduction also, he hoped, would make it clear that just as when Kish was introduced, it was his son Saul, mentioned only in the following sentence, who was the protagonist, here, too, it was Mordecai's ward, mentioned only in the following sentence, who would be the protagonist of this new story.[35]

The second decision reflected in this introduction is the family history that Marduka gave to his heroes. He had their ancestor be exiled along with Jehoiachin, a decade prior to the destruction of the Temple. This asserted the nobility of Mordecai, since it was the nobles who were exiled with Jehoiachin.[36] Thus the hero was given a genealogy stretching back four generations, long enough to bridge the gap between the exile at the very beginning of the sixth century and the reign of Xerxes in the early fifth century.[37] Having Mordecai descend from a noble family, but not one from the Davidic dynasty or even from the tribe of Judah, and indeed from the same tribe as Saul, was one final way of subverting conventional views on power and hierarchies before the story even got under way.

---

[34] 1 Samuel 9:1; see the comments of Adele Berlin, *Esther*, JPS Bible Commentary (Philadephia: JPS, 2001), 24–25, and Amit, "The Saul Polemic," 653; Jon Levenson writes: "Mordecai's genealogy is highly reminiscent of the introduction of Saul in 1 Sam 9:1, more so than coincidence allows" (*Esther*, 56–57).

[35] See the insightful analysis of Yitzhak Berger, "Esther and Benjaminite Royalty: A Study in Inner-Biblical Allusion," *JBL* 129 (2010), 628–29.

[36] Elias Bickerman, *Four Strange Books of the Bible: Jonah, Daniel, Koheleth, Esther* (New York: Schocken, 1967), 209. This explanation is found already in the tenth-century Karaite commentaries to Esther; see Michael G. Wechsler, "An Early Karaite Commentary on the Book of Esther," *HUCA* 72 (2001), 116 and 129 with n. 60. The commentary says, אשר הג׳: כאן מן התאנים הטובות "*who was exiled*: he was among the 'good figs,'" a reference to Jeremiah's claim (Jeremiah 24) that those exiled with Jehoiachin in 597 were the "good figs," and those left until 586 were "bad figs." Wechsler notes similar comments in the unpublished commentaries of Salmon b. Yeruham and Yefet b. ʿAli, as well. For a different explanation of the chronistic notice – the alleged "Wisdom" nature of the narrative – see Shemaryahu Talmon, "Wisdom in the Book of Esther," *VT* 13 (1963), 430–31. Stern, "Esther and the Politics of Diaspora," 48, claims that the point of the introduction is to criticize Mordecai for being an "exilic Jew". This depends on larger claims which I find entirely unconvincing, and which will be discussed below.

[37] The introduction of Mordecai in Esther 2:5–6 (-בֶּן שִׁמְעִי-בֶּן יָאִיר בֶּן מָרְדֳּכַי וּשְׁמוֹ הַבִּירָה בְּשׁוּשַׁן הָיָה יְהוּדִי אִישׁ מִירוּשָׁלַיִם הָגְלָה אֲשֶׁר, יְמִינִי אִישׁ קִישׁ) is often held up as proof that the story is non-historical; the argument goes that if Mordecai were exiled with Jehoiachin, even as an infant, he would be around 110 years old by the time Xerxes came to the throne, and so it is impossible that he played the role he is said to have played or that he would have a young beautiful (virginal) cousin. This is based on a mistaken reading of the text; see my article "The Exile of Kish: Syntax and History in Esther 2:5–6," *JSOT* 37 (2012), 45–56, for a full discussion.

A story written in Hebrew, with heroes modeled on Saul rather than David, with no loyalty to the city of Jerusalem other than a distant family memory, and set entirely in the Diaspora with no expectation of a return to Yehud – this was a story that was sure to enrage those who believed that leadership depended on blood and geography and that Jewish destiny depended on physical and genealogical separation.

PART 2

Entering the fray
Esther as a political book

CHAPTER 5

Persian law and Persian king in the book of Esther

1. The personal is political

The book of Esther opens by making a bold claim about life in the Diaspora: the personal is inextricably intertwined with the corporate, or, to borrow a phrase, the personal is political. The entire narrative rests on the premise articulated by Carol Hanisch in 1969: "One of the first things we discover ... is that personal problems are political problems. There are no personal solutions at this time. There is only collective action for a collective solution."[1] The book does not judge this sentiment. The conflation of the personal with the political is to be neither bemoaned nor applauded; it simply is. It is the reality of minority existence, and the reality of all non-dominant peoples. Every individual represents the group, be it an ethnicity, a religion, a race, or a nationality. In Esther, this truth operates on two levels, internally to the story and externally. Within the story, the plot hinges on Vashti being held to represent all women, and Mordecai (in chapter 3) held to represent all Jews.[2] Outside of the story, the text's power rests on the claim that Xerxes represents the Achaemenid Empire, in that he is the empire personified, and Mordecai and Esther are the Jews personified.[3]

This is one of the central lessons of chapter 1 in Esther: the blurred lines – which are on occasion eviscerated altogether – between public and private.

[1] Carol Hanisch, "The Personal is Political," reprinted in Shulamith Firestone and Anne Koedt (eds.), *Notes from the Second Year: Women's Liberation* (New York: Radical Feminist, 1970), 76–78.

[2] A rabbinic statement, attuned to this aspect of the story, claims that this was the reason why Mordecai told Esther not to reveal her nationality: he saw in chapter 1 that the Persian bureaucracy favored collective punishment, and was concerned that if the king ever turned on Esther, and knew that she was Jewish, he might exact punishment from all the Jews (Targum Sheni to 2:10).

[3] This point is made by many recent commentators, and we will soon return to it. See, for a good example, Timothy S. Laniak, *Shame and Honor in the Book of Esther*, SBL Dissertation Series 165 (Atlanta: Scholars, 1998), 158 (about Mordecai) and 174–77 (about Esther), and LaCocque, *Esther Regina: A Bakhtinian Reading*, 20–22, who writes that the characters "wittingly disappear behind their people's becoming."

Marduka seems to be observing that when imperial power flows from a single individual, there is in fact no difference at all between the will of the king and the will of the empire. It turns out that the king is not the exception here, and that for everyone, the individual is subsumed under the collective. You are who you belong to. This is a constant challenge for a minority living within the empire, and much of the story, indeed, revolves around questions of personal, that is, collective, identity.[4]

To a large extent, therefore, we can read the portrait of the king as sketched in chapter 1 as the author's opening statement about the character of the empire as a whole. The chapter identifies the king strongly with "the law." The word used for "law" is *dāt*, a Persian word in its origin, borrowed into Hebrew during the Persian period.[5] Three times in the first chapter, the law is appealed to (1:8, 1:13–15, and 1:18–22), and each reveals another facet of the absurdity of the imperial law.

The first appearance of *dāt* deals with the party thrown by Xerxes: "He let everyone drink from vessels of gold, each vessel different from the others, and there was much royal wine, as much as the beneficence of the king; the drinking was according to the law (*ka-dāt*): no one coerced."[6] It is difficult to see how the drinking could be "according to the law" if no one coerced; is it really a law at all?[7] The simplest way to make sense of it seems to be to conclude that the law was that everyone could drink as much, or as little, as he wanted. One might object: why bother making a law then? The same legal reality ("no coercion") could be created by simply not making a law in the first place! But this seems to be just the point: this was a law devoid of purpose.[8] The purpose of making the law was just to be able to say that there was a law. This points to an infatuation with law for its own sake, as opposed to law for the sake of creating a functioning society. For the Jews

[4] Mira Morgenstern, *Conceiving a Nation: The Development of Political Discourse in the Hebrew Bible* (University Park, PA: Pennsylvania State University Press, 2009), 177–78, emphasizes the theme of the blurred lines between public and private in Esther. Beal, *The Book of Hiding*, 15, writes: "as the story opens ... one quickly realizes that, in this kingdom, parties have something to do with national politics, and that national politics has something to do with sexual politics."

[5] On the word and the concept in Persian, see Rüdiger Schmitt, "Dāta," in *Encyclopædia Iranica*, www.iranicaonline.org/articles/data (accessed February, 2013).

[6] Sharp, *Irony and Meaning in the Hebrew Bible*, 69, observes that this passage, although ostensibly allowing the attendees to drink *or not drink* as they wish, in fact "characterizes the unrestrained license of the Persian officials at Ahasuerus's drinking party."

[7] According to *Black's Law Dictionary*, 5th edn. (St. Paul: West, 1983), 457: "Law, in its generic sense, is a body of rules of action or conduct prescribed by *controlling authority*, and having binding legal force. That which must be obeyed and followed by citizens *subject to sanctions or legal consequences* is a law" (emphasis added).

[8] Contrast the overly serious interpretation of this law by Yoram Hazony, *The Dawn: Political Teachings of the Book of Esther*, revised edn. (Jerusalem: Shalem Press, 2000 [orig. 1995]), 16.

this would have been particularly ludicrous; this was a people who prided themselves on the "wisdom" of their law: "Who is such a great people, which has just laws and statutes such as this instruction I am giving you today?"[9]

The second occurrence of *dāt* in the chapter is in response to Vashti's "crime." In the story, Xerxes, drunk on his 187th consecutive day of feasting, sent his advisors to call Vashti into the men's party to show off her great beauty. Apparently not willing to be so debased – the party was being attended, after all, not just by nobles but by all the people of the Fortress of Susa – Vashti refused to come.[10] Xerxes was understandably mad, and called his advisors to ask what to do. This was, the book assures us, what he always did when faced with a problem:[11] "Then the king said to the wise men, who knew the times – for this was the king's way, before all who knew law (*dāt*) and judgment ... what should be done, according to the law, to Queen Vashti because she did not obey the word of the king, brought by the eunuchs" (1:13–15). Wise advisors might have helped Xerxes see that this was a personal matter that would be best worked out between husband and wife.[12] They might have pointed out that he was drunk, and this was no time to be making important decisions, and that perhaps in the morning he would see things in a different light.[13] But Xerxes was blessed with advisors who firmly believed that there was nothing merely personal, certainly not in the king's life. As Brenner puts it: "He is portrayed as husband first, ruler later – is this how politics should work?"[14]

This brings us to the third occurrence of *dāt* in the chapter. Xerxes' advisor Memucan validated the king's intuition that his personal problem was in fact an imperial issue:

---

[9] Deuteronomy 4:8.

[10] For Vashti's rationale, see the twelfth-century French commentator Joseph Qara (see his comments on 1:12, quoted in the commentary of the French Sages, in תורת חיים: מגילת אסתר, 33–34), and, similarly, Bickerman, *Four Strange Books of the Bible*, 285–86; Fox, *Character and Ideology in the Book of Esther*, 167–69.

[11] See the comments of Rashi on 1:13. For a different interpretation, see Jean-Daniel Macchi, "The Book of Esther: A Persian Story in Greek Style," in Ehud Ben Zvi, Diana V. Edelman, and Frank Polak (eds.), *A Palimpsest: Rhetoric, Ideology, Stylistics, and Language Relating to Persian Israel*, Perspectives on Hebrew Scriptures and its Contexts 5 (Piscataway, NJ: Gorgias, 2009), 114–15.

[12] Again, Hazony, *The Dawn*, 17–19, takes Vashti's refusal to come to the party as a serious challenge to the king's authority, and his response as a perfectly legitimate one.

[13] See the commentary of the French Sages in תורת חיים: מגילת אסתר, 41: "Usually, if a queen angers a king, just between the two of them – since no damage results for the world at large, it is appropriate that the anger should subside and the wrath pass."

[14] Brenner, "Who's Afraid of Feminist Criticism?," 48.

> Vashti did not only wrong the king, but all the officers and all the peoples in all the king's provinces! For this matter of the queen will spread among the women, who will then disparage their husbands, saying, "Xerxes said to bring Queen Vashti to him, and *she* didn't come!" So this day, the wives of the officers of Persia and Media, who have heard about the matter of the queen, will speak to the officers, with sufficient contempt and wrath. So if it pleases the king, let a royal proclamation be issued, and let it be written in the laws (*dāt*) of Persia and Media, and let it never be abrogated, that Vashti would not come to King Xerxes, and so the king was to give her queenship to another better than herself. And let the order of the king, which he shall make, be heard in his whole kingdom – though it be very large! – and all the women will honor their husbands, great and small (1:17–20).

Not surprisingly, Xerxes' ego was massaged by this reassurance. The fact that his wife did not obey him was not a problem in their relationship, or, worse, in his ability to wield power and dominance in his household; indeed, this was the leading edge of a potential insurrection on an imperial scale. Fortunately, he and his advisors knew just what to do: make a law! And thus the husband who was not obeyed by his wife made a law that all husbands were to be obeyed by their wives.

The chapter concludes with a note of absurdity regarding the details of this new law: "he sent letters to all the king's provinces ... that every man should rule in his own house, and speak the language of his people" (1:22). Was the king prepared to enforce this rule? The midrash points out the absurdity: if a man complains to the imperial court that his wife insists on speaking *her* native tongue, and won't serve what *he* wants for dinner, will the courts really step in?[15] The fourth-century Rava commented that the law was so ridiculous that it undermined the king's credibility in the eyes of his subjects, and that had this not done so, they would have quickly rushed to kill the Jews when they got the later decree to that effect.[16] R. Pinhas, as quoted in the midrash, went further: "because of this decree Xerxes became a laughingstock in the world."[17]

---

[15] Esther Rabbah 4:12. On the issue of languages, see also above, pp. 32–34.

[16] B. Megillah 12b: אלמלא אגרות הראשונות, לא נשתייר משונאיהן של ישראל שריד ופליט. אמרי, "מאי האי דשדיר ?לן להיות כל איש שורר בביתו?! פשיטא! אפילו קרחה (או: קדחה) בביתיה פדכשא להוי!" "Were it not for the first letters [those of chapter 1], not a single survivor would be left from the enemies of Israel [i.e., from Israel]: everyone said, 'What is this that he is sending us – that each man should be in charge of his household?! This is obvious! Even a bald man (or: a domestic servant) is a ruler in his own house!'" The reading and translation are based on the discussion in Segal, *The Babylonian Esther Midrash*, vol. 1, 288–90. See also Levenson, *Esther*, 53.

[17] Esther Rabbah 4:12. Similarly, Morgenstern, *Conceiving a Nation*, 177–78, writes that "this law actually weakens Ahauerus' ability to administer his own empire." On the absurdity of the law here, see also LaCocque, *Esther Regina*, 9.

For the Persians – as described here by the Jews – *dāt* serves as a bulwark against supposed threats to the imperial order: it is brandished against Vashti in chapter 1, against Mordecai in chapter 3, and, in the same chapter, against all Jews.[18] But since the story makes clear that none of these three members of the alleged axis of evil (Vashti, Mordecai, and the Jews) were actually threats at all,[19] the *dāt* looks like an absurdity, an all-powerful weapon targeting innocents. Far from being the defender of a justly ordered society, *dāt* in the hands of these Persians is a terrifying force wreaking nothing but havoc.

Finally, the *dāt* is openly and explicitly flouted in chapters 3 and 4. Haman accused the Jews of being a people who "did not obey the *dāt* of the king" (3:8). For Haman, these are grounds for the annihilation of this people. In the story to this point, however, the reader knows that there has been no evidence of such disobedience, and so Haman's accusations seem to be a trumped-up charge. In the following chapter, much to our surprise, Queen Esther the Jew does indeed flout the *dāt* of the king: she says she will enter the king's throneroom "against the law (*dāt*)." As the reader knows (or is soon to find out), this one open betrayal of the *dāt*, far from condemning the Jews to destruction, begins the process of their salvation. Again, the *dāt* is a terrifying behemoth which, once inspected, shows itself to have no real consequences.

The absurdity and triviality of the law, along with its potentially terrifying omnipresence and omnipotence, is a theme that continues into the next chapter: there is a law to gather all beautiful virgins to the palace in the quest for a new queen (2:8) and a law for how women should prepare themselves to meet the king (2:12). As Elsie Stern observes, what is most striking about the book as we continue reading, however, is that matters of the gravest import – such as genocide and its thwarting – are handled by the very same legal system and same legal mechanisms as the accoutrements of beauty for the king's concubines. The harem and warfare are equally matters of state interest, if the king is the state.[20]

2. The character of the king

Within chapter 1 in particular, though, the portrayal of the law serves to call the entire empire into question. The king is all-powerful, in a sense: his mere word can legislate the dominion of half of the population of his empire

---

[18] Beate Ego, "The Book of Esther: A Hellenistic Book," *JAJ* 1 (2010), 296–97.
[19] The story sets up Vashti and Mordecai as parallel in many ways. See the discussion below, pp. 72–73.
[20] Stern, "Esther and the Politics of Diaspora," 35.

over the other. But this was not his idea; it came from the least of his advisors. The king, with all his power, is a puppet.[21] He is controlled by his advisors, and takes refuge behind the seemingly august institution of the "law," which turns out, on closer inspection, to be merely more pomposity and swagger than substance. Since the personal is political, the empire as a whole can be seen in similar terms. The empire is a farce, a fraud: it is rhetoric and bureaucracy, with no real substance. Hiding behind the elaborate system of laws, advisors, consultations, and decrees is nothing at all.[22] The king and his advisors at times seem to inhabit a web of mere words and wills, in which they discuss with the utmost seriousness the fine points of law while the rest of the world continues operating as always, in blissful oblivion of these pseudo-scholastics.

What prevents this from being a true comedy is that despite the farcical nature of the law, the king's words *may* have real consequences. By the end of the chapter (although it is not explicitly stated), the males of the empire presumably possess no more power than they had beforehand, but Vashti really is no longer queen. Her fate was sealed by words spoken between the king and his advisors, patently ridiculous and yet frightfully effective. This is the essential paradox of the story: as readers we must be terrified of Xerxes and of the Persian Empire, even while laughing at them.[23] We know them to be ludicrous and we know their speeches to be hollow, but their decrees can have deadly consequences. What makes Xerxes terrifying is not that he is evil – he is not – but that there is such life-and-death power in the hands of such a buffoon.

As the story goes on, it emerges that there is one figure from Israel's past to whom Xerxes is in particular being compared. When Xerxes, at the beginning of chapter 2, finds himself alone, deprived (by his own hand) of his queen, his "lads" have quite a brilliant suggestion: "The lads of the king, his attendants, said, 'Let them seek (*yevaqshu la-melekh*) beautiful virgin girls (*ne'arot betulot*) for the king ... and the girl whom the king is most enamored of shall reign in place of Vashti.'" Perhaps we should not

---

[21] Xerxes' inability to decide anything on his own has been emphasized by a number of recent commentators; see, e.g., Fox, *Character and Ideology in the Book of Esther*, 29, and Alexander Green, "Power, Deception, and Comedy: The Politics of Exile in the Book of Esther," *Jewish Political Studies Review*, 23 (2011), 63–64. I am indebted to Ari Mermelstein for the reference to Green's paper.

[22] The image of the Wizard of Oz comes to my mind in this context. The power exists entirely because people believe that it does; there is no substance behind the loud voice. The author of Esther is playing the role of Dorothy, pulling back the curtain to reveal the pathetic individual whose bombast so intimidates his subjects.

[23] This analysis is drawn especially from Fox, *Character and Ideology in the Book of Esther*, 173–76.

Table 5.1 *Esther compared with 1 Kings 1*

Esther	1 Kings 1
Nathan	Mordecai
Bathsheba	Esther*a*
Solomon	Jewish people
David	Xerxes

a For more on the implications of this comparison, see p. 74 below.

give these unnamed lads too much credit for their suggestion, however, since they seem to have lifted some of the phraseology directly from an earlier passage, regarding a senile King David. In that context, we read, "His servants said to him, 'Let them seek (*yevaqshu ladoni ha-melekh*) a virgin girl (*na'ara betula*), that she may service the king and be a nurse for him and lie in his lap, and my lord the king shall be warm."[24]

To confirm that Xerxes is being compared to David in his senility, there is another scene later in the story which again evokes the same image. In chapter 4 of Esther, Mordecai orders Esther to go to the king and advocate on behalf of her kin, the Jewish people. This is reminiscent of the next scene in the last act of David's life. After Adonijah declares himself king, the court divides. Some who had been among David's most loyal supporters were allied with Adonijah, but others, including the prophet Nathan, opposed Adonijah's attempt to reign.[25] Nathan approached Bathsheba, David's wife, and gave her instructions on approaching the king, to make a desperate plea on behalf of her own kin – her son Solomon.[26] In other words, the stories have four characters in parallel, as shown in Table 5.1.

We have already discussed (in the previous chapter) the anti-Davidic streak in the story of Esther. It seems implausible, though, that the author would really claim that David and Xerxes were fundamentally comparable; David was still a cultural hero in Israel. Instead, the point appears to be that Xerxes, *even in his prime*, is akin to David in his teetering old age. David, in

---

[24] Esther 2:2–4 and 1 Kings 1:2. This parallel was noted by R. Judah ha-Nasi, as quoted in b. Megillah 12b; R. Judah ha-Nasi relies on the parallel to claim that in the case of David, parents were offering their daughters to be his consort, whereas in the case of Xerxes, parents hid their daughters to avoid them being taken to the king.

[25] The summary here is what the text reports. For a thoughtful analysis of the development of the story, including compelling observations about the power and roles of the characters involved, see Joyce Willis, Andrew Pleffer, and Steven Llewelyn, "Conversation in the Succession Narrative of Solomon," *VT* 61 (2011), 133–47.

[26] These parallels were discussed by Amos Frisch, "בין מגילת אסתר לספר מלכים," *Mehqerei Hag*, 3 (1992), 28.

the last chapter of his life, is a pawn in the hands of shrewder operators around him. Adonijah, Bathsheba, and Nathan are all angling for power as David's life comes to an end.

At the beginning of Kings, David himself occupies a strange position. All acknowledge that his word is law – but all agree that he is incompetent actually to make decisions. The game becomes one of manipulation. The one who can best manipulate the king – who wields the power but is actually just a puppet – will emerge the victor in this game. This, according to Esther, is *always* the reality in Susa. It will be Haman who at first plays this game most successfully, but he will later be bested at his own game by Mordecai and Esther.[27]

---

[27] On Xerxes' abdication of the responsibilities of decision-making, nominally the job of the king, see Fox, *Character and Ideology in the Book of Esther*, 173.

CHAPTER 6

Modeling heroes

Daniel, Esther, and Mordecai

1. Jewish identity, overt and covert: Daniel vs. Esther

At the beginning of the book of Daniel, we meet Jews who live in the court of the foreign king. Exiles already, they have new Babylonian names bestowed upon them by their overlords, as part of what appears to be a systematic effort to strip them of their native Jewish identities. The protagonist, Daniel, undertakes to halt this process:

> Daniel decided that he would not be defiled by the rations of the king or by the wine he served, and asked the chief officer that he not be defiled ... Daniel said to the waiter whom the chief officer had appointed for Daniel, Hananiah, Mishael, and Azariah, "Please test your servants for ten days: let them give us seeds (*zero'im*) that we shall eat, and water that we shall drink, and our appearances and the appearances of the lads eating the king's rations will be seen by you – and as you see fit, you can then do with your servants." He listened to them regarding this issue, and tested them for ten days, and at the end of ten days, their appearance was good, healthier of flesh than all the lads who were eating the king's rations. So the waiter would take away their rations and their drinking wine, and give them seeds (*zer'onim*). (Daniel 1:8–16)

Nothing in particular is said here about the kashrut of the food being served.[1] It seems likely that rather than there being a specific legal problem with the food and drink provided by the king, the problem was one of symbolic acculturation. Daniel saw the idea of literally living on food provided by the king as defiling, culturally rather than legally.

---

[1] For lucid discussions of the possible explanations for Daniel's decision, with further references, see John E. Goldingay, *Daniel*, Word Biblical Commentary 30 (Dallas: Word, 1989), 18–19; John J. Collins, *Daniel*, Hermeneia (Minneapolis: Fortress, 1993), 141–43. Both Goldingay and Collins read Daniel's refusal to partake of the king's food as a rejection of assimilation, as is suggested here, as well. Further insightful discussion of this can be found in Nathan Macdonald, *Not Bread Alone: The Uses of Food in the Old Testament* (Oxford University Press, 2008), 198–203.

What Daniel is willing to eat is seeds. In their natural state, these are anti-cultural foods. They bespeak no acculturation, because they reflect no culture. Daniel and his friends can be read against the foil of Enkidu in the Mesopotamian epic of Gilgamesh. In that story, Enkidu is a human created in a "natural" state, living among the animals and aligning himself with them in their perpetual conflict with humans.[2] Through the machinations of Gilgamesh and the harlot Shamhat, Enkidu is no longer able to live among the animals in the wild, and Shamhat invites him to join her in her trip back to Uruk to live among humans. On their way back to Uruk, Shamhat brings Enkidu to a tavern, and tries to get him to eat. At that point we read the following:

> They set bread before him,
> They set beer before him.
> He looked uncertainly, then stared,
> Enkidu did not know to eat bread,
> Nor had he ever learned to drink beer!
> The harlot made ready to speak, saying to Enkidu:
> Eat the bread, Enkidu, the staff of life,
> Drink the beer, the custom of the land.[3]

This episode plays a central role in detailing Enkidu's transition from "wild man" to "friend of the king." To undergo this transition, Enkidu has to learn to eat and drink like a man. The foods chosen by the storyteller, beer and bread, represent the paradox of basic human foodstuffs. These are, in Mesopotamian culture, the most basic of foods – "the staff of life." On the other hand, even these most basic of foods are not "natural." They are the synthesized counterparts of wheat and barley: for humans to eat these staples, they have to be processed – they are "the custom of the land." The wheat has to be ground into flour, mixed with water, allowed to rise, and baked; the barley has to be allowed to ferment. Animals eat foods in their natural states; even the simplest of human foods are far removed from these states.[4]

---

[2] The story of Enkidu has much to say about how to read the story of the Garden of Eden, as both seem to explore similar themes of human vs. animal, exemplified by clothes vs. naked, "natural" food vs. produced food, and the ceaseless conflict for survival that pitted mankind against the animal world tout court.

[3] The translation is from Benjamin R. Foster, *The Epic of Gilgamesh: A New Translation, Analogues, Criticism* (New York and London: W. W. Norton, 2001), 14.

[4] Again, when Adam is expelled from Eden, the verdict is that he shall "eat bread by the sweat of his brow." Both components of this statement – the fact that it is bread that is being consumed rather than

In fact, Lévi-Strauss argued that cooked food is the marker of civilization in the thought of humans around the world.[5] Myths of the origins of fire, on this account, are actually myths of the origins of civilization itself.[6] To take one example from outside of mythology: the Hanunoo tribe in the Philippines "regard as 'real' food only that which is prepared for human consumption by cooking ... Real foods such as pre-ripe bananas, root crops, cereals, cucumbers, tomatoes, and onions are never eaten raw. A *meal* must include cooked food. In fact, meals are usually enumerated by the term: pag'apuy, 'fire making.'"[7]

Clearly this was true in Mesopotamia, where Enkidu's transition from barbarian to civilized human is epitomized by his first consumption of cooked, processed – that is, human – foods. The Jewish story of Daniel, set as it is in the court of the Babylonian king, seems to be a sophisticated reversal of the acculturation of Enkidu. Where Enkidu *joins* Mesopotamian society by consuming beer and bread, Daniel *refuses to join* the same society by refusing the bread (*patbag*) and adopting a "natural" diet of seeds and water. It is not the law that is at stake, but Daniel's very identity.[8] He resists the acculturation, and resists the sacrifice of his Jewish identity, by resisting the king's food.[9]

At least in part, the story in Daniel 1 is the reason why refusal of foreign food becomes the symbolic act of resistance par excellence in later Second Temple times.[10] Judith, Tobit, and the Maccabees also reject the food of

---

fruits in their raw states, and the fact that hard work is required to produce such processed foods – represent the "expulsion from nature" that the story seems to be claiming as the fundamental of human existence.

[5] Claude Lévi-Strauss, *Introduction to a Science of Mythology*, vol. 1: *The Raw and the Cooked*, tr. John and Doreen Weightman (New York: Harper & Row, 1969 [French orig. 1964]).

[6] Lévi-Strauss, *ibid.*, 66–78 and *passim*, provides a fascinating selection of such myths.

[7] H. C. Conklin, "The Relation of Hanunóo Culture to the Plant World," unpublished Ph.D. dissertation (Yale University, 1954), 185, quoted in Lévi-Strauss, *The Raw and the Cooked*, 336. Lévi-Strauss' argument has been criticized for focusing entirely on the cultural import of cooking, while neglecting the biological benefits; for a corrective, confirming Lévi-Strauss' insights about the significance of cooking for humanity, see Richard W. Wrangham, James Holland Jones, Greg Laden, David Pilbeam, and NancyLou Conklin-Brittain, "The Raw and the Stolen: Cooking and the Ecology of Human Origins," *Current Anthropology*, 40 (1999), 567–77, and Richard W. Wrangham, *Catching Fire: How Cooking Made us Human* (New York: Basic, 2009).

[8] Mary E. Mills, "Household and Table: Diasporic Boundaries in Daniel and Esther," *CBQ* 68 (2006), 415–17.

[9] A similar analysis was provided by David Moshe Freidenreich, "Foreign Food: A Comparatively-Enriched Analysis of Jewish, Christian, and Islamic Law," unpublished Ph.D. dissertation (Columbia University, 2006), 67–69, as I learned from Jordan D. Rosenblum, *Food and Identity in Early Rabbinic Judaism* (Cambridge University Press, 2010), 37–38.

[10] As Shalom Holtz observed, at the very beginning of the exilic period, Ezekiel also refuses to be "defiled" by his food (Ezekiel 4:9–17, esp. v. 14). Here the issue is not the foreignness of the food, but this may be seen as relevant to the broader issue of food as "defiling" in exile.

their oppressors.[11] "The circumstances of the exile and the post-exilic period ... combined with established beliefs about defilement contributed to a heightened food consciousness among the exiles."[12] In rejecting foreign nourishment, they all demonstrate that the foreign cultures cannot penetrate their bodies: resistance is incarnated, physically, in their flesh.

Esther seemingly has no such qualms. "Unlike Daniel, Esther has agreed to a foreign lifestyle, eating, dressing, and sleeping according to foreign ways."[13] She resists nothing: not foreign food, not foreign bodies, not foreign culture.[14] On the contrary, Esther seems focused on convincing everyone that she is no threat, that her body contains not a shred of resistance. She gives up all semblance of a Jewish identity; indeed, she does not share that aspect of her identity with anyone.[15]

If one chooses not to resist, like Esther, there are two paths of accommodation open.[16] One is the abdication of responsibility, the abandonment of identity, the *passive* allowance of external forces to influence one's very being; the other is the *active* solicitation of such influences. As opposed to the first method, in the second method the self retains control, the individual remains the arbiter of its being. The highest tension in the book is in chapter 4, where Mordecai appeals to Esther to act on behalf of the Jews. Esther, though, demurs, and explains that she cannot violate the law against going uninvited to the king's throne room in order to save her people; Mordecai insists that she must. Mordecai claims that her primary loyalty must be to her people of origin; Esther says that she is loyal first and foremost to the law of the Persians, as personified by her own husband, the king. The tension rests on just this question: which path of accommodation has Esther chosen? Which of these descriptions better characterizes Esther's identity after five years in the palace? Has she given up her identity entirely, or has she carefully cultivated it secretly, overlaying it with many other layers of adopted identities?

---

[11] Daniel and his friends, Hanaiah, Mishael, and Azariah, are referred to explicitly in 1 Maccabees 2:51, 59–61. See also Pace, "Diaspora Dangers, Diaspora Dreams," 23–24 n. 7, pointing to Tobit 1:10–11, 1 Maccabees 1:62–63, and 2 Maccabees 5:27.

[12] Nathan Macdonald, "Food and Drink in Tobit and Other 'Diaspora Novellas,'" in Mark Bredin (ed.), *Studies in the Book of Tobit: A Multidisciplinary Approach* (London: T. & T. Clark, 2006), 165–78, at 169.

[13] Mills, "Household and Table," 417.

[14] See Jon D. Levenson, "The Scroll of Esther in Ecumenical Perspective," *Journal of Ecumenical Studies*, 13 (1976), 440–51; Frederic W. Bush, "The Book of Esther: *Opus non gratum* in the Christian Canon," *Bulletin for Biblical Research*, 8 (1998), 44–45.

[15] Esther 2, *passim*.

[16] This distinction was made by Hazony, *The Dawn*, 29–33. Much of the following paragraph was inspired by Hazony's sharp analysis.

2. Mordecai vs. Esther?

Esther is described in terms of abject passivity through the first few chapters of the story. She is taken to the king, about which she had no choice; she voices no opinion as to how she wishes to dress or adorn herself, but submissively does whatever Hegai, head of the harem, recommends;[17] everyone adores her; the king finds in her whatever it was he was looking for, and assertiveness was certainly high on the king's list of qualities to avoid in the next queen. She says not a word about the food she is to eat, the man she is to marry, or the physical or social spaces she is to occupy. One could reasonably conclude that Esther has ceded control over her very identity to others – many others, in fact.

Later in her story, however, it appears that Esther may not have been such a passive character after all. Indeed, this is just the question posed to her by Mordecai in chapter 4, when he informs her of the plight of the Jews – her countrymen and countrywomen. Has she abandoned her identity entirely, replacing her earlier persona with an entirely new character, crafted by those around her? Or has she simply allowed others to see what they wished, concealing her true self while ever negotiating the new and the old?[18]

It is clear what Mordecai wants the answer to be. He himself spends the first chapters of the book in a carefully constructed hybridity. He is introduced as "a Jewish man" (*ish yehudi*), in a manner that suggests out-sider status; indeed, following on the description of the unified empire in chapter 1 – in which *everyone* attends the king's banquet – the very presence of an ethnic marker may suggest that this man is not fully Persian.[19] He reveals this aspect of his identity only when it becomes relevant, and only under pressure. In chapter 2 he is one who "sits at the gate," the same

---

[17] Hazony, *The Dawn*, 35–39. Regarding the interpretation of this submissiveness, it is instructive to contrast the approaches of Fox, *Character and Ideology in the Book of Esther*, 37, who sees it as proof of Esther's innate passivity, and Levenson, *Esther*, 62, who sees it as shrewdness on Esther's part: after all, who would know better than Hegai what would please the king? It is true that the use of "harem" here is not entirely appropriate, as the very presence of the male Hegai shows, but the word captures something of the life of the women in the "contest." For discussion, see Elna K. Solvang, "The First Orientalist? Fantasy and Foreignness in the Book of Esther," in Steven Holloway, JoAnn Scurlock, and Richard Beal (eds.), *In the Wake of Tikva Frymer-Kensky*, Gorgias Précis Portfolios 4 (Piscataway, NJ: Gorgias, 2009), 199–213.

[18] On the divided loyalties of Esther brought to the fore in chapter 4, see Laniak, *Shame and Honor in the Book of Esther*, 95–96.

[19] Morgenstern, *Conceiving a Nation*, 167–68, suggests that the description of the exile after the description of the opulence of the court "gives rise to the suspicion that the grandeur described at the beginning of the narrative has been acquired through the (unmentioned) suffering of other people."

expression used (in Aramaic) at the end of Daniel 2 to indicate that Daniel was a member of the royal bureaucracy. Mordecai, too, was apparently a royal employee.[20] At the same time, it is difficult to escape the sense that the description of Mordecai "at the gate" is meant to emphasize his liminality: he is neither within the palace nor outside of it, but ever negotiating his position.[21]

Indeed, at the end of chapter 2, he distinguishes himself in his line of work, discovering a plot against the king and conveying the information, through Esther, to the king himself, which leads to the arrest and execution of the plotters. In so doing, Mordecai shows himself to be not just submitting to the crown for lack of a method of resistance, but actively supporting the king, protecting him from threats and thereby earning his gratitude. Mordecai is seen at this point as very much a willing friend of the crown, an actively loyal subject of the king.[22]

When Haman comes to power, however, Mordecai takes a stand. Why exactly he refuses to bow to Haman has long been a source of speculation, and I have nothing to add to the speculation already in print.[23] What is clear, however, is that his stand is a principled one, and has something to do with his Jewish identity.[24] It is also clear that his Jewish identity had not, until this point, been public knowledge: "Although [his colleagues] spoke to him, day after day, he did not listen to them. They told Haman – to see if Mordecai's excuse would stand, *for he told them that he was a Jew*" (3:4). He told them that he was a Jew as a way of explaining his behavior to his colleagues, and they, not very helpfully, were now going to bring that explanation to Haman himself to see whether this was a legitimate excuse.

Again, the point is epitomized by his being "at the gate." It is his presence at the gate that causes the trouble with Haman (3:2–4): the fact that he was close to the palace is what incensed Haman. Had he chosen to leave the area entirely, and go to "the city of Susa" with the rest of the Jews (see 4:14), there would have been no tension. Being "at the gate" means being too close to be entirely marginalized, but not inside, either. When he discovers Haman's plot, he goes "up to the gate" in sackcloth and ashes. He can go no further. He is no longer an insider, and in fact, now does not even aspire to enter the

[20] See, for example, Levenson, *Esther*, 56; Berlin, *Esther*, 31–32; Fox, *Character and Ideology in the Book of Esther*, 38–39, with references.
[21] Morgenstern, *Conceiving a Nation*, 172.   [22] Hazony, *The Dawn*, 29–33.
[23] See the discussions in the commentaries, *ad loc.*, and Macchi, "The Book of Esther," 117–19.
[24] Sandra Beth Berg, *The Book of Esther: Motifs, Themes, and Structure* (SBL Dissertation Series 44 (Missoula, MT: Scholars, 1979), 98–99.

gate. He has cast his lot with those *outside* the gate; someone whose identity was always "at the gate" can choose to do that.

Mordecai here has charted a careful course in identity-construction. Early on, he did not share his Jewishness with his colleagues and, not surprisingly, instructed his niece not to share hers, either. But there comes a point at which he believes that the Jew, closeted though he may be, has to reveal himself in order to act on behalf of principles, and people, held dear.[25] The ascent of Haman was such a time, according to Mordecai. In the tenth century, Saadia perceived the lesson imparted:

> The masses among the nation ought not believe that once they are sub-jugated to foreign kings, they are free to obey them no matter what they command, even when it conflicts with religion. It is incumbent upon them to know that they are obligated by the religion, and have no permission to violate it, and that God decreed his religion upon them and demands that they worship him with all their strength.[26]

Through his relationship with the empire and the king, as it develops over the narrative, Mordecai demonstrates that loyalty to the empire is a policy to constantly be scrutinized. As a general principle, it is a good idea: as the episode of Bigtan and Teresh shows, those who "lift a hand against the king" stand a good chance of being killed. On the other hand, the transition from chapter 2 to chapter 3 also shows that loyalty does not always pay (although this is rectified later): immediately after Mordecai saves the king's life, we read, "After these things, the king promoted . . ." We as readers of course expect the object to be Mordecai, who has just shown us all why he deserves a promotion. But our expectations are foiled, and it is Haman who receives the promotion in Mordecai's place. This reversal sets the stage for a series of reversals between the Jews and their enemies, and in particular between Mordecai and Haman, throughout the rest of the story.[27]

---

[25] Hazony, *The Dawn*, 91–92. A sensitive reading of the character of Esther, seen as an example of "coming out," is provided by Joshua A. Berman, "*Hadassah bat Abihail*: The Evolution from Object to Subject in the Character of Esther," *JBL* 120 (2001), 647–69.

[26] Yehuda Ratzaby, "מפירוש ר' סעדיה למגילת אסתר," in Shaul Yisraeli, Norman Lamm, and Isaac Rafael (eds.), ספר יובל לכבוד מורנו הגאון רבי יוסף דוב הלוי סולובייצ'יק (Jerusalem and New York: Mossad ha-Rav Kook and Yeshiva University, 1984), 1153–78, at 1163; Yehuda Ratzaby, "שרידים מפירוש ר' סעדיה למגילת אסתר," *Sinai*, 104 (1989), 196–97; Hebrew in M. L. Katzenelenbogen, מגילת אסתר: תורת חיים (Jerusalem: Mossad ha-Rav Kook, 2009), 314.

[27] On the theme of reversal, see Berg, *The Book of Esther*, 106–13, Michael V. Fox, "The Structure of the Book of Esther," in Alexander Rofé and Yair Zakovitch (eds.), *Isaac Leo Seeligmann Volume: Essays on the Bible and the Ancient World* (Jerusalem: Rubinstein, 1983), vol. III, 291–303 (Berg had a

In fact, the reversal here cuts even deeper against Mordecai. In 3:1, we read of Haman's promotion: "King Xerxes made Haman, son of Hammedata, the Agagite, great. He lifted him up (*n-ś-*) and he placed his chair (*kissē*) above the chairs of the officers who were with him." This reminds us of 2 Kings 25:27–28: "Amel-Marduk, king of Babylon, in his accession year, lifted up (*n-ś-*) the head of Jehoiachin, king of Judah, from prison. He spoke kindly to him, and placed his chair (*kissē*) above the chairs of the kings who were with him in Babylon." The similarities between these passages are too striking to be coincidental.[28] But they are jarring, as well: the character associated with Jehoiachin is supposed to be Mordecai, not Haman! This adds to the sense of unjunst reversal at the beginning of chapter 3: Haman gets something which by all rights should belong to Mordecai.

In any event, Mordecai has shown that his loyalty to the crown is contingent: when the empire is helping him, or when it could help him in the future, he is the epitome of loyalty. But when the empire rises up as a threat to his identity, to his very life, he stands in opposition to it. He refuses to bow to Haman, flouting an explicit order of the king.

In the context of Esther, this reversal in Mordecai's loyalties is an opportunity to make another point about law in the empire. Mordecai is following in the footsteps of an earlier character, who also took a principled stand against a royal decree: Vashti.[29] Although they may seem like an odd pairing, clearly Mordecai and Vashti play similar roles in the story (to a point).[30] They both refuse to do what the king commanded. In both cases, a royal official suggests punishing not just them, but the entire class of people whom they are seen to represent (women, Jews). But the fates of the two are vastly different: Vashti falls from power, never to be heard from again, whereas Mordecai goes unpunished and it is his nemesis, Haman, who soon falls.[31] What is the value of the rule of law if it is unpredictable and inconsistent? After all the *dāt* in chapter 1, we see in chapters 2 and 3 that it is indeed a façade.

---

pre-publication copy of Fox's study when she wrote her book), and Abraham Winitzer, "The Reversal of Fortune Theme in Esther: Israelite Historiography in its Ancient Near Eastern Context," *Journal of Ancient Near Eastern Religions*, 11 (2011), 170–218, esp. 173–88.

[28] The connection was observed by Frisch, "בין מגילת אסתר לספר מלכים," 26.

[29] On the principles involved in Vashti's refusal, see above, n. 10.

[30] Beal, *The Book of Hiding*, 47, suggests that these comparisons "suggest a kind of 'feminization' of Mordecai and 'Judaization' of Vashti." On the feminization of the Jews, see the discussion of Esther's gender, below.

[31] See Dmitri M. Slivniak, "The Book of Esther: The Making and Unmaking of Jewish Identity," in Yvonne Sherwood (ed.), *Derrida's Bible (Reading a Page of Scripture with a Little Help from Derrida)* (New York: Palgrave Macmillan, 2004), 142–43.

Mordecai's identity politics are thus a complicated matter, truly those of one who "sits at the gate." Normally toeing the line and exemplifying loyalty, he nonetheless shifts his affiliations when he believes the times require it. He goes to Esther with the same expectations of her.[32] Although it was on his instructions that she has spent the past five years *not* resisting, he now demands that she reveal who she truly is.[33] This is the moment of the story with the most narrative tension.[34] Who *is* Esther at this point? She has spent the past five years in the palace of the king, without (as far as we know) any contact with even a single Jew, much less the Jewish community. Even if the original plan had been to simply conceal her Jewish identity, rather than to obliterate it, is it not likely that the neglect of that aspect of her identity has doomed it?

Esther indeed wavers between allegiance to the empire and its rules – represented, after all, by her own husband – and her loyalty to the people of her youth.[35] As Arnon Atzmon observed, there is a telling interchange between Mordecai and Esther in chapter 4, where each uses the same word – *'am* "people" – to refer to a different group.[36] Mordecai sends a message that Esther should "go into the king's presence to beg for mercy and plead with him for her people (*'am*)." She replies that she cannot: "All the king's officials and the people (*'am*) of the royal provinces know that for any man or woman who approaches the king in the inner court without being summoned the king has but one law." He appeals to those he presumes to be her "people" – the Jews; she refers to the "people" with whom she identifies, and who deny there being any special status open to any group within the kingdom ("the king has but one law").

When Mordecai presses her, however, she shows a decisiveness heretofore undetected within her submissiveness. Mordecai's influence is seen to be profound, if veiled. She, like her mentor, has carefully shielded her secret until its revelation can be beneficial. Elsie Stern writes,

---

[32] See Arnon Atzmon, "וַיִּשְׁנֶהָ. . .לְטוֹב (אס' ב 9): על פרשנות וזהות במגילת אסתר," *Bet Miqra*, 57 (2012), 110.

[33] LaCocque, *Esther Regina*, 61, comments that "There is clearly a time not to speak and a time to break the silence. This kind of maneuvering reflects the diasporic world. Circumstances constantly change, demanding constant adaptation from the Jews."

[34] As we progress, there is but one more moment at which the reader (at least once) can plausibly be unsure of what is to come, and that is when Esther approaches the king unbidden in chapter 5. It is a remarkable feat of storytelling that after the events of chapter 6 – which, strictly speaking, did not affect the major storyline of the book at all – the tension has been diffused, and, as Zeresh is quoted as saying at the end of that chapter, it is clear to everyone that Haman's fall is imminent.

[35] Her moment of indecision is described poignantly by Hazony, *The Dawn*, 143.

[36] Atzmon, "וַיִּשְׁנֶהָ. . .לְטוֹב," 410.

In Esther . . . Jewish identity is something that must be actively revealed; if it is not broadcast, it will not be known. Not only is Jewishness invisible in Esther, it is also potentially irrelevant. Outside of the conflict with Haman and the threatened violence that it sets into motion, the Jewishness of the Jewish characters does not affect their status, their access to power, their actions, or their worldview.[37]

When Esther does act, it is with a remarkably intricate balancing act. "On the third day, Esther *donned royalty* and stood in the inner courtyard of the palace . . . When the king saw *Queen Esther* standing in the courtyard, she found favor in his eyes . . . The king said to her, 'What would you like (*mal lākh*), Queen Esther?'" There are intertextual resonances here for the Jewish reader: King David greeted his wife, Bathsheba, with the same question, "What would you like?" (*mah lākh*) in 1 Kings 1.[38] It appears that the use of this key phrase by the author of Esther was meant to call attention to the whole suite of allusions discussed above. By deploying the question *mah lākh* in the mouth of a king, said to his wife, the author is strongly urging us to think harder about the other story in which the phrase appears in similar usage. This technique, of using a particular phrase or word to call our attention to broader parallels of plot and theme, may be called an "allusive keyword," and we will see its use repeatedly in Second Temple literature.[39]

The use of *mah lākh* also focuses our attention on the parallels between Esther and Bathsheba. This suggests that Esther here is playing the role of the wise and manipulative female, acting, like Bathsheba, behind the scenes, but essentially deciding on who will rule and who will fall. This is possible for Esther only because of who she appears to be: she dons royalty; Xerxes is impressed not by the girl Esther whom he once chose, but by *Queen Esther* who stands regally outside; he addresses her as the queen, as well. In order to save the Jews, Esther must look and act like a Persian queen.[40]

On the other hand, the process is described in spatial terms that foreground the issues of inside vs. outside, and make it clear that the moves Esther made were complex. The king is described as exemplifying the empire in every way in this narrative: "and the king was sitting on his royal throne, in his royal palace." Esther pauses on her way in: "she stood in

---

[37] Stern, "Esther and the Politics of Diaspora," 42.

[38] 1 Kings 1:16; see Frisch, "בין מגילת אסתר לספר מלכים," 28.

[39] See below, Chapter 9 and esp. Chapter 11.

[40] Sharp, *Irony and Meaning in the Hebrew Bible*, 81: "In saving her people, Esther has simultaneously consolidated her political power and moved irrevocably into a diaspora from which there is no return. She has become fully vested as Queen of Persia and queen of paradox." Somewhat different is the analysis of Beal, *The Book of Hiding*, 47–49 and elsewhere, according to whom "The closer one looks, the less fixed [Esther's] image appears."

the inner courtyard of the palace, *facing* the palace." She is facing it, but has not gone in. But Xerxes does not see Esther the Jewess; he sees *Queen* Esther ("when the king saw Queen Esther standing in the courtyard"), and he beckons her to enter. This is, after all, where she belongs, does she not? She enters. In the conception of the narrative, her entry shows that she has been fully acculturated, and is *therefore* able to save her own people, with whom she also identifies. Not only is being a good Persian citizen not excluded by being a good Jew, but it just may be the best way to further Jewish interests within the empire.[41]

In this respect, Esther differs from Mordecai despite their many similarities. When Mordecai made his stand, it was decisive in what it revealed: literally shedding his Persian garb, he donned sackcloth and ashes in overt identification with the oppressed minority (4:1–2). No longer playing along, Mordecai has now broken resolutely with his former complicated sense of identity. If in the past his colleagues had not necessarily known him to be Jewish, since he did not wear that aspect of his identity on his sleeve,[42] now there is no mistaking his identification with the Jews and his identity as a Jew. Esther, on the other hand, in order to identify with the Jews – that is, in order to save her people – acts all the more like a Persian queen. In this sense, her identity is even more intricately wrought than that of Mordecai. Whereas the male makes a clear choice, the female lives forever in a state of multifaceted refraction. Never will it be clear to the casual observer who she really is.

As the story unfolds, the author deploys epithets and titles in order to make this difference clear. Mordecai is "Mordecai the Jew" six times in the book. Crucially, the first appearance of this epithet is in the mouth of Haman, who says (5:13), "all this is worth nothing to me as long as I see Mordecai the Jew sitting at the royal gate." From that point on, Mordecai is called "the Jew" five more times, including the last three times he is mentioned in the book (9:29; 9:31; 10:3). The reader is free to imagine that Mordecai has, in a sense, been liberated: no longer bound by his earlier concerns, he is now overtly Jewish, wearing his identity, and his loyalties, openly.

---

[41] Cf. W. Lee Humphreys, "A Lifestyle for the Diaspora: A Study of the Tales of Esther and Daniel," *JBL* 92 (1973), 216; Susan Niditch, *Underdogs and Tricksters: A Prelude to Biblical Folklore* (San Francisco: Harper & Row, 1987), 144–45; Hazony, *The Dawn*, 4. See also Charles D. Harvey, *Finding Morality in the Diaspora? Moral Ambiguity and Transformed Morality in the Books of Esther*, BZAW 328 (New York and Berlin: De Gruyter, 2003).

[42] See Esther 3:4, discussed above, p. 70.

When the threat from the empire is turned back, Mordecai returns to his dual loyalties. His loyalties are not one-sided. He ends the book wearing two hats: "Mordecai the Jew was second to King Xerxes" (10:3). He is, overtly and emphatically, both "the Jew" and "second to the king."[43] His loyalty to the Jewish people can no longer be misconstrued as a lack of loyalty to the empire. Although Mordecai had established his loyalty to the king in chapter 2 by saving the king's life, his loyalty is called into question in chapter 3 when he refuses to bow to Haman "because he was a Jew." Haman claimed that loyalty to the Jews meant disloyalty to the empire: since Mordecai did not bow down, "[the Jews] do not follow the laws of the king" (3:8). As the story develops, however, it is Haman who is hanged as a traitor, and Mordecai whose loyalty to the crown is established beyond a doubt.[44] The story concludes with the most explicit claim possible of Mordecai's dual loyalties: it turns out that the Jews can be both "separate" and "spread out"; they can be both loyal to their own group and loyal to the empire as a whole.

Esther, however, never emerges from the palace at all. The very fact that she is "Esther" is noteworthy, since we were told early on that she had another, Jewish, name – Hadassah.[45] Unlike other Jews with both Hebrew and foreign names, however, she is never again called by her Jewish name. Joseph remains "Joseph" even after being named Tzafenath-Paneaḥ; Daniel, Hananiah, Mishael, and Azariah are all usually referred to by their Hebrew names, as well. But Esther is always Esther, never again Hadassah.[46] Toni Morrison's Beloved pleads: "I want you to touch me on my inside part and call me my name."[47] Hadassah is never called by her name.

Furthermore, she "lives happily ever after" as the queen of Persia, forever married to a foreigner, never taking the stand that Daniel took and requesting different food, never demanding accommodation of any kind. This is despite the fact that in chapter 9 she, along with Mordecai, ordains a Jewish

---

[43] The medieval Judeo-Arabic writers translate *mishneh la-melekh*, literally "second to the king," as *wazīr* "vizier"; see Wechsler, *Strangers in the Land*, 319 with n. 380.

[44] For the development of this theme in Esther and other Second Temple Jewish texts, see Johnson, "Novelistic Elements in Esther," 587–88; see also Ego, "The Book of Esther," 296–97.

[45] The precise etymology of "Esther" is irrelevant to this point; see above, Chapter 1, n. 85.

[46] This was observed by Tanḥum ha-Yerushalmi: "Esther was a Persian by-name by which she was called, and eventually predominated and became famous due to its being that by which she was known to the king and his servants – indeed, do you not see that she is called by no other name other than it throughout the rest of the book?" See Wechsler, *Strangers in the Land*, 218.

[47] Toni Morrison, *Beloved*, reprint edn. (New York: Knopf, 2006 [orig. 1987]), 136, discussed by Homi K. Bhabha, *The Location of Culture* (London and New York: Routledge, 1994), 16.

holiday and writes letters to the Jews throughout the empire beseeching them to observe it. She is a leader of the Jews – by virtue of being thoroughly acculturated within the palace.

Her identity until the end will be "Queen Esther" – Persian name, Persian role – with one notable exception: at the very end of the story, after the narrative has essentially come to an end, the book reports Esther's last act: "Queen Esther, daughter of Avihayil, wrote . . ." (9:29). Not since chapter 2 have we heard of Esther's father, and we can be forgiven for thinking that she had not thought of him in many years, either. The man was gone before she ever became queen, and no hint of Avihayil's influence was perceptible on his daughter, who was now thoroughly Persianized. Yet the author indicates with this sobriquet that we would be mistaken if we thought him to be irrelevant to his daughter's identity. At the end, she is not just Queen Esther of Persia, but also – in some sense – the daughter of Avihayil.

One of the questions posed by the character of Esther is, "Must one have a clear, integrated sense of one's own identity in order to act in transformative ways?"[48] She herself provides a strongly negative answer to this question: Esther has a clear but thoroughly balkanized sense of her own identity, and this is what allows her to act "in transformative ways."[49]

It is likely that the difference between the male and female characters here is not accidental. It was with the female that the Jews of the Diaspora likely identified. The female may be taken as a symbol of the less powerful and less confrontational, but potentially more subversive and more effective in resisting.[50] Few Jews in the Persian Empire would be prepared to take the assertive stand that Mordecai took, much less the death-defying stand that Daniel took.[51] But Esther illustrates a "feminine" option, and in this she is not alone within Second Temple, or earlier biblical, literature:

---

[48] Beal, *The Book of Hiding*, 49.

[49] See also the brief but poignant remarks of Athalya Brenner, "Esther Politicised in a Personal Context: Some Remarks on Foreignness," *European Judaism*, 32 (1999), 4–10.

[50] Sidnie Ann White, "Esther, a Feminine Model for Jewish Diaspora," in Peggy L. Day (ed.), *Gender and Difference in Ancient Israel* (Minneapolis: Fortress, 1989), 161–77, makes the attractive argument that Esther the feminine heroine is a model for national life in Diaspora: she is fundamentally subservient, but capable of triumphing if she deploys her influence and manipulates those with the power appropriately (see esp.*ibid.*, 167). An interesting argument regarding the political use of gender in Esther (as well as in Judith and Susanna) is by Tal Ilan, *Integrating Women into Second Temple History* TSAJ 76 (Tübingen: Mohr Siebeck, 1999), 127–53, but her dating of the books is tendentious. For further comments on "the guile of Esther," see Green, "Power, Deception, and Comedy," 68–71.

[51] On the similar dynamic within Daniel 1, see Berg, *The Book of Esther*, 144, and Pace, "Diaspora Dangers, Diaspora Dreams," 29: "Sometimes, one could accommodate the whims of the dominant regime, as did Daniel and his fellow-exiles when they studied Babylonian lessons. Nevertheless, at other times a stand

Esther, Ya'el, and Judith save themselves and the Jewish people by seducing and deceiving a powerful male gentile. They are all highly valued within the Jewish hermeneutic tradition, and, to the best of our knowledge, never condemned for their deviousness in achieving victory over stronger male adversaries. We would like to suggest that the Jews identified themselves as a people with these heroines, and thus as female, with the appropriation of tactics of survival that belonged "by nature" to women. [52]

Indeed, as a number of recent writers have pointed out, the question of Jewish distinctiveness is one raised explicitly by Haman in chapter 3: "There is a people, scattered and separate among the people" (3:8). Are they scattered among the other peoples, or separate from everyone else? Are they different or the same? Morgenstern writes that they are the same as every other people in the Persian Empire, in that they are different; Beal identifies this as "the paradox of diaspora identity: to be *dispersed* and *one* simultaneously."[53] It is striking that Haman himself has an identity conflicted much like Mordecai's: an Agagite, he dreams of being Persianized. This is most clearly seen in the reward he dream up for himself, described in chapter 6, in which he all but reveals that he wants to be king of Persia.[54] Beal therefore continues: "Despite his clear delineation of us and them, there is in Haman's speech on the 'Jewish problem' (3:8) also an inadvertent admission of the problematics embedded in his own logic: this one, isolatable, ethnic divergence ('One people diverge') in the order of things is admittedly also 'scattered and divided' among all the people everywhere."[55]

---

must be taken, as when Daniel, Hananiah, Mishael, and Azariah stood the test of the food laws." The difference is one of degree: Daniel took a harder and faster stand than Mordecai did.

[52] Daniel Boyarin, "Tricksters, Martyrs, and Collaborators: Diaspora and the Gendered Politics of Resistance," in Daniel Boyarin and Jonathan Boyarin, *Powers of Diaspora: Two Essays on the Relevance of Jewish Culture* (Minneapolis: University of Minnesota Press, 2002), 37.

[53] Morgenstern, *Conceiving a Nation*, 162; Beal, *The Book of Hiding*, 48–49.

[54] Adele Berlin, "The Book of Esther and Ancient Storytelling," *JBL* 120 (2001), 11–14.

[55] Beal, *The Book of Hiding*, 49.

CHAPTER 7

Hero models

Joseph and Saul

1. Identity politics: returning to Joseph

As has already been mentioned, the story of Esther has to be read on the background of the story of Joseph in Genesis. That story threw down the gauntlet regarding Jewish life in the Diaspora.[1] When Jews in the eastern parts of the Persian Empire searched their national memories for precedents for how to negotiate Jewish life in a foreign land, their most obvious model was Joseph. This was noted by James Kugel: "Surely the story of Joseph's forcible removal from his homeland to Egypt must have resonated with the Jews' own experience of captivity and exile in Babylon and, in a more general way, with the sufferings of foreign domination that they experienced after their return, first under Persian rule, then under successive foreign regimes centered under Hellenistic Egypt and Syria."[2] According to Kugel, however, there was no positive reaction to Joseph in the later biblical books: "Yet there is scant biblical evidence for such rehabilitation ... In any case, it is truly only in the corpus of extrabiblical Jewish writings known as the apocrypha and pseudepigrapha of the Hebrew Bible that one encounters such a 'rehabilitated' Joseph."[3] Surprisingly, Kugel here overlooks the use of the Joseph story in the later books of the Bible. Although in Daniel the reaction to Joseph is indeed a negative one, the author of Esther uses Joseph as a role model to be emulated – at least up to a point.

As was discussed in Chapter 1 above, some of the stories of Daniel (most especially Daniel 2) are themselves modeled on Joseph, but correct his

---

[1] For some skeptical remarks regarding this point, see John Van Seters, "The Joseph Story – Some Basic Observations," in Gary N. Knoppers and Antoine Hirsch (eds.), *Egypt, Israel, and the Mediterranean World: Studies in Honor of Donald B. Redford* (Leiden: Brill, 2004), 374–75.
[2] James L. Kugel, *In Potiphar's House: The Interpretive Life of Biblical Texts* (San Francisco: HarperSanFrancisco, 1990), 18.
[3] *Ibid.*

perceived failings and improve on a man seen as deeply and fundamentally flawed. The author of Esther was different in this regard: he depicted his heroes, both Mordecai and Esther, as new Josephs. The two stories share numerous details of plot, some more obvious than others. Many of the parallels were already observed in the midrashic literature,[4] and others have been added by modern scholars.[5]

- A Jew rises to prominence in a foreign land: Joseph in Potiphar's household, and Mordecai as a member of the bureaucracy – "sitting at the gate."
- Two courtiers challenge the king and are punished, and through them the hero becomes known to the king: Joseph is brought to the king after having interpreted the dreams of the royal butler and baker, who were themselves imprisoned; Mordecai earns his reward by reporting the plot of Bigtan and Teresh.
- There is a downturn in fortunes (Joseph in jail, Haman's decree) followed by even greater success (both Joseph and Mordecai as "second to the king").
- The heroes demonstrate their capability through opposition to divination (for Joseph, this is traditional Egyptian dream interpretation; for Mordecai, these are the lots cast by Haman, which Mordecai overcomes).[6]
- The heroes earn royal power.

---

[4] There is a long list in Midrash Abba Gurion, p. 11b, Panim Aherot B, pp. 64 (two occurrences), 66, and 72, and Esther Rabbah, 7:7 (note that this passage is apparently part of the "ancient Midrash" within Esther Rabbah; on this point and the other texts mentioned here, see Chapter 13 below).

[5] The most thorough discussion of this relationship is Berg, *The Book of Esther*, 124–36. For other discussions of this literary connection, see two early studies by L. A. Rosenthal, "Die Josephgeschichte, mit den Büchern Ester und Daniel verglichen," *ZAW* 15 (1895), 278–84, and "Nochmals der Vergleich Ester, Joseph – Daniel," *ZAW* 17 (1897), 125–28, and the more detailed study by Moshe Gan, "מגילת אסתר באספקלריית קורות יוסף במצרים," *Tarbiz*, 31 (1962), 144–49, as well as Niditch, *Underdogs and Tricksters*, 126–28. See also Louis H. Feldman, "Hellenizations in Josephus' Version of Esther," *Proceedings of the American Philosophical Society*, 101 (1970), 144–45 with n. 4, and esp. 157 with n. 34; Edward L. Greenstein, "A Jewish Reading of Esther," in Jacob Neusner, Baruch A. Levine, and Ernest S. Frerichs (eds.), *Judaic Perspectives on Ancient Israel* (Philadelphia: Fortress, 1987), 229; and the detailed analysis in Jonathan Grossman, "'Dynamic Analogies' in the Book of Esther," *VT* 59 (2009), 397–99. According to Jona Schellekens, "Accession Days and Holidays: The Origins of the Jewish Festival of Purim," *JBL* 128 (2009), esp. 125–28, the Joseph allusions constitute a "secondary type scene" within Esther. This, however, depends on a highly unlikely reconstruction of the original book. Hans-Peter Mathys, "Der Achämenidenhof im Alten Testament," in Bruno Jacob, and Robert Rollinger, (eds.), *Der Achämenidenhof/The Achaemenid Court: Akten des 2. Internationalen Kolloquiums zum Thema "Vorderasien im Spannungsfeld klassischer und altorientalischer Überlieferungen", Landgut Castelen bei Basel, 23.–25. Mai 2007*, Classica et Orientalia (Wiesbaden: Harrassowitz, 2010), 236–39, uses these parallels to suggest a Persian date for the Joseph story, but this is unconvincing.

[6] Winitzer, "The Reversal of Fortune Theme in Esther," 180.

- The reversal of fortunes has to do with the king's sleeplessness: Pharaoh's disturbing dreams are what lead him to call for interpreters, and eventually to the release of Joseph from prison; Xerxes' inability to sleep in chapter 6 is the turning point of the narrative.
- The drama climaxes with a banquet where the invitees do not know the (Jewish) identity of the host: Joseph's brothers sit at his table without knowledge of who is hosting them, and Haman's downfall comes at a banquet at which he learns of Esther's ethnicity.

Lest these plot similarities not convince a reader, the author included verbal clues as to the intertextual connection, so that the allusions could not be missed (see Table 7.1).[7]

Although not every one of these pairs is convincing individually, the overall impression is clear: the author of Esther wants his readers to be thinking about Joseph at every turn. Some of the parallels may suggest specific ways of reading the story of Esther. Thus, Joseph's resistance to Potiphar's wife serves as a precedent for Mordecai's resistance to bowing to Haman (Esther 3:4 = Genesis 39:10, parallel no. 3 in Table 7.1). In parallels nos. 1 and 2, Mordecai plays the role of Joseph, but the role of Pharaoh is, significantly, shared by Haman and Xerxes. Some of the parallels link Esther, rather than Mordecai, to Joseph: thus it is Esther who throws the banquet at which her Jewishness is revealed.

Beyond the specific interpretations suggested by these allusions, however, is the more basic, and more important, point: the author of Esther modeled his story on the story of Joseph. Like Joseph, Esther adopts the role of the foreign potentate whole-heartedly, never asking, as Daniel did, for different food or special accommodations.[8] As in the case of Joseph, the role that Esther plays turns out to be critically important for the rescue of the Jews, and it would not have been possible for Esther or Joseph to effect the rescues they did had they not subverted their Jewishness altogether. Carolyn Sharp noted that Joseph was valuable to the Israelites specifically because he was not overtly Israelite;[9] the same could be said of Esther.

Yoram Hazony argues that three biblical books, Daniel, Nehemiah, and Esther, all accept the lesson of Joseph that in order to survive the exile, collaboration with the state is necessary. But "they rejected the ending to the

---

[7] See Gabriel Haim Cohen, "Introduction [to Esther]," in חמש מגילות, Da'at Miqra Commentaries (Jerusalem: Mossad ha-Rav Kook, 1990), 13 (in the pagination that begins again for Esther), for a fuller list of parallels, including some which are not as striking, but which – in light of the certain parallels – were also presumably intentional.

[8] See the comments of Sharp, *Irony and Meaning in the Hebrew Bible*, 66; Hazony, *The Dawn*, 89.

[9] See Sharp, *Irony and Meaning in the Hebrew Bible*.

Table 7.1 *Esther and the Joseph narrative*

Book of Esther	Joseph narrative	Parallel no.
Haman took the garments and the horse and he clothed (*va-yalbesh*) Mordecai. He had him ride in the city square and he called in front of him (*va-yiqra le-fanav*), "This is what shall be done to the one whose honor the king desires!" (6:11).	He had him ride in the second chariot he had, and they called in front of him (*va-yiqre'u le-fanav*) "Abrek!" (41:43).	1
The king removed (*va-yasar*) his ring (*tabba'to*) which he had taken from Haman, and gave it (*va-yittenah*) to Mordecai (8:2).	Pharaoh removed (*va-yasar*) his ring (*tabba'to*) from his hand and gave (*va-yitten*) it to Joseph, and he clothed (*va-yalbesh*) him (41:42).	2
When they continued to talk to him day after day (*yom va-yom*), he refused to listen to them (*ve-lo shama' 'aleihem*) (3:4).	When she continued to speak to him day after day (*yom yom*), he refused to listen to her (*ve-lo shama' 'eleha*) (39:10).	3
For how (*eikhakha*) can I endure to see the calamity that is coming to my people (*ba-ra'a asher yimtsa et 'ami*)? How (*eikhakha*) can I endure to see the destruction of my kindred? (8:6).	For how (*eikh*) can I go back to my father if the lad is not with me? I fear to see the evil that would come upon my father (*ba-ra'asher yimtsa et avi*) (44:34).	4
In the third year of his reign, he made a feast for all his officers and servants (1:3).	On the third day – Pharaoh's birthday – he made a feast for all his servants (40:20).	5
Let the king appoint overseers (*yafqed peqidim*) (2:3)	Let Pharaoh appoint overseers (*yafqed peqidim*) over the land (41:34)[a]	6

[a] My thanks to Moshe Bernstein for pointing out this parallel.

Joseph story as the only possible outcome. Surely, they argued, one should have been able to achieve favor and wield power in Egypt – and yet have been strong enough, when the moment of terror came, to defy the idol and deliver one's people."[10] In fact, the differences of opinion among these three are far greater than Hazony believes, but he is certainly correct to put them all in dialogue with Joseph and with each other.

Hazony argues well that in reviving the model of Joseph, the author of Esther espouses a philosophy of power. In order to accrue power in a foreign land, the Jew must be prepared to play power politics together with the foreigners. Daniel, Nehemiah, and Mordecai are all involved in the royal

[10] Hazony, *The Dawn*, 135.

bureaucracy, and all rise to great heights there. They differ, however, on a critical question, relevant to all Jews (and, indeed, all minorities) who participate in imperial society: how much of their original identity – in this case, their Jewish identity – are they prepared to sacrifice in order to participate?

Joseph, it will be recalled, represents an extreme model in this regard. Once in Egypt, he turns his back on his family with a shocking finality.[11] Apparently convinced that all members of his household were at least complicit in the vicious treachery committed against him – including his father, who had, after all, *sent* him to check on his brothers – he lives a life in Egypt of remarkable solitude. As a slave, then as a prisoner, then as an interpreter of dreams, and finally as a prince, he cuts a figure of austere alone-ness. He is accompanied by no one, has no friends, cultivates no relationships. Alone he falls, alone he rises; failure and success are his alone. Not only does he not develop new relationships within Egyptian society, but he actively dissolves his old ties to his family and his ancestry. Or, perhaps, he perceives that these ties have already been dissolved, and he sets about eradicating them from his identity altogether. He names his first son "Manasseh," from a Semitic root meaning "to forget," and he explains: "for the Lord has made me forget all my toils *and my whole family*" (Genesis 41:51). The second son, on the other hand, is named "Ephraim," "for the Lord has made me prosper in the land of my affliction" (41:52).

He has not erased his identity within himself. At least early in his Egyptian career, he refrains from sleeping with Potiphar's wife, on the grounds that his master had been good to him, "so how could I do this great wicked thing, and sin before God?"[12] Even later, he still thanks "the Lord" for his successes, and does call Egypt "the land of my affliction." But he thanks the Lord for helping him to forget his past and for helping him prosper in his new land. Here we have the ultimate irony of conscious forgetting: he has "forgotten" his past so well that what he is most grateful for is that he no longer remembers it. But does Joseph, before his brothers arrive in Egypt, really not remember his past? What Joseph exemplifies here is not forgetfulness in the usual sense, which is a passive process by which memories are actually erased. Joseph models *active* forgetting, in which the memories, seared into the very essence of the individual, are consciously marginalized. Can this really work? Can a memory as powerful as one's

---

[11] See Yoel Bin-Nun, ‏"הפילוג והאחדות – כפל הטעות המרה והלם הגילוי: מפני מה לא שלח יוסף (שליח) אל אביו?"‏ *Megadim* 1 (1986), 20–31.

[12] Genesis 39:9; my thanks to Moshe Bernstein for drawing my attention to this passage in this context.

entire childhood be marginalized within one's identity? These may well be the very questions that the first half of the Joseph narrative asks.[13]

As a model of Jewish life, Joseph was difficult to embrace. In speaking to his brothers, he exclaims, "By the life of Pharaoh – you are spies!" Biblical characters typically swear by God, or by the life of God,[14] but Pharaoh here has replaced God. In Joseph's mind, Pharaoh plays that role: he is the all-powerful sustainer of life.

Indeed, one could argue that within the narrative, *Joseph* actually plays the role of God. After all, he does sustain life, choosing who shall live and who shall die. Joseph himself asks the question: "Am I in place of God?" (50:19).[15] There are other hints that suggest that Joseph sees himself, if not as a God, then as God's avatar on earth. When Joseph clandestinely has the brothers' silver placed in their sacks, his brothers exclaim (42:28), "What is it that God (*elohim*) has done to us?" To makes things worse, Joseph's steward says, "Do not fear: your god and the god of your father gave you a treasure in your sacks" (43:23). Joseph asks indignantly, in much the manner of God, how his brothers could wrong him, since he knows all (44:15), and Judah's response (44:16) admits that Joseph is, in a sense, in place of God: "What can we say to my lord? What can we speak, and how can we acquit ourselves? God has discovered his servants' sin!" Since in Egypt the Pharaoh did participate in the divine, the idea that Joseph would see himself in the same light is not surprising.

The most explicit statement in this regard was uttered by Joseph earlier, in a manner that seems designed to obscure the issue of who *really* is God in this story. While yet in prison, when his co-prisoners, the butler and the baker have mysterious dreams, Joseph says, "Well, ĕlōhîm has solutions. Tell the dreams to me!"[16] And much later, when ruling in Egypt, with his family around him, the Egyptians say to him, "You have given us life (*heḥeyitanu*)!"[17] Regarding Joseph's final rhetorical question – "am I in the place of God?" – Sharp concludes: "The implicit claim is that Joseph is not in the place of God, yet the audience knows that he has functioned in a quasi-divine role, omniscient and able to manipulate life-and-death matters

---

[13] Clarke E. Cochran, "Joseph and the Politics of Memory," *Review of Politics*, 64 (Summer 2002), 421–44. Once Joseph's brothers arrive, they obviously change his thinking and the course of the story.

[14] For the religious significance of which deity one swears by, see, e.g., Isaiah 19:18: "On that day, there will be five cities in the land of Egypt speaking Canaanite and swearing by the Lord of Hosts."

[15] This was observed by Sharp, *Irony and Meaning in the Hebrew Bible*, 56, and many of the points in this paragraph are drawn from her discussion, *ibid.*, 55–61.

[16] Genesis 40:8. The significance of this verse in this regard was reiterated to me by David Silber in some of the conversations we have had about the book of Esther, from which I gained immeasurably.

[17] Genesis 47:25. I am indebted to Shalom Holtz for the importance of this verse in this context.

unseen."[18] Indeed, we note that God himself has disappeared from the story: there is no divine discourse in Egypt (37:1 – 46:2).[19] If there is any god in Egypt, it is Joseph.

We will return to the question of God within Esther, but for now it is sufficient to note that Joseph is an extreme example of a Jew who, while remaining a Jew, has given up much of his overtly Jewish identity in order to take part in the political life of his new land. He dresses as an Egyptian, is married to an Egyptian, and speaks Egyptian – well enough that his brothers, who communicate with him through a translator, never seem to suspect that he is not a native Egyptian. Esther adopts Joseph as a role model whole-heartedly.

Daniel represents the other pole: a Jew who never sacrificed anything. He ate what he wanted, refusing the king's food (chapter 1); he requested help from God in interpreting the king's dreams, and openly thanked God, praising him to the king, when that help arrived (chapter 2); he preached on matters of religion to the king, convincing Nebuchadnezzar to acknowledge the almighty power of the God of Israel (chapter 4); he flouted a decree against prayer and insisted on praying as he wished, *at his window*, to his God, confident that if he were caught, God would intervene on his behalf (chapter 6). The author of Esther vehemently disagrees with this approach. His characters, as has been seen above, sacrifice nearly everything, from their names to their choices of food and spouse.[20]

Politically, Daniel also provides a contrast. In Daniel 6, the prayers Daniel offers are in the direction of Jerusalem (6:10–11). It is surely no coincidence that the beginning of the book of Daniel (in stark contrast to the beginning of Esther) narrates the siege of Jerusalem and details of the exile of the Jews to Babylonia: the book of Daniel takes exile to be a thoroughly lamentable and hopefully brief episode in the history of the Jews. In Esther, on the other hand, diaspora life is simply a reality to be navigated.[21]

---

[18] Sharp, *Irony and Meaning in the Hebrew Bible*, 60.

[19] André Neher, *The Exile of the Word* (Philadephia: JPS, 1980), 24–27; see also LaCocque, *Esther Regina*, 16–17; Neher's interpretation is that when in exile, one is distanced from God.

[20] Macchi, "The Book of Esther," 117, suggests rather implausibly that the author portrayed the marriage between Esther and Xerxes as strained in order to avoid a positive depiction of a mixed marriage.

[21] It seems gratuitous to argue that at the end of Esther, "in the midst of the joy of salvation, the reader is reminded of the mourning over the destruction of the Temple and Jewish national life in the land of Israel," and that "close attention to the hidden level reveals the narrator's criticism of the Jews of Shushan for remaining in Persia and not returning to their own country" (Grossman, "'Dynamic Analogies,'" 410 and n. 43). It may be true that some readers would have arrived at these thoughts, but only readers who would have condemned the Persian Jews for living in Persia before reading the book;

2. Redeeming Saul

One more set of intertextual references is deployed by the author of Esther, and again, the use of these references is for political purposes. Many details in the story serve to bind the heroes of this story to Saul.[22] The connection to Saul is suggested when we are first introduced to Mordecai and Esther, as was discussed above. The introduction of Mordecai is reminiscent of that of Saul, and even contains names (Shimei and Kish) known to have been names of individuals within Saul's family, as well.[23] Since Mordecai's genealogy is traced back only to his great-grandfather, who lived through the beginning of Neo-Babylonian rule and the early sixth century BCE, no direct genetic connection is claimed between Mordecai (and Esther) and Saul, however. Instead, the two are merely being associated. The mantle of Saul is then worn by Esther when the queen does not disclose her identity: "Esther did not tell her origin and her people" (Esther 2:20) reminds the reader of Saul, of whom it was said, "the matter of the kingship he did not tell" (1 Samuel 10:16).[24]

   Certainly the most important connection between the two, as the narrative unfolds, is that whereas Saul lost his kingship for failure to massacre Agag, king of the Amalekites (a story told in 1 Samuel 15), Mordecai succeeds by killing Haman *the Agagite*. Numerous writers have seen that at the root of the conflict between Mordecai and Haman is an old ethnic feud between the tribe of Saul and the tribe of Agag the Amalekite.[25] The tenth-century Karaite commentator Salmon b. Yeruham already commented regarding Mordecai's introduction:"The meaning of *yemini* is 'from Benjamin' . . . This expression is fronted in order to make known that just as Saul, Mordecai's ancestor, vanquished Amalek, so too Mordecai, descendant of Saul, vanquished the descendant of Amalek – that is, Haman, identified as a descendant of Agag when it calls him 'the Agagite.'"[26] The claim is that the actions of Mordecai and Esther redeem the missteps of

---

in both ancient and modern times, it tends to be the Jews living in Israel who do so. In the book itself, there is not a hint to this effect, and even the analogies to the book of Joshua discussed by Grossman, if they are found compelling, can be interpreted in precisely the opposite direction. For more on this mode of interpretation, motivated more by contemporary Zionism than by philological or interpretive considerations, see below, Chapter 10, nn. 9–10.

[22] See above, pp. 49–53, for some initial observations relevant to this theme.

[23] For detailed discussion of the characters named, see Berg, *The Book of Esther*, 64–66.

[24] This allusion was noticed by the Rabbis; see b. Megillah 13b and Esther Rabbah 6:12.

[25] For two examples, see Laniak, *Shame and Honor in the Book of Esther*, 73–75, and Hagedorn, "The Absent Presence," 53–54.

[26] Salmon's commentary, which is extant in manuscript, is quoted by Wechsler, *Strangers in the Land*, 216–17 n. 108, from where the present translation was taken with modifications.

Saul, their tribesman, half a millennium ago.[27] As another midrash puts it, relying on a parallel between 1 Samuel 15:28 and Esther 1:19: "with this formula her grandfather lost the monarchy – as it says, 'it shall be given to your fellow who is better than you' – and with this formula the monarchy returned to her – as it says, 'the king shall give her queenship to her fellow better than her.'"[28]

Thus, one of Saul's early mistakes was his failure to act decisively when faced with challenges to his authority at the beginning of his reign. Instead, the text says, "he remained silent (*maḥărish*)."[29] This is exactly the challenge Mordecai hurls at Esther in 4:14: "if you indeed remain silent (*taḥărishi* . . .)." In that same passage, Mordecai tells Esther that if she *does* – like Saul – remain silent, "you and your father's household (*beit avikh*) will perish." Samuel had originally told Saul that the entire nation of Israel was looking expectantly at Saul "and his father's household" (*beit avikha*).[30] On that occasion, the nation's hopes were dashed by Saul's failures. Esther has the chance to redeem her father's household – the House of Saul.

In concluding his plea for action, Mordecai tells Esther that what she must bring is *revaḥ ve-hatsalah*. The concept of *revaḥ* is not one with positive resonances for Saul. "Relief" (*revaḥ*) eluded Saul when he was king, and he was able to achieve it only by relying on the upstart David: "David would take the lyre and play by hand, and bring relief (*ravaḥ*) to Saul so that he had it good, and the evil spirit would depart from him. By imploring Esther to bring the *revaḥ* to the Jewish people, Mordecai is entreating her to rectify that which Saul could never do.[31]

Finally, as many have noted, in the battles at the end the Jews "do not touch the spoils" (9:15). This is despite the fact that in 8:11, they were explicitly given permission to plunder their enemies. This seems to be an explicit correction of the mistakes made under Saul in 1 Samuel 15, when the Israelites, in direct violation of religious orders, brought back spoils of war

---

[27] The argument in the following paragraph is drawn from Berger, "Esther and Benjaminite Royalty," 630.

[28] Esther Rabbah 4:9 and Abba Gurion, p. 9a; see also Targum Rishon and Targum Sheni to 4:14.

[29] 1 Samuel 10:27.   [30] 1 Samuel 9:20.

[31] This, again, is drawn from Berger, "Esther and Benjaminite Royalty," 632–35. Intriguingly, these two passages – 1 Samuel 16:23 and Esther 4:14 – are brought together in a discussion of the semantics of רוח by Tanḥum ha-Yerushalmi in his *Kitāb al-Bayān*, but he does not explicitly comment on the relationship between the texts as going beyond the lexical; the relevant passage is cited and translated in Wechsler, *Strangers in the Land*, 325–26 and n. 9.

from Amalek. They atone for that here by *refraining* from plundering when they are permitted to plunder.[32]

The import of these parallels is less readily apparent, but clearly Mordecai and Esther are depicted as completing the work begun – and left unfinished – by Saul, and thus clearly they are seen as rectifying his faults and righting his wrongs. André LaCocque finds it most important that the ultimate completion of this process takes place *outside of Israel*, as if to say that in the new reality, even those jobs which seem to be nation-based and relevant mostly to the old national existence in the land of Israel will now be executed in the Diaspora.[33] If so, this returns us to the claim made in the previous chapter: the emphasis on the Benjaminite heritage of the heroes is not a serious attempt to rehabilitate the line of Saul, but a polemic against the hopes for a resurrection of the Davidic dynasty during the Persian period.[34] In all, the use of the Saul imagery allows the author of Esther to claim that redemption, thought by some to be possible only in the land of Israel and with a Davidic king on the throne, will actually be realized by the anti-David, in the land of exile.

Yitzhak Berger has drawn attention to another complex of allusions linking Esther to the narrative of Saul and, again, serving as a corrective to the faults seen in the first Benjaminite king. Berger points to the story in 1 Samuel 20, in which Saul hosts a feast on one day, and then another feast the next day (v. 27). Whereas the first one passes uneventfully, at the second the host, Saul, becomes enraged at one guest, Jonathan, for betraying him and protecting David. Jonathan concludes that "[Saul] definitely intends evil" (v. 7, and see v. 33) and rises angrily from the feast (v. 34). All this is reprised in Esther. There, Esther hosts two banquets, on successive days; the first passes uneventfully, while at the second, the king rises angrily and leaves, and Haman observes that "the king definitely intends evil against him" (Esther 7:7).[35] Berger concludes that the similarities are meant to connect the narratives in a way that emphasizes the differences between

---

[32] William McKane, "A Note on Esther ix and I Samuel xv," *JTS* 12 (1961), 260–61; Berg, *The Book of Esther*, 67; Laniak, *Shame and Honor in the Book of Esther*, 137 n. 28. Sharp, *Irony and Meaning in the Hebrew Bible*, 67–74, argues that the slaughter depicted in chapter 9 is like a sort of holy war, exemplified by the fact that they didn't touch the spoils – but not quite: it is actually a poor imitation of one.

[33] LaCocque, *Esther Regina*, 18–19.

[34] A similar suggestion was made by Berg, *The Book of Esther*, 68–70.

[35] The same Hebrew expression is used: *kaletah ha-ra'ah me-et ha-melekh* and *kaletah ha-ra'ah me-'imo*. For the motif of the angry king, see also Tessa Rajak, "The Angry Tyrant," in Tessa Rajak, Sarah Pearce, James Aitken, and Jennifer Dines (eds.), *Jewish Perspectives on Hellenistic Rulers* (Berkeley: University of California Press, 2007), 110–27.

them. Whereas Saul had "determined to do evil" against a fellow Israelite, Esther caused Xerxes to "determine to do evil" against the mortal enemy of Israel, Haman.[36]

Following this line of thought, and following further the trail of allusions to Saul, brings us to the end of the book of Esther. The very last line of the book (10:3) informs us: "For Mordecai the Jew was second to King Xerxes and great among the Jews; he was well received by his many brethren, seeking favor for his people and advocating peace (*shalom*) for all his kin (*zaro*)." The collocation of *shalom* "peace" with *zera* "seed, kin" is rare, and the only real parallel to the final phrase of the book is in 1 Kings 2:33. There Solomon, in the final stages of consolidating his power over Israel (i.e., in the final stages of massacring all real or potential threats to his rule), advises Benaya to assassinate Joab at the altar of God. By way of explanation, Solomon says: "There will be peace (*shalom*) for David and his kin (*zaro*), his household and his throne, forever, from God." This contrast shows the superiority of the "reign" of Mordecai over that of David, in a way similar to that seen above regarding Esther. When Mordecai is in power, he (like Esther) does not turn on fellow Jews, as David did. Like Solomon, he seeks peace for his kin, but he defines "kin" more broadly: rather than contrasting "his kin" with other families within Israel, as Solomon does, he regards "his kin" as including all Jews.[37]

There is a further contrast between Solomon's statement and the statement about Mordecai that deserves comment, although it may perhaps be so obvious that it needs none. Solomon envisioned a peace "from God," whereas the peace in Esther is brought about by Mordecai. It is true that the absence of God from the last line of Esther is certainly no surprise, absent as he has been throughout the entire book. But this very point is worthy of further consideration.

---

[36] Berger, "Esther and Benjaminite Royalty," 636–37, and see *ibid.*, 637–40, for a more extended argument regarding the motif of ‏כלתה רעה מעם‎* in the continuation of the Saul and David story, as well.

[37] Frisch, "‏בין מגילת אסתר לספר מלכים‎," 30; Berger, "Esther and Benjaminite Royalty," 642–43.

CHAPTER 8

Diaspora revisions
Rethinking the Exodus and rethinking God

1. Reprising, and transmuting, the Exodus

By way of considering this theme further, I would like to take a detour
through a related cluster of intertextual motifs underlying Esther: the
Exodus.[1] I would submit that Esther, like the Exodus, is very much a
story of redemption, but that Esther is in many ways an anti-Exodus.

As was discussed in Chapter 1, many Jews in the Second Temple era
anticipated another Exodus experience. The author of Esther made it clear
that his story could not be read without calling to mind the original
Exodus – and by extension, the expectations of another exodus – and
rapidly and thoroughly subverts these expectations. Although the action
in the narrative spans a decade in the life of Xerxes, the climax, which takes
up most of the text of the story, is focused on a three-day period. These days
happen to include the fourteenth and fifteenth days of Nisan, the very days
which traditionally celebrated the Exodus. The chronology is spelled out in
a number of verses: "The royal scribes were called, in the first month, on the
thirteenth day, and all that Haman commanded was written . . . : to destroy,
to kill, and to wipe out all the *yehudim*, youth to elder, children and women
on one day, on the thirteenth day of the twelfth month – namely Adar – and
plunder their booty."[2] The action moves quickly from that point.
Apparently immediately, Mordecai knows of the plot (and its background)
and reacts: "Mordecai knew all that was done . . . and he approached in
front of the royal gate."[3] After a brief dialogue between Mordecai and
Esther, Esther conceives of a plan, whose first stage is to be enacted by
Mordecai:

---

[1] Humphreys, "A Lifestyle for the Diaspora," 216 n. 17, points to the Exodus as a crucial background
story for Esther. Carey A. Moore, "Esther Revisited Again: A Further Examination of Certain Esther
Studies of the Past Ten Years," *HAR* 7 (1983), 173–76, rejected the Exodus narrative as a significant
intertext for Esther, but has been rightfully overruled by subsequent scholarship.
[2] Esther 3:12.   [3] Esther 4:1–2.

Esther said to respond to Mordecai, "Go gather all the *yehudim* found in Fort Susa, and fast for me – don't eat or drink for three days, night and day, and I and my maidservants will fast thus, too. Thus will I approach the king – against the law, but if I am lost, I am lost." Mordecai passed, and did all that Esther had commanded him.[4]

If this conversation occurred on the 13th of Nisan, as seems to be implied, the three days could either begin that same day, or the next; Esther's reference to "night and day" in that order may imply that she thought it should begin that evening. This would be the evening of the 14th of Nisan, and the fast would continue for the 14th, the 15th, and the 16th. Alternatively, the fast could begin immediately, and continue on 13–15 Nisan. It would be on either the 15th or the 16th, then, that Esther takes the next step: "On the third day, Esther donned royalty . . ." (5:1). That evening Esther holds her first banquet (5:4–5), and the following day (5:8) she holds the second, at which Haman is revealed and killed. On the evening in between (either 16 or 17 Nisan), the king cannot sleep (6:1).[5]

Surely no one could miss the coincidence that the story of the salvation of the Jewish people in this new book was also effected on Passover. Indeed, some scholars have seen the connections as running much deeper. Gerleman saw thirteen elements that the stories had in common: (1) foreign court; (2) mortal threat; (3) deliverance; (4); revenge; (5) triumph; (6) establishment of a festival; (7) Esther is adopted, as was Moses; (8) Esther's ethnic origins are unknown to Xerxes, as were Moses' to Pharaoh; (9) Haman is an Amalekite, as the Amalekites fought against Moses; (10) Esther is Mordecai's spokesman, as Aaron was Moses'; (11) Esther is reluctant to help her people, as was Moses; (12) Esther appears in front of the king numerous times, as did Moses; (13) thousands of enemies die in Persia, as they did in Egypt.[6] Not all of these are compelling, even in

---

[4] Esther 4:15–17.

[5] The specific dates were analyzed in detail by Wechsler, for whom they were significant for the Christological prefiguration he finds there; see Michael G. Wechsler, "Shadow and Fulfillment in the Book of Esther," *Bibliotheca sacra*, 154 (1997), 275–84. In a thorough but idiosyncratic discussion of the dates, utilizing a fairly convoluted means of calculating and positing multiple calendars within Esther, Nina L. Collins ("Did Esther Fast on the 15th of Nisan? An Extended Comment on Esther 3:12," *RB* 100 [1993], 533–61, esp. 548–49) concluded that the night the king could not sleep was actually 14 Nisan. She compared this, then, to Exodus 12:30, according to which Pharaoh woke in the middle of the 14th night of Nisan ("Pharaoh woke up that night"). On this reading, too, Esther's first banquet was on the 14th, but her second – and climactic – banquet, which led directly to the salvation of the Jews, was on the 15th, just like the first *pesah*; and see also J. A. Loader, "Esther as a Novel with Different Levels of Meaning," *ZAW* 90 (1978), 417–21.

[6] Gillis Gerleman, *Esther*, Biblischer Kommentar: Altes Testament 21 (Neukirchen-Vluyn: Neukirchener, 1973), 14–23.

the aggregate, but some are indeed suggestive, and when they are coupled with the confluence of dates, it is impossible to believe that this is a coincidence.

These connections operate on two levels. On the one hand, they compel the reader to read the stories together, and in light of each other. Thus, one can argue compellingly that both Exodus and Esther mercilessly ridicule a king who believes himself to be omnipotent, and nearly (or actually) divine.[7] One may also claim that in light of the Exodus narrative, Esther can be read more comfortably as sacred scripture, interacting with earlier sacred texts rather than standing outside the tradition.[8]

On the other hand, the differences between the two narratives are all the more striking because of the elements they share.[9] The book describes a "salvation" with no God. Whereas Moses saved the Jews by exiting the palace, Esther saves the Jews by entering *into* the palace. Moses rebelled against the system; Mordecai and Esther work within the system and end as powerful representatives of the system.[10] Whereas the Exodus story is deadly serious, Esther sees the farcical elements in the world and can laugh at them.[11] Most importantly, the Jews in the book of Esther stay just where they were: still in Persia and the other 126 provinces of the empire.

How are we to interpret this series of inter-narrative reversals? How are we to make sense of this? One way is to see Esther as reflecting on and responding to the Exodus: "Surely there is a staggering difference between the events of Sinai and the events of Susa . . . The Purim decree seems to be scripture, but it is not. It is a flawed imitation with none of the authority given the real Scripture by its divine source."[12] According to this approach, Esther is a book which deconstructs itself. It constructs an impressive edifice and then reveals it to be nothing but a façade.

An alternative approach is to understand that the claim made in Esther is that God's covert operation in Persia was the equivalent of his overt operation in Egypt.[13] Thus, the Esther story takes itself very seriously – as seriously as the Exodus is taken. The changed details in the narrative are just

---

[7] William Whedbee, *The Bible and the Comic Vision* (Cambridge University Press, 2008), 187–90.

[8] Beal, *The Book of Hiding*, 117.

[9] See the perceptive comments of LaCocque, *Esther Regina*, 92–93 and 108–09.

[10] M. E. Andrews, "Esther, Exodus and Peoples," *Australian Biblical Review*, 23 (1975), 25–28, cited in Moore, "Esther Revisited Again," 175.

[11] Mary E. Mills, *Biblical Morality: Moral Perspectives in Old Testament Narratives*, Heythrop Studies in Contemporary Philosophy, Religion, & Theology (Aldershot: Ashgate, 2001), 75.

[12] Sharp, *Irony and Meaning in the Hebrew Bible*, 76.

[13] Loader, "Esther as a Novel with Different Levels of Meaning," 418 and 421.

details, but the themes and dominant ideas are the same: this, too, tells a salvation history, and God's differing modes of operation reflect nothing more than a multi-talented deity.

A third approach, which seems to do the most justice to the text, sees Esther as reflecting, wryly rather than triumphantly, on how times have changed. While the author might *want* overt action (or any action!) by God in the world, and while he might *prefer* that Israel be geographically redeemed in an ideal world, with a miraculous return to Israel, he has no expectation of such developments. Life has been desacralized. There is no God, there are no miracles. There are yet Jews, and there is hard work and shrewd planning; with these, and leaders such as Mordecai and Esther, the Jews can effect their own salvation, even if it is not quite of the type that God used to effect.

Even the holiday created as a result is "not quite" of the type that resulted from the Exodus. It is a holiday decreed by two Persianized Jews, whose authority rests on their royal appointments, not any religious standing they have, and they make no attempt to get approval from the Judean high priest or other authorities.[14] The holiday is created by an act of writing. It cannot escape the reader's attention that the same writing that was used earlier to absurdly decree the dominance of males in their homes and to cruelly ordain the destruction of all of world Jewry is now being used to promulgate a Jewish festival. The writing is performed by the same scribes; the promulgation is performed by the same horsemen. In short, it is difficult to take this writing as entirely sincere and genuine. The fact that the new holiday has the imprimatur of the Persian bureaucracy on it is a striking statement about the Jews' relationship to the empire.[15]

In every respect, the redemption in Esther is indeed a pale shadow of what "redemption" used to mean. Not only is there no geographic movement – as the Babylonian rabbi Rava commented nearly a millennium later, "We are still the slaves of Xerxes!" – but there is no real change in the status of the Jews. This is one of the most remarkable elements of the story: its radical focus on the present. This is true with regard to the biographies of the characters: it is striking that no one in the story has children, except for Haman, and his are all killed. Mordecai and Esther, and even Xerxes, have no descendants, and there is therefore no hint of a promise for the future.

The focus on the present also precludes any serious discussion of the past. The book makes no particular effort to explain why the Jews are living in

---

[14] LaCocque, *Esther Regina*, 90–95.
[15] Sharp, *Irony and Meaning in the Hebrew Bible*, 77; Stern, "Esther and the Politics of Diaspora," 50.

Persia – how they got there to begin with, or why they did not move back to Palestine with the returnees of the late sixth century,[16] or when and why they moved (presumably) from Mesopotamia to Susa.[17] The one mention of the exile in the book is the reference to the exile of Jehoiachin in the introduction of Mordecai, and its purpose there is to emphasize Mordecai's nobility (since it was the nobles who were exiled with Jehoiachin), rather than to lament the Jews' state of being.[18] The obvious contrast is Daniel 1, which begins by rehashing the story of the destruction of the Temple and the exile at the hands of Nebuchadnezzar, king of Babylon.[19] Such an introduction orients the reader immediately: what follows in Daniel is a life lived under protest, in which the protagonists are not where they are supposed to be, and life itself is not as it is supposed to be.

The different time-frames envisioned by the two books – that seen by Daniel, which stretches from the past, shattered by tragedy, to the future, full of promise and hope, and that seen by Esther, which sees only the present and the most elementary desire to survive it – are described in other terms, in the context of diaspora literature, by Homi Bhabha:

> The present can no longer be simply envisaged as a break or a bonding with the past and the future, no longer a synchronic presence . . . Unlike the dead hand of history that tells the beads of sequential time like a rosary, seeking to establish serial, causal connections, we are now confronted with what Walter Benjamin describes as the blasting of the monadic moment from the homogenous course of history, "establishing a conception of the present as the 'time of the now'".[20]

The same is true regarding the nature of the redemption in Esther. In response to Haman, Mordecai and Esther outmaneuvered the villain, and he is no more. But will there be no more Hamans in the world? Joseph, one model for Mordecai and Esther, was successful, throughout the entire end of the book of Genesis, in protecting his kin, the Jews. The book of Exodus begins with a terrifying turn, however: "A new king, who did not know Joseph, came to power" (Exodus 1:8). With the new king comes a new era, indeed, a new world for the Jews. The security they enjoyed under Joseph's

---

[16] See the comments of Naḥmanides in his *hiddushim* on Bavli Megilla 2a for an appreciation of this.
[17] See Shlomo Dov Goitein, ‏עיונים במקרא: בחינתו הספרותית והחברתית‎ (Tel Aviv: Yavneh, 1967), 62; Joseph Tabory, "‏התקופה הפרסית בעיני חז"ל‎," *Millēt*, 2 (1984), 75–76.
[18] See above, Chapter 4, n. 36.
[19] This is observed by Lawrence M. Wills, *The Jew in the Court of the Foreign King: Ancient Jewish Court Legends*, Harvard Dissertations in Religion 26 (Minneapolis: Fortress, 1990), 80.
[20] Bhabha, *The Location of Culture*, 4; the embedded quotation is from Walter Benjamin, "Theses on the Philosophy of History," in *Illuminations* (London: Jonathan Cape, 1970), 265.

protection evaporates with his disappearance.[21] And so we may ask: after the deaths of Mordecai and Esther, after the death of Xerxes, when "a new king" comes to power in Persia "who knows not Mordecai and Esther," what will be the fate of the Jews?[22] Will there be another Haman? Will the Jews survive?

The book's answer appears to be that there may very well be another Haman. Nothing has changed about the world over the course of the ten chapters of Esther: the absurd world of chapter 1 is the same world occupied in chapter 10. "Even though the story ends happily for the Jews, the narrative offers no guarantee that this course of events will repeat itself next time. This is perhaps the most chilling piece . . ."[23] With no God, one can only hope for survival until the next generation. This is not mere fatalism, though: in diaspora, one tends to view the present as the "time of the now."

On the other hand, the book seems to claim that the holiday has all the gravity as any other religious celebration. It is not a frivolous celebration, but one that cuts deep at what Jewish life in the Diaspora can be. This can be seen from yet one more allusion, this time buried in the formulation of the holiday itself. In 9:29–31, we read of the institutionalization of the new festival: "Then Queen Esther daughter of Avihayil and Mordecai the Jew wrote with full authority, to confirm this second Purim letter . . . words of peace and truth, to establish these days of Purim in their times, as Mordecai the Jew and Queen Esther obligated them to do, and as they have obligated themselves and their descendants to observe the fasts and lamentations."[24] The "fasts" referred to here were recognized by Ibn Ezra to be a reference to Zechariah 8:19, where "the fast of the fourth (month)," "the fast of the fifth (month)," "the fast of the seventh (month)," and "the fast of the tenth (month)" are all mentioned.[25] Ibn Ezra explains that the logic is that once the people have shown themselves willing to adopt new religious practices in

---

[21] Klara Butting, "Esther: A New Interpretation of the Joseph Story in the Fight against Anti-Semitism and Sexism," in Athalya Brenner (eds.), *Ruth and Esther*, A Feminist Companion to the Bible (Second Series) (Sheffield Academic, 1999), 248.

[22] Sharp, *Irony and Meaning in the Hebrew Bible*, 79.

[23] Stern, "Esther and the Politics of Diaspora," 45.

[24] This passage is riddled with translational, and possibly textual, issues which do not affect the point being made here. For detailed discussions, see Berlin, *Esther*, 92–93, and Fox, *Character and Ideology in the Book of Esther*, 123–28 and 286–87.

[25] The same position is taken by Tanḥum ha-Yerushalmi (text from Wechsler, *Strangers in the Land*, לג; translation modified from that given by Wechsler,*ibid.*, p. 317): ואמא ט'אהר אלנץ פהו אנהם ית'בתון ד'לך אליהם כמא ת'בתו אלציאמאת אלתי כאנו פי אלשבעים שנה אלתי בין צום ראשון ובית צום הרביעי וצום החמישי וכו' כמא באן פי ספר זכריה ולד'לך קאל באלג'מע אסתסננוהא. "the exoteric meaning (*ẓāhir al-naṣṣ*) of the text is that they enjoined upon themselves these just as they had enjoined upon themselves the

response to historical events – as they adopted those four fasts in response to the destruction of the Temple – they should also adopt the new festival of Purim.[26]

In fact, Ibn Ezra's insight is deeper than that. Zechariah does not just mention the fast days, but foretells that they "will be joy and happiness for the house of Judah, good festivals; but you must love truth and peace." Michael Fishbane writes, "the old divine promise that the four fast-days would become a time of joy and festivity was considered to be fulfilled in the days of Esther."[27]

I would submit a less dramatic interpretation, building on the same point. Mordecai and Esther do not claim that the fasts are to be abolished. What they argue, though, is that *just as* people observe the fasts commemorating the destruction of the Temple, they ought to celebrate the feasts commemorating the salvation in exile. If history is meaningful – and clearly people who observe the four fasts each year think it is – then Purim, too, should be on their calendar. This is said to be "words of peace and truth." Zechariah had said that "truth and peace" would be needed to abandon the fasts for festivals, and while that may not have yet arrived, surely this, too, is "peace and truth." Although the redemption of Esther may disappoint some, with its lack of supernatural elements and lack of any real progress, the book claims that it is a truly redemptive story, deserving of a festival on par with – if radically different from – Passover.

2. Finally: life without God

We can return now to the fact that the redemption, and the story as a whole, is *desacralized*. The ineluctable calling to mind of the Exodus story that Esther required leads to further reflections on the absence of God from the entire book.[28] That God is absent from the book of Esther is probably the best-known fact about the book, but its significance must be reevaluated.

---

fasts which were introduced during the seventy years between the First Temple and the Second Temple, i.e., the 'fast of the fourth month, the fast of the fifth month, and so on', as is made clear in the book of Zechariah – and this is why it says 'the fasts' in plural."

[26] See also H. L. Ginsberg, *Five Megilloth and Jonah: A New Translation* (Philadelphia: JPS, 1969), 88, and Berlin, *Esther*, 93. For a contrasting view, see Samuel E. Loewenstamm, "Esther 9:29–32: The Genesis of a Late Addition," *HUCA* 42 (1971), 117–24, and for further discussion, see Berg, *The Book of Esther*, 42–44 and 54–56 nn. 45–55.

[27] Fishbane, *Biblical Interpretation in Ancient Israel*, 503–05.

[28] On the significance of the absence of God, in particular when the story is compared with the Exodus, see Lori Hope Lefkovitz, *In Scripture: The First Stories of Jewish Sexual Identities* (Lanham: Rowman and Littlefield, 2010), 118–19.

In the first part of his provocative book *The Disappearance of God: A Divine Mystery*, Richard Elliott Friedman argues that the Tanakh, read from beginning to end according to the Jewish order, reveals the gradual disappearance of God from the world, from history, and even from the text. On Friedman's reading, God disappears from the world step by step: the last person to whom he is said to "reveal" himself is Samuel in the late eleventh century; the last person to whom God is said to "appear" is Solomon in the mid-tenth century; the last public miracle performed is the fire for Elijah on Mt. Carmel, and this is swiftly followed by God's refusal to appear to Elijah on Mt. Sinai; the last personal miracle is performed for Hezekiah in the late eighth century; by the book of Esther, God is absent entirely.[29]

This is a wonderfully insightful reading of the Bible, and significant for the method of reading (canonically) as much as for the results. The results are more nuanced than Friedman implies. The book of Daniel appears to constitute a major exception to the trend, and Friedman marginalizes the significance of the book for that reason.[30] It is noteworthy that although Daniel is filled with miracles, these are mediated through angels and other divine beings and omens. God has withdrawn, to a large extent, from the world of Daniel, as well. Generally speaking, therefore, the conclusions reached are impressive. Friedman does, however, overstate the unanimity of biblical voices when he writes: "Gradually from Genesis to Ezra and Esther, there is a transition from divine to human responsibility for life on earth. The story begins in Genesis with God in complete control of the creation, but by the end humans have arrived at a stage at which, in all apparent ways, they have responsibility for the fate of their world."[31] It is true that in many important ways, Ezra and Esther belong together. But in joining the two books, important differences between these texts are blurred. With regard to God, although he does not appear as a character in Ezra, he is said by the narrator to be directly manipulating history, by inspiring the kings to act in certain ways.[32] As already discussed, similar views of history and theology are to be found in Jeremiah, Chronicles and Second Isaiah, as well.[33]

Esther is altogether different. It affords not even a nod in the direction of God, no admission that such a being exists, much less that it has any influence of the lives of the people on earth. The absence of God in Esther, rather than being the natural culmination of a trend evident

---

[29] Richard Elliott Friedman, *The Disappearance of God: A Divine Mystery* (Boston: Little, Brown, 1995), 27–29, 78–85, and *passim*.
[30] *Ibid.*, 26. [31] *Ibid.*, 30. [32] See Ezra 1:1 and 6:22.
[33] See Chapter 1, above, and Koller, "Negotiating Empire."

throughout the Bible, is a radical fact. It is a fact about the book observed by all readers, whose significance may, yet, be underestimated.[34]

The fact of God's absence from Esther can be – and has been – understood in multiple ways. One school of interpretation minimizes the literary and theological significance of this fact by claiming some external reason for the absence of God's name. Saadia Gaon and Ibn Ezra suggested that the author knew that scribes would translate this text into many languages for distribution across the empire, and feared that any divine names would be replaced by the names of other gods. To avoid this, the author refrained from mentioning the deity altogether.[35] Gordis suggested that the author undertook to write his book in the form of a Persian chronicle (examples of which we unfortunately do not have).[36]

Another approach, found already in rabbinic literature, takes the absence of God as a positive statement made by the author. The Rabbis, and numerous other readers since, understood the literary absence of God to be merely a surface-level fact, and in fact to be a subtle argument for the hiddenness of God, rather than his absence. A Talmudic comment (in B. Hullin 139b) playfully asks, "What is the source for Esther in the Torah?" The answer given is that Esther was foretold in Deuteronomy 31:18: "I will indeed hide (*haster astir*) my face on that day." In part this is a pun, linking the name Esther to the Hebrew phrase "I will indeed hide" (*haster astir*), but in part it is a serious theological claim: where did the Torah foretell a story with no God? In Deuteronomy 31, where God promised that one day he would hide his face from his people.[37] Most modern interpreters of the book read similarly.[38]

---

[34] For a discussion see Kristin de Troyer, "Is God Absent or Present in the Book of Esther? An Old Problem Revisited," in Ingolf U. Dalferth (ed.), *The Presence and Absence of God: Claremont Studies in the Philosophy of Religion, Conference 2008* (Tübingen: Mohr Siebeck, 2009), 35–40, esp. 37.

[35] See Saadia's introduction to Esther, first published in Ratzaby, "מפירוש ר' סעדיה למגילת אסתר," 1159, reprinted in Katzenelenbogen, תורת חיים: מגילת אסתר, 316, and Ibn Ezra's introduction to Esther, *ibid.*, 1. For a detailed analysis, see Moshe Zipor, מדוע לא נכתב שם ה' במגילת אסתר? עיון במקורות הקדומים ובדברי חכמי ימי הביניים," *Bet Miqra*, 56 (2011), 58–70. Similar, but less compelling, is the suggestion of Paton (*Esther*, 95–96) that the concern was that inebriated Jews would desecrate the megillah on Purim.

[36] Robert Gordis, "Religion, Wisdom and History in the Book of Esther: A New Solution to an Ancient Crux," *JBL* 100 (1981), 359–88.

[37] See further below, Chapter 15.

[38] For a lucid discussion, with representative references, see Fox, *Character and Ideology in the Book of Esther*, 237–44; for a few examples among recent commentators, see Bush, *Ruth, Esther*, 323–26, Abraham D. Cohen, "'Hu ha-goral': The Religious Significance of the Book of Esther," *Judaism*, 23 (1974), 87–94, Levenson, *Esther*, 18–21, Harald Martin Wahl, "'Jahwe, wo bist Du?' Gott, Glaube, und Gemeinde in Esther," *JJS* 31 (2000), 1–22, and Morgenstern, *Conceiving a Nation*, 174–75; see also the apodictic statement of Isaac Kalimi, "The Place of the Book of Esther in Judaism and Jewish Theology," *Theologische Zeitschrift*, 59 (2003), 200–01.

A different reading of God's literary absence takes it to be an argument not for his *hiddenness*, but for the possibility of his actual absence. The most eloquent modern defender of this reading is Michael Fox:

> The author is carefully creating and maintaining uncertainty. That is why he hints of God's role, but only obliquely ... This carefully crafted indeterminacy is best explained as an attempt to convey uncertainty about God's role in history. The author is not quite certain about God's role in these events (are *you?*) and does not conceal that uncertainty. By refusing to exclude either possibility, the author conveys his belief that there can be no definitive knowledge of the workings of God's hand in history. Not even a wonderful deliverance can prove that God was directing events; nor could threat and disaster prove his absence.[39]

The author of Esther goes beyond Fox's questions, however, and makes it abundantly clear not only that God was not playing a role in his story, but that his place had been usurped by humans in multiple ways. In some ways, the role of God has been taken over, grotesquely, by the Persian king Xerxes; in other ways, God's jobs are performed by the Jews – Mordecai, Esther, or the entire Jewish people.[40]

As we enter the world of the story, we encounter a grandiloquent description of a court on display. Xerxes makes a feast whose explicit purpose, at least according to the narrator, is "to show the riches of his glorious kingdom and the honor of his excellent majesty" (1:4). The ostensible audience of the grandeur is "all his princes and his servants, the powerful of Persia and Media, the nobles and princes of the provinces" (1:3), but the literary audience is us. We are then treated to a detailed list of what we would have been most impressed with, if only we had ourselves been privy to this: "white cotton, and blue wool, bordered with cords of fine linen and purple, upon silver rods and pillars of marble; the couches were of gold and silver, upon a pavement of green, and white, and shell, and onyx marble" (1:6). This display, incredibly, went on for six months.

Numerous readers have seen in these verses allusions to the Temple and its predecessor, the Tabernacle. In particular, the architectural motif of tapestries spread over columns was the mode of construction of the

---

[39] Fox, *Character and Ideology in the Book of Esther*, 247.
[40] Hazony, *The Dawn*, 246, writes: "A number of events suggest that Mordechai and Esther understood this shift of responsibility from God to man – taking initiative not only in political actions, but also in making critical philosophical and religious determinations in order to give moral force to these actions."

Tabernacle, as described in Exodus.[41] The Jerusalem Temple is called a *birah* in 1 Chronicles 29. King David is quoted as having said, "the citadel (*birah*) does not belong to man, but to God" (29:1). Indeed, throughout the Hebrew Bible, only two places are called a *birah*: the Fortress of Susa and the Temple in Jerusalem.[42] More striking are the materials named: the "blue wool" (*tekhelet*), "fine linen" (*butz*), and purple (*argaman*). These are materials especially associated in the Israelite mind with the Temple. The combination of *tekhelet* and *argaman* appears nineteen times in the description of the Tabernacle in Exodus 25–28 and 35–40, and again in the description of the Temple in 2 Chronicles 3:14 – and only twice in the rest of the Bible outside of Esther.[43] The reference to *tekhelet* and *argaman* in the *birah* in Susa would ineluctably, then, conjure up images of the Temple in the mind of the Jewish reader.

Furthermore, the words used to praise the palace and its accoutrements are nearly hymnic in their tenor. In Psalms we find God being praised for his "greatness": "Great is God and exceedingly praised; his <u>greatness</u> (*gedulah*) cannot be understood" (Psalm 145:4). In Esther 1 it is Xerxes' greatness that is on display, as he shows off "the honor of the glory of his greatness (*gedulah*)" (1:3). Just as entrance into the Holy of Holies is prohibited in the Temple, entrance into the throne room is prohibited – on pain of death![44] Whereas in Esther 1, the king flaunts "the richness of the glory of his kingship (*kevod malkhuto*)" (1:4), it is just this "glory of the kingship," belonging to God, which is praised by the psalmist in Psalm 145:11–12.[45]

But if this is a Temple, are we to understand that Xerxes is comparable to God? The text makes it clear that, on the contrary, the king in this *birah*, while wielding overwhelming – nearly divine – power, is a comical image of a true monarch. Indeed,

---

[41] See, e.g., Exodus 26:31–32 and 40:18–19 This point is pressed hard by L. B. Paton, *A Critical and Exegetical Commentary on the Book of Esther* (Edinburgh: T. & T. Clark, 1908), 139.

[42] For Susa, see Esther, *passim*, but also Daniel 8:2 and Nehemiah 1:1; for the Temple, see Nehemiah 2:8 and 7:2, and also 1 Chronicles 29:19. In Ezra 6:2, "the citadel in Ecbatana, in the province of Media," is also mentioned, using Aramaic *birta*. On the passages in Nehemiah, see also below, Chapter 10.

[43] See Exodus 25:4; 26:1, 31, 36; 27:16; 28:5, 6, 8, 15, 33; 35:6, 23, 35; 36:8, 35, 37; 38:23; 39:1, 3; 2 Chronicles 2:13, 14. The two other occurrences are in Jeremiah 10:9 and Ezekiel 27:7.

[44] See Hayyim Angel, "*Hadassa Hi Esther*: Issues of Peshat and Derash in the Book of Esther," *Tradition*, 34 (2000), 87, with further references to modern scholars who have noted this.

[45] These observations were inspired by Laniak, *Shame and Honor in the Book of Esther*, 50. Laniak's later claim that the statement in Esther 1:12 וַיִּקְצֹף הַמֶּלֶךְ מְאֹד is significant because "In the Bible, the root קצף is used of God almost exclusively, except in late books like Esther and Daniel" (*ibid.*, 57), is false (unless one grants "almost" a generous definition; see 2 Kings 5:11 and Genesis 40:2 and 41:10, for example – but see above, regarding the connection between Pharaoh in Genesis 40–41 and the book of Esther).

[t]he king was probably viewed as a comical figure by the audience because of his decadent tastes and propensity for writing unrealistic laws while in the midst of celebration. Although the ancient readers (or hearers) of Esther may have found him amusing, they would also have recognized that he provides the main danger for the protagonists and is the driving force of suspense.[46]

Once more, the Joseph story provides an important intertext for reading Esther. Throughout the story of Joseph's sale, Genesis 37, God is not mentioned, and through a series of apparently fortuitous coincidences, including a chance encounter with a mystery man, Joseph eventually meets his brothers in a spot alongside the caravan routes that lead to Egypt.[47] Later on, however, Joseph informs his brothers – and the readers – that in fact the complicated sequence of events which brought him down to Egypt was a divine plan in action: "Now, it was not you who sent me down here, but God!"[48] One could expect the same sort of denouement at the end of the story of Esther, but no character makes this claim.[49] The question of divine involvement is never addressed directly within Esther, as opposed to Genesis. In light of the pervasive parallels between the stories of Joseph and Esther, the author of Esther must have expected his readers to be waiting for the literary revelation of God at some point in the story. By not providing it, he seems to be making a strong statement that he cannot, because God has refrained from revealing himself. He could say about God's involvement in the world, channeling Iago, "Demand me nothing: what you know, you know. From this time forth I never will speak word."[50]

Other aspects of the book also hint that in the author's mind, God is not just hidden, but *has been replaced*. According to Esther 9:2, the Jews had their ways with their enemies: "no man stood in their way." This is an expression that readers have encountered before. It was promised in Joshua 10:8 ("no man of them will stand in your way") and fulfilled in Joshua

---

[46] Kevin McGeough, "Esther the Hero: Going beyond 'Wisdom' in Heroic Narratives," *CBQ* 70 (2008), 57. Beal, *The Book of Hiding*, 17–18, writes that on the basis of the descriptions of the parties, "a picture is developing in which all ostensible power, from greatest to least, is consolidated around and identified with the king, and with the palace at Susa as its central, physical location."

[47] The coincidences work out so well that here, too, readers have seen God's hand directing events. See, e.g., the comment of the Tanhuma Va-yeshev §2 (quoted by Rashi in his commentary on 37:15): "the man – this is [the angel] Gabriel."

[48] Genesis 45:8; see also 50:20.

[49] When Mordecai says to Esther, "who knows – perhaps you have achieved royalty for just this moment" (4:14), some have seen a statement regarding the divine hand in history (Gan, "מגילת אסתר באספקלריית קורות יוסף במצרים," 144). But it seems just as reasonable to take it as a statement of uncertainty (cf. מִי יוֹדֵעַ רוּחַ בְּנֵי הָאָדָם הָעֹלָה הִיא לְמָעְלָה וּמִי יוֹדֵעַ הֶחָכָם יִהְיֶה אוֹ סָכָל in Qoh 2:19, וּמִי יוֹדֵעַ in Qoh 3:21, and כִּי מִי־יוֹדֵעַ מַה־טּוֹב לָאָדָם בַּחַיִּים in Qoh 6:12) regarding the theological import of the events transpiring (my thanks to Tzvi Novick for fine-tuning this point).

[50] Shakespeare, *Othello*, Act v Scene 2.

21:42–43 ("no one from all their enemies stood in their way") and 23:9 ("no one stood in your way").[51]

Again, though, the similarities highlight the stark contrast between Joshua and Esther in this regard.[52] In Joshua 10, it was God who said that "no man will stand in your way,"and he explained: "for I have delivered them into your hand." In Joshua 21 the point is made even more emphatically: "God allowed them to rest all around, as he had sworn to their fathers, and no one from all their enemies stood in their way – God delivered all their enemies into their hand." The first phrase in this verse, "God allowed them to rest (*va-yanaḥ*)," is also significant. God's ultimate promise regarding life in the land of Israel was that they would achieve *menuḥah* "rest" there: "For you have not yet reached the rest (*menuḥah*) and the inheritance which the Lord your God is giving you. But when you shall cross the Jordan, and dwell in the land which the Lord your God is giving you as an inheritance, he will cause you to rest from all the enemies around, and you shall dwell securely."[53] The claims made in Joshua 21 reached their pinnacle with the construction of the Jerusalem Temple, when Solomon said: "Blessed is the Lord, who gave rest (*menuḥah*) to his nation Israel, like all that he said."[54] Despite this history, the Jews in the Persian period, without the Temple and outside the land, could only have been ambivalent about these promises of *menuḥah*. Was this lost forever? The author of Esther claims that the events of his story accomplished *menuḥah*, however, far from the Promised Land: "They rested (*noaḥ*) from their enemies … on the thirteenth day of Adar, and resting (*noaḥ*) on the fourteenth day … and resting (*noaḥ*) on the fifteenth day of the month, making it a day of feasting and rejoicing … like the days on which the Jews rested (*naḥu*) from their enemies."[55] To clinch the point, Solomon's blessing on the dedication of the Temple verse goes on to say, "not a thing was forsaken (*lo nafal davar*) from all that he said." The same expression is found in Joshua 21:43: "not a thing was forsaken (*lo nafal davar*) from all the good that God had spoken to the house of Israel."A clear link is thereby established between these passages, implying strongly that the dedication of the Temple is the culmination of the process of conquering the land.

The same expression is used in Esther, too, but in an altogether different context: describing the reward due to Mordecai, which is the first good thing to happen to the Jews in the book, and the harbinger that from this point on the Jews' success was relentless and unavoidable, Xerxes says to

[51] Levenson, *Esther*, 120.   [52] Ego, "The Book of Esther," 292–93.   [53] Deuteronomy 12:9–10.
[54] 1 Kings 8:56.   [55] Esther 9:16–22.

Haman, "Do not forsake a single thing (*al tappel davar*) from all that you said."[56] This is as if to say, "Once again the promise of *menuḥah* 'rest' has come true, but this time it is not *in* the land, it is out of the land; this time, it is not *through* the Temple, but in its absence; this time, the agent of *menuḥah* is not God, but Xerxes."

Elsewhere in the book, the role of God is played not by the king, which is a reversal of the grossest kind, but by the Jews. Here it could be said that the Jews have taken over for God. For example, a number of times in the Bible, the "fear of God" falls on people: "the fear (*pahad*) of the Lord fell on the people";[57] "for the fear (*pahad*) of the Lord was upon them";[58] "fear (*pahad*) of the Lord was on the kingdoms of the lands";[59] "the fear (*pahad*) of the Lord was upon them";[60] "the fear (*pahad*) of God was upon all the nations of the lands when they heard that God was fighting against the enemies of Israel."[61] In Esther, however, in the absence of God, it is the "fear of the Jews" falls on the people of the land: "Many of the people of the land were Judaizing, because the fear (*pahad*) of the Jews had fallen upon them."[62]

This chapter began with the claim that in the world of this story, the personal and the corporate are inextricably intertwined. To make this point one final time, the expression "fear of the Jews" is replaced just a few verses later by something slightly different: "All the officers . . . were glorifying the Jews, because the fear (*pahad*) of Mordecai had fallen upon them."[63] LaCocque concludes on the basis of these passages that according to the story of Esther, "the community is endowed with numinous immunity, and the wise courtier replaces the inspired leader or prophet. Consequently, the diaspora Jews do not feel under any compulsion to go as pilgrims to a center of divine power, such as the Temple, as they themselves have become, so to speak, that very powerhouse."[64]

The same point emerges from the establishment of the festival by Mordecai and Esther. They daringly establish "a universally observed Jewish holiday, the only one . . . not associated with Palestine."[65] As part of the celebration of this new festival, the Jews are asked to send "presents" (*mattanot*) to the poor. Tzvi Novick has observed that elsewhere in the Bible, "presents" (*mattanot*) are "not so much shared as relinquished,

---

[56] Winitzer, "The Reversal of Fortune Theme in Esther," 182–84 and 186, discusses the expression *'al tappēl* within the book of Esther, contextualizing it within appearances of the root נפל in the book.

[57] 1 Samuel 11:7.   [58] 2 Chronicles 14:13.   [59] 2 Chronicles 17:10.   [60] 2 Chronicles 19:7.

[61] 2 Chronicles 20:29.   [62] Esther 8:17. See LaCocque, *Esther Regina*, 91.

[63] Esther 9:3. LaCocque points out that 1 Chronicles 14:17 replaces the phrase פחד ה' with פחד דויד, but there is actually a referential ambiguity in that verse, which reads, "David went out in all the lands, and the Lord placed his fear (פחדו) on all the nations." LaCocque, *Esther Regina*, 91.

[64] *Ibid.*, 92.   [65] Gordis, "Religion, Wisdom and History in the Book of Esther," 375.

whether to descendants, or, more commonly, to God or to God's priestly representative."[66] In this case, too, the position usually occupied by God has been usurped by the people.

Finally, a single city is differentiated in this celebration, but here it is not Jerusalem that is marked as unique, but Susa.[67] Not all diaspora Jews felt that Jerusalem could be, or had been, eclipsed. The Jews in Persian-period Elephantine, in southern Egypt, turned to the Jerusalem leadership for assistance and approval regarding the (re)construction of their temple.[68] Not surprisingly, the Jewish Temple at Elephantine was oriented toward Jerusalem, as well.[69]

The reality depicted in Esther is starkly different than that depicted anywhere else in the Bible. History operates without God. God has been replaced by the king, by the Jews, by the leader of the Jews. His Temple is no more; it has been replaced by the palace of a foreign king. Jerusalem is a past and possibly future center of Jewish life, but certainly not a present center. This is not a cause for lament; it is a fact about the new reality to which the Jews must adapt. "The most remarkable aspect of the book is not God's absence itself, but the fact that this absence does not induce defeat and despair."[70] The Jews' success no longer depends on their fidelity to traditions, but on their ability to navigate competing loyalties and to negotiate complex identities. They must be loyal citizens and also strong and loyal Jews. They hope for redemption, but of a temporary and limited sort. They are pragmatic in their politics, flexible in their affiliations, and adaptable in their religious practices. Their aspirations are for life to go on as usual, and this is the remarkably prosaic – and yet boundlessly joyous – conclusion to the book:

> King Xerxes imposed a tax on the land and the islands of the sea. The whole account of his might and power, and the story of Mordecai's advance – when he was promoted by the king – they are written in the Chronicles of the kings of Media and Persia. For Mordecai the Jew was second to King Xerxes, great among the Jews; he was well received by his many brethren, seeking favor for his people and advocating peace for all his kin.

---

[66] Tzvi Novick, "Charity and Reciprocity: Structures of Benevolence in Rabbinic Literature," *HTR* 105 (2012), 35.

[67] Esther 9:17–19.   [68] *TAD*, vol. A, 4.8.

[69] Bezalel Porten, "The Structure and Orientation of the Jewish Temple at Elephantine: A Revised Plan of the Jewish District," *JAOS* 81 (1961), 38–42. For more on the bonds between the Elephantine community and the Jerusalem Temple, see Knowles, *Centrality Practiced*, 42.

[70] Hazony, *The Dawn*, 247.

As a literary tactic, this ending is reminiscent of the conclusion to the epic of Gilgamesh, in its eleven-tablet Standard Babylonian version. There, after eleven tablets regarding questions of the nature of humanity, the meaning of friendship, and, above all, the implications of mortality, we read the following lines (XI 314–19):

> They arrived in Uruk-Haven.
> Gilgamesh said to Urshanabi, the ferryman:
> "O, Ur-shanabi, climb Uruk's wall and walk back and forth!
> Survey its foundations, examine the brickwork!
> Were its bricks not fired in an oven?
> Did the Seven Sages not lay its foundation?

A square mile is city, a square mile date-grove, a square mile is clay-pit, a square mile the temple of Ishtar: three square miles and a half is Uruk's expanse.[71]

After his quest for "something more," Gilgamesh arrives at the conclusion that mundane success is all he can hope for in life. It may not be transcendentally redemptive, but it is real life. In an earlier version of the epic, this was poignantly expressed to Gilgamesh by the barmaid Siduri:

> "O Gilgamesh, where are you wandering?
> The life that you seek you will never find:
> when the gods created mankind, they dispensed death to mankind,
> and kept life to themselves.
> But you, Gilgamesh, let your belly be full,
> enjoy yourself always by day and by night!
> Make merry each day,
> dance and play day and night!
> Let your clothes be clean,
> let your head be washed, may you bathe in water!
> Gaze on the child who holds your hand,
> Let your wife enjoy your repeated embrace!"[72]

The conclusion of the epic literarily dramatizes the ordinariness of the redemption experienced by Gilgamesh. By proudly recording the size and the neat arrangement of his city, Gilgamesh can claim the only real achievement available to him.[73]

---

[71] In the Standard Babylonian edition, this concluding passage brings the reader back to the beginning of the text, which started very similarly; my thanks to Shalom Holtz for emphasizing the importance of this point.

[72] This is from the Old Babylonian Sippar tablet, ii 14′ – iii 13.

[73] For this interpretation of the end of Gilgamesh, and the emphasis on "normal life as the form of existence that provides meaning," especially in the Old Babylonian version, see Tzvi Abusch, "The Development and Meaning of the Epic of Gilgamesh: An Interpretive Essay," *JAOS* 121 (2001),

A similar sentiment is expressed by the conclusion to Esther. In diaspora, "redemption" can only mean survival, triumph over evil, and the chance to go on. The mundane – the taxes imposed over the empire – is the witness to that redemption.[74] For now, all is well in the empire, and so all is well for the Jews.

617–18, as well as William Moran, "The Gilgamesh Epic: A Masterpiece from Ancient Mesopotamia," in Jack M. Sasson (ed.), *Civilizations of the Ancient Near East* (New York: Scribner, 1995), vol. IV, 2336.

[74] Shalom Holtz made the sharp observation that earlier, Jeremiah had a "mundane" vision of the meaning of redemption: he emphasizes the sounds of weddings and millstones (25:10 and elsewhere), real estate transactions (32), and other trappings of everyday life.

PART 3

Early reactions
Rejection, subversion, correction

CHAPTER 9

A tense embrace
The reception of Esther in Hellenistic Alexandria

There is no way of knowing how quickly the story of Esther traveled through the Near East. The burden of this section will be to demonstrate two related claims. First, the story circulated widely, in either written or oral form, and was known in Palestine and even in Jewish Egypt within Hellenistic times, by the second century BCE at the latest. Second, the reaction to the story within Palestine was harshly negative. Evidence for the book's spread will not come from enthusiastic reviews or laudatory citations, therefore. Instead, we will be hunting for more oblique indications that the story was known, even if not approved.

I. 2 Maccabees

The earliest and most important evidence for the reception of Esther – more specifically, for the holiday of Purim – comes from the very end of 2 Maccabees. There we read that the Day of Nicanor is established, "To mark the thirteenth day of the twelfth month (called 'Adar' in Aramaic), one day prior to the Mordecaian Day (*tēs Mardochaikēs hēmeras*)" (15:36). What exactly people did on this Mordecaian Day, and why the author of 2 Maccabees uses this odd name, is not clear.[1] It is clear, though, that there was a holiday being celebrated, and that it was well enough known to serve

---

[1] The significance of this notice for the history of Purim was emphasized in particular by Bezalel Bar-Kokhba, "על חג הפורים ועל מקצת ממנהגי הסוכות בימי הבית השני ולאחריו," *Zion* 62 (1997), 387–89; see also Bar-Kokhba, "חג הפורים בימי הבית השני ומגילת אסתר ב"אסיה": "גישה היסטורית" ו"היסטוריה אורתודוכסית"," *Sinai*, 121 (1998), 42–44, and Dov Herman, "מתי נכללה מגילת אסתר בכתבי הקדש?" *Beit Mikra*, 48 (2003), 326–327. Schellekens, "Accession Days and Holidays," 115–34, has argued that in fact "the Day of Mordecai" was the original name of the festival, and that the entire book of Esther is propaganda for the Mordecaian dynasty, like the book of Samuel is propaganda for the Davidic dynasty. This fails to convince, however, since there never was a Mordecaian dynasty; the book would thus be reduced to an apology for something which never occurred.

as a point of reference for the book's readers. It is also possible that the reference to 14 Adar in this context is not a mere chronological touchstone, but a covert argument for the legitimacy of instituting new holidays to commemorate physical salvations: just as Mordecai did it with 14 Adar, we (Hasmoneans) are doing it with 13 Adar.[2] "The 'Mordecaian Day' was known, then, at least in parts of the Jewish Hellenistic Diaspora ... If this was the case in the far west, what can be deduced about the Jews of the Babylonian-Persian Diaspora?"[3]

Interestingly, no reference to this holiday is found in 1 Maccabees. In this regard, it is worth reflecting on some of the salient ideological differences between the two books of Maccabees. One difference is reflected in the books' treatment of Nicanor. According to 2 Maccabees, Nicanor is honorable and a friend of Judah. He is compelled to turn against Judah because of his king's command, but it is not something he relishes.[4] This may be reflective of a larger theme in 2 Maccabees: the non-Jews, even the Seleucids themselves, are not evil. Even Antiochus himself repents![5] In sharp contrast, 1 Maccabees consistently paints non-Jews as thoroughly hostile to Jews.[6]

Within 2 Maccabees, when Nicanor does attack the Jews, against his better judgment, he is, of course, defeated. It is this defeat which is to be celebrated on the 13th of Adar, the day before the Mordecaian Day. The political overtones of invoking the story of Mordecai seem to resonate clearly in the new holiday. Just as in the story of Mordecai in Persia, the celebration of the Jewish victory within 2 Maccabees is not a statement of anti-imperialism, and bespeaks no broader desire to create conflict between Jews and non-Jews. On the contrary, the Jews would prefer to live at peace with their neighbors and are by nature and inclination cooperative citizens of the wider empire, and fight only when those who should be friends choose to turn on them. In this light, the absence of any such reference on the part of the more militant author of 1 Maccabees is unsurprising.

---

[2] This claim was made by Burns, "The Special Purim," 13–15. Burns' further argument that since Nicanor is said "to have threatened to desecrate the Temple," and "even to have likened himself to the God of the Jews," he is being caricatured "as a *nouveau* Haman," is unconvincing, since there is no evidence that Haman was viewed in this way.

[3] Bar-Kokhba, "חג הפורים בימי הבית השני ומגילת אסתר ב"אסיה": "גישה היסטורית והיסטוריה אורתודוכסית"," 389.

[4] See 2 Maccabees 14:23–25.

[5] See 2 Maccabees 9 and Steven Weitzman, *Surviving Sacrilege: Cultural Persistence in Jewish Antiquity* (Cambridge, MA: Harvard University Press, 2005), 42–43.

[6] See Seth Schwartz, "Israel and the Nations Roundabout: 1 Maccabees and the Hasmonean Expansion," *JJS* 42 (1991), 16–38, and Steven Weitzman, "Forced Circumcision and the Shifting Role of Gentiles in Hasmonean Ideology," *HTR* 92 (1999), 46–47 and n. 46.

The different ideologies of the two books of Maccabees may in part reflect their different places of origins.[7] 2 Maccabees, which does allude to the Day of Mordecai, is a product of the Diaspora.[8] 1 Maccabees, on the other hand, composed (most likely) in Israel itself, contains no mentions of Purim or Esther.[9] Diaspora Jews may have more readily identified with the story of Esther and with its way of handling the fundamental problem of being a minority. Jews in Palestine, on the other hand, may have found it difficult to sympathize with the problems faced by the protagonists in the story. They could, of course, have simply returned "home" to Jerusalem.

Indeed, further allusions to Esther were identified in 2 Maccabees by Daniel Schwartz. First, the tower on which Antiochus executed Menelaus was fifty cubits tall.[10] Second, there is a reference to a three-day fast in 2 Maccabees.[11] Both of these parallels point to deeper connections between the stories. The execution of Menelaus cannot but remind us of the execution of Haman. In both cases, the foreign king, who has been turned against the Jews by a rogue loyalist, realizes that he has been duped, and has the "scoundrel" executed on a structure fifty cubits high. The height of the execution tower may serve as an allusive keyword, of which we will see more below. In using such a tactic, the author deploys a key word or phrase in order to cue the reader to think about the two stories in light of each other.

The three-day fast, too, is far more striking a parallel than a superficial numerical equivalence. Judah Maccabee declared the three-day fast in preparation for meeting the king, just as Esther declared her fast in preparation for meeting the king. The similarities highlight the vast differences between the stories, as well. The heroes could not be more different in the tactics they utilize to challenge the foreign ruler. Esther meets the king as submissive and seductive, as part of her plan to manipulate the king into preserving her people. Judah meets the king on the battlefield, "to stand up even to death for the laws, the temple, the city, their country, and citizens."[12] The dichotomy is reminiscent of a claim

---

[7] See the discussion of Malka Zeiger Simkovitch, "Greek Influence on the Composition of 2 Maccabees," *JSJ* 42 (2011), 293–310, who argues that 2 Maccabees is Temple-centric, but not Israel-centric.

[8] For an extended discussion of this point, see Daniel R. Schwartz, *2 Maccabees*, CEJL (Berlin: De Gruyter, 2008), 45–56.

[9] For more on the attractiveness of Purim in the Diaspora, see Burns, "The Special Purim," 13. Burns writes that 2 Maccabees was likely composed in Judaea, which is not true.

[10] 2 Maccabees 13:5; see Daniel R. Schwartz, ספר מקבים ב': מבוא, תרגום ופירוש (Jerusalem: Yad Yitzḥak Ben Zvi, 2004), 250 and 285; Schwartz, *2 Maccabees*, 450.

[11] 2 Maccabees 13:12, and Esther 4:16; see Schwartz, *2 Maccabees*, 452.   [12] 2 Maccabees 13:14.

made by Edward Said about exiles: "It is not surprising that so many exiles seem to be novelists, chess players, political activists, and intellectuals. Each of these occupations requires a minimal investment in objects and places a great premium on mobility and skill. The exile's new world, logical enough, is unnatural and its unreality resembles fiction."[13] These allusions to Esther, then, reveal two important facets of the intertextuality. First, the author of 2 Maccabees knew Esther well enough not only to mention the Day of Mordecai, but also to refer to some of the distinctive motifs in the story, such as the fifty-cubit tree of death, and the three-day fast before meeting the king.[14] By the same token, however, the differences between the texts emerge starkly from their juxtaposition in this way. Where Esther can be read as meek and submissive, 2 Maccabees replaces her with the militant Judah Maccabee. Jonathan Goldstein saw a similar dynamic even in the reference to "the Mordecaian Day." He proposed that the hero chosen was Mordecai, and not Esther, in order to stress the parallel between Judah Maccabee and Mordecai. To this André Lacocque added that the choice of Mordecai was based not only on gender, but on the nature of their heroism: Esther is subversive and manipulative, rather than confrontational and combative.[15] The Hasmoneans, who tended toward the confrontational and combative, would not have been laudatory toward Esther. Mordecai, who at least stood up to Haman, however, could well be seen as a precedent for Hasmonean refusals to partake of Seleucid ways of life.

In sum, the reference to the Mordecaian Day in 2 Maccabees, and possibly the further allusion contained in the detail of Menelaus' execution tower, show first and foremost that the story of Mordecai was known in Alexandria in the late second century BCE. Beyond mere knowledge, these references may also enable us to see some of the differences within the book's reception, differences between Hasmonean Palestine and the Diaspora. Going further, the references provide grounds for speculation, but little basis for any further conclusions.

---

[13] Edward Said, "Reflections on Exile," in *Reflections on Exile and Other Essays* (Cambridge, MA: Harvard University Press, 2002), 144.

[14] For other possible allusions to Esther, see Schwartz, *2 Maccabees*, 450, 471–72, and 483.

[15] Jonathan Goldstein, *II Maccabees*, AB 41A (Garden City, NY: Doubleday, 1983), 502; LaCocque, "The Different Versions of Esther," 308. See also Schwartz, *2 Maccabees*, 511–12, and the broader discussion of gender above, pp. 77–78. In a very different, text-critical, vein, Torrey, "The Older Book of Esther," 16, uses the reference to "the day of Mordecai" to support his contention that the older version of the story climaxed with the ascension of Mordecai.

2. Greek Esther

More revealing than the elusive references in 2 Maccabees is the Greek version of Esther, and in particular the large sections of the Greek text which have no parallel in the Hebrew text. There are six blocks of text, conventionally labeled A through F, found in all known Greek versions of Esther and without any parallel in the Hebrew text.[16] These six blocks can be grouped into three pairs. Additions A and F, found at the very beginning and very end of the book, are a dream that Mordecai had and its interpretation, revealed to him at the end. Addition A also contains another short narrative of an attempt on the king's life, foiled by Mordecai – just like the narrative present in both the Hebrew and the Greek versions of chapter 2. Additions B and E are the texts of, respectively, the letter that Haman sent out against the Jews, and the letter that Esther and Mordecai sent out allowing the Jews to defend themselves. Addition C contains prayers uttered by Mordecai and Esther for the salvation of the Jews, and Addition D tells an expanded version of the story of Esther's approach to the king.[17]

The origins of these "Additions" is somewhat mysterious, and just calling them "Additions" already stakes out a position on one contested issue. Some scholars have argued that the term is a misnomer, and that in fact the Hebrew MT and the Greek version should be seen simply as divergent branches on a family tree on which the last common ancestor is not recoverable.[18] This is not a compelling view, however, and it does seem clear to me that these six passages were literally *added* onto the book. Evidence for this comes from the redundancies which resulted: in the Greek text, Mordecai is introduced twice, and twice he discovers the plot to kill the king, for example. Some of the other differences between the MT

---

[16] The earliest fragment of any text of Esther in Greek is POxy 4443, from the first–second centuries CE, now in the Ashmolean Museum, Oxford, which contains part of Addition E. See Katharina Luchner, "4443. LXX, Esther E.16 – 9.3," in M. W. Haslam, A. Jones, F. Maltomini, and M. L. West (eds.), *Oxyrhynchus Papyri 65*, Graeco-Roman Memoirs 85 (London: Egypt Exploration Society for the British Academy, 1998), 4–8. A high-resolution photo of the fragment is available at the Oxyrhynchus Online Image Database, at http://163.1.169.40/gsdl/collect/POxy/index/assoc/HASH5833/32d0419f.dir/POxy.v0065.n4443.a.01.hires.jpg (accessed January, 2011).

[17] For a brief insightful summary, see Sidnie White Crawford, "Additions to Esther," in David Noel Freedman, Allen C. Myers, and Astrid B. Beck (eds.), *Eerdman's Dictionary of the Bible* (Grand Rapids, MI: Eerdmans, 2000), 426–27.

[18] Such a position was argued by Torrey, "The Older Book of Esther," 4–5 and 1–40 *passim*, for example, as well as by Carey A. Moore, "A Greek Witness to a Different Hebrew Text of Esther," *ZAW* 79 (1967), 351–58, and H. J. Cook, "The A-Text of the Greek Version of the Book of Esther," *ZAW* 81 (1969), 374–75.

and the Greek are more difficult to understand,[19] but whether they arose within Hebrew or in the translation process is a secondary question.

The significance of the Additions found in the Greek version of Esther would be greatly increased if we could locate their times and places of origins. Although certainty is not possible, a consensus has developed around an old theory that Additions A, C, D, and F were originally composed in Hebrew or Aramaic, whereas Additions B and E were composed in Greek.[20] At least the Semitic Additions were presumably composed in Palestine.[21]

In 1944, C. C. Torrey summarized the consensus regarding one major theme of the Additions: "The main reason for making the additions, it is commonly said, was the wish of the Greek-speaking Jews of Egypt to give to the story of Esther the religious atmosphere that is so sadly lacking in the Hebrew version."[22] This rewriting has to be situated within the different types of "rewritings" going on in Second Temple Judaism. Emanuel Tov observed that this is part of a large constellation of rewritings from this

---

[19] See esp. Almut Hintze, "The Greek and Hebrew Versions of the Book of Esther and its Iranian Background," *Irano-Judaica*, 3 (1994), 34–39, who argues for the view held by Torrey, Moore, and Cook (see n. 18 above) on the basis especially of the divergent proper nouns in the two versions.

[20] Torrey wrote in 1942 that "A, C, D, and F . . . are all of them translations from Semitic, as is obvious and beyond question when they are examined" (review of A. E. Brooke, Norman McLean, and H. St. John Thackeray (eds.), *The Old Testament in Greek*, *JBL* 61 [1942], 131; see also "The Older Book of Esther," 2). See Carey A. Moore, "On the Origins of the LXX Additions to the Book of Esther," *JBL* 92 (1973), 382–93; R. A. Martin, "Syntax Criticism of the LXX Additions to the Book of Esther," *JBL* 94 (1975), 65–72. See also Emanuel Tov, "The 'Lucianic' Text of the Canonical and the Apocryphal Section of Esther:," 11; Tov, "Three Strange Books of the LXX: 1 Kings, Esther, and Daniel Compared with Similar Rewritten Compositions from Qumran and Elsewhere," in Martin Karrer and Wolfgang Kraus (eds.), *Die Septuaginta – Texte, Kontexte, Lebenswelten: Internationale Fachtagung veranstaltet von Septuaginta Deutsch (LXX.D), Wuppertal 20.–23. Juli 2006*; (Tübingen: Mohr Siebeck, 2008), 369–93; Emanuel Tov, "The LXX Translation of Esther: A Paraphrastic Translation of MT or a Free Translation of a Rewritten Version?," in Alberdina Houtman, Albert de Jong, and Magda Misset-van de Weg (eds.), *Empsychoi Logoi – Religious Innovations in Antiquity: Studies in Honour of Pieter Willem van der Horst* (Leiden: Brill, 2008), 516–19; Clines, *The Esther Scroll*, 69 and 186 n. 3; Moore, *Daniel, Esther, and Jeremiah: The Additions*, AB 44 (Garden City, NY: Doubleday, 1977), 155–56. Elias J. Bickerman, "Notes on the Greek Book of Esther," *PAAJR* 20 (1951), 114–15, disputed the idea that the Additions were originally written in Hebrew, claiming instead that "the authors of these pieces wanted precisely to produce this impression." This is impossible to disprove, but the arguments of Moore and Martin do as well as can be hoped in this regard. Either way, Bickerman's secondary point regarding the high literary quality of the Greek produced in Jerusalem stands; cf. also Elias J. Bickerman, "The Colophon of the Greek Book of Esther," *JBL* 63 (1944), 356–57.

[21] Bickerman, "Notes on the Greek Book," 102, wrote that "the Greek Esther . . . is not the *Megillat Esther* . . . couched in Greek language and letters, but its adaptation designed for the Diaspora."

[22] Torrey, "The Older Book of Esther," 1–2; Torrey himself disputes this notion, but I find it compelling. In this study (see esp. pp. 24–25), Torrey argues that the Greek represents (a translation of) the original (Aramaic) form of the book. For a restatement of the older view, see Gordis, "Religion, Wisdom and History in the Book of Esther," 362.

period, observable within the LXX as well as in much other contemporary literature.[23] Sidnie White Crawford describes one type of rewriting in a manner that nicely captures the dynamic of the present example: this is an example of "works in which the scribal manipulation of the base text is so extensive that a recognizably new work is created. In these words the base text is still clearly identifiable, but the new work has a separate purpose or theological *Tendenz*."[24]

There was presumably more than one reason for these changes, and the new *Tendenz* need not be reducible to a single idea. One theme discernible in the new version of the Esther story is a political one, especially because of the explicit editorializing at the end of the assassination attempt narrated in Addition A. According to this line (A 17), Haman "enjoyed great favor with the king, and he sought to harm Mordecai and his people because [Mordecai prevented the plot] of the eunuchs of the king." This makes the point, as Noah Hacham showed, that "hatred of the Jews derives ... from hatred of the king; hatred of the the king, i.e., the attempt to harm him, is both the cause and the result of hatred of Mordecai and the Jews; and it is the Jews who are loyal subjects of the king."[25] Hacham situates this claim in the context of Hellenistic and Roman-era Jewish responses to charges of misanthropy; the claim of LXX Esther is that "the genuine reason for hatred of the Jews derives from their firm alliance with the lawful regime."[26] The alliance between the Jews and the regime, representing the host nation as a whole, is seen at other points in the text as well.[27] Later on, for instance, in the establishment of the holiday of Purim, we read that "both now and hereafter, it may represent deliverance for us and the loyal Persians, but that it may be a reminder of destruction for those who plot against us."[28]

For our purposes, however, more significant than the political import of the new version of the book is the "religious atmosphere" to which Torrey referred, and which pervades the Additions, starting with the very idea of Mordecai as a dreamer.[29] As a dreamer, and especially as a dream

---

[23] Tov, "The LXX Translation of Esther," 522–24.

[24] Sidnie White Crawford, *Rewriting Scripture in Second Temple Times*, Studies in the Dead Sea Scrolls and Related Literature (Grand Rapids, MI: Eerdmans, 2008), 14.

[25] Noah Hacham, "*Bigthan and Teresh* and the Reason Gentiles Hate Jews," *VT* 62 (2012), 334–35.

[26] *Ibid.*, 348–49.

[27] The centrality of the monarchy in the Additions is discussed in Tessa Rajak, *Translation and Survival: The Greek Bible of the Ancient Jewish Diaspora* (Oxford University Press, 2009), 183–85.

[28] Hacham, "*Bigthan* and *Teresh* and the Reason Gentiles Hate Jews," 339.

[29] See also, Clines, *The Esther Scroll*, 174; Kristin De Troyer, *Rewriting the Sacred Text: What the Old Greek Texts Tell us about the Literary Growth of the Bible*, Text-Critical Studies 4 (Atlanta: SBL, 2003), 26–28; Atzmon, "וישׁנה. . . לטוב," 111.

interpreter, Mordecai is brought in line with Daniel and, crucially, with their predecessor Joseph.[30] The details of the dream (including "combat with fearsome beasts and the miraculous rescue of the righteous minority") also have much in common with Daniel 7, even suggesting to some that "chap. A may have come from the same period as the apocalyptic visions in Daniel, that is, the second century B.C.E."[31] Certainly the author of Addition A was biblically oriented: the dream contains many intertextual references to other biblical books. These include use of the imagery of the dragon, fountain, battle, and the contrast between dark and light from Jeremiah 28.[32] Jill Middlemas has well argued that these intertextual allusions have the effect of emphasizing that Esther, as rewritten in Greek, is part of the grand narrative of biblical history.[33]

The interpretation of the dream in Addition F adds to the connection to the Joseph story. Within the Bible, and even within the Joseph story, there are different types of dreams. Unlike Pharaoh's dreams, Joseph's own dreams are transparent. Their meaning is immediately clear, even if it is not clear how the reality foretold in the dream will come about. As the story unfolds, however, the referents of the dream become self-evident – just as in Mordecai's dreams, as he discovers, and reveals to the readers, in Addition F:[34]

---

[30] George W. E. Nickelsburg, *Jewish Literature between the Bible and the Mishnah: A Historical and Literary Introduction*, 2nd edn. (Minneapolis: Fortress, 2005), 203. For a nuanced discussion of the intertextuality of Daniel 2, Daniel 5, and the Joseph narrative, which uncovers an original closer relationship than exists in the stories' current form, see Segal, "From Joseph to Daniel," esp. 142–45. Note that Tobit, too, has been seen as modeled on the Joseph story (see the references to the work of Irene Nowell in Richard A. Spencer, "The Book of Tobit in Modern Research," *Currents in Research: Biblical Studies*, 7 [1999], 158). It is difficult for me to accept the claim of Chris Seeman, "Enter the Dragon: Mordecai as Agonistic Combatant in Greek Esther," *Biblical Theology Bulletin*, 41 (2011), 3–15, that Mordecai is depicted in the Greek text as an ambivalent character, in whom the biblical echoes are meant to satirize those connections as much as suggest them.

[31] Levenson, *Esther*, 40. Moore, too, connected Addition A to Daniel – focusing, however, on Daniel 8 ("A Greek Witness to a Different Hebrew Text of Esther," 388–89). For further discussion, see Anne E. Gardner, "The Relationship of the Additions to the Book of Esther to the Maccabean Crisis," *JSJ* 15 (1984), 1–8.

[32] Jobes, *The Alpha-Text of Esther*, 188–193; Arnon Atzmon, "חלום מרדכי: מהוספה למדרש," *JSJ* 6 (2007), 129; Jill Middlemas, "The Greek Esthers and the Search for History: Some Preliminary Observations," in Bob Becking and Lester L. Grabbe (eds.), *Between Evidence and Ideology: Essays on the History of Ancient Israel Read at the Joint Meeting of the Society for Old Testament Study and the Oud Testamentisch Werkgezelschap, Lincoln, July 2009*, Oudtestamentische Studiën 59 (Leiden: Brill, 2011), 158. One example not noted is in A 11, where the text says that Mordecai had the dream "on his heart," a description perhaps reminiscent of what Jacob did after hearing about Joseph's dreams in Genesis 37:11.

[33] See Middlemas, "The Greek Esthers," 156–59, and 145–63 *passim*.

[34] Joseph Tabory, "השפעת תרגום השבעים למגילת אסתר על הספרות הרבנית," *Sidra*, 24–25 (2010), 489.

Mordecai said, "These things have come from God, for I remember about the dream I saw concerning these matters – not even a word of them has failed to be fulfilled! There was the little spring that became a river, and there was light and sun and abundant water: Esther is the river, whom the king married and made queen; the two dragons are myself and Haman; the nations are those that gathered to destroy the name of the Judeans; and my nation, this is Israel, who cried out to God and were saved! The Lord saved his people, delivering us from all these threats of treachery, and performed signs and great wonders which have not happened among the nations."

Furthermore, the last line just quoted says that God "performed signs and great wonders (*ta sēmeia kai ta terata ta megala*), which have not happened among the nations."[35] The Greek phrase "signs (*sēmeia*) and wonders (*terata*)" must represent an original Hebrew אֹתוֹת וּמוֹפְתִים, since this is the Greek expression consistently used in the LXX to translate that Hebrew phrase.[36] This is significant, inasmuch as Hebrew אֹתוֹת וּמוֹפְתִים is uniquely associated with the Exodus and the events leading up to it,[37] especially in Deuteronomy[38] and Jeremiah,[39] but also already in Exodus.[40]

The interpretation of the dream also shifts the battle lines to "the Jews against the Gentiles."[41] According to the story as told in the MT, the Jews are at peace with everyone except those who actively want to kill them. Ethnically this is restricted to Haman the Agagite, and his ethnicon has been understood from early on (on the basis of the Amalekite king Agag) as a reference to the Amalekites, Israel's ancient enemy. The conflict, then, is severely circumscribed. According to the Greek version, however, Haman is not an Agagite/Amalekite, but a Macedonian.[42] This would appear to make the Jews squarely at odds with the majority population surrounding them.[43]

---

[35] Greek Esther F 6.   [36] I am indebted to Rori Picker Neiss for suggesting this.

[37] The only time אֹתוֹת וּמוֹפְתִים appears in a context other than the Exodus is Isaiah 8:18.

[38] See Deuteronomy 4:34; 6:22; 7:19; 26:8; 29:2; 34:11.

[39] See Jeremiah 32 [LXX 39]:20–21 ὃς ἐποίησας σημεῖα καὶ τέρατα ἐυ γῇ Αἰγυπτῷ.

[40] See Exodus 7:3, where the LXX reads σημεῖα καὶ τέρατα "signs and wonders."

[41] See esp. F 7. Bickerman, "The Colophon of the Greek Book of Esther," 360; Bickerman, *Four Strange Books of the Bible*, 220; Sidnie White Crawford, "The Additions to Esther," in *New Interpreter's Bible*, 12 vols. (Nashville: Abingdon Press, 1994–2004), vol. III, 948 and 970. Bickerman, "Notes on the Greek Book of Esther," 126, situates this attitude in the reign of Alexander Janneus.

[42] See Addition E 10 but also 9:24. In the rest of the instances throughout the LXX and the AT, Haman is called a "Bougaios," which has been discussed by Michael G. Wechsler, "The Appelation BOUGAIOS and Ethnic Contextualization in the Greek Text of Esther," *VT* 51 (2001), 109–14. Wechsler argues that the term refers to the Beja tribes, a harshly negative association in Ptolemaic Egyptian thought.

[43] It is therefore not surprising that Josephus omits this identification; see Feldman, "Hellenizations," 165. Bickerman ("The Colophon of the Greek Esther," 361–62) at first saw in the promulgation of the Greek Esther a purposeful propaganda campaign by the Jewish leadership in Jerusalem, meant to encourage the Jews in Alexandria to adopt an "anti-alien" stance.

However, Haman is not held up, even in the Greek text, as the paradigmatic non-Jew: he is denounced by Ahashverosh as a traitor (E 10–14),
who uses Haman's ethnicity as an explanation of his faults: "Haman son of
Hamadathos, a Macedonian who was in truth not of Persian descent ...
made it his business to deprive us of our rule and our breath." Despite the
potential significance in Ptolemaic Alexandria of the fact that the Jews'
enemy in the story is a Macedonian, then, this possibility is held up but then
subverted by the narrative itself.[44]

This may have been too subtle for some readers, however. It certainly
seems that the Additions are more nationalistic and more apocalyptic than
the Hebrew text, which itself is rather unobjectionable for foreign overlords
(with the exception of the less-than-flattering depiction of the king himself).
Indeed, comparing the biblical texts of Esther to Josephus' paraphrase of the
story shows that Josephus censored much more of the Additions than of the
base text of Esther, apparently because they in particular would have been
offensive to Josephus' Roman audience.[45]

Addition C contains the prayers of Mordecai and Esther, and Esther's in
particular is worthy of notice in this context.[46] The queen here laments the
Jews' existence in exile and blames their own sins for the lamentable
situation: "we have sinned against You, and You have handed us over to
our enemies" (C 17). Esther bemoans her own situation as queen. The
position is abhorrent first of all because of her intermarriage: "You know
that I ... abhor the bed of the uncircumcised, and of any foreigner"

---

[44] See Bickerman, "Notes on the Greek Book of Esther," 120. A somewhat different reading of the
ethnicon "Macedonian" for Haman, which winds up in much the same place, is offered by Sara
R. Johnson, *Historical Fictions and Hellenistic Jewish Identity: Third Maccabees in its Cultural Context*
(Berkeley: University of California Press, 2004), 44.

[45] Louis H. Feldman, *Judaism and Hellenism Reconsidered*, JSJ Suppl. 107; Leiden: Brill, 2006), 511–12
(discussing C 19–22) and 599–603. The question of which text(s) of Esther Josephus had in front of
him has long exercised scholars; see the literature in Feldman, "Hellenizations," 143–44 n. 1, and in
particular Bickerman, "Notes on the Greek Book of Esther," 104; also briefly in Louis H. Feldman,
"Flavius Josephus Revisited: The Man, his Writings, and his Significance," *ANRW* 11.21/2 (1984),
803–04. As mentioned above, there is a debate as to whether the different versions of the Esther story
reflect alternatives to the MT or revisions of that text. This is true even with regard to Josephus:
Bickerman, for example, argued that Josephus preserves a version of the Greek Esther which at points
better reflects the original translation than the current LXX ("Notes on the Greek Book of Esther,"
104); Feldman assumes that where Josephus and the LXX differ, Josephus has consciously revised the
text ("Hellenizations"); Bar-Kokhba assumes that Josephus had the Greek text in front of him, but
recalled the Hebrew text from his youth (על חג הפורים ועל מקצת ממנהגי הסוכות, 392 n. 18); Dalley
assumes that Josephus reflects a version of the story independent of the MT (*Esther's Revenge at
Susa*, 114).

[46] See Johnson, *Historical Fictions and Hellenistic Jewish Identity*, 161–62, who notes that "[t]he Greek
versions of Esther, by contrast, are profoundly concerned with religion," and discussing Esther's
prayer in detail. See also Crawford, "The Additions," 959.

(C 26).[47] But it is also deplorable in its own right: "You know … that I abhor the symbol of my lofty position which is on my head when I am seen in public – I abhor it like a menstruous rag!" (C 27).[48] Certainly, Esther protests, perhaps just a bit too much, that she has kept the laws of the Torah to the extent possible: "Your servant has never dined at Haman's table, nor have I extolled the king's banquet or drunk the wine of libations" (C 28).[49]

Addition D describes Esther's entry into the throne room. Anxious, she faints when the king looks at her, and her husband revives her and assures her that the prohibition against approaching the king uninvited does not apply to royalty.[50] It must be said that this scene violates the narrative's integrity and undermines Esther's heroism. Not only do we wonder how the queen could have not known the rules that applied to her, but the bold resolve displayed in chapter 4 turns out to have been pointless, having been predicated on a mistaken belief about the law. The motivation for this addition was not to amplify the themes of the book, but to bring the book more in line with Hellenistic romances. These texts habitually included explicit soliloquies and confessions of emotions, and numerous protestations of piety. Fainting due to overwhelming emotion was a common theme, for both males and females.[51]

With this review of the Additions complete, we can turn to the question of their significance. It is true, in a sense, as Isaac Kalimi has written, that the Additions "testify to the popularity of the book [of Esther] in the late Commonwealth era."[52] This needs to be nuanced in important ways, however, and the nuance has been provided already by Elias Bickerman.[53]

---

[47] Crawford, "The Additions," 959, points out that intermarriage was a top agenda item for Nehemiah, as well, thus providing another example of the Additions bringing Esther in line with what was expected of a good biblical book in Judea.

[48] The offensiveness to non-Jews was apparently noted by Josephus, who omitted this line (see Feldman, "Hellenizations," 164).

[49] See also Nickelsburg, *Jewish Literature between the Bible and the Mishnah*, 204. I do not know what the significance of "Haman's table" is precisely. Is his table worse than the king's table? Why?

[50] This scene became one of the most famous scenes in medieval and early modern (Christian) paintings of the book of Esther. For Jews familiar only with the Hebrew text, this would have been unfathomable, since no similar scene appears there.

[51] Michael V. Fox, "Three Esthers," in Sidnie White Crawford and Leonard J. Greenspoon (eds.), *The Book of Esther in Modern Research*, JSOT Suppl. 380 (London: T. & T. Clark, 2003), 59.

[52] Kalimi, "The Place of the Book of Esther in Judaism and Jewish Theology," 193 (see also Burns, "The Special Purim," 21: the Greek additions are evidence of "the widespread proliferation of the Purim festival among Greek-speaking Jewish communities both in Judaea and in the Diaspora"). Incidentally, Kalimi's treatment of the rabbinic material in "The Place of the Book of Esther in Judaism and Jewish Theology," 194, is unreliable. Cf. also the claim of Clines, *The Esther Scroll*, 174 (echoed by Bush, *Ruth, Esther*, 275), that these transformations "affirm[ed] its canonical status." On the contrary: if it were canonical, it would not be in need of change, and change may well not be licit.

[53] Bickerman, "Notes on the Greek Book of Esther," 108–13.

These Additions certainly do show that the book was being read, but they also show that although some people *wanted* it to be an admirable book, it was not seen as a book to be esteemed in its current form. To earn that esteem, the book would have to be improved and enhanced in certain fundamental respects. The Additions point up just what needed to be changed.[54]

In short, "the primary effect of the LXX expansions as a whole is . . . *to assimilate the book of Esther to a scriptural norm,* especially as found in Ezra, Nehemiah, and Daniel."[55] The Hebrew text of Esther presents a very different view of post-exilic Jewish history than that found in those three biblical books, and it was this difference that provoked the need for "correction" by means of the Additions.[56]

It is not only the Additions which "correct" the Hebrew text – although they provide the most striking examples – but the Greek version as a whole.[57] It will suffice to mention in this context that the Greek translator has "corrected" the "deficiency" of the lack of God's name throughout, by inserting it at points where it seems natural (6:1 and 6:13). Again, this is an attempt to "normalize" Esther.[58] To take another example: when Esther first becomes queen, the Hebrew text reports that she did not reveal her ancestry, in accord with Mordecai's instructions to her. With this, the

---

[54] In a slightly different context, Shlomo Dov Goitein wrote: "What our Sages add. . .draws our attention to what is missing in the original." See Goitein, עיונים במקרא, 60; so, too, Bush, *Ruth, Esther,* 275.

[55] Clines, *The Esther Scroll,* 169 (emphasis in the original). A different view is to be found in Erich S. Gruen, *Heritage and Hellenism: The Reinvention of Jewish Tradition,* Hellenistic Culture and Society 30 (Berkeley: University of California Press, 1998), 177–86; Gruen argues regarding the prayers (Addition C) that "Like Mordechai, the queen protests too much" (*ibid.,* 185), and that the effect is to purposely *detract* from the characters of Mordecai and Esther. For methodological remarks on this reading, see Daniel R. Schwartz, "How at Home were the Jews of the Hellenistic Diaspora?," *Classical Philology,* 95 (2000), 353.

[56] The addition of prayers to a narrative seems to have been a common phenomenon and could serve varied purposes. See the discussion of Wright, *Rebuilding Identity,* 12–14, for a survey of such examples.

[57] Bickerman ("Notes on the Greek Book of Esther," 101–02) emphasized that it is illegitimate to speak of the Greek Additions as if they could stand on their own. Instead, the entire Greek version of Esther must be treated as a whole, and the "Additions" are integral parts of that telling.

[58] This example is complicated by the AT, where God's name also appears. As noted above, this may be original, in which case we have to reckon with a process of the original mentions of God being removed by the author of the MT version, and those later being restored by the LXX editor. Alternatively, they may have been copied back into the AT from the LXX, along with the Additions. I find the latter possibility to be more likely, but obviously uncertain. Another example may be the date of the festival, which in MT Esther is the day *after* the military victory, but in LXX Esther is the day of the victory: Bickerman (*Four Strange Books of the Bible,* 220) attributes this to the fact that the translator "was used to Hellenic celebration of the anniversary day of a battle," while Burns suggests ("The Special Purim," 17) that this is an attempt to "indirectly [liken] Purim to Hanukkah and to the Day of Nicanor, recent Hasmonean celebrations of strategic victories."

Greek agrees ("she did not reveal her ancestry, for so Mordecai had commanded her"), but the Greek version then continues: "for so Mordecai had commanded her, to fear God and to do his commandments, just as when she was with him; so Esther did not change her way of life."[59] Furthermore, the Greek version makes it clear that despite being in the palace, Esther was always faithful to her Jewish faith; in 2:20, we read, "For so Mordecai had commanded her: to fear God and to do his commandments, just as when she was with him. So Esther did not change her way of life."[60]

When Mordecai discovers Haman's plot to kill the Jews, rather than imploring Esther to go to the king on the grounds that "perhaps" she became queen for just this reason, Greek Mordecai is far more direct: "Remember your humble days ... call upon the Lord and speak to the king about us – deliver us from death!"[61] Finally, one more example will make it clear how deeply the story has been altered in the Greek version. In place of the Hebrew's enigmatic opening verse in chapter 6, "On that night, the king's sleep was elusive," the Greek makes God's involvement as explicit as possible: "But the Lord kept sleep from the king that night." The effect of all these references is not only felt by the reader, but is reflected even in the advice delivered to Haman by his wife Zeresh. She tells her husband: "You will never be able to ward off [Mordecai], because a living God is with him."[62]

Where can we situate the Additions, and Greek Esther as a whole? In order to use the text for the purposes of intellectual history, we need to know something of its origins, its time and place of composition. Fortunately, the text includes a colophon, unique in the Greek Bible, informing us about these facts. The colophon states that in the fourth year of Ptolemy and Cleopatra, two men named Dositheos and Ptolemy, who said they were priests, arrived from Jerusalem. They brought with them the book of Esther, called "the letter about Purim (Phrouai)," and they explained that it had been translated by one Lysimachus in Jerusalem. The Ptolemy and Cleopatra involved must have been Ptolemy XII, who came to the throne of Egypt in 80 BCE, and thus this Greek book of Esther reached Alexandria in 77 or 76 BCE.[63]

---

[59] 2:20 in the Old Greek. [60] Halvorson-Tayler, "Secrets and Lies," 483.
[61] 4:8 in the Old Greek. [62] 6:13 in the Old Greek.
[63] Bickerman, "The Colophon of the Greek Book of Esther," 331. Actually, Bickerman gives the year as 78/77, but this was corrected to 77/76 by Bar-Kokhba, "על חג הפורים ועל מקצת ממנהגי הסוכות בימי הבית השני ולאחריו," 389–90 n. 13. Others have preferred identifying the king as Ptolemy IX Lymachus, yielding a date of 113, but see the discussion and references by Bickerman and Bar-Kokhba in the studies just mentioned. The recent effort by Aven, *Three Versions of Esther*, chapter 4, to date the translation to 142 BCE relies too heavily on a deterministic approach to intellectual history, in my view.

Regarding the history of the book's reception, and on the basis of this text alone, one could claim that Purim was unknown in Alexandria before this point,[64] or that only the festival was known but not the story justifying it.[65] These possibilities are ruled out, however, by the references to Esther in 2 Maccabees, which predates Greek Esther by a number of decades.[66]

Purim, along with a version of Esther similar to the MT, may have become popular in Alexandria for many of the same reasons why the book was produced in the exilic community of Persia, to begin with: here, too, there were Jews who were culturally integrated into the surrounding (in this case Hellenistic) society, who spoke only the common language of their neighbors (in this case Greek), and who were involved in the bureaucracy of the city and of the wider empire. Here, too, the Jews could be victims of vicious rulers, as they had been violently reminded in the massacre of 217 BCE. And as Bickerman noted, "A Hebrew-reading Jew of Greek culture found everything he could desire in the Book of Esther . . . The reader was happy to find in a Hebrew book motifs familiar from the Greek school."[67] The dependence on the foreign power, and the unquestioned assumption that Jewish life would continue outside of Israel, would have made Purim an attractive festival and Esther an attractive book.[68]

Unlike the Jewish community in Persia and Mesopotamia, however, the Alexandrian Jews were geographically close to the Jews in Israel, and to a large extent under the influence of the latter. One scholar neatly summarized the Alexandrian Diaspora ideology: "obey the Torah, venerate the Temple of Jerusalem, but speak Greek, and put your hopes in the Ptolemaic Dynasty."[69] The colophon to Greek Esther may indicate that the Palestinian Jews deemed it important that the Jews of Alexandria receive a copy of their new and improved version of Esther – with at least Additions A, C, D, and F – which brought the book and its associated festival back in

---

[64] So Bickerman, "The Colophon of the Greek Book of Esther," 349–51.

[65] So Torrey, "The Older Book of Esther," 26–27, as well as Burns, "The Special Purim," 18 and 21 (and see also 32), if I am reading him correctly.

[66] For the date, see again Schwartz, *2 Maccabees*, 14.

[67] Bickerman, *Four Strange Books of the Bible*, 205–06.

[68] Gordis, "Religion, Wisdom and History in the Book of Esther," 381, notes that "undoubtedly, the festival made headway more rapidly in the diaspora than in Palestine."

[69] Jonathan A. Goldstein, "The Message of 'Aristeas to Philokrates' in the Second Century B.C.E.: Obey the Torah, Venerate the Temple of Jerusalem, but Speak Greek, and Put your Hopes in the Ptolemaic Dynasty," in Menachem Mor (ed.), *Eretz Israel, Israel, and the Jewish Diaspora: Mutual Relations – Proceedings of the First Annual Symposium of the Philip M. and Ethel Klutznick Chair in Jewish Civilization, Held on Sunday–Monday, October 9–10, 1988*, Studies in Jewish Civilization 1 (Lanham, MD, and Omaha, NE: University Press of America and the Center for the Study of Religion and Society, Creighton University, 1991), 1–23.

line with what was, to their minds, normative Jewish ideology and practice. In other words, this was probably a revised edition produced by Palestinian Jews and sent to Alexandria to correct the edition which circulated there previously.

It may well have been in Alexandria itself that Additions B and E were added.[70] These, as mentioned, were probably composed originally in Greek, and do not serve primarily to change the ideological value of the book.[71] Instead, their goal appears to be primarily literary, since the current fashion in Greek historiography was to quote documents verbatim.[72] These documents, then, bring the book in line with expectations for a Hellenistic historiographic work. This type of revision may well have been done by the Jews of Alexandria, steeped as they were in Greek literature and historiographical praxis. On the other hand, the Greek-speaking Jews of Palestine could also have added these texts in order to emulate this aspect of Hellenistic historiographic practice. Some slight evidence for this latter possibility comes from the fact that Josephus utilizes Additions B and E in his retelling; they were, apparently, part of the version of the text either in the Palestine of Josephus' youth or the Rome of his adulthood.

---

[70] This has been argued most convincingly on the basis of lexical evidence by Anna Passoni Deel'Acqua, "The Liberation Decree of 'Addition' E in Esther LXX: Some Lexical Observations Starting from a New Papyrus (POxy LXVI, 4443). New Evidence for the 'Egyptian Flavour' of this 'Addition,'" *Admantius*, 10 (2004), 72–88. The view is far older: Torrey, "The Older Book of Esther," notes that B and E "are composed in Greek such as was commonly written in Egypt in the second century B.C.," and that they were composed specifically for the consumption of the Alexandrian audience.

[71] However, it is worth considering the claims of Polaski regarding the image of "writing" in an imperial context in Daniel 5–6; see Donald C. Polaski, "*Mene, Mene, Tekel, Parsin*: Writing and Resistance in Daniel 5 and 6," *JBL* 123 (2004), 649–69. Note also Sharp, *Irony and Meaning in the Hebrew Bible*, 63–64, about Darius' writing in Daniel 6, esp. the conclusion: "Thus texts can kill, but texts can also preserve life. Writing can confine or writing can liberate. It all depends who the author is" (64). This is dramatically brought to the fore in Esther, and especially in the Greek version, where we can read the words of death and the words of life.

[72] See Bickerman, "Notes on the Greek Book of Esther," 119–20, who asserts that this historiographical trend began with Timaeus (c. 250 BCE); see also Bickerman, *Four Strange Books of the Bible*, 222.

CHAPTER 10

Subvert or ignore
Canonical re-contextualization and outright rejection of Esther

1. The correction of Esther in the canon

Retelling stories was a common phenomenon in the Jewish society of the Second Temple period.[1] Those who retold stories, adding and subtracting passages, rearranging component parts, and editorializing freely, were clearly motivated by a desire to put their own stamp on the stories being told. In some cases, they may have wanted to amplify themes already in the text, or clarify amibiguities. Those who added sections to Esther in an effort to alter its tenor and theme were engaged in an effort to counter a possible reading of the text. Rather than openly combating the story, they retold it, making it explicit how the story is to be understood.

The most subversive interpreters of Esther, however, may have been those responsible for its position in the canon of the Hebrew Bible.[2] Who this was cannot be said, but I will argue that looking at Esther in the context of the Bible radically alters one's perspective on the book, and in fact inverts many of the central themes of the book. The last three books in the Bible, according to a text cited in the Bavli (Bava Batra 14b), are "the Scroll of Esther, Ezra, and Chronicles." Although clearly the books are sequenced chronologically (on the basis of the events they describe), there may also be an ideological significance to having Ezra immediately follow Esther. To

---

[1] For surveys, see White Crawford, *Rewriting Scripture in Second Temple Times*, and Daniel K. Falk, *The Parabiblical Texts: Strategies for Extending the Scriptures in the Dead Sea Scrolls*, T. & T. Clark Library of Biblical Studies, Companion to the Qumran Scrolls 8, Library of Second Temple Studies 63 (London and New York: T. & T. Clark, 2007).

[2] It should be noted that the order to be discussed here, in which Ezra-Nehemiah follows Esther, is not the order in the LXX, in which 1 and 2 Esdras precede Esther. This discussion is relevant only for the order in the Hebrew Bible, as prescribed in the Talmud and as practiced by the Masoretes.

elaborate, it is worthwhile to step back to look, once again, at the relationship between the book of Esther and the story of Joseph.

This relationship has already been discussed with regard to uncovering the themes of the book of Esther, and the use to which the author mobilized the precedent of Joseph.[3] The aftermath of the story of Joseph was singled out as a challenge for the author of Esther: one could argue, after all, that the end of Joseph's saga bodes badly for anyone who would emulate him. Joseph is successful, within his own lifetime, at securing favorable treatment for his kin within Egypt. When he dies, however, everything changes: "A new king arose over Egypt, who did not know Joseph" (Exodus 1:8). All of Joseph's success bears no fruit for later generations. It is meaningful only as long as the guarantor himself is alive.

As discussed earlier, if Mordecai and Esther are to some extent modeled on Joseph, the alert reader must ask the same question. What will happen when Esther is no longer queen, and Mordecai is no longer vizier? What will happen when Xerxes is no longer king? Will there not be "a new king over Persia, who did not know Esther and Mordecai"? The book's answer, as discussed in the previous chapter, seems to be that this may well be true. For the Jews in exile, "success" is surviving to another day. That the book of Esther ends with nothing other than the mundane (the notorious taxes of chapter 10) bespeaks the book's conviction that "redemption" has been redefined in the current context. Survival is the ultimate redemption, and it is something which may not be taken for granted; the Jews' right to just survive may well be challenged in every generation.

A canonical perspective on the Bible has a different answer to the question, "What will be when there is 'a new king over Persia'?" Immediately following the story of Esther, which takes us to the twelfth year of Xerxes (473 BCE), is the book of Ezra and Nehemiah. The juxtaposition is striking. Within the terms of the narrative, Ezra's odyssey begins just fifteen years after Esther ends, in the seventh year of the reign of Artaxerxes (458 BCE). Thirteen years later, in 445, Nehemiah, an important member of the court of Artaxerxes in the Fortress of Susa, asks for permission to leave in order to assist his brethren in rebuilding Jerusalem.

Within the terms of history set by the book of Esther, Esther and Mordecai may have lived to see these developments, but Ezra and Nehemiah represent a response to the threats presented by Diaspora life which stands in stark opposition to that offered by Esther. Whereas Esther, like Joseph, had advocated manipulation of the foreign system from within

---

[3] See Chapters 3 and 7.

to the benefit of the Jews, Ezra and Nehemiah, like Moses, advocate the activist rejection of Diaspora altogether.

One might claim, therefore, that Ezra and Nehemiah are to Esther and Mordecai as Moses was to Joseph. Indeed, perhaps Genesis meant to hold up Joseph not as a hero, but as a warning, an example *not* to be followed.[4] He may be the foil for the true history of the story of Israel in Egypt: Moses, who, although also a child of the system, does not work from within, but breaks free.[5] Joseph left his home behind, naming his son Manasseh, it will be recalled, to thank God for helping him forget his ancestry.[6] Moses has no need to leave anything behind in order to be fully Egyptian, and only when he leaves Egypt does he name his son "Gershom," a reflection of his sense that he has been "a stranger in a strange land" (Exodus 2:22).

While Joseph opted to embrace his new Egyptian identity whole-heartedly, finding rootedness in the culture in which he finds himself, Moses retains his sense of foreignness, never assimilating, but remaining a perennial outsider. Thus Joseph and Moses present two models of Jews in the court of the king of Egypt. A diaspora Jew can go the route of Joseph, and rise to great heights within the system, but this may come at a great cost: the individual's very identity may be lost in the process. Alternatively, one can go the way of Moses and reject the court, leaving the foreign land and taking the people along. Perhaps, the story of Joseph and Moses argues, while Joseph can save people's lives, only Moses can bring redemption to the world.

The author of Esther attempted to resurrect the character of Joseph. Searching for a model for Jewish life in the Diaspora, he settled on Joseph and argued that this was the right type of hero for current circumstances. Redemption, in the deep sense, was not a viable option, and all that could be hoped for, as in the days of Joseph, was survival.

The canonizers of the Hebrew Bible, however, juxtapose the story of Esther to the stories of Ezra and Nehemiah. By doing so, they remind readers that the only reason why Joseph's story did not end in abject failure and the destruction of the nation of Israel was that Moses arose. Esther and Mordecai, too, could only have postponed the inevitable. In exile, nothing is secure, certainly not beyond the lifetime of individuals. Persia is a country governed by laws, but the book of Esther itself pointed out how absurd those laws could be at times, and with what caprice they could be enacted and enforced – or not enforced.

---

[4] See above, Chapter 3, n. 21.   [5] Wildavsky, *Assimilation versus Separation*, esp. 126–29.
[6] See Cochran, "Joseph and the Politics of Memory," 421–44.

The only solution to this problem, therefore, is the tack taken by Ezra and then Nehemiah. Being an important member of the administration in Susa, like Mordecai and Esther and like Ezra and Nehemiah, is not sufficient. When Nehemiah hears of the degraded status of the Jews in Jerusalem, he does not attempt to utilize his influence at court to improve the situation from afar; instead, he requests to be relocated, so that he can personally aid the Jerusalemites. Thus, he provides the antidote to Esther. Rather than resigning oneself to a diaspora existence, it is possible simply to get up and move.[7]

Reading the two books together makes it difficult to avoid reading Nehemiah as a character in the model of Mordecai and Esther. Nehemiah introduces himself as being in the Fortress of Susa (1:1), where he hears bad news about the Jews (1:2–3). He, like Mordecai, reacts with typical mourning activities – sitting, crying, mourning (1:4). Unlike Mordecai, however, Nehemiah explicitly prays to God, as well. When Nehemiah is with the king, Artaxerxes realizes that something is bothering his official, and asks what he can do for him (2:2). Nehemiah hesitates, prays to God, and then offers his request, beginning, "If it pleases the king and if your servant seems good to you" (2:3). These are the very expressions which Esther deploys to great effect, most notably in beseeching the king to save her people (7:3). When placed in the same position, Nehemiah, using a similar introduction, asks to leave exile altogether. The contrast is stark.

In this light, the use of Exodus imagery in the book of Ezra becomes more significant. We discussed above the echoes of the Exodus to be heard in the march conducted by Ezra to the Promised Land.[8] When Ezra-Nehemiah is read after Esther, as in the canonical order, the reader cannot help but hear, once again, the progression of Joseph-to-Moses. The more radical elements of Esther's politics are thus undermined. It can be granted that Esther is another Joseph figure, but the fatal flaw in the Esther-Joseph method is now brought to the forefront: there will inevitably be "a new king over Persia, who does not know Esther." The solution to this problem is to be found in the persons, and the decisions, of Ezra and Nehemiah. In other words, the only solution to the problem of Diaspora is to return home.

---

[7] For the following, see esp. Binyamin Lau, קריאה במגילה – אסתר (Tel Aviv: Yedi'ot Aḥaronot and Sifre Ḥemed, 2011), 71–74.
[8] See above, Chapter 2.

It should be emphasized that this is *not* the perspective of the author of Esther, who clearly does *not* mean to criticize his story's heroes. For the author of Esther, Mordecai and Esther are positive figures, not characters held up for criticism or ridicule. This is important to stress because some recent writers have suggested that the book of Esther actually means to criticize the Jews in Persia for failing to move to Yehud when they were allowed to. On this reading, Mordecai and Esther are not positive figures, since they exemplify the collective failings of the Jewish community in fifth-century Persia. Such a suggestion, however, goes against the basic grain of the entire book. Indeed, some sophisticated exponents of this reading have admitted as much, arguing that this is the difference between the surface meaning of the book and the "deeper" meaning.[9] But this does not seem to me to be a legitimate way of reading. It amounts to a claim that the book has a clearly articulated ideology, but that this is precisely the opposite of what it actually means to say. The hermeneutic utilized can be concisely summarized. Esther seems to legitimate Jewish life in the Diaspora; Jewish life in the Diaspora is illegitimate;[10] therefore Esther must be mocking the view that legitimates Jewish life in the Diaspora.[11]

On the contrary, I assume that the book of Esther takes Jewish life in exile as a fact to reckon with. There is no indication that this is a positive development in the history of the Jewish people, but the author is pleading with his contemporaries to reconcile themselves to it. The same resistance to this notion encountered in some modern scholars was also found in antiquity, however. Some refused to accept that such a life was all that could be achieved, and searched for solutions grander than mere survival. Assigning Ezra-Nehemiah as a sequel to Esther makes this point: there *is* a grand solution, but the Jews will have to leave Susa to accomplish it. Just as Moses had to leave Egypt, the Jews will have to leave Persia and effect their own redemption.

---

[9] The most methodical attempt at such a reading is Jonathan Grossman, *Esther: The Outer Narrative and the Hidden Reading*, Siphrut 6 (Winona Lake, IN: Eisenbrauns, 2011); see also Lau, קריאה במגילה – אסתר, 12–13, and Menachem Leibtag, "Megillat Esther: Its 'Hidden' Message," available at www.tanach.org/special/purim.txt (accessed September, 2011).

[10] It will be noted that the exponents of this view are all Israeli scholars, who seem to have particular difficulty in accepting the existence of a biblical book which does not reject Diaspora life altogether. Contemporary readings of Esther, as a subject of inherent interest, are obviously beyond the mandate of this book, but they will provide rich material for analysis. See, for instance, the interpretation propounded by Rabbi Shlomo Aviner, analyzed by Julia Schwartzmann, "The Book of Esther – A Case Study of Ideological Interpretation," *Shofar* 29 (2011), 124–47.

[11] See, for e.g., Grossman, *Esther*, 240: "Despite the ultimately happy ending, it seems unlikely that the story advocates coming to terms with Jewish existence in exile."

2. Qumran

Despite the Greek translation and the canonization of the book as a prequel to Ezra-Nehemiah, both of which re-read Esther in light of other biblical books and thus take the sting out, other groups of Jews in the Second Temple period preferred simply to ignore the book altogether. It has often been noted that alone of all the biblical books, Esther has never been found at Qumran.[12] This has raised the question of what the sectarians' attitude toward the book was.

One could, of course, raise the possibility that they just did not know of the book. After all, it was presumably written in the east (Persia or Mesopotamia), and maybe it just had not reached Israel by the second century BCE. We have already seen, however, that it was known in Alexandria in the second century. Furthermore, evidence from Qumran does show that the book of Esther was known: a number of texts seem to allude to, or simply utilize phraseology from the book.[13] One striking example is the use of the expression שְׁאֵלָתִי וּבַקָּשָׁתִי "request and wish" (Esther 5:7), which, within the Bible, appears only in Esther. The words are paired in a Qumran psalm, as well: הט אוזנכה ותן לי את שאלתי / ובקשתי אל תמנע ממני "incline your ear and give me my *request/my wish* do not refuse me" (11QPsalms[a] 24:4–5). Another example may be 4Q171 ii 18–19, which refers to רשעי אפרים ומנשה אשר יבקשו לשלוח יד בכוהן ובאנשי עצתו "the wicked ones of Ephraim and Manasseh, who will attempt to harm the Priest and the men of his council." The expression לשלוח יד "to harm," with a person as the object, is found only twice in the Bible, in Esther 2:21 and 6:2, so perhaps this usage, too, is due to the influence of Esther;[14] note that both actually have the complete clause *בקש לשלוח יד "sought to harm," strengthening the claim of a conscious allusion.[15]

---

[12] I set aside here the question of 4Q550 (esp. a–e), which are certainly not copies of the book of Esther itself. For recent studies and discussion, see the references and discussion in Moshe J. Bernstein and Aaron Koller, "The Aramaic Texts and Hebrew and Aramaic Languages at Qumran: The North American Contributions," in Devorah Dimant with the assistance of Ingo Kottsieper (eds.), *The Dead Sea Scrolls in Scholarly Perspective: A History of its Research*, STDJ 99 (Leiden: Brill, 2012), 184–86.

[13] See esp. Shemaryahu Talmon, "Was the Book of Esther Known at Qumran?" *DSD* 2 (1995), 249–67. Compare the apparent use of Esther 5:3, 6, 7:2 (עד חצי המלכות ותעש "up to half the kingdom, and it shall be done") in Mark 6:23, which shows knowledge of the book on that (much later) author's part. Contrary to the assertion of Burns, "The Special Purim," 31 n. 73, this does not "indicate that the book of Esther had attained 'canonical' status." It does, however, show knowledge of the text.

[14] David Katzin, "The Time of Testing: The Use of Hebrew Scriptures in 4Q171's Pesher of Psalm 37," *Hebrew Studies*, 45 (2004), 139–40.

[15] I am again indebted to Moshe Bernstein for this observation.

Ben-Dov has added another example from 4Q267 (one copy of the Damascus Document, 4QD^b), in which the scribe accidentally wrote מיום ליום ו[מחדש לחדש], instead of just מיום ליום as he was supposed to. The complete phrase is drawn from Esther 3:7, but it is meaningless in its new context. This shows, as Ben-Dov puts it, that the scribe's "acquaintance with the Book of Esther must have been so profound that characteristic words from its text occurred in his mind while copying other compositions."[16] Moshe Bernstein pointed out that the same phrase, [מיום] ליום ומחדש לחדש, appears in the enigmatic 4Q306 i 2. Here, too, the meaning may be different from that in Esther (perhaps "every day and every month"?).[17]

So then why are there no copies of Esther at Qumran, and why did Purim not make its way onto the Qumran calendar? The book was certainly not considered authoritative within the Qumran community. The festival of Purim, explicitly ordained in Esther 9, was not on the Qumran calendar. Some have suggested that the calendar was the primary objection that the Qumran group had to the book of Esther, since according to their calendar Purim would have fallen on the Sabbath every year.[18] It is theoretically possible that the sect possessed copies of this book, which they did not deem to be authoritative, and that these copies have been lost only by accident. Certainly it is unlikely that we have part of every book they had. It would, however, be special pleading to rely on allegedly lost copies. Furthermore, not only are no copies known, but we know from the calendar that they did not practice what the book preaches. More than that, in no other text do the Qumran writers refer to Esther as authoritative, appeal to its legal or theological or religious authority, or in any other way indicate that it is a book they turn to for guidance.[19]

---

[16] Jonathan Ben-Dov, "A Presumed Citation of Esther in 4QD^b," *DSD* 6 (1999), 282–84.

[17] Another example discussed by Talmon is the citation of Esther 8:15 in Genesis Apocryphon 20:31. This example is discussed below, pp. 141–46. I omit it here, since the Genesis Apocryphon is almost certainly not a text composed by the Qumran community. The knowledge of Esther on the part of the author of the Apocryphon, therefore, can tell us nothing about the knowledge of Esther in Qumran.

[18] This point was developed by Roger Beckwith, *The Old Testament Canon of the New Testament Church: And its Background in Early Judaism* (London: SPCK, 1985), 211–14, as I learned from both James C. VanderKam, "Authoritative Literature in the Dead Sea Scrolls," *DSD* 5 (1998), 385 (according to whom this is the primary reason for the Qumran rejection of the book of Esther), and Bush, *Ruth, Esther*, 273–74.

[19] The vexed term "canonical" is avoided here, because if a canon must be closed to be a canon, the term is inappropriate to the situation at Qumran, where authoritative books were still produced. For good discussion of the term, see Eugene C. Ulrich, "The Notion and Definition of Canon," in Lee Martin McDonald and James A. Sanders (eds.), *The Canon Debate* (Peabody, MA: Hendrickson Publishers, 2002), 21–35. To some extent, terminology has proven to be an obstacle here, since

It is more likely, then, that the people of Qumran knew Esther, but rejected it. Why would they have done so? Sectarian concerns have here been detected by some, but it seems likely that many of the concerns that the sect may have had would have been shared by other Palestinian Jews, as well,[20] and that the situation in Qumran may not have differed much from the situation elsewhere in Jewish Palestine.[21]

One obvious point of contention was intermarriage. Some scholars have argued that the Qumran sect had to reject the book of Esther because of the intermarriage of Esther. This would have especially troubled a group that held Jubilees to be sacred, since that book rules that intermarriage is punishable by death for everyone involved (30:7–10).[22] But is this consideration important *only* for the Qumran community? Jubilees was a book that certainly was influential outside of that isolated community, even if its precise sphere of influence is difficult to gauge. More importantly, Jubilees is far from a lone voice within Second Temple Palestinian Judaism. Although it is not clear whether there was an earlier biblical prohibition

"canon" and "canonical" are judged by some scholars to be anachronisms in discussions of Second Temple times. See, e.g., Eugene C. Ulrich, "Qumran and the Canon of the Old Testament," in J.-M. Auwers and H.J. de Jonge (eds.), *The Biblical Canons*, Bibliotheca Ephemeridum theologicarum Lovaniensium 163 (Leuven: Leuven University Press and Peeters, 2003), 57–80; Hanne von Weissenberg, "'Canon' and Identity at Qumran: An Overview and Challenges for Future Research," in Anssi Voitila and Jutta Jokiranta (eds.), *Scripture in Transition: Essays on Septuagint, Hebrew Bible, and Dead Sea Scrolls in Honour of Raija Sollamamo* (JSJ Suppl. 126; Leiden and Boston: Brill, 2008), 629–40, with further references. I am not sure whether this is correct or not, but it is beside the point: the question is whether the book of Esther was deemed to be "sacred." In other words, the question is not so much what people did with the book, as much as what they thought about it.

[20] This question is raised by James A. Sanders, "Canon: Old Testament," *ABD*, vol. 1, 842: "The complete lack of a representative fragment of Esther may or not be significant with regard to whether or not that book was included in the Qumran biblical canon, or yet at the time in the general Jewish canon."

[21] Thus, contrary to the assertion of Isaac Kalimi: "the absence of the book of Esther altogether from among the Dead Sea Scrolls *cannot be a model* representing the general attitude of the Jewish people toward the book . . . The *majority* of Jewish people, however, had a very different approach this [sic] fascinating book" ("Fear of Annihilation and Eternal Covenant: The Book of Esther in Judaism and Jewish Theology," in Isaac Kalimi (ed.), *Jewish Bible Theology: Perspectives and Case Studies* [Winona Lake, IN: Eisenbrauns, 2012], 231–32). Kalimi's paper does not distinguish properly between texts from different times and different places, and instead presupposes (and then finds) a homogenous Jewish approach to the book.

[22] So recently Isaac Kalimi, "The Book of Esther and the Dead Sea Scrolls' Community," *Theologische Zeitschrift* 60 (2004), 101–06. The biblical exegesis lying behind the formulations in this passage in Jubilees is insightfully explicated by Christine Hayes, "Intermarriage and Impurity in Ancient Jewish Sources," *HTR* 92 (1999), 16–18. See also Robert H. Eisenman and Michael O. Wise, *The Dea Sea Scrolls Uncovered* (Shaftesbury, Dorset, and Rockport, MA: Element, 1992), 100, who note "the militant xenophobia and apocalyptic nationalism of the Community"; they conclude that the idea that Esther "could marry . . . a foreign potentate, even in order to save her people . . . would have been anaethema to a Community or movement such as this."

on intermarriage,[23] Ezra's reaction to the news of intermarriage within his community leaves little doubt as to where this prominent Jewish leader of the Second Temple era stood on the issue: "I tore my clothes and coat, I ripped hair out of my head and beard, and I sat desolate."[24]

Indeed, railing against intermarriage was certainly a common literary practice, whether or not the practice was actually common and a pressing social concern in later Second Temple times.[25] Texts relevant to this issue include the biblical book of Malachi, the book of Enoch (both 6–11 and the Book of Watchers), the Genesis Apocryphon (especially the section therein entitled "the book of the words of Noah"), the Aramaic Levi Document, Miqṣat Maʿaśē ha-Torah (MMT), the Testament of Kohath, and the Temple Scroll, as well as the particularly strong words of Tobit.[26] Of course, many of these texts in their original forms are known from Qumran, and some are even Qumran compositions. The wide range of texts which discuss

---

[23] See Ezra 9:10–12. For discussion, see Shaye J. D. Cohen, "From the Bible to the Talmud: The Prohibition of Intermarriage," *HAR* 7 (1983), 23–39, and Hayes, "Intermarriage and Impurity in Ancient Jewish Sources." My thanks to Shlomo Zuckier for pressing me to clarify this point.

[24] Ezra 9:3, and see Ezra 9–10 and Nehemiah 13 at length. See recently Saul M. Olyan, "Purity Ideology in Ezra-Nehemiah as a Tool to Reconstitute the Community," *JSJ* 35 (2004), 1–16, for a discussion of these passages (with important references to the work of Hayes), and the summary chart, *ibid.*, 16, which shows how deep the opposition to intermarriage was according to Ezra and Nehemiah; see also the brief discussion in Lawrence H. Schiffman, *Who Was a Jew? Rabbinic and Halakhic Perspectives on the Jewish–Christian Schism* (Hoboken, NJ: Ktav, 1985), 14–16. It is not of fundamental importance whether the narratives of Ezra and Nehemiah are factual. "The fictiveness of our sources, a real constraint on our ability to reconstruct the struggle for cultural survival as it actually unfolded, is something we can turn to our advantage when it comes to understanding the role of imagination in that struggle" (Weitzman, *Surviving Sacrilege*, 10).

[25] See Martha Himmelfarb, "Levi, Phinehas, and the Problem of Intermarriage at the Time of the Maccabean Revolt," *JSQ* 6 (1999), 1–24.

[26] See Armin Lange, "Your Daughters do not Give to their Sons and their Daughters do not Take for your Sons (Ezra 9:12): Intermarriage in Ezra 9–10 and in the Pre-Maccabean Dead Sea Scrolls," *BN* 137 (2008), 17–39, and 139 (2008), 79–98. For the Testament of Kohath (i 6–7), see Edward M. Cook, "Remarks on the Testament of Kohath from Qumran Cave 4," *JJS* 44 (1993), 209–10. In MMT, the relevant passage is B 75–82, taken by Qimron and Strugnell as a ban on priests marrying non-priests (*Qumran Cave 4, V: Miqṣat Maʿaśe ha-Torah*, Discoveries in the Judean Desert 10 (Oxford: Clarendon, 1994), 171–74), but interpreted by Baumgarten and Schiffman as a ban on intermarriage (Baumgarten is cited in *ibid.*, 171 n. 178a; see Lawrence H. Schiffman, "Prohibited Marriages in the Dead Sea Scrolls and Rabbinic Literature," in Steven D. Fraade, Aharon Shemesh, and Ruth A. Clements (eds.), *Rabbinic Perspectives: Rabbinic Literature and the Dead Sea Scrolls*, STDJ 62 (Leiden: Brill, 2006], 121–22). For Tobit in particular, and further discussion of biblical antecedents, see Thomas Hieke, "Endogamy in the Book of Tobit, Genesis, and Ezra-Nehemiah," in Géza G. Xeravits, and József Zsengellér, (eds.), *The Book of Tobit – Text, Tradition, Theology: Papers of the First International Conference on the Deuteronomical Books, Pápa, Hungary, 20–21 May, 2004, JSJ* Suppl. 98 (Leiden: Brill, 2005), 103–20. It must be admitted that as in MMT, it is not entirely clear from Tobit whether the restriction is to Jews broadly speaking, or whether marriage is to be restricted even further, to members of the same "tribe." Of course, then intermarriage would certainly be prohibited, but this would not be literary evidence of the issue as a live one.

the issue shows, however, that the virulent anti-intermarriage view was quite widespread.[27]

Other considerations, too, may have led to the rejection of the book on the part of Palestinian Jews. Esther fasted, and asked that all other Jews fast, on the 13th through the 15th of Nisan – including, of course, the first day of Passover.[28] This is a calendrical detail that would have offended all Jews equally. The fact that the Jews fasted through the *seder* is mentioned explicitly in later rabbinic literature, as well.[29]

Esther also makes no mention of the already-standing Second Temple in Jerusalem.[30] Indeed, the book seems to believe in the possibility of a commendable Jewish existence without regard for a Temple, or for the land of Israel, at all. For the Qumran community this would have been senseless. While they had moved to the desert because they could not venerate the Temple in its current form, their religious lives still in principle revolved around the Temple. If the physical Temple was inaccessible to them, their own community would have to stand in for the Temple.[31] But religious life without a Temple was inconceivable! The focus on the Temple was certainly not unique to the Qumran community, although one might claim that they dealt with their own loss of control over the Temple in a

---

[27] Lange, "Your Daughters do not Give to their Sons," *BN* 139 (2008), 85. See André Lacocque, *The Feminine Unconventional: Four Subversive Figures in Israel's Tradition* (Minneapolis: Fortress, 1990), 63. It should be emphasized, though, that this survey gives voice only to the views circulating in Persian, Hellenistic, and Roman-era Palestine. The views of Diaspora Jews remain unknown. For criticism of the assumption that Tobit must be diasporic, see, e.g., John J. Collins, "The Judaism of the Book of Tobit," in Géza G. Xeravits and József Zsengellér (eds.), *The Book of Tobit – Text, Tradition, Theology: Papers of the First International Conference on the Deuteronomical Books, Pápa, Hungary, 20–21 May, 2004, JSJ* Suppl. 98 (Leiden: Brill, 2005), 23–40. Joseph A. Fitzmyer, *Tobit*, CEJL (Berlin and New York: De Gruyter, 2003), 50–54, concludes that "the likelihood is that it was composed within Palestinian Judaism" (p. 54). In a recent study of the halakha found in Tobit (esp. 1:6–8), Devorah Dimant ("The Book of Tobit and the Qumran Halakhah," in Devorah Dimant and Reinhard G. Kratz [eds.], *The Dynamics of Language and Exegesis at Qumran*, Forschungen zum Alten Testament, 2nd Series.35 (Tübingen: Mohr Siebeck, 2009), 121–43) concluded that "Tobit may not be the work of a Diaspora Jew, but of a Jewish author living in the Land of Israel, well versed in the halakhic practices current there. Accordingly the Book of Tobit may have been composed in the land of Israel, but was addressed to Jews living outside of it" (p. 140). Also relevant is the older theory of J. T. Mílik ("Le patrie de Tobie," *RB* 73 [1966], 522–30) that the book was primarily an apology for the Tobiads. I am indebted again to Tzvi Novick for pressing on Tobit and forcing me to rethink it in this context.

[28] Again, see Kalimi, "The Book of Esther and the Dead Sea Scrolls' Community."

[29] See below, pp. 199–200. For more on this, and discussion of the specific dates, see above, pp. 90–92.

[30] For an appreciation of this, see again the comments of Nahmanides at the beginning of his Talmudic commentary on the tractate Megillah.

[31] See the texts cited by Lawrence H. Schiffman, "Temple, Sacrifice and Priesthood in the Epistle to the Hebrews and the Dead Sea Scrolls," in Florentino García Martínez (ed.), *Echoes from the Caves: Qumran and the New Testament* (Leiden: Brill, 2009), 165–76.

particularly dramatic way. By the end of the Second Temple era, Jews throughout Palestine and, indeed, throughout the world held the Temple to be of paramount significance in Jewish political and religious life.[32]

The priestly Sadducees were Temple-oriented, and the Pharisees apparently focused their influence on Temple rites and practices, as well. The lack of interest in the Temple and its worship in Esther may well have bothered the Qumran sect, but it is likely that it bothered all other Palestinian Jews, as well.[33] The derogation of – or, better, blithe disregard for – Jerusalem by Mordecai and Esther in the founding of a new festival for all Jews from India to Nubia (Esther 9:20–23) could also not have failed to offend.[34] Especially offended would have been those who were prepared to give their lives to protect the sanctity of the Temple. The Hasmoneans, rulers in Jerusalem, would thus have had little patience for a book like Esther.[35] There also would have been political umbrage taken here. The Hasmoneans portrayed the dedication of the Jerusalem Temple as a festival for Jews throughout the world and explicitly hoped for an ingathering of exiles.[36] Esther, too, proclaims a festival for all Jews throughout the world, and does not so much as hint that life in Persia is a temporary state of affairs.

Indeed, the most fundamental of Esther's themes (as described in Part 2 above) would have found no audience among Palestinian Jews in the Hasmonean era. The idea of peaceably integrating into the imperial network, even at the expense of religious fidelity, would not have found any audience under the Hasmoneans.[37] Esther advocates, or at least tolerates, major concessions with regard to religious practice in the name of "loyalty." Her intermarriage is only the most prominent sign of her assimilation. Certainly she was not eating only kosher, or observing the Sabbath, while serving as queen of Persia. One might reply, but she had no choice. Not

---

[32] See Chapter 12 below, and see Martin Goodman, *Judaism in the Roman World: Collected Essays*, Arbeiten zur Geschichte des antiken Judentums und des Urchristentums 66 (Leiden: Brill, 2007), 47 (and see also *ibid.*, 33–34 n. 3). Note that his citation, *ibid.*, 52, of Cicero, *Pro Flacco* 28:66–69 to prove that Jews also in Asia Minor, Rome, and Babylon all venerated the Jerusalem Temple goes beyond the evidence; nothing there is said regarding the eastern Diaspora. For further discussion of this passage, see Anthony J. Marshall, "Flaccus and the Jews of Asia (Cicero 'Pro Flacco' 28:67–69)," *Phoenix* 29 (1975), 139–54.

[33] For an attempt at a finer-grain analysis, see below, pp. 156–58.

[34] Bickerman, "The Colophon of the Greek Book of Esther," 359, notes the difference between Hanukkah and Purim in this regard; he writes that "Purim appears to have been a work of private propaganda."

[35] See Eyal Regev, "Ḥanukkah and the Temple of the Maccabees: Ritual and Ideology from Judas Maccabeus to Simon," *JSQ* 15 (2008), 110–14.

[36] See 2 Maccabees 2:18 and Regev, "Ḥanukkah and the Temple of the Maccabees," 104.

[37] I find the claim that "The success of the Hasmoneans' subaltern idealism reified the story of Purim, thus enhancing its relevance to contemporary Jewish civilization" (Burns, "The Special Purim," 19) very difficult to understand on multiple levels.

true, thunder the Hasmoneans! One always has a choice. One can choose to martyr oneself rather than submit to the coercion, and this is precisely what is modeled in the stories of 2 Maccabees.[38]

The ethos animating the martyrdom stories in 2 Maccabees, in which people martyr themselves rather than violate the law, stands violently opposed to the ethos of accommodation exemplified by the actions of Esther in the palace. On the other hand, Maccabees has much in common with the stories in Daniel 1–6.[39] This may be related to a further difference, whose significance it is difficult to exaggerate. In the books of Maccabees, God is invoked repeatedly and explicitly, showing that the idea of a God no longer operating, or operating only under the cover of darkness, was not a popular one in Hellenistic Palestine.

The suggestion is, then, that the Jews in Palestine were familiar with Esther, but many of them, at least, could not accept the book as sacred for many good reasons.[40] In fact, it is nearly inconceivable that any group of Jews in Palestine could have received the book affectionately. This apparently secular book, which attributes salvation to flawed religious figures operating with no God and no providence, violating Passover and the ban on intermarriage explicitly and probably all the other laws implicitly, probably raised the curiosity of some Jews, the interest of the less sophisticated among the populace who did not worry about such niceties, and the ire of the political and religious elites. It is no wonder that the book was not found at Qumran. It is a wonder that it is found anywhere at all.[41]

---

[38] See esp. chapters 6–7.

[39] The ethos of martyrdom in 2 Maccabees has been much studied. See esp. Jan Willem van Henten, *The Maccabean Martyrs as Saviours of the Jewish People*, JSJ Suppl. 57 (Leiden: Brill, 1997), and Mark W. Whitters, "Martyrdom as Cultic Death in the Books of Maccabees: Antecedents and Later Developments," in Jeremy Corley and Vincent Skemp (eds.), *Studies in the Greek Bible: Essays in Honor of Francis T. Gignac, S.J.*, CBQMS 44 (Washington, DC: Catholic Biblical Association, 2008), 97–119, with references to further literature.

[40] Ben Sira does not mention Mordecai or Esther. Some have seen the value of this to be doubtful, since he mentions few figures from Second Temple times (Bar-Kokhba, "חג הפורים בימי הבית השני," 54), but others conclude that Ben Sira seems not to have known of Esther (along with Ruth, Shir ha-Shirim, and Daniel); see Aharon Oppenheimer, "אהבת מרדכי ושנאת המן ?פורים בימי הבית השני ולאחריו," *Zion* 62 (1997), 410; Shnayer Z. Leiman, *The Canonization of Hebrew Scripture: The Talmudic and Midrashic Evidence*, Transactions of the Connecticut Academy of Arts and Sciences 47 (Hamden, CT: Published for the Academy by Archon Books, 1976), 29. Leiman (*ibid.*, 151 n. 139) does quote the view of Eberharter, however, who detected literary influence of Esther on Ben Sira, which would be interesting if true. For a denial that Ben Sira provides a list of his "canon," see Armin Lange, "'The Law, the Prophets, and the Other Books of the Fathers (Sir, Prologue): Canonical Lists in Ben Sira and Elsewhere?," in Géza G. Xeravits and József Zsengellér (eds.), *Studies in the Book of Ben Sira: Papers of the Third International Conference on the Deuterocanonical Books, Shime'on Centre, Pápa, Hungary, 18–20 May, 2006*, JSJ Suppl. 127 (Leiden and Boston: Brill, 2008), 55–80.

[41] Cf. Bar-Kokhba, "חג הפורים בימי הבית השני ומגילת אסתר ב"אסיה"," 50, who discusses Talmudic views opposed to Esther; his points are even more true with regard to Qumran.

CHAPTER II

Criticism by adaptation
Rewriting Esther in Hellenistic and Roman times

One of the more fascinating phenomena regarding the reception of Esther is the number of attempts made to "clean up" the book. In these, an author writes a new story that is meant to be a correction to Esther. The similarities must be striking enough that the connection is clear, but the story will take a different direction, or propound a different ideological vantage point, than the original does. By necessity, recognizing such rewritings is a matter of luck and of looking in the right places. It is likely that there are further examples which I have not yet recognized, but the four examples presented here are valuable in their own right, and suggestive regarding the larger dynamics of the reception of Esther.

1. Rewriting Esther 1: Judith

Much has been written about the similarities and contrasts between the books and the heroines of Esther and Judith. The origin of Judith is very uncertain.[1] It may possibly be a product of the Alexandrian community,[2] but more likely is that it is an originally Semitic work which was popular in the Alexandrian community.[3] There is a long tradition associating the story

---

[1] See Gruen, *Diaspora*, 165–66 and 321 n. 103.

[2] Jan Joosten, "The Original Language and Historical Milieu of the Book of Judith," *Meghillot*, 5–6 (2008), *159–*176; arguments that the book of Judith may not have been originally in Hebrew were also mounted by Jeremy Corley, "Septuagentalisms, Semitic Interference, and the Original Language of the Book of Judith," in Jeremy Corley and Vincent Skemp (eds.), *Studies in the Greek Bible: Essays in Honor of Francis T. Gignac, S.J.*, CBQMS 44 (Washington, DC: Catholic Biblical Association, 2008), 65–96.

[3] Some have suggested that it is a much older text: for a Persian-period origin, see recently Ziony Zevit, "Dating Ruth: Legal, Linguistic, and Historical Observations," *ZAW* 117 (2005), 588–89, and earlier Jehoshua Grintz, ספר יהודית: תחזורת הנוסח המקורי (Jerusalem: Bialik, 1957), 15–55; my thanks to Moshe Bernstein for the latter reference. Jan Retsö, *The Arabs in Antiquity: Their History from the Assyrians to*

with the Hasmoneans.[4] Although there are many elements that would have to be discussed in order to give a full accounting of the book of Judith – including its use of other biblical stories, such as that of Yael, and its political meaning in the second century BCE – I will here focus only on how the book relates to the story of Esther.

Both Judith and Esther feature Jewish heroines who save their people, and both do it by getting as close as possible to the leader of those threatening the Jews. In both, the salvation is effected by the means of a banquet in the home of that leader. A good place to begin contrasting the works is their foreign policies. The political differences begin with geography. Esther is a diaspora book, whereas Judith is set in the land of Israel. The Jews there are governed within the book by a high priest, from the Temple in Jerusalem.[5] Judith argues that foreign rule is never benevolent, and that obedience to it is only a posture to be adopted until it can be overthrown. If such obedience comes into conflict with loyalty to the Jewish tradition, however, it is the loyalty to tradition that must take precedence, and at that point, all pretenses of dual loyalties must immediately cease. The differences between this ideology and the one propounded by Esther are subtle, but all the more important for that reason. Judith obeys the king as a ruse, as long as his commands are not in conflict with her traditions. Esther, on the other hand, obeys because she is a loyal citizen. What is for Judith a mere façade is for Esther a way of life.[6]

Other details suggest that the author of Judith was consciously trying to "correct" the deficiencies evident in Esther.[7] The most blatant example is that Judith brings kosher food with her when she goes to dine with the foreign potentate. This stands in sharp contrast to Esther, who apparently

the Umayyads (New York: RoutledgeCurzon, 2003), 145–47, sees an ancient Jewish story about the campaign of Tiglath-Pileser III in the 730s BCE as lying behind the military campaign description in Judith 1:21–26.

[4] Weitzman, *Surviving Sacrilege*, 52–53.

[5] Sidnie White Crawford, "Esther and Judith: Contrasts in Character," in Sidnie White Crawford and Leonard J. Greenspoon (eds.), *The Book of Esther in Modern Research*, JSOT Suppl. 380 (London: T. & T. Clark, 2003), 67.

[6] *Ibid.*," 68–69. White Crawford has suggested that the reason why Esther was canonized and Judith was not was specifically the depiction of gender roles in the two stories. Esther the character is feminine throughout, relying on her beauty, wits, and intelligence to deliver the Jewish people from annihilation. Judith, although seductive and beautiful, is more activist and, indeed, uses a sword to deliver her people from the threat looming over them. See also White Crawford, "Esther not Judith: Why One Made it and the Other Didn't," *Bible Review* 18.1 (2002), 22–31, 45, as well as Adolpho Roitman and Amnon Shapira, "ספר יהודית כסיפור-בבואה "מתקן" של מגילת אסתר," *Beit Mikra* 49.4 (2004), 137 n. 37. Below it will be argued that the canonization of Esther had more to do with the book's politics than with its perspectives on gender, but this difference is worthy of note for its own sake.

[7] Roitman and Shapira, "ספר יהודית כסיפור-בבואה "מתקן" של מגילת אסתר," 127–43.

eats whatever she is fed in the palace. This does align Judith, to a large extent, with Daniel, who also refuses the royal food.[8] The second example, from the theological plane, is the principle of providential reward and punishment. This is a principle that is never expressed at all within Esther, but is stressed often in Judith. It is a theme in the speeches of both Achior and Judith herself.[9] The very fact that Judith prays to God already sets her apart from Esther.

Indeed, there are close points of contact between the Greek Additions to Esther and the book of Judith. (Some scholars have even dated the Additions on this basis, arguing that they, like Judith, must be products of the second century BCE.[10]) The Additions are texts that bespeak a deep discomfort with the trajectory and the characters of the Esther story, and Judith does the same. If the book of Judith is the product of the Hasmonean world, there is yet another connection between this text and the Additions to Esther. Both the Additions (at least A, C, D, and F) and Judith may be texts composed in Palestine *for* the Alexandrian Jewish community, or at least primarily consumed there. Both texts aim to create the type of religious worldview preferred by the Hasmoneans and reflected so strongly in the book of Judith: resistance to foreign rule, refusal to compromise on religious values, and willingness to undergo martyrdom.[11]

In sum, both the Additions to Esther, discussed above, and the book of Judith may represent attempts to correct Esther by rewriting her. One rewrites her from within, and the other from without. Neither is content to leave her alone, and insists that a flawed story such as Esther's must be corrected in the public sphere.

---

[8] See above, Chapter 6.   [9] Judith 5:17–18 and, e.g., 8:25.

[10] Moore, *Daniel, Esther, and Jeremiah*, 220–22, points out many similarities between, on the one hand, Additions C and D in particular and, on the other hand, the book of Judith – both, on his view, composed in second-century BCE Palestine. For more on these connections, see C. P. van der Walt, "The Prayers of Esther (LXX) and Judith against their Social Backgrounds – Evidence of a Possible Common *Grundlage*," *Journal for Semitics = Tydskrif vir Semitistiek* 17 (2008), 194–206; van der Walt suggests situating both texts in Judea in the aftermath of Antiochus' defilement of the Temple.

[11] Seeing Judith in the context of Hasmonean-era religious debates is also instructive: Benedikt Eckhardt, "Reclaiming Tradition: The Book of Judith and Hasmonean Politics," *JSP* 18 (2009), 243–63, argues that whereas the Hasmoneans had claimed Mattathias as a zealous ancestor, building on the model of Phineas (1 Maccabees 2), Judith responds with a different model of zealousness, which utilizes Simeon's act in Genesis 34 as a model. She is a better hero, in that Judith calls on God repeatedly, and there is a delicate balance between crediting God and crediting Judith with her actions; Mattathias never calls on God (although see 1 Maccabees 3:18–22 for Judah Maccabee as a divinely inspired warrior).

2. Rewriting Esther 2: 3 Maccabees

Another attempt to clean up Esther by rewriting it may be the Alexandrian historical novel of 3 Maccabees, whose relationship to Esther has been well studied. There seems to be a complex relationship between the books. The relationship between the two texts was first discussed thoroughly in 1924 by R. B. Motzo,[12] who drew attention to numerous points of similiarity between the books. Not all of Motzo's points have stood up to later criticism, and more recent scholars have tended to see many of the similarities as merely reflective of broader trends in Greek literature during the first century BCE.[13] The most compelling evidence for a literary connection depends on literary usages unique to the books, and these do exist. Most prominently, only in these two texts does anyone threaten to destroy places "with fire and spear";[14] in Addition E 24, the king threatens that any locale which does not fulfill his instructions will be destroyed with "spear and fire," and in 3 Maccabees 5:43, the king says he will destroy the army of Judah Maccabee with "fire and spear." This can be seen as an allusive keyword. The key phrase is deployed in order to remind the reader of the text being alluded to, with the expectation that the more widespread literary connections between the texts will then become evident.

Once we look, it is readily apparent that there are broad similarities in the plot outlines of the two books. In 3 Maccabees, Ptolemy IV Philopator, having defeated Antiochus III at Raphia and been saved from assassination by a Jew, Dositheus, visits the Jerusalem Temple in celebration. He wishes to enter the Temple, but the high priest Simon and the other priests beseech him not to defile their Temple with his entry. When Ptolemy ignores them, Simon prays for God to stop him, and his prayers are answered: God strikes him within the Temple, and he has to be dragged out by his attendants just to save his life.

The king, returning home, then plots to kill all the Jews in Alexandria, ordering all those who will not renounce their faith to report to the hippodrome, where they will be trampled by drunken elephants. God foils

---

[12] R. B. Motzo, "Il rifacimento Greco di Ester e il III Maccabei," in *Saggi di storia e letteratura giudeo-ellenistica*, Contributi alla scienza dell' Antichità 5 (Florence: Le Monnier, 1924), 272–90.

[13] For thorough and insightful discussions, see Johannes Magliano-Tromp, "The Relations between Egyptian Judaism and Jerusalem in Light of 3 Maccabees and the Greek Book of Esther," in C. M. Tuckett (ed.), *Feasts and Fasts*, Contributions to Biblical Exegesis and Theology 53 (Leiden: Peeters, 2009), 57–76, and Noah Hacham, "3 Maccabees and Esther: Parallels, Intertextuality, and Diaspora Identity," *JBL* 126 (2007), 769–72.

[14] See especially Hacham, "3 Maccabees and Esther," 765–85, and Magliano-Tromp, "The Relations," 66–67.

Ptolemy's plans again and again, and finally the Jewish leader Elazar offers a lengthy prayer for salvation. The elephants turn and trample the army behind them, and the king then repents. He encourages them to build a synagogue and to establish an annual festival commemorating the events of the day.

The similarities of plot are obvious. Both begin with the story of a Jew saving the king from assassination. In both, the king decrees the destruction of the Jews, and then rescinds the decree and promulgates a decree favoring the Jews. In both, the abolition of the decree of destruction results in the establishment of an annual festival. Both take place in the Diaspora.[15]

The religious outlook of 3 Maccabees is less compromising in relation to that of the author of Esther. Unlike Esther, this book is Temple-centric and priestly-oriented. The Jews in general are not willing to sacrifice anything for their faith, and are prepared to martyr themselves instead. The salvations are effected through prayer and direct divine intervention, and the narrator makes the involvement of God explicit: "Now this was an active interference of the unconquerable Providence which assisted the Jews from heaven."[16] Indeed, it is clear that the authors of 3 Maccabees and of Esther were not in agreement on fundamental questions. The author of 3 Maccabees seems hell-bent on showing that the Alexandrian Jews were unquestionably Greek, and yet also, simultaneously, unquestionably Jewish.[17] Esther, of course, is prepared to entertain the possibility that in order to preserve the loyalty to the regime, which is paramount, loyalty to Judaism must sometimes give way.

It may not be surprising, then, that 3 Maccabees also cannot countenance the establishment of a festival whose celebration is earthy and mundane, and requires no study of Torah. In place of a festival like Purim, a festival is established, "not for drinking and gluttony, but because of the deliverance that had come to them through God."[18] It is difficult not to see this as an oblique criticism of Purim.[19]

---

[15] See Hacham, "3 Maccabees and Esther," 767, where other parallels are also adduced.

[16] This is from 4:21, and similar sentiments are found throughout the text.

[17] Uriel Rappaport, "3 Maccabees and the Jews of Egypt," *JQR* 99 (2009), 555.

[18] 3 Maccabees 6:36.

[19] Burns, "The Special Purim," 21, crediting Nickelsburg with this insight. This is rejected by Hacham, "3 Maccabees and Esther," 771, on the grounds that similar "festival foundation stories" are found elsewhere as well. Hacham argues that there is a latent polemic here, but it is not against the Dionysian cult, an insight that he developed in "3 Maccabees – An Anti-Dionysian Polemic," in Jo-Ann A. Brant, Charles W. Hedrick, and Chris Shea (eds.), *Ancient Fiction: The Matrix of Early Christian and Jewish Narrative*, SBL Symposium Series 32 (Atlanta: SBL, 2005), 167–83. I find it difficult, despite this, to not see this as a covert criticism of the foundation of Purim.

Recent scholars have added a very interesting wrinkle to this argument. Although Esther may have been one model for the book of 3 Maccabees, the Additions – and in particular, Addition E – are modeled after 3 Maccabees. The evidence for this claim comes in large part from the theory of diaspora existence and relations advocated in that book.[20] In particular, MT Esther presupposes a reality in which the king himself is incompetent, but not evil, and harbors no intent to harm the Jews, and in which the Jews are secure enough to describe killing non-Jews. In 3 Maccabees, on the other hand, the king himself persecutes the Jews, the Jew who saves the king's life is an apostate, and Jews are not described as killing non-Jews, but only traitorous Jews.[21]

On this reading, then, the author of Additions B and E was deeply uncomfortable with Esther's portrayal of Jewish–Gentile relations, and on all counts found precedent for his own preferred reality in 3 Maccabees. In composing Additions B and E, therefore, he attempted also to alter the outlook found in Esther regarding these issues, and therefore "these Additions, which voice the difficulty of Jewish life in the Diaspora, are in dissonance with the viewpoint emerging from the Hebrew."[22] In sum, then, the book of 3 Maccabees may be seen as another attempt to rewrite, and thus to correct, the book of Esther. In the wake of 3 Maccabees, another author was inspired to use this text to subvert Esther from within, composing the Additions to the book itself and thus attempting an even more subversive correction of the problematic text.

3. Rewriting Esther 3: Genesis Apocryphon

We turn now to a more covert example of retelling. Embedded within a longer text, the example to be studied here proves to be remarkable for a number of reasons. Above, we saw the likelihood that the Qumran community harbored antipathy for the book of Esther. The Genesis Apocryphon, however, found among the Dead Sea Scrolls, does seem to allude to Esther. This text was not composed by the Qumran community, and so it cannot be used as evidence for the beliefs and ideas of that group;[23]

---

[20] Hacham, "3 Maccabees and Esther," 781–85.   [21] See also Burns, "The Special Purim," 19–21.

[22] Hacham, "3 Maccabees and Esther," 783.

[23] In this context, this point was made by Talmon, "Was the Book of Esther Known at Qumran?," 251–52.

instead, the text must be studied on its own, as an example of the richness of biblical interpretation and narrative retelling in antiquity.[24]

The Apocryphon's retelling of the story of Abram and Sarai in Egypt (found originally in Genesis 12:10–20) seems to be based on the book of Esther; in keeping with the principle of the allusive keyword, this is signified by the inclusion of the phrase לבוש שגי די בוץ וארגואן "much clothing of fine linen and purple" (20:31). The extended story, which stretches over columns 19–20 of the text, is as follows.

Soon after Abram and Sarai's arrival in Canaan, there was a famine in the entire land. They decided to journey to Egypt. On the night when they entered Egypt, Abram had a terrifying dream, in which he saw two trees, a cedar and a date-palm. The palm tree was very beautiful. Men arrived, looking to cut down the cedar tree, but it was saved by the palm tree, who exclaimed that the two were grown of the same root. When Abram awoke, he told the dream to Sarai, and also instructed her regarding its significance. People would try to kill him, and it would be up to Sarai to save him by claiming that they were brother and sister. Sarai was scared, but the two of them continued on to Egypt.

After five years in Egypt, there were three Egyptians in Abram's house for instruction in the ways of wisdom. Abram was teaching them the teachings of Enoch, and apparently in the course of the conversation, Sarai emerged and impressed the Egyptians with her beauty and her wisdom. The Egyptians returned to Pharaoh, and one, Hirqanosh, burst into song in praise of this wondrous woman. After praising her physical beauty and form, insisting that "no virgins or brides who enter the bridal canopy exceed her beauty," he concluded by noting her great wisdom. Pharaoh immediately sent for Sarai, and tried to kill Abram. Sarai saved him by claiming that he was her brother, and instead Pharaoh simply married Sarai.

Abram broke down in tears when she was taken away. He and Lot passed that night, and many nights thereafter, crying and praying. In response to Abram's prayers, God sent afflictions to the palace, which tortured Pharaoh and his entire household for two years. For that entire time, Pharaoh was not able to sleep with Sarai because of the divine afflictions. After two years, Hirqanosh arrived at Abram's home with the request that Abram pray on behalf of Pharaoh. Lot burst out, "My uncle Abram cannot pray for the king, while his wife Sarai is with him! Go tell the king to send his wife away

---

[24] For a collection of papers on the biblical interpretation and narration in the Genesis Apocryphon, see Moshe J. Bernstein, *Reading and Re-Reading Scripture at Qumran*, STDJ 107 (Leiden: Brill, 2013), vol. 1.

from him, to her husband, and then he will pray for him and he will be cured."

Hirqanosh conveyed to Pharaoh that Sarai was actually a married woman, and advised that she be returned immediately. Pharaoh angrily summoned Abram, who prayed that Pharaoh be healed. The plague was removed, and the king gave Sarai many gifts, including Hagar and "much silver and gold, much clothing of fine linen and purple (*levush sagi di buts ve-argavan*)."[25]

Our discussion must begin with the expression "much clothing of fine linen (*buts*) and purple (*argavan*)." This phraseology is drawn from Esther 8:15, which reports that "Mordecai left the presence of the king in royal clothing of blue and white, with a large gold crown and a mantle of fine linen (*buts*) and purple (*ve-argaman*)." The fact that Genesis Apocryphon uses this phrase is particularly striking because, other than in Esther, it appears nowhere else in the Bible or in other ancient Semitic texts.[26]

The author of this section of the Apocryphon was probably not using the phrase from Esther as a mere literary flourish. Rather, he was drawing attention to the commonalities between the story he had just told and the story in Esther; in other words, we have here another allusive keyword. In both stories, a woman is taken to the king's palace for the purpose of marriage; she has a male relative who should be her caretaker and protector; as a result of what befalls the woman, her male relative is rewarded with riches. By deploying an allusive keyword, the author of the Apocryphon is drawing the readers' attention to the connections between the two *biblical* stories. In fact, readers have long noted that there are certain parallels and connections between the stories of Abram and Sarai in Egypt on the one hand and Esther on the other;[27] Jonathan Grossman presented the chart of comparisons between two as shown in Table 11.1.

---

[25] The text, with translation and full commentary, can be found in Joseph A. Fitzmyer, *The Genesis Apocryphon of Qumran Cave 1 (1Q20): A Commentary*, 3rd edn., Biblica et Orientalia 18/B (Rome: Pontifical Biblical Institute, 2004), 98–102.

[26] Joshua Finkel, "מחבר המגילה החיצונית לבראשית הכיר את מגילת אסתר," in Yigael Yadin and Chaim Rabin (eds.), מחקרים במגילות הגנוזות: ספר זיכרון לאליעזר ליפא סוקניק ז"ל (Jerusalem: Hekhal ha-Sefer, 1961), 178–79. Even in rabbinic literature, the phrase appears only in discussions of the verse in Esther. The phrase בוץ וארגוון does appear in an Aramaic poem from Byzantine Palestine describing the décor at Xerxes' banquet. This attestation is particularly telling, since the phrase had apparently become deeply associated with the book of Esther, but its location within the story was malleable. See Joseph Yahalom and Michael Sokoloff, שירת בני מערבא: שירים ארמיים של יהודי ארץ- ישראל בתקופה הביזנטית (Jerusalem: Israel Academy of Sciences and Humanities, 1999), 192 (line 24).

[27] Finkel, "מחבר המגילה החיצונית לבראשית הכיר את מגילת אסתר," 163–68.

Table 11.1 *Esther 2 and Genesis 12*

Thematic element	Taking of Esther to Xerxes' palace (Esther 2)	Taking of Sarai to Pharaoh's palace (Genesis 12)
Male–female relationship	He was foster father to Hadassah – that is, Esther – and when her father and mother died, Mordecai adopted her as his own daughter (2:7).	Abram and Nahor took to themselves wives, the name of Abram's wife being Sarai (11:29).
A family exiled from its land	Who had been exiled from Jerusalem in the group that was carried into exile along with King Jeconiah of Judah (2:6).	Abram went down to Egypt to sojourn there (12:10).
Description of the woman as beautiful	The maiden was shapely and beautiful (2:7).	I know what a beautiful woman you are (12:11).
The king's servants encourage him to take a wife	The king's servants who attended him said, "Let beautiful young virgins be sought out for your majesty" (2:2).	Pharaoh's courtiers saw her and praised her to Pharaoh (12:15).
Man requests of the woman not to reveal her identity	Esther did not reveal her people or her kindred, for Mordecai had told her not to reveal it (2:10).	Please say that you are my sister (12:13).
Taking of the woman to the king's palace	Esther, too, was taken into the king's palace (2:8).	The woman was taken into Pharaoh's palace (12:15).
The king discovers the hidden connection between the man and the woman	For Esther had told (הגידה) how he was related to her (8:1).	Why did you not tell me (הגדת לי) that she was your wife? (12:18).
The king enters into dialogue with the man	Mordecai presented himself to the king (8:1).	Pharaoh sent for Abram and said ... (12:18).
The king bestows wealth on the man	Mordecai left the king's presence is royal robes of blue and white, with a magnificent crown of gold and a mantle of fine linen and purple wool (8:15).	And because of her, it went well with Abram: he acquired sheep, oxen, asses, male and female slaves, she-asses, and camels (12:16).

Note: This table is slightly adapted from the one presented in Grossman, *Esther*, 67.

The important question, of course, is what purpose these comparisons may serve. There are numerous points that can be made. The comparisons between the stories make the most critical contrast stand out even more. The fates of the two women involved cannot be more different. Sarai, after a long period of abduction, is returned to her husband. Esther, on the other hand, remains married to the king of Persia forevermore.[28]

The author of the Genesis Apocryphon also perceived the connection between the two stories. Rather than constructing an elaborate chart to explain these connections, he deploys the most subtle of tactics, the allusive keyword, to indicate that he sees the relationship between the stories. This one key phrase is meant to conjure up a whole network of associations in the minds of his readers. In our case, the author of the story in the Apocryphon uses the phrase "fine linen and purple wool" as just such an allusive key-word. This is meant to call the biblical expression "fine linen and purple wool" to mind, and thus ineluctably refer to the story of Esther. Since the story being told is about Abram and Sarai in Egypt, the points of compar-ison and contrast are thus evoked.

The similarities between the two biblical stories have just been discussed. In the mind of the author of the Apocryphon, however, these are not interesting for questions of literary or intellectual history, and certainly not as a mere literary flourish. Instead, the juxtaposition of the two stories is a way of extolling Abram and castigating Mordecai. Indeed, when the two characters are juxtaposed, and their stories are seen to be parallel in so many ways, their behaviors are seen to be vastly different. Abram is, first, warned by God in a dream that his life will be put at risk and saved only by the intervention of Sarai. When his wife is taken, he describes how he wept and prayed all night, beseeching God to protect Sarai in the palace. Sarai is indeed miraculously protected from the advances of Pharaoh, and even-tually is returned to Abram. Mordecai, on the other hand, has no particular reason to fear the king, yet when Esther is taken we hear nothing of his reaction. He coolly goes on with his life, only periodically checking on Sarai's wellbeing in the palace. Furthermore, whereas Abram went to great lengths to prevent Sarai from being taken in the first place, and successfully hid her for five years, Mordecai seems to make no such effort. Instead, Esther is simply taken from his home, with no objection, no fight, and no opposition. Not surprisingly, and perhaps (one might claim) as a result of Mordecai's failure to pray on her behalf, Esther is not protected from the king's advances, and engages in sexual relations with the Gentile. Perhaps – as another result? – Esther is never returned to Mordecai, but is damned to live the rest of her days as the unwilling consort of a heathen king.

---

[28] Grossman, *Esther*, 66.

Table 11.2 *Esther and the story of Abram in the Genesis Apocryphon*

Thematic element	Esther	Apocryphon
Woman	Esther	Sarai
Male protector	Mordecai	Abram
King	Xerxes	Pharaoh Zoan
Divine guidance	*None*	*Warning of imminent danger*
Attempts to provide security	*None*	*Sarai is hidden for five years*
Her fate	**Taken to the king's palace as a wife**	**Taken to the king's palace as a wife**
Protector's reaction	*Calm*	*Weeping and prayer*
Result for her	*She is married to the king*	*She is protected from the king*
Result for him	**Fine linen and purple wool**	**Fine linen and purple wool**
Final result	*Lives in the foreign palace forever*	*Is returned to her Israelite family*

These similarities and differences can be summarized in Table 11.2, where the commonalities are shown in **bold** type; those differences which seem to be judgmental are in *italics*.

It appears that the story of Abram in the Apocryphon has been composed as a "corrective reflection" on the Esther story. This was not necessarily the primary goal of the story, or the motivation for its composition, but the Esther connection clearly provided the author with some of the material for his narrative. The plot lines are similar enough to demand comparison, but the comparison highlights the claim that Mordecai did not act properly, and therefore condemned his female ward to a lifetime of alienation from her people (an issue that bothered other ancient readers, as well).[29] Abram, on the other hand, models perfect behavior in his response when Sarai is taken, and thus earns the same riches and power that Mordecai earns, exemplified by the "fine linen and purple wool," but he earns his wife back, as well.

---

[29] For example, a Byzantine-era Aramaic poem from Palestine corrects this deficiency in Mordecai's (and Esther's) behavior: "when the royal decree was issued / to ingather all the virgins / she entered a room that she would not be seen/ that she would not be defiled by the laws of the heathen. / An angel sat in the window of the upper story / appearing to passers-by how she looked. / The guards ran and told the king / and soon thereafter were sent to Mordecai / 'Old man, old man, why did you not say that you have a daughter?' . . . " The text is from Yahalom and Sokoloff, שירת בני מערבא, 188. See also the (approximately contemporary) Targum Sheni, in its translational paraphrase of Esther 2:8, with a similar story.

4. Rewriting Esther 4: the story of Janneus

Another example of the use of the allusive keyword can be seen in a tale preserved in Bavli Qiddushin 66a. Again, this is a short passage embedded within a longer text, and in this case the longer text is from centuries later. The short episode to be discussed is cited in its literary context for a legal nicety concerning the value of rumors and witnesses in establishing that a married woman has had a sexual affair with another man. In order to establish his legal claim that even a single witness, if he is credible, may be believed in such a case, the fourth-century Talmudic sage Abbaye quotes a story about Janneus.

Modern scholars have often observed that this story seems to originate in some sort of historical narrative, and we will return to this question below. What has not been often observed, however, is that the story alludes to, and takes much of its meaning from, the book of Esther.[30]

In the story, the king, Janneus, throws a grand banquet to celebrate a military victory and to commemorate the construction of the Temple centuries earlier. At the banquet, a malicious advisor named El'azar ben Po'irah advises the king to provoke the Pharisees by making them swear by the frontlet on his forehead, the emblem of the office of the high priest. Provoked, an elder, Judah ben Gudgeda,[31] arises and proclaims: "It is enough that you have the royal crown (כתר מלכות)! Leave the crown of priesthood to the descendants of Aaron!" His demand, we are told, was based on a rumor (which turns out to be unfounded) that Janneus' mother had been a captive, and that Janneus himself was thus disqualified from priestly service. The king himself does not know how to respond, but the same wicked El'azar again comes up with advice: massacre all the Pharisees, on the grounds that the actions of Judah are representative of what they all think. After some deliberation, Janneus is convinced, and kills all the Pharisees.

There is, once again, an allusive keyword, a key phrase that alerts the reader to see Esther as the intended intertext here: when reporting the rumor about Janneus' mother, the text says, "the matter was investigated (ויבוקש הדבר) and was not found to be true (ולא נמצא)." This sentence closely

---

[30] A recent sophisticated treatment of this story is Vered Noam, "The Story of King Jannaeus (*b. Qiddushin* 66a): A Pharisaic Reply to Sectarian Polemic," *Harvard Theological Review* (forthcoming, 2013); I thank Dr. Noam for sharing a copy of her paper with me prior to its publication. Noam discusses the text in full philological and bibliographical detail; see esp. *ibid.*, nn. 19–23 for references to the voluminous earlier literature.

[31] *Ibid.*, n. 12.

resembles – in fact, reverses – the line from Esther 2:23, regarding the plot of Bigtan and Teresh: "the matter was investigated (וַיְבֻקַּשׁ הַדָּבָר) and it was found to be true (וַיִּמָּצֵא)."[32] Furthermore, the two antagonists in the story, El'azar b. Po'irah and Judah b. Gudgeda, are introduced with clauses very similar to the introduction of Mordecai in Esther 2:5: "there was one wicked person there (והיה שם אחד איש), evil and troublemaking, and his name (ושמו) was El'azar b. Po'irah," and "there was (שם היה) one elder there, and his name was (ושמו) Judah b. Gudgeda." Finally, the expression "royal crown" (כתר מלכות) is unique to the book of Esther within the Hebrew Bible.[33]

Again, these verbal similarities alert us to deeper connections: the plot lines closely mirror those of the Esther story. Both stories open with elaborate royal banquets. There is a wicked advisor, who convinces the king to provoke "the Jews" (which, from the perspective of the story, was a term equivalent to "the Pharisees"). In Esther, Haman appears and says that the king has ordered everyone to bow down to him. Whether or not the king had in fact ordered this, clearly it was publicized by Haman himself. The provocation itself is related: in Esther, Mordecai refuses to *get up* in front of Haman (לא קם); Janneus provokes the Pharisees by abjuring them (הקם להם).[34] If the author of this story shared in the rabbinic claim that Haman forced the people to commit idolatry by bowing down to him,[35] there is the added similarity that both Haman and Janneus utilize religious paraphernalia to force the people to do acts of political obeisance: Janneus abjures the people with the *tzitz*, the priestly frontlet.

In both stories, a single individual resists: Judah stands up and protests verbally; Mordecai will not bow down. In both, the king does not react, but the wicked advisor – El'azar or Haman – persuades the king that such an offense to his honor cannot be tolerated. In both, the advisor's chosen means of dealing with the insurrection is to massacre the group to which the rebel belongs – the Pharisees in one story, the Jews in general in the other. Of course, the stories turn out very differently: Janneus is successful in

---

[32] This was noted by Israel Levi, "Les sources talmudiques de l'histoire juive: I. Alexandre Jannée et Simon ben Schetah; II. La rupture de Jannée avec les Pharisiens," *REJ* 35 (1897), 222, brought to my attention by Noam, "The Story of King Jannaeus," n. 39.

[33] Noam, "The Story of King Jannaeus," text at n. 38.

[34] For this interpretation of הקם להם, see *ibid.*, n. 10, and Moshe J. Bernstein, "Oaths and Vows in the Pentateuchal Targumim: Semantics and Exegesis," in Aharon Maman, Steven E. Fassberg, and Yochanan Breuer (eds.), *Sha'arei Lashon: Studies in Hebrew, Aramaic and Jewish Languages Presented to Moshe Bar-Asher* (Jerusalem: Bialik Institute, 2007), vol. II, 20–41, and the many references in both, esp. Saul Lieberman, תוספתא כפשוטה (New York and Jerusalem: Jewish Theological Seminary, 1995), vol. VII, 397 n. 14.

[35] See, e.g., Esther Rabbah 7:6 and 7:8. See the comments of Elliott Horowitz, *Reckless Rites: Purim and the Legacy of Jewish Violence* (Princeton University Press, 2006), 157.

Table 11.3 *Esther and the Janneus story*

Thematic element	Esther	Janneus story
King	Xerxes	Janneus
Wicked advisor	Haman	El'azar ben Po'irah
Opening act	Elaborate royal banquet	Elaborate royal banquet
Advice of the advisor no. 1	Provoke the Pharisees by making them swear by the *tzitz* (הקם להם)	[Provoke the Jews by making them bow down because of the idol]
Noble protestor	Mordecai	Judah ben Gudgeda
Protest	Ignores king's decree	Questions king's legitimacy as priest
Advice of the advisor no. 2	Kill the protestor's group	Kill the protestor's group
Result	Jews are saved	Pharisees are massacred

killing the Pharisees, whereas Haman's plot is thwarted. Perhaps this is exemplified by the reversal of the phraseology, from Esther's "the matter was investigated and found to be true" to "the matter was investigated and not found to be true" in the story of Janneus.[36] Again, the similarities may be summarized in a chart; see Table 11.3.

As mentioned, the story in Qiddushin is fascinating for other reasons. First, its language is archaic, or archaizing, utilizing the *waw ha-hippukh* form often: *va-yomer ... va-yomer ... va-yevuqqash ... va-yibbadelu ... va-yomer ... va-toṣeṣ ... va-yeharegu* "he said ... he said ... it was sought ... they separated ... he said ... it burst forth[37] ... they were killed." A full history of this form is not necessary at this point;[38] suffice it to say that it is not found in Mishnaic Hebrew at all. Thus, these attestations suggest that the text that Abbaye is citing is not a rabbinic text, but something different, and probably older.[39]

[36] This idiomatic allusion was noted by M. H. Segal, *Grammar of Mishnaic Hebrew* (Oxford: Clarendon, 1927), 62 n. 1.

[37] The word ותוצץ is a difficult one. It is analyzed by Jastrow as being from the root צו"ץ and meaning "burst forth." MS Munich 95 reads ותיועץ, and MS Vatican 111 reads ותיועץ, but was then corrected to ותוצץ. MS Oxford Opp. 248 (367), however, reads ותוצץ.

[38] But see Mark S. Smith, *The Origins and Development of the Waw-Consecutive: Northwest Semitic Evidence from Ugarit to Qumran*, HSS 39 (Atlanta: Scholars, 1991).

[39] See Segal, *Grammar of Mishnaic Hebrew*, 16 and 72; J. N. Epstein, מבוא לנוסח המשנה (Jerusalem: Magnes, 2000 [orig. 1964]), vol. 11, 677; Elisha Qimron and Raphael Nir, פרקים בתולדות הלשון העברית (Tel Aviv: Open University, 2004), vol. 11, 71; Noam, "The Story of King Jannaeus," *passim*.

Adding to the intrigue regarding this text is that it seems to report the historical event more accurately than Josephus does.[40] It likely contains some real historical memories, although they are couched in literary, and even symbolic terms. Besides the use of the Esther story as a literary frame, Baumgarten has pointed to the symbolic names deployed: El'azar b. Po'irah, who opened a gap (*pa'ar*) in Israel, and Judah b. Gudgeda, who caused the nation to split into factions (*gedudim*).[41]

These facts may indicate that it is quite an ancient fragment being quoted by Abbaye – and it should be emphasized that Abbaye cites it for halakhic reasons, rather than as history for its own sake. Chaim Rabin drew the conclusion that this episode and perhaps one or two others preserved in rabbinic literature are "likely to be quotations from ancient works of history, saga, and pious tales, of the type which we still have in such books as Judith, Susannah, Jubilees, and I Maccabees, and now in the Aramaic Genesis Apocryphon. That literature, as a whole, was pre-Tannaitic, and we have so far no evidence of similar works having been composed within the early Rabbinic community."[42]

The analysis offered here suggests that this text is not to be classified as "history." Rather than being a dry chronicle containing a straightforward historical account, we clearly are dealing with a literary text, which has cast the story of Janneus in light of the story of Esther and has told the story in partly symbolic terms, utilizing names that are symbolic rather than historical.[43] Beyond this, of course, all is speculation; it cannot be known how old this text is or what circles produced and transmitted it. Perhaps the most fascinating question is how the Babylonian sage Abbaye came to cite it – to

---

[40] M. J. Geller, "Alexander Jannaeus and the Pharisee Rift," *JJS* 30 (1979), 202–11. A harshly negative verdict regarding the story's historicity may be found in Joshua Efron, *Studies on the Hasmonean Period*, Studies in Judaism in Late Antiquity 39 (Leiden: Brill, 1987), 176–90. Efron's discussion is part of his long polemic – which consistently overstates its case – that the Bavli corrupts all information about the Hasmoneans. See the much more nuanced arguments of Albert I. Baumgarten, "Rabbinic Literature as a Source for the History of Jewish Sectarianism in the Second Temple Period," *DSD* 2 (1995), 14–57, esp. 36–52.

[41] Baumgarten, "Rabbinic Literature as a Source for the History of Jewish Sectarianism," 45.

[42] Chaim Rabin, "The Historical Background of Qumran Hebrew," in Chaim Rabin and Yigael Yadin (eds.), *Scripta Hierosolymitana* 4; *Aspects of the Dead Sea Scrolls*, Scripta Hierosolymitana 4 (Jerusalem: Magnes, 1958), 155–56. See also the literature cited in Daniel R. Schwartz, *Studies in the Jewish Background of Christianity*, Wissenschaftliche Untersuchungen zum Neuen Testament 60 (Tübingen: J. C. B. Mohr (P. Siebeck), 1992), esp. chapter 1, "On Pharisaic Opposition to the Hasmonean Monarchy, " 48 n. 22.

[43] A much fuller analysis of the genre of this text is provided by Noam, "The Story of King Janneus." She observes that the text alludes heavily to the story of Korah in Numbers 16–17, and develops this connection as providing much of the story's meaning. She hypothesizes that the story is drawn from a lost Pharisaic polemical book, a claim I find compelling.

all appearances, from memory. Were there other such texts which the Amoraim studied? Is this fragment unique because it was the only time such a text was cited in the course of a halakhic discourse, or was it actually unique?

More relevant for our inquiry is the light this sheds on the reading of the book of Esther presupposed in the Janneus story modeled on it. Again, the story reads like a not-very-hidden polemic against the type of politics practiced by Mordecai in the book of Esther. One may stand up to the royal authorities, as Mordecai did, and this may appear to be a heroic act. Certainly this is the impression one has of Judah b. Gudgeda when he arises to criticize the king fearlessly. The king, if he is a benign monarch, may even be willing to tolerate such criticism! But there is no accounting for the power behind the throne. Mordecai and Esther were fortunate to escape with their lives, and with the lives of their contemporaries. Do not emulate them! This is the message of the Judah b. Gudgeda story. He *did* play Mordecai to El'azar b. Po'irah's Haman, but the results were catastrophic. The stakes are simply too high for such risks, and the behavior of Mordecai, though successful once, must not provide the model for future Jews.

CHAPTER 12

Adoption

Esther in the eastern Diaspora and in the canon

1. Dura Europos

There is unfortunately no evidence from the eastern Diaspora that is contemporaneous with the texts from Palestine discussed in the previous chapters. From a few centuries later, however, we do have some evidence, and what is available seems to show that the book of Esther was already treated there with great respect. It was held to be a very significant *religious* book. It must be admitted that when we find the situation in second- and first-century BCE Palestine to be different from that in third-century CE Syria, there is no sure way of telling whether the operative variable is chronology or geography. Certainty may eternally elude us as to whether the operative distinction is between the communities in Israel and in the Diaspora, or between earlier and later communities. I see no alternative to agnosticism here.

From the third century CE, we have evidence specifically from the synagogue paintings from Dura Europos in northern Syria. The Esther panel in the synagogue is immediately notable because of its position: it is just to the left of the niche for the Torah, in an obvious place of distinction.[1] It is difficult to avoid the impression that the Jews of Dura, living under Persian rule in the eastern Diaspora, would have been particularly drawn to the Esther story as a tale with particular personal meaning (see Figure 12.1).[2]

---

[1] For a detailed description, see Rachel Hachlili, *Ancient Jewish Art and Archaeology in the Diaspora*, Handbuch der Orientalistik, part 1: Der Nahe und Mittlere Osten 35; Leiden: Brill, 1998), 119–21. The prominent position accorded to the Purim panel was noted by Burns, "The Special Purim," 24, Bezalel Narkiss, "סיפורי מגילת אסתר בבית הכנסת של דורא אירופוס," in I. S. Recanati (ed.), חמש מגילה ככתבה: המגילות – הגות, אמנות, עיצוב, קובץ מאמרים (Jerusalem: Ministry of Education Department of Publications, 2008), 67–68.

[2] Rachel Hachlili, "The Dura-Europos Synagogue Wall Paintings: A Question of Origin and Interpretation," in Zeev Weiss, Oded Irshai, Jodi Magness, and Seth Schwartz (eds.), *"Follow the Wise": Studies in Jewish History and Culture in Honor of Lee I. Levine* (Winona Lake, IN: Eisenbrauns, for the Jewish Theological Seminary of America and the Hebrew University, 2010), 417.

Figure 12.1 The Esther panel from the synagogue at Dura Europos.

There has been much debate regarding the existence of any unifying theme or themes within the synagogue paintings.[3] Jaś Elsner argues that the art of Dura Europos – not only in the synagogue, but in the Temple of Bel, the Mithraeum, and the Christian religious space, as well – was fundamentally an act of resistance against Roman cultural hegemony.[4] He argues that the Jewish space in particular exemplifies this resistance through its art. The art, he claims, serves as public broadcasts of Jewish texts and values, and along the way belittles the other religions found in the local environs.[5]

In constructing his argument, Elsner omits mention of the Esther panel, and it at first appears to contradict his thesis. Here, after all, is a picture which depicts a Jewish queen comfortably seated behind her Gentile husband on the right side of the panel. The queen's kinsman is seen triumphantly parading on a horse on the left side, depicting a story in which Jews did well in a foreign empire.[6] A closer look reveals details which appear

---

[3] For an overview with bibliography and a compelling suggestion, see Joseph Gutmann, "Early Synagogue and Jewish Catacomb Art and its Relation to Christian Art," *ANRW* ii.21/2 (1984), 1315–28. Hachlili's article provides a thorough survey of the interpretive options regarding the paintings as a group; see Hachlili, "The Dura-Europos Synagogue Wall Paintings," 403–20.

[4] Jaś Elsner, "Cultural Resistance and the Visual Image: The Case of Dura Europos," *Classical Philology* 96 (2001), 269–304, and esp. 281–99 on the synagogue.

[5] *Ibid.*, 299.

[6] The textual basis for this depiction (along with the textual bases for many of the other "frescoes" in the synagogue) has long been sought. The left half of the panel clearly refers to Esther 6, but the right half is enigmatic in its reference; for a theoretical discussion with references to literature on the subject, see Annabel Jane Wharton, "Good and Bad Images from the Synagogue of Dura Europos: Contexts, Subtexts, Intertexts," *Art History* 17 (1994), 1–25, esp. 11–18 on the Purim panel and a suggestion to read it "midrashically"; similarly in Annabel Jane Wharton, *Refiguring the Post Classical City: Dura Europos, Jerash, Jerusalem and Ravenna* (Cambridge University Press, 1995), 44–49; see also the discussion in Lee I. Levine, *The Ancient Synagogue: The First Thousand Years*, 2nd edn. (New Haven: Yale University Press, 2005), 252–56, as well as references in Gutmann, "Early Synagogue and Jewish Catacomb Art."

actually to confirm Elsner's hypothesis.[7] The most imposing figure is that of Mordecai on the left; Mordecai himself (like all the humans in the synagogue paintings) is shown frontally,[8] and he is riding a horse which is shown in profile. The various components of his attire are reflexes of standard Parthian artistic practices, and thus Mordecai is garbed as a proper Parthian nobleman. Haman, on the other hand, is depicted as a Roman charioteer, a character seemingly appropriate for one shown leading a horse. Dalia Levit-Tawil therefore suggested that this image is meant as "an allegory for the triumph of Persian-backed Jews over Rome."[9] The Persian king is depicted as fully in control on the right side, and if read as commentary on current events, this may suggest support for Shapur I.[10] Esther, positioned over the king's left shoulder, may then represent the supportive role that the Jews were prepared to play for the Persian monarch.

Far from challenging Elsner's thesis, then, the Purim panel seems to support it. The artist appears to have used the story of Esther as a vehicle to reflect on the Jews' position in contemporary society. There are enemies of the Jews, represented by Haman (the Roman), but these can be beaten and subordinated to the Jews with the support of the good Gentiles, represented by Ahasuerus (the Sasanian). The depiction of the monarch is striking, if he is represented as a positive figure in this painting; in much of rabbinic literature, he is condemned as a buffoon at best, and an illegitimate and wicked king at worst.[11] In third-century Syria, then, the story of Esther found new resonance.

One might object that this analysis presupposes something about how the Dura Europos paintings convey meaning. In particular, some of the foregoing assumes that the paintings can be read as reflecting on contemporary realities. There is a methodological question regarding how to

---

[7] For analyses of the depictions of the king and queen, see Dalia Levit-Tawil, "The Enthroned King Ahasuerus at Dura in Light of the Iconography of Kingship in Iran," *Bulletin of the American Schools of Oriental Research* 250 (1983), 57–78, and Dalia Levit-Tawil, "Queen Esther at Dura: Her Imagery in Light of Third-Century C.E. Oriental Syncretism," *Irano-Judaica* 4 (1999), 274–97; see also Narkiss, "סיפורי מגילת אסתר," 51–69.

[8] See Bernard Goldman, "A Dura-Europos Dipinto and Syrian Frontality," *Oriens Antiquus*, 24 (1985), 279–300; further, see Hachlili, *Ancient Jewish Art and Archaeology*, 177–78 with references.

[9] Dalia Tawil, "The Purim Panel in Dura in the Light of Parthian and Sasanian Art," *JNES* 38 (1979), 93–109; for a very different (and probably mistaken) view, see Shalom Sabar, "The Purim Panel at Dura: A Socio-Historical Interpretation," in Lee I. Levine and Zeev Weiss (eds.), *From Dura to Sepphoris: Studies in Jewish Art and Society in Late Antiquity JRS* Suppl. 40; Portsmouth, RI Journal of Roman Studies, 2000), 154–63.

[10] Gutmann, "Early Synagogue and Jewish Catacomb Art," 1326–27.

[11] For some sources and historical discussion, see Geoffrey Herman, "Ahasuerus, the Former Stable-Master of Belshazzar, and the Wicked Alexander of Macedon: Two Parallels between the Babylonian Talmud and Persian Sources," *AJS Review* 29 (2005), 283–97.

interpret this art. Clearly the paintings must be read as midrash, as fundamentally referential to the biblical stories and not to the real world.[12] This
does not exclude the power the art would have had for its contemporary
audiences because of particular resonances and allusions.[13] It may also be
noted that the *dipinto* under the queen labels her אסטיר "Esther";[14] perhaps
the phonetic spelling indicates that the painter of this *dipinto* has encountered Esther not textually, but orally. For such a community, living in exile
like Esther and hearing her tale of vindication, the story was a live one.

2. Canonization

In light of all that has been said in this chapter to this point, the most
difficult question may well be: how did Esther get into the canon of the
Hebrew Bible? Because so little is known about the canonization process,
there is no easy way to answer this question. It cannot be said with any
degree of certainty when the canonization of the entire Bible, much less of
any individual book, took place.[15]

---

[12] Joseph Gutmann, *Speculum*, 67 (1992), 504 (in a review of Kurt Weitzman and Herbert Kessler, *The Frescoes of the Dura Synagogue and Christian Art* [Washington, DC: Dumbarton Oaks, 1990]); see also Joseph Gutmann, "Introduction," in Joseph Gutmann (ed.), *The Dura-Europos Synagogue: A Re-Evaluation (1932–1992)*, South Florida Studies in the History of Judaism 25 (Atlanta: Scholars, 1992), xxiv.

[13] Martin S. Jaffee, "The Hermeneutical Model of Midrashic Studies: What it Reveals and What it Conceals," *Prooftexts*, 11 (1991), 67.

[14] See the reproduction in Hachlili, *Ancient Jewish Art and Archaeology in the Diaspora*, 405. For comments on the *dipinti* and their origins and functions, see Hachlili, "The Dura-Europos Synagogue Wall Paintings," 417.

[15] Josephus (*Against Apion* 1.37–41) writes that there are twenty-two sacred books. Many have assumed that there were therefore two books in the rabbinic Bible not in Josephus' Bible, but others have claimed that Judges and Ruth, and Jeremiah and Lamentations, were each counted as one. For references, discussion, and the latter position, see Sid Z. Leiman, "Josephus and the Canon of the Bible," in Louis H. Feldman and Gohei Hata (eds.), *Josephus, the Bible, and History* (Detroit: Wayne State University Press, 1989), 50–58, esp. 54. Josephus writes that "[f]rom Artaxerxes to our own time" (ἀπὸ δὲ Ἀρταξέρξου μέχρι τοῦ καθ' ἡμᾶς χρόνου) "the complete history has been written, but has not been deemed worthy of equal credit with the earlier records" – i.e., these later books are non-biblical. The question of whether the expression "from Artaxerxes to our own time" includes Artaxerxes' own time is of crucial importance, since, as Leiman notes, Josephus elsewhere (*Antiquities* 11.184) identifies the monarch in the Esther story as Artaxerxes. Although this phrase is in fact ambiguous, Bar-Kokhba claims that the first clause actually resolves this problem: ἀπὸ δὲ τῆς Μωυσέως τελευτῆς μέχρι Ἀρταξέρξου "from the death of Moses until *that of* Artaxerxes," explicitly including Artaxerxes' own time in the "biblical" era (Bar-Kokhba, "חג הפורים בימי הבית השני," 52 n. 52). On the other hand, John M. G. Barclay, *Against Apion*, Flavius Josephus: Translation and Commentary 10 (Leiden: Brill, 2007), 30 n. 163, notes that the text has been emended, and τῆς removed, by most twentieth-century scholars, based on the Latin. This then makes it seem that biblical history ends before Artaxerxes, although Barclay himself claims that it goes into his reign (to include Esther) but not to his death. Still, it must be said that all this relates only to the question of whether the text of Josephus *could* have

It may well be that the book of Esther can be helpful in conceptualizing this process. It appears to be all but impossible that Palestinian Jewish leaders would have stamped Esther with any sort of seal of approval. As we have seen, the intellectuals seem to have been alternately correcting, subverting, and ignoring the text. It is likely that a finer-grain analysis would allow us to see the differences within Palestinian Jewish society.[16] Rather than using a top-down approach, Esther's inclusion in the canon should probably be explained as a result of the popularity of Purim and the fact that it is a wonderful story, to which many people were drawn.[17]

Who were these people? One possibility is to look to the Diaspora. The community in Alexandria apparently liked the book.[18] It does not seem probable that the Masoretic canon is a product of the Alexandrian community, however, or of any Diaspora community. Another possibility, therefore, is to locate the origins of the book within Palestinian society, if groups not represented by the texts thus far surveyed can be identified.

The Pharisaic views on Esther may have been different from the reactions discussed in the previous chapters. Whereas the Hasmoneans, for example, drew their power from the priestly classes in Jerusalem, and the Qumran sect represented an extreme fringe worldview, the Pharisees may well have adopted a different attitude. For direct evidence of the practice of Purim within Pharisaic circles we are forced to wait until the first century CE. Such evidence comes in the form of a line in Megillat Ta'anit, which lists Purim among the festivals, to be celebrated on the 14th and 15th days of Adar. This text not only reveals the celebration of Purim, but shows that it was a relatively important festival. The text rules that on that day one is enjoined

---

Esther included in the biblical canon; there is still no evidence that he actually did so. The more popular view recently has certainly been that Josephus included Esther, but this cannot be proven (cf. Oppenheimer, "חג הפורים", 416, and Bar-Kokhba, "אהבת מרדכי ושנאת המן'? פורים בימי הבית השני ולאחריו", בימי הבית השני," 51–52 n. 51). For more on the ambiguities of Josephus' canon in the *Against Apion* passage, see Steve Mason, "Josephus and his Twenty-Two Book Canon," in Lee Martin McDonald and James A. Sanders (eds.), *The Canon Debate* (Peabody, MA: Hendrickson Publishers, 2002), 110–27.

[16] Leiman, *The Canonization of Hebrew Scripture*, 200–01 n. 634, argues that (a) the book is discussed as early as R. Zechariah b. ha-Kazzab (dated to the second half of the first century CE), (b) the Greek translation of 77 BCE "probably indicates" that the Hebrew was canonical by then, and (c) the exilic character of the book makes it unlikely that the book would have been canonized under the Hasmoneans, and that therefore (d) it was likely canonized in the early second-century BCE. I agree that (c) is intuitive; with (b) I disagree (see above); regarding (a) it should be noted that R. Zechariah only discusses details of the practice of reading Esther on Purim, and celebration of Purim need not presuppose the recognition of Esther as sacred scripture. The encyclopedic knowledge Leiman brings to the question is relevant here, because despite it he is compelled to admit that the evidence for canonization of Esther by even the first century CE is virtually non-existent.

[17] White Crawford, "Esther and Judith," 69.   [18] See Chapter 9 above.

not only "not to fast" (*de-la le-'it'ana'ah*), but also "not to eulogize" (*de-la le-misped*),[19] a status bequeathed upon only thirteen out of the forty days listed in the text.[20] Since the Pharisees and the Hasmoneans were at odds regarding a number of issues, especially matters of political-religious ideology,[21] it is not implausible that already a century or two before the composition of Megillat Ta'anit, the Pharisees had been celebrating Purim and, presumably, enjoying and sanctifying the book of Esther.[22] How widespread this may have been is unknown.

One way of approaching the history of Purim, even if only as a heuristically useful exercise, is to view the histories of Esther/Purim and Hanukka as mirror images of each other. The festival of Hanukka, founded by the Hasmoneans, underwent fundamental changes under Herod. First, Herod would have had little interest in celebrating the accomplishments of the Hasmoneans, whose position he usurped, or their Temple, which he rebuilt in far grander fashion.[23] Ideologically, as well, a celebration of a militant revolutionary independence movement would find no place within the ideology of Herodian acculturation and accommodation.

The reverse could be expected to occur in the history of Purim and its etiological narrative, Esther. For the Hasmoneans and their followers, many of its central themes were anathema, but for the Herodians (and perhaps the Pharisees), the themes of acculturation to the empire and cooperation with the imperial power were very attractive. Indeed, Herodian princesses such as Berenice and Drusilla were married repeatedly to foreign potentates; Esther may have served as a useful precedent for such actions.[24] The popularity of Esther in its "Masoretic" version may also have been promoted by the

---

[19] Text in Vered Noam, מגילת תענית: הנוסחים, פרשם, תולדותיהם, בצירוף מהדורה ביקורתית (Jerusalem: Yad Ben-Ẓvi, 2003), 47.

[20] Bar-Kokhba, "על חג הפורים ועל מקצת ממנהגי הסוכות בימי בית השני," 391.

[21] See esp. Schwartz, *Studies in the Jewish Background of Christianity*, 44–56; also James C. VanderKam, "The Pharisees and the Dead Sea Scrolls," in Jacob Neusner and Bruce D. Chilton (eds.), *In Quest of the Historical Pharisees* (Waco, TX: Baylor University Press, 2007), 225–36, esp. 228–32.

[22] Noam raises the possibility that the very fact that the festival is mentioned in Megillat Ta'anit may show that the book was not "biblical," since as a rule it is extra-biblical festivals which are enumerated (מגילת תענית, 303–04). She concludes, however, that this is not a necessary conclusion, and that Purim was included since it, too, was a day on which "miracles were done for Israel" (p. 304).

[23] See the detailed discussion of the fate of Herodian Hanukka and its reinterpretation in Moshe Benovitz, "הורדוס וחנוכה," *Zion* 68 (2003), 5–40.

[24] For a nuanced analysis of Herodian intermarriages, arguing that they may have been defensible, at least on some interpretations of Jewish law, see Eyal Regev, "Herod's Jewish Ideology Facing Romanization: On Intermarriage, Ritual Baths, and Speeches," *JQR* 100 (2010), 202–06. See also Eisenman and Wise, *The Dead Sea Scrolls Uncovered*, 101.

Pharisees. The Pharisees thrived under Herod,[25] who persecuted the Sadducees relentlessly, and perhaps here we see at least a faint trace of a line that can be drawn to connect the dots between the Pharisees in the Hasmonean era and the later Bible inherited by the Rabbis. Of course, Herod himself did not (I assume) have a hand in shaping the Bible, but as Marx said, "The ideas of the ruling class are in every epoch the ruling ideas, i.e. the class which is the ruling material force of society, is at the same time its ruling intellectual force."[26] The Herodian age, therefore, may be the appropriate time to locate the canonization of Esther.

Thus far I have tried to sketch a possible answer to the question of who in late Second Temple Palestine would have preserved and sanctified the book of Esther. If we move down in history, the terms of the question are fundamentally altered. After the destruction of the Temple, the line between "homeland" and "diaspora" was redefined. In this world, the heart of the homeland was destroyed, and even living in the homeland meant living under foreign rule. With the loss of the Temple, the dichotomy between Palestine and the Diaspora crumbled.[27] If the Jewish state no longer existed, all Jews essentially lived in the Diaspora.[28] Now a diaspora book was just what was needed, and Esther was available. It is possible that in this period, the Jews in Palestine searched their Scriptures for guidance as to how to live a religious life without a Temple, and found the model of Esther and Mordecai.

Evidence of a real shift in identity lines may be visible in the fact that in the Great Revolt of 67 CE, the Diaspora communities of Mesopotamia remained uninvolved,[29] but they participated in the Palestinian Jews' revolt against Trajan in 115–17.[30] This may indicate that there was a change in

---

[25] See Joachim Schaper, "The Pharisees," in William Horbury, W. D. Davies, and John Sturdy (eds.), *The Cambridge History of Judaism,* vol. III: *The Early Roman Period* (Cambridge University Press, 1999), 416–21.

[26] Karl Marx and Friedrich Engels, *The German Ideology, Part One: With Selections from Parts Two and Three, Together with Marx's "Introduction to a Critique of Political Economy",* ed. and intro. C. J. Arthur (New York: International Publishers, 1970), 64–65.

[27] See Martin Goodman, "Diaspora Reactions to the Destruction of the Temple," in James D. G. Dunn (ed.), *Jews and Christians: The Parting of the Ways, A.D. 70 to 135* (Tübingen: J. C. B. Mohr (P. Siebeck), 1992), 27–38, but note that in his work, "Diaspora" = "Western Diaspora." I am indebted to a suggestion by my student Nadav Recca regarding the loss of the Temple for sharpening my thought on this issue.

[28] Schwartz, "How at Home were the Jews of the Hellenistic Diaspora?," 357.

[29] The sole exception was the Jews of Adiabene, noted by Josephus, *Jewish War,* 2.520; see also 2.388–89. See Martin Goodman, "Trajan and the Origins of Roman Hostility to the Jews," *Past & Present* 182 (2004), 9.

[30] The latter Jewish revolt may show that the communities in the western Diaspora (Alexandria, Cyprus, Cyrene), Palestine, and Mesopotamia were in ideological, and perhaps even operational, cooperation, but this is not certain, owing to the many more basic uncertainties surrounding this

relations among Jews throughout the region in the late first century CE. The process may have begun earlier, however. Already in the last century of the Second Temple era, world Jewry seems to have begun to see Jerusalem not just as a political capital of a Levantine state, but as the symbolic center of Judaism. In the first part of the first century CE, with the Temple still standing, Philo of Alexandria wrote that Jerusalem "is my home, and it is the capital not of the single country of Judea, but of most other countries also."[31]

This process of making Jerusalem the capital of world Jewry was primarily the work of Herod and his grandson, Agrippa. Herod's international outlook encouraged him to look to the Jews throughout the eastern Mediterranean and the Near East for support. His construction projects gave those supporters physical results on the ground to which they could point, or even make pilgrimage, with pride.[32] Agrippa continued these policies, acting as the political representation of Jewish populations everywhere. When this Judean king visited the city of Alexandria, he was received there as "king of the Jews"; he also argued on behalf of the Alexandrian Jews at the Roman court.[33] Other first-century sources describe pilgrimage to Jerusalem from around the world.[34] In the west, Jewish names in first-century Cyrene, Libya, included Judah, Simon, Elazar, and Jonathan, revealing that community's affinity for the nationalist Hasmoneans.[35] In the east, the Mesopotamian Jewish community is said to have had a close

revolt. According to T. D. Barnes, "Trajan and the Jews," *JRS* 40 (1989), 145–62, the revolt was sparked by Trajan's Parthian campaign, making the Mesopotamian connection less surprising. On the other hand, William Horbury, "The Beginnings of the Jewish Revolt under Trajan," in Peter Schäfer (ed.), *Geschichte – Tradition – Reflexion: Festschrift für Martin Hengel zum 70. Geburtstag* (Tübingen: J. C. B. Mohr (Paul Siebeck), 1996), vol. 1, 283–304, sees a messianic component to the revolt, and Goodman, "Trajan and the Origins of Roman Hostility to the Jews," 25–26, links it to frustration over the prolonged inability to rebuild the Temple. If the latter is correct, the involvement of Jews in the western Diaspora is understood, but that of Jews of the eastern Diaspora remarkable.

[31] Philo, *Legatio*, §§281–82.

[32] For a discussion of Herod in this regard, see Peter Richardson, *Herod: King of the Jews and Friend of the Romans* (Minneapolis: Fortress, 1999), 264–72.

[33] Menachem Stern, "The Jewish Diaspora," in Shmuel Safrai and Menachem Stern in co-operation with David Flusser and W. C. van Unnik (eds.), *The Jewish People in the First Century: Historical Geography, Political History, Social, Cultural and Religious Life and Institutions*, CRINT 1.1 (Philadelphia: Fortress, 1974), 122–33.

[34] Acts 2:9–11; Josephus, *War*, 7.43. See Shmuel Safrai, "Relations between the Diaspora and the Land of Israel," in Shmuel Safrai and Menachem Stern in co-operation with David Flusser and W. C. van Unnik (eds.), *The Jewish People in the First Century: Historical Geography, Political History, Social, Cultural and Religious Life and Institutions*, CRINT 1.1 (Philadelphia: Fortress, 1974), 195–98.

[35] Stern, "The Jewish Diaspora," 134. Recall, too, that earlier, Jason of Cyrene had written the five-volume chronicle of the Hasmomeans which, in condensed form, has survived as 2 Maccabees.

relationship with Agrippa's grandfather Herod; the first high priest appointed by Herod was Hananel, a Babylonian.[36]

Throughout the Diaspora, the "half-shekel" was collected in every city; apparently, huge sums of money were brought in from all regions in which Jews lived, including Babylonia.[37] These donations funded not only the sacrifices, but also the upkeep of Jerusalem, increasing the Diaspora Jews' attachment to that city. They were conceived of as a real tax, not a gift. All Jews were citizens of world Jewry, and like all citizens, they contributed to their capital, in this case Jerusalem.[38] Naturally, after 70, Jews everywhere were subject to the "Jewish tax" imposed by the Romans.[39]

All this is to say that the transition of homeland–diaspora relations in the Jewish world was not only the result of the cataclysmic event of 70. Rather, it was a transition that was a century in the making. Gradually, Jews had developed a self-consciousness as a people which transcended geographical borders. It was, until 70, a self-consciousness centered on Jerusalem. With the loss of that center in 70, and then, even more traumatically, the expulsion from Judea in the wake of the Bar Koseba revolt in 135, the transition took a slightly different turn. Rather than all Jews being citizens of Jerusalem, all Jews, including those in Jerusalem, were diaspora Jews. They all had to struggle, as a people, to navigate a world ruled by others. In this world, Esther was the perfect biblical book.

---

[36] Stern, "The Jewish Diaspora," 172.
[37] Josephus, *Antiquities* 18:312–13; see Safrai, "Relations between the Diaspora and the Land of Israel," 189–91.
[38] Safrai, "Relations between the Diaspora and the Land of Israel," 191.
[39] Stern, "The Jewish Diaspora," 133.

PART 4

Rabbinic readings
Moving Esther from the periphery to the center

CHAPTER 13

Introduction to the rabbinic literature on Esther

Before examining in detail the ways in which rabbinic literature interpreted and grappled with Esther, a word is in order regarding this literature. The texts to be discussed originated in various regions of the world – from Mesopotamia to Western Europe, from various eras – from the third through the eleventh centuries CE, and consist of various genres – biblical translations, legal literature, homiletics, and commentaries. Despite this wide variety regarding so many factors, there is still an obvious and deep continuity that runs throughout the entire body of literature called "rabbinic."

The rabbinic exegetical literature that is the raw material for Chapters 14 and 15 is found to some extent in the literature of the Tannaim – the Rabbis in Roman Palestine, primarily in the second century CE – but far more in the literature produced by their successors, the Amoraim, and even later heirs to the rabbinic traditions.

Babylonian Esther Midrash

In Babylonia, this literature was produced from the third century through the seventh century or so, and is preserved in the Babylonian Talmud, known as the Bavli. Extraordinarily, the Bavli preserves a running midrashic commentary on Esther – possibly the only such running midrash in the Bavli[1] – known now as the "Babylonian Esther Midrash."[2] It is not only that the midrash is preserved in the Bavli, but that it is Babylonian in origin: the

---

[1] The only possible additional example is the lengthy discussion in b. Sotah 11b–13a on Exodus 1–2; this is embedded in a longer biblically oriented discussion, on which see Günter Stemberger, "Midrasch in Babylonien, am Beispiel von Sota 9b–14a," *Henoch*, 10 (1988), 183–203.

[2] See Eliezer Segal, *The Babylonian Esther Midrash*, vol.1, 1: "there is nothing else [in the Bavli] that compares with the scope of the present work." For Babylonian midrash, and its relationship to it Palestinian predecessors, see Joseph Heinemann, אגדות ותולדותיהן: עיונים בהשתלשלותן של מסורות (Jerusalem: Keter, 1974), 163–79, and Eliezer Segal, *From Sermon to Commentary: Expounding the*

most important characters in the midrash are Rav, Samuel, and Rava.[3] Besides this concentrated text, there are also many references to, and comments on, the book of Esther scattered through the rest of the Bavli which originated in disparate times and places but which found their way into this sixth- or seventh-century work.

In general, it is not possible to be certain regarding the reliability of the Bavli's attributions of individual comments to particular rabbis. There is a voluminous literature on this subject.[4] I have followed the position that I judge to be the most reasonable: although the attributions cannot be taken as entirely reliable, they represent a good-faith effort on the part of the Rabbis to record the genealogy of various statements. Confusion between closely related rabbinic authorities no doubt was common, but dismissing the attributions altogether is an exaggerated response to these problems.

Eretz Israel Midrashim

From the west, we have, first, the legal literature of the Mishnah, Tosefta, and Palestinian Talmud (the Yerushalmi), which contains numerous comments on Esther. Richer as sources for interpretations are numerous midrashic collections, which are more numerous for the book of Esther than for any other book of the Bible. These have been expertly surveyed, with

---

Bible in Talmudic Babylonia, Études sur le christianisme et le judaïsme 17 (Waterloo, Ontario: Wilfrid Laurier University Press for the Canadian Corporation for Studies in Religion, 2005), 1–8 and *passim*, and the references throughout.

[3] See the thorough discussion of the sources of this midrash in Avraham Weiss, על היצירה הספרותית של האמוראים (New York: 'Horev' Yeshiva University, 1962), 276–294, who emphasizes that the Bavli had radically reformed the Palestinian sources at its disposal. Segal (*The Babylonian Esther Midrash*, vol. III, 256–59) also catalogs and discusses the Babylonian elements in the Midrash. Furthermore, recent studies of this text by Börner-Klein and Bodendorfer have done much to demonstrate the "Diaspora" nature of the midrashic readings therein. See Dagmar Börner-Klein, *Eine babylonische Auslegung der Ester-Geschichte: Der Midrasch in Megilla 10b–17a*, Judentum und Umwelt 30 (Frankfurt am Main: Peter Lang, 1991), esp. 271–74 (with a comparison to bSot 9b–14a); Gerhard Bodendorfer, "Der Babylonische Ester-Midrasch: Diaspora 'positiv denken', ohne sie zu verklären," *Kirche und Israel*, 18 (2003), 134–49; Gerhard Bodendorfer, "Die Diaspora, die Juden und die 'Anderen,'" in Ekkehard W. Stegemann and Klaus Wengst (eds.), *"Eine Grenze hast Du gesetzt": Edna Brocke zum 60. Geburtstag* (Stuttgart: Kohlhammer, 2003), 193–214. Note the programmatic statement of Bodendorfer, "Die Diaspora," 194: "In bMegilla 10b–17a schließlich hat ein Redaktor – vielleicht im 6. Jh. n. – eine Fülle von Materialien aus babylonischen und palästinischen Quellen aufgenommen, um daraus ein Kunstwerk eines Diasporamidrash zu schaffen, der die Frage der jüdischen Identität in der 'Fremde' beantworten sollte."

[4] See the references in the first footnotes of Sacha Stern, "Attribution and Authorship in the Babylonian Talmud," *JJS* 45 (1994), 28–29, and Yaakov Elman, "How Should a Talmudic Intellectual History be Written? A Response to David Kraemer's *Responses* (Review of *Responses to Suffering in Classical Rabbinic Literature* by David Kraemer)," *JQR* 89 (1999), 371–82.

detailed textual discussions, by M. B. Lerner,[5] so a brief overview of only the major midrashim preserved on Esther will suffice here.

1. Esther Rabbah

The fullest midrash on Esther, this text was shown by Zunz and Albeck to be actually a fusion of an ancient midrash and later additions to it. The ancient midrash (essentially the first part of the text, sections 1–5, plus some passages from the latter half, covering only through Esther 4:7)[6] is a classical midrashic text, and thus dates probably to the sixth century CE. The additions, on the other hand, which draw on later midrashim as well as the tenth-century chronicler Yosippon, date from no earlier than the eleventh century and possibly as late as the thirteenth.

The ancient midrash is full of "proems" (*petiḥta'ot*), like all classical midrashim. In these introductory sections, various Rabbis introduce the book, or a section of the book, through citation of various biblical passages. The significance of recognizing the late additions may be illustrated with a single example. As already discussed, the dream in the Greek Addition A portrays the two as mighty dragons, engaged in such combat as threatens to destroy the entire world.[7] This dream found its way, through the Latin Vulgate, into medieval Hebrew literature when it was translated and included in the tenth-century chronicle Yosippon. From there, it was brought back into midrashic literature, appearing in the second half of Esther Rabbah.[8]

2. Abba Gurion

Extant in numerous manuscripts, and edited in the late nineteenth century by Solomon Buber, Abba Gurion is later than Esther Rabbah but, perhaps because of its relative brevity, was more popular than the earlier and longer midrash.[9] Bialik showed that this was probably not an original midrash at all, but instead an eclectic work of probably no later than the tenth century,

[5] Myron Bialik Lerner, "The Works of Aggadic Midrash and the Esther Midrashim," in Shmuel Safrai, Zeev Safrai, Joshua Schwartz, and Peter J. Tomson (eds.), *The Literature of the Sages, Second Part: Midrash and Targum, Liturgy, Poetry, Mysticism, Contracts, Inscriptions, Ancient Science, and the Languages of Rabbinic Literature* (Assen and Minneapolis: Van Gorcum and Fortress, 2006), 176–229.

[6] See esp. *ibid.*, 181–82, for an exact delineation of the components of the text.

[7] See above, Chapter 9.

[8] For this process of transmission, see Atzmon, "חלום מרדכי: מהוספה למדרש," 127–40, and Tabory, "השפעת תרגום השבעים למגילת אסתר על הספרות הרבנית," 485–502.

[9] Lerner, "The Works of Aggadic Midrash," 190–91.

with short comments borrowed from Esther Rabbah and Panim Aherot B (see below), and longer sections taken from midrashim now lost.[10] Despite this derivative nature of the work, it is valuable since the original sources are often no longer extant.

3. Panim Aḥerot B

MS Oxford-Bodleian 155, which Solomon Buber used as his base text for Abba Gurion, follows that text with other midrashic texts, each introduced by the copyist with the phrase *panim aḥerot* "another version." This infelicitous title was then copied by Buber;[11] we were bequeathed numerous texts with the name "Panim Aḥerot," and given little choice but then to number them sequentially. Panim Aḥerot A is not a full midrash, but a homiletic essay; Panim Aḥerot B, on the other hand, is an important early midrash on Esther 1–7. It likely dates from the seventh century CE.[12]

4. Pirqe de-Rabbi Eliezer

While not a midrash on Esther per se, Pirqe de-Rabbi Eliezer, an eighth-century work from Eretz Israel,[13] retells the story of Esher and Mordecai, richly embellished aggadically, in chapter 49 of the work.

Targum

Many exegetical traditions about Esther are also found in the rich Targumic literature to the book. The Targum, an Aramaic elaboration of the biblical text, was recited in the synagogue along with biblical readings.[14] Because of its public nature, and the popularity of Esther, there are numerous manuscripts of Targum to Esther preserved. For good reason, these are seen as representing two Targumic traditions; among Targumic fragments that have been preserved in the Cairo Geniza and published in recent years there may be evidence of yet another tradition. The Targumim on Esther are suffused with midrashic additions and interpretations. Again, reliable surveys of this literature exist, in Alexander's article in the *Anchor Bible*

---

[10] *Ibid.*, 192.   [11] Although not entirely accurately; see *ibid.*, 195–96.   [12] *Ibid.*, 201.

[13] See the discussion of Moshe David Herr, "Pirkei de-Rabbi Eliezer," in Fred Skolnik (ed.), *Encyclopaedia Judaica*, 2nd edn., (Detroit: Macmillan Reference USA in association with the Keter Publishing House, 2007), vol. XVI, 182–83.

[14] For introductions and overviews of Targumic literature, see Philip S. Alexander, "Targum, Targumim," *ABD*, vol. VI, 320–31.

Dictionary and in Grossfeld's translation of both major traditions,[15] so only brief remarks are necessary here.

1. Targum Rishon

The large number of midrashic interpretations in this text are mostly woven into the translation itself, rather than standing outside the Aramaic rendering of the text.[16] Bernard Grossfeld published a critical edition of this Targum, together with a translation, from MS Paris 110,[17] and the translation of a different manuscript (Madrid 116-Z40) is available in Grossfeld's *Two Targums of Esther*.

The language of the Targum is Late Jewish Literary Aramaic, and therefore is not really of assistance in assigning a provenance or specific date to the text. It is accepted that it was composed in Eretz Israel – along with most expansive Targumim – and guesses for the date range over the sixth, seventh, and eighth centuries CE. Given the nature of the Targum, it is difficult to know whether this was intended for liturgical use or was only of literary nature.[18] This question has implications for the dating (or may depend on the dating), since the use of Aramaic as a functional language among the Jews in Eretz Israel declined beginning with the Islamic conquest.

2. Targum Sheni

This Targum, too, was published by Bernard Grossfeld, on the basis of MS Sassoon 282, the oldest known manuscript,[19] and has been the subject of a number of insightful studies, most recently that by Beate Ego.[20] The literary form and exegetical nature of the text were studied systematically by Robert

---

[15] *Ibid.*, vol. VI, 328, on the Esther Targumim; Bernard Grossfeld, *The Two Targums of Esther: Translated, with Apparatus and Notes*, Aramaic Bible 18 (Collegeville, MN: Liturgical Press, 1991), 1–25.

[16] See Arnon Atzmon, "התרגום לאסתר: התרגום המדרשי או המדרש התרגומי?," *HUCA* 80 (2009), ט.

[17] Bernard Grossfeld, *The First Targum to Esther: According to the MS Paris Hebrew 110 of the Bibliotheque Nationale* (New York: Sepher-Hermon, 1983).

[18] Atzmon, "התרגום לאסתר," יג.

[19] Bernard Grossfeld, *The Targum Sheni to the Book of Esther: A Critical Edition Based on MS Sassoon 282 with Critical Apparatus* (New York: Sepher-Hermon, 1994).

[20] See esp. Beate Ego, *Targum Scheni zu Esther: Übersetzung, Kommentar und theologische Deutung* (Tübingen: Mohr Siebeck, 1996), and Beate Ego, "All Kingdoms and Kings Trembled before Him: The Image of King Solomon in Targum Sheni on Megillat Esther," *Journal of the Aramaic Bible*, 3 (2001), 57–73.

Hayward.[21] Atzmon showed that in this Targum, the midrashic interpretations are often set apart from the translation proper, and speculated that the
translation may have first circulated, as a relatively straightforward Targum,
without the midrashic additions.[22] Indeed, the sources of this Targum have
long been sought, and dates for the text range from the fourth century to the
eleventh century, primarily on the basis of different estimations regarding
literary dependencies.[23] It has been argued that Midrash Panim Aḥerot B
served as a source for this Targum,[24] but this means only that the Targum
Sheni, like the Targum Rishon, likely dates from no earlier than the seventh
century.

3. Fragments

Remains of what may be a third Targumic tradition, preserved in the Cairo
Geniza, have been published in recent years.[25] These contain aggadic
material not found in the other extant Targumim, and have provided us
with further information about the lore that circulated about Esther in late
Byzantine and early Islamic Palestine.

Liturgical poems

Also of use for discerning what tales Jews were telling about Esther over the
course of the first millennium CE are liturgical poems. Many such poems
were preserved in the Cairo Geniza,[26] and these can be mined for the
information they preserve.

Conclusion regarding "rabbinic" texts

As can be seen from the above survey, the various texts utilized here are not
all "rabbinic" in the sense of having been composed formally by Rabbis.

---

[21] Robert Hayward, "Targum a Misnomer for Midrash? Towards a Typology for the Targum Sheni of
Esther," *Aramaic Studies*, 9 (2011), 47–63, and Robert Hayward, "Profile Targum Esther Sheni,
Excerpt from: *Database of Anonymous and Pseudepigraphic Jewish Literature of Antiquity, c. 200 BCE to c.
700 CE*, ed. A. Samely, R. Bernasconi, P. Alexander, and R. Hayward," *Aramaic Studies*, 9 (2011),
65–82.

[22] Atzmon, "התרגום לאסתר, יד."   [23] See Grossfeld, *The Two Targums*, 19–21.

[24] Atzmon, התרגום לאסתר, יא."

[25] Rimon Kasher and Michael L. Klein. "New Fragments of Targum to Esther from the Cairo Geniza,"
HUCA 61 (1990), 89–124; Avraham Tal, "קטעי תרגום אסתר מן הגניזה והעדות שהם מעידים," in
Moshe Bar-Asher and Hayyim E. Cohen (eds.), *Mas'at Ahron: Studies Presented to Ahron Dotan*
(Jerusalem: Bialik, 2010), 139–71.

[26] See esp. Yahalom and Sokoloff, שירת בני מערבא.

The Talmudim of course were, as were the midrashim. The Targumim, however, have their origins in the synagogues of Byzantine-era Palestine, as do the liturgical poems. These last two categories further differ in being anonymous, and are also performative in origin, rather than literary (although see above regarding the Targum).

The dates of these texts vary, too, from Amoraic times, and earlier for some of the traditions preserved within the classical rabbinic texts, to nearly a millennium later. Thus, we have interpretations and views from the second to the thirteenth centuries, and texts from the sixth through the thirteenth. Geographically, the range is also disturbingly large, stretching from Mesopotamia to Spain.

Despite these many variables and differences, however, it will be seen in the ensuing discussion that the commonalities within this literature far outweigh the differences detectable therein. In the footnotes, references will be given to the various texts being drawn upon, and even when a particular motif appears in one text or another, and not widely, it will be evident that it is part of an approach to the book of Esther that spanned what appears to be the expanse of Jewish culture for a thousand years.

One final note on this issue needs to be sounded. It has, in past years, become fashionable to cast the rabbis as interlopers within first-millennium CE Jewish society. Clearly, there were (as there always are) gaps between the religious elites and the populace at large. On the other hand, a study such as this one, surveying the exegetical traditions explicit in rabbinic texts and implicit in more popular texts such as Targumim and liturgical poems, can show that these gaps did not extend to the way in which Jews read the biblical books or the religious values that animated that reading.

CHAPTER 14

Biblicizing Esther

In discussing the effects of canonization on how people read a book, Moshe Halbertal observes that such a context affects the assumptions readers bring to the book. A *biblical* book can no longer be different; it can no longer stand outside the body of tradition. "When [a book] was introduced into the body of Scriptures, however, it was required to give up its unique and heretical message. The moment it became part of the scriptural canon, the exegete was obligated to make it consistent with the rest of the Scriptures. The new reading means that the original meaning will be lost."[1] This section will trace the dynamics of this process within rabbinic readings of Esther. The Rabbis faced all the same problems with the book that their predecessors had faced: a lack of religious observance, lack of God, lack of nationalism; there was also the overriding problem of the place of the book within the biblical canon. It is no surprise, therefore, that there is more exegetical literature devoted to Esther in the rabbinic corpus than to any other biblical book except for Genesis.

The book of Esther appears to be so vastly different from the rest of the biblical books that it is difficult to conceive of it as speaking in the same voice as the rest of the Bible. This point will immediately provide one key to understanding some of the rabbinic readings of the book: the Rabbis read the Bible as a single book, not as a collection of books. This necessitated a certain mode of reading, and led to a presumption that there would not be a chasm of difference between texts within the Bible.

Two aspects of rabbinic exegetical literature will be especially emphasized in this chapter and the next one, because these are underappreciated. First, the Rabbis did not consistently read atomistically, and in fact often are seen to be reading and commenting on larger literary units. In our case, much of the rabbinic attention will be directed to the broad themes of Esther as a

---

[1] Moshe Halbertal, *People of the Book* (Cambridge, MA: Harvard University Press, 1997), 24. My thanks to Ari Mermelstein for reminding me of the relevance of Halbertal's discussion for my own analysis.

whole. This is, of course, not to exclude atomistic readings, which certainly exist in abundance, but it is to focus our attention on the fact that the Rabbis were attuned to broader issues, as well.

Second, much of the rabbinic interpretation is not focused on the relevance of the biblical text for the Rabbis' own time. Although, once again, there are of course such contemporizing readings within rabbinic literature, much of their exegesis is academic in nature: they are interested in interpreting the Bible, as a whole and in all its details, for the sake of plumbing the meaning of the sacred texts. Let us now turn to the details, and see how the Rabbis re-read Esther as part of the canon.

1. Esther as part of the grand biblical story

In a story told in both the Yerushalmi and the Bavli, we read that the Rabbis wanted to include the book of Esther in their collection of sacred scriptures, but felt legally constrained to reject it. "Esther wrote to the Sages, 'Enshrine me forever.' They responded, 'Have I not written thrice for you' (Proverbs 22:20) – thrice, but not four times!" In the end, however, they relented; the book was able to be included after the Rabbis found biblical evidence that the narrative belonged. They expounded the verse "The Lord said to Moses, write this, a remembrance, in the book" (Exodus 17:14) in a way that foretold three *future* iterations of the war between Israel and Amalek. The three would be found throughout the Bible, one in the Torah, one in the Prophets, and one in the Writings. The inclusion of Esther in the Writings is therefore necessary, to fulfill the triple prophecy of Exodus.[2]

In other words, the inclusion of the book of Esther within Scripture depends on our being able to find Scriptural license for it. Here the Rabbis are grappling, nearly explicitly, with the claim that Esther cannot be a biblical book because it is so un-biblical. The book can be granted admittance to the Bible only if it can be shown that the Bible itself licensed the inclusion of a book of this sort. Esther can be biblical only if the Bible recognizes Esther.[3]

---

[2] B. Megillah 7a; cf. the slightly different version in y. Megillah 1:5 (70d), where the emphasis appears to be on the problematics of new *commandments* (my thanks to Moshe Bernstein for emphasizing this difference).

[3] A different motif, present elsewhere (see, e.g., y. Megillah 1:5 (70d); cf. b. Megillah 7a), has the discussion revolve around the question of preserving bad national memories. For some discussion of this text with historical comments, see Joseph Tabory, מועדי ישראל בתקופת המשנה והתלמוד (Jerusalem: Magnes, 1995), 324; see also Dov Herman, "מתי נכללה מגילת אסתר בכתבי הקדש?," 326–28.

To put it differently, we might say that the Sages here pose the question: was the "biblical age" not over before Esther's time? Was there really room for another book in the canon? A different midrash makes this concern explicit, and even claims that this anxiety over whether the story of Esther was truly like other biblical stories was actually a concern of Mordecai himself: "[Mordecai] said: 'I am not moving from here [from the gate of the king, wearing sackcloth and ashes], until God performs miracles for me like he did in the past!"[4]

The notion that Esther is, so to speak, "post-biblical" does not appear to have been a chronological one. According to the Rabbis, the book of Ezra-Nehemiah dates from even later than Esther, and yet its place in the Bible was never questioned.[5] The objection to Esther is not that the book is too late, but that it simply does not belong. It is a book that seems to stand outside of the biblical tradition, outside of the commonalities that make the Bible into a cohesive collection.

Shlomo Dov Goitein observed that all the narratives in the Bible seem to tell a single epic story: "how the Israelites received the land of Israel, how they lost the Land, and how they returned and received the Land again." "Esther," he noted, "does not fit this framework at all."[6] The biblical narrative centers on the Land, God, Temple, and political autonomy. Esther seemingly acknowledges none of these themes, and therefore would seem to have no place in the Bible. The Talmudic texts just cited, therefore, are to be read as the Rabbis searching for a way to see Esther as part of the grand story which comprises the Bible. If Esther can be found to be referred to in earlier parts of Scripture, then it cannot be un-biblical. Scripture must tell one story, and Esther must somehow be part of that story.

These texts tell that the Rabbis succeeded in inserting Esther into the biblical framework by seeing her story as another example, destined to be the final one, of the abiding conflict between Israel and Amalek. In some midrashim, this conflict is traced back to the conflict between Jacob, ancestor of Israel, and Esau, ancestor of Amalek (Genesis 32:16). Haman is linked to Esau not only by blood, but by attitude and by a particular verb:

---

[4] Panim Aherot B, p. 35b.

[5] Similarly, the rabbinically instituted law of lighting Hanukkah candles was never challenged on the grounds that new laws are not allowed, as observed by Isaac Boaz Gottlieb, "המדרש על :"ונהפוך הוא" עיוני מקרא ופרשנות, כרך ח: מגילת אסתר," in Shmuel Vargon, Amos Frisch, and Moshe Rahimi (eds.), מנחות ידידות והוקרה לאלעזר טויטו (Ramat Gan and Elkanah: Bar Ilan University Press and Mikhlelet Orot, 2008), 131. See, however, the question (b. Shabbat 23a) regarding the *blessing* recited when lighting the Hanukkah candles: "Where were we commanded?"

[6] Goitein, עיונים במקרא: בחינתו הספרותית והחברתית, 59.

"just as Esau 'disdained' (*va-yivez*) so too his descendant Haman 'disdained' (*va-yivez*)." Indeed, the word *va-yivez* appears only twice in the Hebrew Bible, once in Genesis 25:34 regarding Esau and once in Esther 3:6 regarding Haman. The midrash argues that this links the two through time, by virtue of their ties of blood and attitude.

More usual in the rabbinic texts is the view that the conflict with Amalek is a story that began not with Esau but with the war in Exodus 17; it then continued in Deuteronomy 25 with the injunction never to forget what Amalek did to Israel, was picked up again in the story of Saul's war against Amalek in 1 Samuel 15, and found its conclusion with the annihilation of the family of Agagites in Esther.

By making Esther a final component in the enduring war between Israel and Amalek, the Rabbis have reframed the question of Esther's place within the biblical narrative, and opened the door for Esther's inclusion there.[7] The conflict with Amalek is itself part of a larger theme in the Bible, since the war that Israel is commanded to wage against Amalek is tied to the conquest of the Land.[8] There is, therefore, an obvious irony in the claim that the war against Amalek was completed outside the land of Israel, in Persia. This entirely re-orients the story of Esther. Rather than being a diaspora story, it is, as the climax of this conflict, what allows the Jews to re-enter the land of Israel. Amalek has been scattered throughout the world, and in order to eradicate them, Israel must follow them to the ends of the earth. Having done so, the Jews can resume their saga, which is continued with the stories of Ezra and Nehemiah and the return to the land.[9]

A related strand of midrashic thought is the claim that the threat by Xerxes and Haman is just another one in a series of threats to Jewish existence, spanning the centuries and foretold long ago. There are numerous rabbinic texts that broach this issue: they desire to show that the threat

---

[7] For a similar approach to some of these texts, see Gottlieb, "המדרש על מגילת אסתר": "ונהפוך הוא"," 132. One midrash uses the Amalek connection to explain why Esther postponed the fateful encounter one final day, to the second banquet: "All descendants of Amalek are accustomed to falling on the next day." For this the midrash quotes Exodus 17:9 – the war of Moses and Joshua against Amalek, which took place "on the morrow" – and 1 Samuel 9:16 – the anointment of Saul, who would fight against the Amalekites, and which also took place "on the morrow."

[8] Deuteronomy 25:19: "When the Lord your God gives you security from all your enemies roundabout, in the land which the Lord your God is giving you as an inheritance, erase the memory of Amalek." See also the formulation of Maimonides, Laws of Kings and their Wars, 1:1: "Israel was commanded three commandments when they entered the land . . . to destroy the seed of Amalek."

[9] See above, Chapter 10.

of Haman and the salvation wrought by Esther and Mordecai fit seamlessly into the broad sweep of Jewish history.[10]

In a different way, the same claim was made of Xerxes: he represents, in many texts, one of the "four kingdoms." The motif of the four kingdoms, which dates back to Hesiod in the eighth century, finds its biblical expression in the book of Daniel (chapters 2 and 7). The Rabbis found hints of this scheme throughout the Bible, however, and Xerxes and the events of the book of Esther are often named as one of the kingdoms.[11] Contextualizing Xerxes as one of the four kingdoms foretold long earlier has the effect of reducing him to a type, rather than allowing him to stand as a unique and unprecedented type of threat, and of asserting that he is not the first or the last to threaten Israel, but, like the rest, will be overcome.

All of the texts seen in this chapter to this point appear to be responding to the same fundamental problem, of which the Rabbis were acutely aware: Esther is, in many ways, different from the rest of the Bible. The story does not involve God, the land of Israel, or Jewish law or teachings, making its claim to be "biblical" a difficult one. The Rabbis overcame these problems in various ways, and redeemed Esther by reading numerous other biblical texts as referring to it. God had planned for Esther from the beginning of time, and had even prepared the method by which to save the Jews from him. Haman is not *sui generis*, but one in a long list of adversaries, and

---

[10] This is, for instance, the theme of an Aramaic poem from Byzantine-era Palestine; here the final event in Jewish history narrated is the story of Esther, but oddly enough, Esther, Mordecai, Xerxes, and Haman are not in the story. Instead, the story is told as a clash between Shimshai the scribe, known from Ezra 4:8 and taken here (as elsewhere) to be Haman's son, and God: Shimshai the scribe arose / himself greatly enriched // He paid ten thousand/ to destroy the nation enriched. // The sculptor took his money / and sunk his ship // He jumbled his end / and his body was crucified" (Yahalom and Sokoloff, שירת בני מערבא, 170–74). Other relevant texts include Esther Rabbah 10:13, Esther Rabbah Petiḥtot §10, Bereshit Rabbah 30:8 (Julius Theodor and Hanokh Albeck, על פי כתבי מדרש בראשית רבא: יד ועפ"י דפוסי המדרש הראשונים, 3 vols. [Berlin: Itskovski, 1912–29, reprinted Jerusalem: Wahrmann, 1965], 273ff. – on which see Eliezer Lorne Segal, "'The Same from Beginning to End': On the Development of a Midrashic Homily," *JJS* 32 [1981], 158–65), Esther Rabbah 9:2, Esther Rabbah Petiḥtot §4; b. Megillah 11a, Esther Rabbah Petiḥtot §12, b. Megillah 13b, Targum Rishon on 3:9, and b. Megillah 16a.

[11] For a general discussion of this motif in rabbinic literature, see Rivkah Raviv, "השפעתו של ספר דניאל על פרשנות המקרא של חז"ל," in Shmuel Vargon, Amos Frisch, and Moshe Rahimi (eds.), עיוני מקרא ופרשנות ח: מנ ידות והוקרה לאלעזר טויטו (Ramat Gan and Elkanah: Bar Ilan University Press and Mikhlelet Orot, 2008), 100–05. For some of the interesting vicissitudes of the motif within midrashim on Esther, see Joseph Tabory, "פתיחות רב ושמואל למדרש 'מגילת אסתר," in David Golinkin, Moshe Benovitz, Mordechai Akiva Friedman, Menachem Schmelzer, and Daniel Sperber (eds.), Torah Li-Shma: Essays in Jewish Studies in Honor of Professor Shamma Friedman (Jerusalem: Bar Ilan University Press, Jewish Theological Seminary of America, and Mekhon Schechter, 2008), 492–99. See Bereshit Rabbah 44:12 (Raviv, "השפעתו של ספר דניאל על פרשנות המקרא של חז"ל," 103–05), Panim Aherot B, p. 28a, and the Byzantine-era Aramaic poem in Yahalom and Sokoloff, שירת בני מערבא, 192 (esp. lines 8–13).

possibly just one in a series of iterations of the war against Amalek. In some fashion, Esther has been brought into the fold, and takes its place in the grand saga that is biblical history.

There is an important difference between the general claim that Haman was one of many and the specific claim that Haman was an iteration of the conflict with Esau/Amalek. The difference is not so much an exegetical one as a political one. In the invocation of Esau, it is impossible not to also hear the Rabbis' own contemporary concerns being echoed in the discussion of the past. A well-known and widely attested rabbinic equation between Esau and Rome, dating at least to the mid-second-century sage R. Akiva, makes the invocation of Esau in this context overtly political.[12] On this reading, by equating Haman with Esau, the Rabbis are actually accomplishing two complementary goals simultaneously. First, they are casting the story of Esther backward in time, securing it the authority of precedent and thus ensuring its acceptance as a legitimate story. Second, they are projecting it forward, *using* its newfound authority to foreshadow their own destiny: in the same way as Esau's descendant Haman was destroyed, Esau's spiritual equivalent, Rome, will also be destroyed, and power will again revert to the Jews.

2. Diaspora

The major thesis of this book has been that Esther is a diaspora book, advocating positions that may have seemed natural (if controversial) to Jews living in the Diaspora, but which would have been anathema to nationalist Jews in the land of Israel. It has further been argued that changing circumstances in the Herodian and later Roman periods allowed Esther to be accepted as a sacred book by all Jews, even in Israel. Despite this, the Rabbis – and, presumably, other contemporary Jews throughout the Roman and Byzantine eras in Palestine, and the Sassanid period in Persia – were deeply uncomfortable with an advocacy of a diasporic lifestyle. In order to redeem Esther, therefore, they had to show why the Diaspora

---

[12] On this equation, see Gerson D. Cohen, "Esau as Symbol in Early Medieval Thought," in Alexander Altmann (ed.), *Jewish Medieval and Renaissance Studies* (Cambridge, MA: Harvard University Press, 1967), 19–48, reprinted in Cohen, *Studies in the Variety of Rabbinic Cultures*, JPS Scholar of Distinction Series (Philadelphia: JPS, 1991), 243–69; Mireille Hadas-Lebel, "Jacob et Esaü, ou Israël et Rome dans le Talmud et le Midrash," *Revue de l'histoire des religions*, 201 (1984), 369–92; Louis H. Feldman, "Josephus' Portrait of Jacob," *JQR* 79 (1988–89), 130–33; and Robert Hayward, "Mules, Rome, and a Catalogue of Names: Genesis 36 and its Aramaic Targumim," in Geoffrey Khan and Diana Lipton (eds.), *Studies on the Text and Versions of the Hebrew Bible in Honour of Robert Gordon, VT* Suppl. 149 (Leiden: Brill, 2012), 309–12.

therein was acceptable, by showing that it was necessary to pave the way for nationalist redemption.

a. Chronology as interpretation

If the book of Esther is going to be part of the grand narrative of the Bible, it is important to discover what part of the story it tells. In order to do that, it is of paramount importance to establish where in the timeline of history the story fits. A late midrash reflects on the importance of chronology for understanding the story of Esther: "We must learn from the words of the prophets how this came to be, that an enemy opposed Israel in the days of Xerxes during their exile, and [we must learn] when during the exile it was, in order to understand the essence, and to learn one thing from another."[13] Indeed, the rabbinic construction of the Persian period is to some extent an exercise in chronography, but is also a statement of historiosophy.[14] The Rabbis' view of the chronology of the time period shaped their view of the meaning of the period. They had a dramatically different conception of the history of Achaemenids from modern scholars. As a result, their understanding allowed them to understand Esther in radically different ways than modern readers do.

b. Method in rabbinic historical reconstructions

The Rabbis were constrained by their exclusive use of the Bible as the source for historical data.[15] Since no biblical book provides a comprehensive chronological framework for the Persian period, as the book of Kings did for the Iron Age, later readers were left without sufficient information to reconstruct that history.[16] The Rabbis knew from the Bible of three named Persian kings: Cyrus, Darius, and Xerxes. A fourth Persian royal name that

---

[13] Midrash Leqaḥ Ṭov, pp. 85–86.   [14] Tabory, התקופה הפרסית בעיני חז״ל, 76.

[15] This was observed by the Tosafists (on b. Megillah 11a, s.v. שלשה מלכו בכל העולם כולו). They ask why the Talmud counted only Ahab, Nebuchadnezzar, and Xerxes as kings who ruled over the entire world, and did not include Alexander the Great. They answer: "Because they are dealing here only with those who are explicitly written." Further on the method used by the Rabbis in reconstructing history, especially as exemplified in Seder Olam, see the studies of Chaim Milikowsky, esp. "Seder 'Olam and Jewish Chronography in the Hellenistic and Roman Periods," PAAJR 52 (1985), 115–39, and "Josephus between Rabbinic Culture and Hellenistic Historiography," in James L. Kugel (ed.), Shem in the Tents of Japhet: Essays on the Encounter of Judaism and Hellenism (Leiden: Brill, 2002), 159–200.

[16] The same principles guided earlier Second Temple-era Jewish historians, as well; for the implications for the understanding of the Persian period in Daniel 9, see Michael Segal, "The Chronological Conception of the Persian Period in Daniel 9," JAJ 2 (2011), 297.

appears in the Bible, Artaxerxes, was taken to be either another name for Xerxes or a dynastic name held by all the Persian kings.[17]

Using the little data available to them, and trying to accommodate prophecies as well as historical narratives, the Rabbis came to the conclusion that the Persian period lasted 52 years altogether. Beginning with the assumption that 490 years passed between the destructions of the First and Second Temples, and subtracting 70 years of exile, the Rabbis concluded that the Second Temple had stood for 420 years.[18] The Greeks were said to have ruled for 180 years, and the Hasmoneans and Herodians for 103 each. That left 34 years after the construction of the Temple for the Persians to reign, and the Rabbis held that 18 years passed after Cyrus came to power and before the Temple was built. Persian rule thus lasted a total of 52 years.

c. Chronological schemes, rabbinic and modern

It may be helpful to summarize in chart form the historical schemes used by modern historians and by the Rabbis, at least of the Babylonian Talmud.[19] For the sake of comparison, let us call the year of Nebuchadnezzar's ascension to power (= 605 BCE in the modern scheme) year "0," and list the historical events in the two centuries following that (see Table 14.1).

The most important number in the rabbinic scheme is 70. Jeremiah had foretold that the Babylonian domination would last 70 years,[20] and much ink was spilled in trying to puzzle out the precise contours of this period. It could begin with the rise of Nebuchadnezzar to power, in which case Belshazzar's second year would mark the completion of 70 years (on the rabbinic counting). Indeed, according to the Talmud, this was the occasion for the party narrated in Daniel 5; since this was a miscalculation, however, Belshazzar was swiftly punished. The period of 70 years could also begin with the initial conquest

---

[17] Compare Esther Rabbah 1:3 with Seder 'Olam, chapter 30 and b. RH 3b–4a, and see Tabory, "התקופה הפרסית בעיני חז"ל," 70.

[18] Seder 'Olam, chapter 28. The total of 490 years is, of course, based on the interpretation of Jeremiah's "seventy years" prophecy in Daniel 9:24, although if Segal's analysis (in "The Chronological Conception of the Persian Period in Daniel 9") is correct, and it appears to me to be convincing, the Rabbis' understanding of the 490 years differs from that reflected in Daniel 9. For discussion of the 490-year schemes reflected in various Qumran texts, see Cana Werman, "Epochs and End-Time: The 490 Year Scheme in Second Temple Literature," *DSD* 13 (2006), 229–55. Only the Rabbis, as far as I can tell, posited that the 490 years would link the destruction of the First Temple to the *destruction* of the Second Temple.

[19] The scheme laid out in Seder 'Olam (chapter 29) differs in some details from that given below, but not in ways that affect the main points to be discussed here.

[20] Jeremiah 25:12 and 29:10. See the discussion in Mark Leuchter, "Jeremiah's 70-year Prophecy and the ששך/לב קמי *Atbash* Codes," *Biblica*, 85 (2004), 503–22.

Table 14.1 *Comparative chronologies, rabbinic and modern*

Event	Modern historians		Rabbinic historiography
	Date BCE	Date counting from ascension of Nebuchadnezzar	
Nebuchadnezzar comes to the throne	605	0	0
Exile of Jehoiachin	597	8	8
Destruction of the Temple	586	19	19
Death of Nebuchadnezzar	562	43	45
Evil-merodach/Amel Marduk	562–560	43–45	45–68[a]
Nergal-šar-uṣur (Neriglissar)	560–556	45–49	DID NOT EXIST
Labashi-Marduk	556	49	DID NOT EXIST
Nabonidus	556–539	49–66	DID NOT EXIST
Belshazzar	553–539[b]	55–66	69–70[c]
Darius the Mede	DID NOT EXIST		71–73[d]
Cyrus	539–530	66–75	73–75
Cambyses	530–522	75–83	DID NOT EXIST
Darius I	521–486	84–120	DID NOT EXIST
Xerxes	485–465	121–41	76–88[e]
Artaxerxes	465–424	141–82	------------
Darius			88–?

[a] The Talmud (b. Megillah 11b) reports a "tradition" that Evil-Merodach reigned for 23 years.
[b] Belshazzar was never king, but co-regent with his father Nabonidus, in charge of Babylon.
[c] Belshazzar's second year is thus 70 years since the beginning of Nebuchadnezzar's rule.
[d] The existence of Darius the Mede is explicitly stated in Daniel 9:1.
[e] Xerxes' third year was thus 70 years since the *first* conquest of Jerusalem by the Babylonians and the exile of Jehoiachin. His latest year mentioned in the Bible was his 12th; see below for the significance of this.

of Jerusalem, and the exile of Jehoiachin; the end would then be in Xerxes' third year. The arrival of that awaited time with no evident redemption, according to the Rabbis, was the reason for the grand party thrown by Xerxes in his third year, as narrated in the first chapter of Esther.

d. Implications of the chronology: Esther and the Temple

One of the most important components of the rabbinic chronological scheme is that according to the Rabbis' calculations, the Second Temple was not yet built in Xerxes' time.[21] This again allows for – indeed, encourages – multiple ways of reading the story as intimately connected to the epic story of the Temple in Jerusalem, including its destruction and reconstruction.[22] Thus, again, the chronology quickly serves to blunt the Diaspora-orientation of the book of Esther, and to bring it more in line with conventional views of exile and the centrality of Israel and the Temple.[23]

One story puts Mordecai squarely in the story of the Temple's reconstruction. In a different tradition, Mordecai son of Yair of the Esther story is equated with another Mordecai, who appears on a list of Jews who moved from Babylonia to Jerusalem with Ezra. The list includes "Jeshua, Nehemiah, Seraiah, Re'eliah, Mordecai *bilshan*, Mispar, Bigvai, Rehum, Ba'ana."[24] According to most readings of this verse, the word *bilshan* after Mordecai's name just refers to another individual, Bilshan.[25] The Rabbis, however, take *bilshan* to be an epithet of Mordecai. This epithet is then derived from *lashon* "language" and taken to indicate that Mordecai was

---

[21] Midrash Abba Gurion (p. 11a) records one surprising view that Xerxes' insistent refusal to allow construction of the Second Temple led to the central conflict of the Esther story. After Mordecai saved the king's life at the end of chapter 2, Xerxes realized that he would owe Mordecai a favor, and that Mordecai would likely take the opportunity to ask for permission to rebuild the Temple. Not willing to grant that request, but also not willing to turn Mordecai away, the king decided to appoint Haman vizier, so that Haman could prevent Mordecai from fulfilling his wish. Thus, immediately after Mordecai saves the king's life, chapter 3 begins, "After these things, King Xerxes promoted Haman." See also Targum Rishon to 5:3 and b. Megillah 15b for related midrashim. According to another version (Panim Aherot B, p. 30b; see also Esther Rabbah 5:2), Xerxes himself would have contemplated allowing the reconstruction of the Temple, but his wife Vashti – scion of the Babylonian royal family (see below, p. 189) – objected, "What my ancestors destroyed, you want to rebuild?!" Along the same lines is the claim by R. Taḥlifa b. b. Ḥana (Esther Rabbah 1:1), who interpreted the name *Ahashverosh* as "the brother of (*ahiv shel*) the head (*rosh*)." He explains that "the head" is Nebuchadnezzar, and that Xerxes and Nebuchadnezzar are "brothers" in the sense that Nebuchadnezzar destroyed the Temple, and Xerxes refused to allow it to be rebuilt; "therefore Scripture compared the two."

[22] According to Neusner, the older part of Esther Rabbah has a single theme: the need to explain, religiously and theologically, why Israel is ruled by foreign despots (Jacob Neusner, "Esther in Esther Rabbah," in Jacob Neusner and Alan J. Avery-Peck [eds.] and William Scott Green and Günter Stemberger [consulting eds.], *Encyclopaedia of Midrash: Biblical Interpretation in Formative Judaism* [Leiden: Brill, 2005], vol. 1, 59–74). Neusner's source division within Esther Rabbah is faulty; see Lerner, "The Works of Aggadic Midrash," 180. His observation that this is a major theme of Esther Rabbah is valuable, however.

[23] For more on rabbinic conceptions of exile and Diaspora, see Chaim Milikowsky, "Notions of Exile, Subjugation and Return in Rabbinic Literature," in James M. Scott (ed.), *Exile: Old Testament, Jewish, and Christian Conceptions* (Leiden: Brill, 1997), 265–96. Segal, *The Babylonian Esther Midrash*, vol. III, 241–44, notes that one of the primary thrusts of the Midrash seems to be to emphasize the "temporary and anomalous period" of Jewish existence prior to the rebuilding of the Temple – certainly a far cry from the ideology of MT Esther!

[24] Ezra 2:2.

[25] The name is attested in an Aramaic epigraph on a cuneiform tablet from Nineveh. See Mohammed Maraqten, *Die semitischen Personennamen in den alt- und reichsaramäischen Inschriften aus Vorderasien* (Hildesheim and New York: G. Olms, 1988), 237, and for the form of the name, see

particularly proficient with languages.[26] Furthermore, this Mordecai is equated with Mordecai, cousin of Esther.[27] How could Mordecai have both returned to Judea with Ezra and lived in Susa to save the Jews? It turns out that not only had Mordecai gone to Judea with Ezra, but Haman was there, as well. There the two clashed over the construction of the Temple. As a result of their clash, they both journeyed to Susa, to plead their cases and continue their conflict.[28] This, then, fills in Mordecai's background, turning him from a circumstantial hero into a grand military and diplomatic figure;[29] it also again links the story of Esther to the drama of the construction of the Temple.

The most dramatic claim that results from this is that Darius II, said to have been the king after Xerxes, was in fact the son of Queen Esther.[30] The

---

Richard C. Steiner, "Why Bishlam (Ezra 4:7) cannot Rest 'in Peace': On the Aramaic and Hebrew Sound Changes that Conspired to Blot out the Remembrance of Bel-Shalam the Archivist," *JBL* 126 (2007), 400.

[26] The Talmud derives בלשן from *bēl lišānī* (b. Menahot 65a: אלא שלא תהא סנהדרין שומעת מפי התורגמן, (דהוה בייל לישני ודריש והיינו דכתיב במרדכי (נחמיה ז) בִּלְשָׁן "master of languages." For this Akkadianism in Jewish Babylonian Aramaic, see Michael Fox, "בייל לישני," *Lešonénu*, 41 (1976–77), 75, and Richard C. Steiner, *Early Northwest Semitic Serpent Spells in the Pyramid Texts*, HSS 61 (Winona Lake, IN: Eisenbrauns, 2011), 6. See also the Aramaic poem from Byzantine Palestine published in Yahalom and Sokoloff, שירת בני מערבא, 186–88: "he was wise / in seventy tongues / /therefore he was called / Mordecai the tongue-man (מורדכיי בילשן) // fifth in the group / who were exiled to Babylon // who were called / who arrived with Zerubavel."

[27] See, e.g., b. Megillah 16b.

[28] Panim Aherot B, p. 28a. See further Tabory, "התקופה הפרסית בעיני חז"ל," 72–73.

[29] For his military accomplishments, see the extended story preserved in the Targum, which tells that Mordecai and Haman were both generals in the Persian army; Mordecai was a very successful one, while Haman was something of a personal failure. The text of this targumic passage is conveniently available in Katzenelenbogen, אסתר מגילת :חיים תורת, 239–41, and see *ibid.*, 239 n. 8 for his sources. See also Ginzberg, *Legends of the Jews*, tr. Henrietta Szold, 7 vols. (Philadelphia: JPS of America, 1909–38), vol. IV, 397–99 and vol.VI, 464 n. 105 for the sources used by Ginzberg. On the diplomatic side, a beraita cited in the Bavli (b. Menahot 64d–65a) tells of a man named Mordecai who resolved sundry halakhic problems related to practices in the Temple. Very similar stories are told in m. Sheqalim 5:1, where the protagonist is named Petahiah (see also y. Sheqalim 5:1). The mishnah there comments, "Why was he called Petahiah? Because he would open matters and interpret them, and knew seventy languages." It seems that in the Babylonian version of the Mishnah, Petahiah was said to also bear the name Mordecai, based on the parallel traditions of the name: b. Menahot quotes, והיינו דתנן 'פתחיה על פתחיה זהו מרדכי' this is what was learned in הקינין זה מרדכי', למה נקרא שמו פתחיה? שפותח דברים ודורשן, ויודע בשבעים לשון the Mishnah, 'Petahiah of the *qinnin* is Mordecai, and why was he called Petahiah? Because he would open matters and interpret them, and knew seventy languages.'" The line פתחיה זהו מרדכי "Petahiah is Mordecai" does not appear in any of the manuscripts, but does appear in printed editions. Rashi in Menahot 65a, s.v. מרדכי, comments, "the one who lived in the days of Xerxes." According to Rashi, therefore, there was only one Mordecai in Jewish history: he appears in Esther, in Ezra-Nehemiah, and again in the Mishnah. The Tosafot (s.v. אמר להו מרדכי) take issue with Rashi's claim, pointing out that he would have had to live for hundreds of years. See Tabory, "התקופה הפרסית בעיני חז"ל," 72–73 n. 24.

[30] See Vayyiqra Rabbah 13:5, in the name of R. Judah b. R. Simon: דריוש האחרון בנה שלאסתר היה טהור מאמו וטמא מאביו "The later Darius was Esther's son; he was pure on his mother's side but impure on his father's side." The Tosafists (Rosh ha-Shana 3b, s.v. בשנת) take to calling him "Darius son of Esther."

Rabbis knew the name Artaxerxes, of course, since he is an important character in the careers of Ezra and Nehemiah; they claim, however, that *Artaḥšasta* (as he is known in Hebrew, a good transcription of Old Persian R̥taxšaca "whose reign is through truth") is a throne name, taken by numerous Persian kings,[31] and that therefore "Cyrus is Darius is Artaxerxes."[32] Crucial for our discussion, though, is that this king is said to have been the one who sponsored the reconstruction of the Jerusalem Temple. As can be seen in Table 14.1, although modern historians know that Xerxes reigned for twenty years, the Rabbis apparently assumed – in consonance with their historiographical assumptions – that he reigned for only twelve, since his twelfth year is the latest year of his reign mentioned in the Bible. His son and successor, then, began reigning in the sixty-ninth year, and his second regnal year was the seventieth year since the destruction of the Temple. It therefore comes as no surprise to read that the Temple was built in Darius' second year.[33]

Thus, through the efforts of Esther, the Jews were saved in one generation.[34] Through her son Darius, they were saved in far grander style in the following generation. Far from being a one-generation wonder, then, Esther is revealed through this reading not only to have saved her own contemporaries, but also to have physically created the Persian king who would usher in the period of the Second Temple.

---

[31] This is in fact correct; see Rüdiger Schmitt, "Artaxerxes," in *Encyclopædia Iranica*,www.iranicaonline. org/articles/artaxerxes-throne-name-of-several-persian-kings-of-the-achaemenid-dynasty (accessed May, 2012).

[32] This triple equation is likely based on Ezra 6:14, where the three names appear together. See already Seder Olam §30, as well as b. Rosh ha-Shana 3b, and see Jason Sion Mokhtarian, "Rabbinic Depictions of the Achaemenid King Cyrus the Great: The 'Babylonian Esther Midrash' (bMeg. 10b–17a) in its Iranian Context," in Carol Bakhos and M. Rahim Shayegan (eds.), *The Talmud in its Iranian Context*, TSAJ 135 (Tübingen: Mohr Siebeck, 2010), 130–32.

[33] See Haggai 1:1; 2:10; Zechariah 1:1; 1:7.

[34] Some midrashim do not seem to shy away from the conclusion that the "salvation" in Esther reversed the calamity of the destruction of the Temple: "R. Berakhiah said in the name of R. Levi, God said to Israel: You cried 'we were orphans with no father' (Eikhah 5:3) – the redeemer that I will raise for you in Media will also be an orphan, as it says, 'for she had no father or mother' (Esther 2:7)" (Abba Gurion, p. 9b; see also Eikhah Rabbah 5:3, where it presumably originated, and Esther Rabbah 6:7). This midrash portrays Esther as the redeemer of Israel, making up for the loss of the Temple. It is thus unsettling to recall that this "redeemer" did not rebuild the Temple or bring the Jews back to their land, but only kept them alive in exile. Below we will see that some Talmudic authorities, such as Rava, denigrated the "redemption" described in Esther, since "we are still slaves of Xerxes!" For R. Levi, though, the salvation of Esther was very much a true salvation. On his reading, the redemption in Susa reversed the destruction of Jerusalem.

3. Great cities of the world: Susa vs. Jerusalem

Since the story of Esther is set prior to the construction of the Temple, there is reason to seek, and find, echoes of the ruined Temple within the story. The Rabbis find such echoes in the notice of the banquet in chapter 1; they claim that the Temple vessels were brought out at Xerxes' feast. This is based on the use of the word "glory" (*tif'eret*) in the depiction of Xerxes' banquet, and also its use in the description of the priestly garments in Exodus 28:2.[35] Building on this claim, the midrash claims that Xerxes' own vessels darkened with shame when they saw the beauty of the Temple vessels.[36]

The idea that the banquet would revolve around questions of the Temple is an idea borrowed, rather brazenly, from Belshazzar's feast in Daniel 5. In that story, the Babylonian king Belshazzar has the vessels from the Temple brought out at the feast, to gloat over the destruction of Jerusalem and the failure of the Jews to rebuild the Temple. The mysterious hand that appears and writes on the wall, however, foretells that Belshazzar will pay with his life for this display of hubris. There are numerous similarities between that story and the story of Xerxes' feast in Esther 1: both tell of grand banquets, thrown in the king's third year of his reign, featuring much wine and at which gold and silver vessels are used. In both stories, the plot hinges on the momentous appearance, or non-appearance, of the queen: in the story of Belshazzar, it is the queen mother who arrives to tell her son about the wise Daniel, and in the story of Xerxes, it is Vashti's refusal to come that sets the plot in motion. Given these similarities, the Rabbis apparently saw that there was license to read one story in light of the other.[37]

Although the textual basis of this reading is evident, it is the political import that is of central significance here; the theme of the Temple vessels strikes me as playing on two central and interrelated themes in the rabbinic reading of Esther. The first is the reconstruction of the Temple, which is a major topic of the book of Esther according to the Rabbis. The second is the

---

[35] Esther Rabbah 2:1; see also b. Megillah 12a, and Targum Rishon to 1:7.

[36] Esther Rabbah 2:11. This is part of a sustained rabbinic attempt to exploit the Temple imagery in the description of the feast in chapter 1. One of the more striking examples of this program is a statement, again of R. Levi's, quoted in the Bavli (Megillah 12b). R. Levi takes the list in Esther 1:14 – *karshena, shetar, atmata, tarshish, meres, marsena, memukhan* – as a series of references to the components of the Temple worship (rather than a list of royal advisors, as it appears to be in context). He then suggests that this was a sentence uttered by the angels in defense of Israel: pointing to the various Temple practices the Jews performed, the heavenly host asked, have the other nations ever offered any of the sacrifices alluded to here?

[37] Raviv, "השפעתו של ספר דניאל על פרשנות המקרא של חז״ל," 117–18.

conflict between Susa and Jerusalem. Where is the seat of sovereignty? Where does royalty reside? From where does power emanate?

There can be no doubt that these questions, cast back as exegetical questions regarding history, were also contemporary questions that plagued the Rabbis and other Jews. In the western world of the time, the rivalry between Rome and Jerusalem was a fundamental one.[38] The popular view among the Jews was presumably that their God had temporarily abandoned them, probably as punishment for unstated sins.[39] For the Romans, on the other hand, the God of Israel had been defeated, and his cult in Jerusalem brought to an end.[40] This was likely the import of carting off the Temple vessels after the Great Revolt, in 70 CE, from Jerusalem to Rome, an accomplishment memorialized in the Arch of Titus. With the vessels forever visible in Rome, shown in their disgrace being carried into exile, the eternal ignominy of Jerusalem was guaranteed.

The Rabbis literarily turned this claim on its head. The vessels may have been carted off into exile, but this indicates nothing regarding the past, or, more crucially, the future. The vessels, even while in exile, are so stunningly beautiful, so surpassingly wondrous, that the grandest vessels in the king's palace darken with shame when confronted with them. Despite the difference in media, seeing our midrash in dialogue with the plastic representation of the same vessels in the Arch of Titus reveals the polemical power of the tale told.

More generally, the Temple and its vessels are the emblems of Jerusalem's centrality. They remind the viewer of Jerusalem's glory and – in the rabbinic conception of history – of the fact that the world was once ruled by the king in Jerusalem. The image of the artifacts of rule from Jerusalem in exile in Susa is, therefore, a powerful symbol of the shift of the locale of authority. This power was both divine and Davidic, and no attempt is made to disentangle those two. In this light, midrashim about the Temple vessels being located in Jerusalem or, as we will soon see, about the very throne of

---

[38] Some rabbinic texts also reflect on a rivalry between Jerusalem and Alexandria, but this seems to have no impact on the reading of Esther in rabbinic literature.

[39] This will be discussed at greater length below. For some discussion, see Jonathan J. Price, "Josephus and the Dialogue on the Destruction of the Temple," in Christfried Böttrich and Jens Herzer (eds.), *Josephus und das Neue Testament: Wechselseitige Wahrnehmungen. II. Internationales Symposium zum Corpus Judaeo-Hellenisticum, Mai 2006, Greifswald*, Wissenschaftliche Untersuchungen zum Neuen Testament 209 (Tübingen: Mohr Siebeck, 2007), 181–94, and Jonathan J. Price, "Some Aspects of Josephus' Theological Interpretation of the Jewish War," in Mauro Perani (ed.), *"The Words of a Wise Man's Mouth are Gracious" (Qoh 10,12): Festschrift for Günter Stemberger on the Occasion of his 65th Birthday*, Studia Judaica 32 (Berlin: De Gruyter, 2005), 109–19.

[40] Jodi Magness, "The Arch of Titus at Rome and the Fate of the God of Israel," *JJS* 59 (2008), 201–17.

the Davidic king being located there are ciphers for the same fundamental question being asked by the Rabbis: has dominion shifted from Jerusalem to Susa? And once again, this is presumably as much a question about the present – has dominion shifted to Rome? – as about the past.

In one text, this comparison is made in the form of a complaint, placed in the mouth of the angels: "Master of the world, the Temple is destroyed, and this wicked one is sitting and making parties?!"[41] In a different text, the question is explicitly posed: where does kingship reside? R. Abu said: "Kingship use to reside in Israel, but when they sinned, kingship was taken from them and given to the nations of the world." This is not the final act in the drama, however: "But tomorrow, when Israel repents, the Holy One, blessed be He, will take it from the idolaters and return it to Israel."[42]

Other texts make the same point less overtly. There are a number of passages which draw attention to elements of the palace in Susa which were uniquely paralleled in the Temple of Jerusalem. Thus, Xerxes gave his guests to drink only in gold vessels, just as "Solomon's drinking vessels were of gold, and all the vessels of the house of the forest of Lebanon were of pure gold."[43] Xerxes' palace in Susa, according to the midrash, was built with marble from a secret quarry; the only other building which is said to have been made of this marble was the Temple built by Solomon.[44]

Extending the comparison beyond explicit mention of the two capitals, Susa and Jerusalem, other midrashim compare the kings Solomon and Xerxes. In these comparisons, it is clear that the two kings stand in for their respective capitals and cultures, and thus that these texts are raising the question of cultural supremacy, pitting Jerusalem against Susa and Israel

---

[41] Esther Rabbah 1:10. The word for "party" is *marzeaḥ*. The same complaint is voiced by God in Esther Rabbah 3:3.

[42] Esther Rabbah 1:13.

[43] 1 Kings 10:21, cited in Esther Rabbah 2:10. On the gold drinking vessels in ancient drinking culture, see Aaron Koller, "The *kos* in the Levant: Thoughts on its Distribution, Function, and Spread from the Late Bronze through the Iron Age II," in Gershon Galil, Ayelet Gilboa, Aren M. Maeir, and Dan'el Kahn (eds.), *The Ancient Near East in the 12th–10th Centuries BCE, Culture and History: Proceedings of the International Conference Held in the University of Haifa, 2–5 May 2010*, Alter Orient und Altes Testament (Münster: Ugarit-Verlag, 2012), 269–90.

[44] Esther Rabbah 2:7. Another text also seems to equate, in a mythical sense, Susa with Jerusalem: commenting on the verse, "On the third day, Esther donned royal clothes" (5:1), the midrash asserts that the "clothes" in question were actually the spirit of God, which rested on Esther at that moment. She entered "the inner courtyard of the palace, which was built corresponding to the palace in Jerusalem. The king was sitting on his royal throne in the palace," and Esther began to pray (Targum Rishon on 5:1). "Palace in Jerusalem" (*bet malka biYrushalayim*) could conceivably be a reference to the royal palace, rather than the Temple, but the fact that Esther prays there, addressing the Master of the World, strongly suggests that she stood in a place where God was present – the Jerusalem Temple.

against Persia, in the persons of Solomon and Xerxes.[45] The connection with Rome is evident here, as well, since other rabbinic texts claim a unique relationship between Solomon and the Roman emperors. "'Two nations in your womb' (Genesis 25:23): Two proud nations are in your womb, each boasting supremacy in its world, each boasting supremacy in its kingdom. Two proud nations are in your womb: Hadrian among the non-Jews, and Solomon among the Jews."[46]

A number of comparisons are clearly meant to denigrate Xerxes at the expense of Solomon. Thus, the Targum Sheni contains a long discussion of the arrival of the queen of Sheba in Solomon's Jerusalem; "whereas Solomon was able to bring the famous Queen of Sheba from the ends of the earth to his royal court, Xerxes could not even bring his wife to his meal."[47]

One motif that appears frequently in the rabbinic texts on Esther is the throne of Solomon. According to the oft-told tale, Xerxes tried to sit on Solomon's throne, which had migrated through much of the Near East on its way to Susa. The throne was adorned not only with precious stones, but

---

[45] For an extended discussion of the image of Solomon in Targum Sheni, see Ego, "All Kingdoms and Kings Trembled before Him," 57–73. A comparison commonly made is between Esther 1:2 ("who ruled from India to Kush"), predicated about Xerxes, and 1 Kings 5:4 ("who controlled the whole Transjordan, from Tiphsah to Gaza"), predicated about Solomon; see Panim Aherot B, p. 28b; Targum Sheni to 1:1; etc., and the discussion in Segal, *The Babylonian Esther Midrash*, vol. 1, 127–34. Another passage (Esther Rabbah 1:14) compares the syntax of "Jerusalem which is in Judah" (Ezra 1:2) to "which is in Susa the Fortress" (Esther 1:2). It should be noted that the meaning of בירה in Mishnaic Hebrew is not identical to the meaning of that lexeme in Biblical Hebrew and in other ancient cognate languages; for full discussion and documentation, see Paul Mandel, "'בירה' כמונה אדריכלי בספרות חז"ל," *Tarbiz*, 61 (1992), 195–217. The Rabbis know well what the word meant in the Bible, however.

[46] Bereshit Rabbah 63:7; see Nicholas R. M. De Lange, "Jewish Attitudes to the Roman Empire," in P. D. A. Garnsey and C. R. Whittaker (eds.), *Imperialism in the Ancient World*, The Cambridge University Research Seminar in Ancient History (Cambridge University Press, 1978), 270.

[47] For a description of the passage in Targum Sheni regarding the queen of Sheba, see Ego, "All Kingdoms and Kings Trembled before Him," 66–67; for the insight regarding the comparison between Solomon and Xerxes, see *ibid.*, p. 69. In a different text, R. Isaac claimed that idolaters never fully enjoy "goodness," but he was challenged on the basis of Esther 1:10, "when the king's heart was 'good' with wine." In response, he emphasized the difference between "when the heart of the king was *like* good (*ke-tov*)." This midrashic reading takes the *kaf* to be the "comparative *kaf*" (*kaf ha-dimmayon*), meaning "like," rather than the temporal adverbial *kaf* meaning "when." The non-midrashic meaning of the text is "when the heart of the king was 'good.'" A contrast is then drawn between the heart of the king here and a passage describing the Israelites in 1 Kings 8:66, "happy and good of heart" – not *like* good, but actually good, according to R. Isaac (Esther Rabbah 3:11). The verse chosen for comparison comes from the end of the story of the dedication of the Temple, and reads in full, "On the eighth day he released the people, and they blessed the king and went to their tents, happy and good of heart." The comparison is obvious: in Susa, after seven days of feasting, everything went wrong, and even the king was only "like" happy; in Jerusalem, after eight days of feasting, everyone was joyous, and filled with actual happiness. They even blessed the king, something the residents of Susa never did.

with magical animals on every step who guarded the throne and instructed the king, as he ascended, how to properly exercise power and govern. Also on the throne were appropriate biblical passages, meant to remind the king of his obedience to God and responsibility to fairness and justice.[48] The connection between the thrones of Xerxes and Solomon was presumably inspired, besides the general theme of juxtaposing these two kings, by the fact that the expression "the throne of his kingship" (*kisse malkhuto*) appears in the Bible only in the context of these two kings, in Esther 1:2 regarding Xerxes and in 1 Chronicles 22:10 regarding Solomon. The story differs, of course, from telling to telling, but one version is as follows.

After the death of Solomon, Shishak came and took the throne as part of the *ketubba* of his daughter.[49] Centuries later, Sennacherib of Assyria came and took the throne from Egypt. Later in Sennacherib's career, he brought the throne with him on his campaign against Jerusalem.[50] When Sennacherib was defeated there, Hezekiah took the throne back, and it was because of the throne that he was so successful a king. A century later, however, Pharaoh Necho defeated and killed Josiah, and then he took the throne. He did not know how the secret mechanisms of the throne worked, however. As a result, one of the lions on the steps struck him on his thigh and he limped – so he was called Pharaoh the Lame.[51] Nebuchadnezzar, on his arrival to Egypt, found the throne and brought it to Babylon. When he tried to sit on it, however, the Israelites cried out, and God had the lion strike him, this time with enough force that the king fell from the throne.[52] This is the background for the mocking lament in Isaiah 14, "How have you

---

[48] Other versions of this tale are found in Panim Aherot B, p. 28a, Targum Rishon, and esp. Targum Sheni on 1:1; see also Ego, "All Kingdoms and Kings Trembled before Him," 65–66. A long description of the throne itself is found in Midrash Abba Gurion pp. 2b–4b, and many other sources related to Esther, such as Kasher and Klein, "New Fragments of Targum to Esther," 99. One can also add the Aramaic poem in Yahalom and Sokoloff, שירת בני מערבא, 192 (line 15: "he sat on his gold throne / it was Solomon's throne"). A fuller description is found in an Oxford manuscript (2797), translated by Moses Gaster in *The Chronicles of Jerahmeel, or The Hebrew Bible historiale*, Oriental Translation Fund, New Series 4 (London: Royal Asiatic Society, 1899), 251–53; see also the sources on this topic collected by Lerner, "The Works of Aggadic Midrash," 194 and 223.

[49] The midrash is here (as elsewhere) assuming that the daughter of Pharaoh who married Solomon was the daughter of Shishak. The Egyptian king's campaign against Jerusalem (reported in 1 Kings 14:25–29) is here understood as the king's collection of the *ketubba* due to his daughter because of the death of her husband.

[50] In fact, in Sennacherib's reliefs depicting his campaign against Judah, he is shown sitting on a throne, watching the battle rage against Lachish. See Julian Reade, *Assyrian Sculpture* (Cambridge, MA: Harvard University Press, 1983), 73. Did the Rabbis have some memory of this? Had they (or recent predecessors) seen Sennacherib's reliefs?

[51] The word for "lame" is נָכֶה *nekheh*, a play on "Necho" (נכה).

[52] This is based on, or inspired by, Isaiah 14:9, regarding the despised king: "he makes [the kings] rise from their thrones."

fallen from the sky, Hellel son of the Morning Star!" Finally, Darius took the throne with him back to Elam after conquering Babylon, but did not sit on it. Xerxes wanted to use the throne, but Israel objected to God: "Eternal master! Do not disgrace your throne of glory!"[53] The king was told, "any king who is not a cosmocrat may not sit on it. Instead, therefore, Xerxes brought in wise men to make a throne like it."[54]

These midrashic comments denigrate Susa relative to Jerusalem, or, to put it differently, exalt Jerusalem at the expense of Susa. Other texts also compare the two cities, but for different purposes. While Susa, as a partial stand-in for Rome, may legitimately be seen as a rival to Jerusalem, the notion that Jerusalem's role had been usurped was not tolerated. The book of Esther leaves room for the suggestion that Susa replaced Jerusalem not only as a political center, but as a *religious* center. The new festival was decreed in Susa, and Susa is the paradigmatic city for a whole class of cities which will have a date of celebration, the 15th of Adar, unique to them. The Rabbis, however, set things right by ruling that the question of which cities will celebrate on the 15th depends not on Susa, but on which cities had walls at the time of Joshua b. Nun, conqueror of the land of Israel.[55] Moreover, they explicitly state that this is done in order to "give honor to Israel": "R. Simon said in the name of R. Joshua b. Levi, they gave honor to the land of Israel, which lay in ruins at that time, and they made it dependent on the days of Joshua b. Nun."[56]

It bears repeating that the Rabbis took the Roman claim of their city's supremacy to be a theological threat. Rome's claim to be the "eternal city" (*aeterna urbs*) was countered by the rabbinic claim that the true Eternal One (Hebrew *netsaḥ*) would in fact destroy Rome.[57] Gerson Cohen articulated well the depth of the conflict reflected here:

> Neither [Rome nor Jerusalem] could accept their existence as mere fact. Each considered itself divinely chosen and destined for a unique history. Each was obsessed with its glorious antiquity. Each was convinced that heaven had

---

[53] This is a citation from Jeremiah 14:21.

[54] Abba Gurion 1b–2b. The "cosmocrat" line, not found in Abba Gurion, is from Esther Rabbah 1:12. See also Panim Aherot A, p. 23a, s.v. בימים ההם.

[55] The political significance of this point was first pointed out to me by Tzvi Novick, to whom I am indebted.

[56] Y. Megillah 1:1 (70a). A different view, of R. Joshua b. Qorhah in t. Megillah 1:1, cited in b. Megillah 2b, does insist that Susa should be the model walled city, but his view does not triumph; see further the comments of Naḥmanides on Megilla 2a regarding the difference between walled and unwalled cities, and Israel and the rest of the world, in this regard.

[57] See the statement of R. Shila in b. Berakhot 58a, as discussed by Lawrence Zalcman, "The Eternal City: Rome or Jerusalem?," *JJS* 48 (1997), 312–13.

selected it to rule the world. Neither could accept with equanimity any challenge to its claims ... As the Jews spoke of an eternal covenant between Israel and God, the Roman could quote the promise of Jove to Rome: "Imperium sine fine dedi."[58]

Of course, rabbinic attitudes toward Rome varied by time, by place, and by personal views. Particularly famous is the debate recorded in the Bavli:

> R. Judah, R. Yose, and R. Shimon [bar Yohai] were sitting, and Judah b. Gerim was sitting near them. R. Judah commenced [the discussion] by observing, "How fine are the works of this people (= Rome)! They have made streets, they have built bridges, they have erected baths." R. Yose was silent. R. Shimon b. Yohai answered and said, "All that they made they made for themselves; they built market-places, to set harlots in them; baths, to rejuvenate themselves; bridges, to levy tolls for them!"[59]

A number of studies have shown that the rabbinic views took a definite turn toward the negative after the failed revolt led by Bar Koseba and put down viciously by Hadrian, but that over the course of the third century there were still different opinions. By the end of the third century, however, a negative attitude toward Rome was firmly entrenched in the rabbinic worldview.[60] Certainly throughout the rabbinic period Rome had to be countered ideologically and literarily, and the texts we are examining here are part of the rabbinic attempt to do so.

4. Attitude toward the king

As discussed earlier, in Esther the empire is incarnated in the person of the king. His will is law; his character is the state. For the Rabbis, therefore, grappling with the character of Xerxes is the process of grappling with the very institution of the foreign monarch, at times benign but always dangerous.

---

[58] Cohen, "Esau as Symbol," 247.

[59] Shabbat 33b. For analysis, see Jeffrey L. Rubenstein, *Talmudic Stories: Narrative Art, Composition, and Culture* (Baltimore: Johns Hopkins University Press, 1999), 108–11 (and chapter 4, *passim*).

[60] See Nahum N. Glatzer, "The Attitude toward Rome in Third-Century Judaism," in Alois Dempf, Hannah Arendt, and Friedrich Engel-Janosi (eds.), *Politische Ordnung und menschliche Existenz: Festgabe für Eric Vögelin zum 60. Geburtstag* (Munich, Beck, 1962), 243–67, reprinted in Glatzer, *Essays in Jewish Thought*, Judaic Studies Series 8 (University, AL: University of Alabama Press, 1978), 1–14; Nahum N. Glatzer, "The Attitude to Rome in the Amoraic Period," in *Proceedings of the Sixth World Congress of Jewish Thought* (Jerusalem: World Union of Jewish Studies, 1975), vol. II, 9–19; Allan Harris Cutler, "Third-Century Palestinian Rabbinic Attitudes towards the Prospect of the Fall of Rome," *Jewish Social Studies*, 31 (1969), 275–85; de Lange, "Jewish Attitudes to the Roman Empire," 254–81; Louis H. Feldman, "Abba Kolon and the Founding of Rome," *JQR* 81 (1991), 239–66; as well as the sources cited above in n. 12.

The chronological scheme within which the Rabbis see Esther impacts their reading of the king. Xerxes may be conceptualized as another example of a well-known type of foreign king. But the Rabbis go beyond that, and systematically portray Xerxes derogatorily, as the *illegitimate* heir to Nebuchadnezzar. They articulate this in two ways. The first is explicit: according to their reconstruction, Xerxes was a usurper to the throne, and Vashti was actually the one of royal blood. In most rabbinic statements, Vashti is said to have been the daughter of Belshazzar, and she uses that fact as a slur against her husband: "Son of my father's stablemaster! My father drank in front of thousands and did not get drunk, and you have gone crazy with your wine!"[61] The Bavli reports that some took Xerxes' usurpation to be an indication of his talent and ambition, while others saw it more cynically, claiming that Xerxes bought the throne and did nothing to earn it.[62]

Comparison with Nebuchadnezzar is also the theme of a statement of Rav's, quoted in the Bavli. To turn again to the name *Ahashverosh*, Rav interprets it as meaning "brother of the head."[63] Rather than emphasizing Xerxes' power, however, this is meant to denigrate him, by comparison with a truly powerful king. Nebuchadnezzar was rightfully called "head" (and Rav appropriately cites Daniel 2:38 – "you are the head of gold" – for this point). Xerxes, on the other hand, is a poor imitation of the "head": "one slew, the other sought to slay; one laid waste, the other sought to lay waste."[64] What Nebuchadnezzar did, such as kill and destroy, Xerxes tried to do, but couldn't.

The question of Xerxes' character is taken up explicitly by the Bavli: "This is a debate between Rav and Samuel. One said he was a shrewd king, and the other said he was a foolish king."[65] It is tempting to think that it was Samuel who said he was a shrewd king, and that Rav said he was a foolish king, if they are reading Esther through their own contemporary lenses:

---

[61] B. Megillah 12b. See Herman, "Ahasuerus, the Former Stable-Master of Belshazzar, and the Wicked Alexander of Macedon," 292–93. In the title and the body of the article, Herman claims that Xerxes was accused of being a former stable-master, but of course it is his father who is thus named in Vashti's statement. For Vashti as the daughter of Belshazzar, see also Panim Aherot B, p. 60.

[62] Bavli Megillah 11a: אמר רב, שמלך מעצמו. אמרי לה לשבח ואמרי לה לגנב "Rav said that he ruled on his own; some said this as praise and some said this to his detriment." Slightly more subtle are the tales told of how Xerxes amassed his wealth (Esther Rabbah 2:1; similarly Targum Rishon on 1:4). One interesting story concedes that Xerxes was as great as Nebuchadnezzar, but insists that there is no direct line of inheritance connecting the two. Instead, Nebuchadnezzar decided just before his death that he did not want to bequeath his immense riches to his son Evil-Merodach, so he buried them under the Euphrates. When Cyrus permitted the reconstruction of the Temple, God revealed the Babylonian's riches to him.

[63] Cf. the view of Rav Tahlifa above, n. 21.   [64] B. Megillah 11a.   [65] B. Megillah 12a.

Samuel is said to have been on good terms with the Persian monarch living in his day, Shapur I,[66] while Rav is credited with a series of harsh criticisms and bitter reflections on the Sasanian regime.[67] On the other hand, it is important to emphasize once again that the Rabbis tended *not* to read through contemporary lenses. They were fully capable of criticizing an ancient Persian king while supporting the current one. This claim, which goes against a well-worn assumption about rabbinic biblical interpretations, has been well articulated in the context of the Rabbis' interpretation of Esther by Jason Sion Mokhtarian, who has argued that "the [Babylonian Esther Midrash] passages do not represent the Sasanian rabbis' taking a stand on 'the burning issues of the day,' but are rather just what they purport to be: . . . exegetical-historiographical traditions."[68]

The view that he was a fool is certainly the more popular one in the rabbinic sources, however, and the Rabbis did not fail to note the ironies in many of his actions. They note, for instance, that "he sought advice regarding his wife, but not regarding an entire nation," and that "he killed his wife because of his friend, and killed his friend because of his wife."[69] Furthermore, "were it not for the first letters [at the end of chapter 1], not a shred of a remnant would be left of the enemies of Israel (= Israel). People said, what's this that is sent to us? That each man should govern his own house?! This is obvious! Even a bald man should be a ruler[70] in his own house!"[71]

---

[66] See, e.g., b. Sanhedrin 98a, and the comments of Yaakov Elman, "'Up to the Ears' in Horses' Necks (B.M. 108a): On Sasanian Agricultural Policy and Private 'Eminent Domain,'" *JSIJ* 3 (2004), 104, 108–09. On Shapur in rabbinic literature, see Jason Sion Mokhtarian, "Empire and Authority in Sasanian Babylonia: The Rabbis and King Shapur in Dialogue," *JSQ* 19 (2012), 148–80.

[67] Moshe Beer, "הרקע המדיני ופעילותו של רב בבבל," *Zion*, 50 (1985), 157–60, reprinted in Beer, חכמי המשנה והתלמוד: הגותם פועלם ומנהיגותם (Ramat Gan: Bar Ilan University Press, 2011), 12–15. On the other hand, Rav was said to enjoy a close relationship with Artavan V, the last of the Parthian kings (b. Avoda Zara 10b–11a); see Yaakov Elman, "Middle Persian Culture and Babylonian Sages: Accommodation and Resistance in the Shaping of Rabbinic Legal Tradition," in Charlotte E. Fonrobert and Martin S. Jaffee (eds.), *The Cambridge Companion to the Talmud and Rabbinic Literature* (New York: Cambridge University Press, 2007), 175; Elman also notes, however (*ibid.*, 193–94) the antipathy that Rav had for some aspects of Persian culture.

[68] Mokhtarian, "Rabbinic Depictions of the Achaemenid King Cyrus the Great," 117.

[69] Panim Aherot B, p. 28b; Esther Rabbah Petiḥtot §9 and 1:1.

[70] For the derivation of פדשכא (an emended reading based on the form פרשכא which appears in one of the most reliable manuscripts) from Persian *padixša* "ruler" (for which the Aramaic שליטא was used as a logogram), see Segal, *The Babylonian Esther Midrash*, vol.1, 289–90 n. 218 (end); see also Mokhtarian, "Rabbinic Depictions of the Achaemenid King Cyrus the Great," 113–14 n. 6.

[71] B. Megillah 12b. Other midrashim (Panim Aherot B, p. 31a; Abba Gurion, p. 9a; Targum Rishon and Targum Sheni to 2:1; b. Megillah 12b) tell different tales of the conversation between Xerxes and Vashti in the aftermath of the drunken party of chapter 1. In one version, the *Rabbis* were the royal advisors, but they recused themselves from deliberations over Vashti's fate, reasoning, "If we tell him to kill her, tomorrow he will sober up and ask us for Vashti!" Once the Rabbis stepped aside, the seven

5. Restoring the model of Diaspora life: reading Esther in light of Daniel

The book of Daniel, unlike the book of Esther, provides unimpeachable models of religious behavior. Daniel and his friends Hananiah, Mishael, and Azariah are unswerving in their religious devotion, as seen both in speech and in action. They refuse all attempts to deter them from righteous perfection, and even succeed in convincing a succession of foreign rulers that the God of Israel is the true and mighty deity.

It is not surprising, therefore, that the book of Daniel helped set the agenda for reading the Bible in the post-biblical period. Ideas from Daniel penetrated rabbinic exegesis of biblical texts from Genesis through Esther.[72]

a. Reading Daniel into the story

Themes and motifs from Daniel permeate the rabbinic readings of Esther. One midrash likens Mordecai to Daniel with regard to their occupations. Following up on the fact that both are said to be "in the gate of the king,"[73] the midrash explains that Mordecai's appointment was consciously modeled on Daniel's position. The newly anointed Queen Esther told her husband that earlier kings had a secret to their success: a righteous Jew at the gate. Xerxes asked for a recommendation, and Esther was quick to nominate her uncle for the position.[74]

advisors named in Esther 1 foolishly jumped at the opportunity to pass judgment on Vashti. This reading restores the Rabbis to their rightful place in society; the Persians, too, recognized their surpassing wisdom.

[72] See esp. Raviv, "השפעתו של ספר דניאל על פרשנות המקרא של חז"ל," 97–118. A brief example is the letter Xerxes sent to his subjects ordering the massacre of the Jews, as quoted in the Midrash Abba Gurion. The letter, which is written in Hebrew, opens with an Aramaic introduction: "to all peoples, nations, and ethnicities, who live in the entire world, may your peace increase!" This introduction was lifted from the opening of the letter written by Nebuchadnezzar quoted in Daniel 3:31, which is the same as the opening of Darius' letter quoted in Daniel 6:26. The fictional letter in full is found in the midrash there, pp. 15a–16a in Hebrew, and a different version on pp 16b–17a in Aramaic. It is a remarkable example of imagined counter-history, for in it Xerxes quickly reviews Jewish history, focusing in particular on the Exodus, casting the Jews as wicked sorcerers with unknown dark powers. Of course, what we actually have here is the Jews imagining what their enemies might say about what are, in their minds, the high points of their past – and thus, presumably, debunking such counter-histories in their own minds. For some brief comments on this genre, which appears in a number of forms in the Esther midrashim, see Lerner, "The Works of Aggadic Midrash," 176, who refers to them as "'anti-Semitic' outbursts and diatribes against Jewish religion and custom." Joshua Berman, "Aggadah and Anti-Semitism: The Midrashim to Esther 3:8," *Judaism*, 38 (1989), 185–96, discusses the sources of the descriptions of Jewish ritual found in some of the midrashim, but does not deal with the counter-historical narratives.

[73] See Esther 2:19, 21, and Daniel 2:49. [74] Panim Aherot B, p. 33a.

The comparison between Mordecai and Daniel may also be part of the point of the speech of Zeresh, as quoted in Esther Rabbah and the Targum Rishon and Targum Sheni, all of which include variations on the line "You cannot hope to kill Mordecai by throwing him into the lions' den: Daniel was saved from that very fate!"[75] One targumic passage quotes a prayer offered by Mordecai, which overtly draws on Daniel 2: "Revealer of Secrets! Reveal the secret to Mordecai, for death has been decreed upon the House of Israel!"[76]

Other examples are more surprising. One midrash claims that Memucan – identified elsewhere by the Rabbis as Haman[77] – was actually Daniel![78] The text explains that he was planted there by God in order to effect the "miracle" of the death of Vashti, necessary for the advancement of the Jewish interests in the story. Thus his name, Memucan, which is taken to mean "appointed," reflects the fact that he was "appointed" to carry out this mission. Others see Daniel later in the story, in the figure of Hatach, who carried messages back and forth between Esther and Mordecai.[79] Both Rav and Samuel identify Hatach as Daniel, although they disagree on why he was named Hatach: according to Rav, it was because he was "cut off" (*ḥatakh*) from his position of greatness; Samuel says it was because all matters of state were "decided" (*ḥatakh*) on the basis of what he says.[80]

Why read Esther in light of Daniel? As discussed at length above, Daniel and Esther provide conflicting models of life in the Diaspora.[81] Of the two, it was the model of Daniel which the Rabbis found to be satisfactory; Daniel, it will be recalled, compromised on none of his religious practices, and instead found success within the empire by excelling at Judaism. Reading Esther as if it were another episode in the book of Daniel, in full agreement on matters of identity and ideology, made the book not just palatable but inspiring. The influence of Daniel on reading Esther is, therefore, far-reaching.

---

[75] Esther Rabbah 9:2; Targum Rishon and Targum Sheni to 5:14.
[76] The Geniza text is T-S B 12.21 1r 12–20, published in Kasher and Klein, "New Fragments of Targum to Esther," 94. The translation here differs from that offered by Kasher and Klein (*ibid.*, 104), which takes the last line (גלי רזין גלא רזא למרדכי, דגזירת מותא כל בית ישראל) to be a narrative post-script to the prayer, rather than part of the prayer. The line, if I understand it correctly, is based on Daniel 2:19.
[77] See b. Megillah 12b.   [78] Panim Aherot B, p. 31a.
[79] For a modern approach to the literary problem of Hatach, see Jonathan Grossman, "The Vanishing Character in Biblical Narrative: The Role of Hathach in Esther 4," *VT* 62 (2012), 561–71.
[80] B. Megillah 15a; see also Targum Rishon to 4:5. Both these suggestions (quoted in the names of Babylonian Amoraim) rely on the interchange of the phonemes /h/ with /ḥ/, which had merged in Babylonian Aramaic.
[81] See esp. Chapters 3 and 6 above.

b. Food habits in Esther and Daniel

In a number of midrashim, Esther is said to have refrained from eating the food served in the palace, an idea explored above in the discussions of Addition C and the book of Judith.[82] This is a motif likely influenced by the refusal of Daniel and his friends to eat the royal food served in Babylon, according to Daniel 1. This comparison is made explicit sometimes: "Nevertheless, she consumed nothing except her own food, and not from the table of the king, just as Hananiah, Mishael, and Azariah did not eat the rations of King Nebuchadnezzar."[83] The two Targumim also emphatically state that Esther did not consume the non-kosher food in the palace.[84] What is taken for granted in these texts is debated in the Bavli: while Samuel argues that she violated the laws of kashrut, because of coercion, Rav suggests that she observed the dietary laws during her entire time in the palace. Strikingly, R. Yohanan claims that Esther became a vegetarian, and cites the story of Daniel 1 for proof.[85]

It is difficult to know precisely what lies behind the opposing views of Rav and Samuel. Elisha Ancelovits observed that Rav is particularly active in formulating the laws regulating which foods cooked by non-Jews may and may not be eaten.[86] Perhaps, then, for him this was a deep-rooted concern not entirely shared by his colleague. Arnon Atzmon observed that the dispute between Rav and Samuel may be the result of differing hermeneutics, but it may also be the result of differing worldviews. Samuel is known to have had a close relationship with the Persian court, and may have been comfortable acknowledging that identities, especially in a diaspora setting, are complex.[87] Here we may see different political views come to the surface in readings of Esther. Whereas most of the Rabbis insisted on absolute fidelity to the law, and could tolerate nothing less in their biblical heroes, Samuel knew from experience that political accomplishment may necessitate compromises of one sort or another, and was prepared to find such compromises being made in Esther, as well. This is not to say that he *advocated* such compromises, only that he found it plausible that they occurred, and read Esther in that light.

---

[82] See above, pp. 118–19 and 136–38.   [83] Panim Aherot B, p. 32b.

[84] This is in their rendering of Esther 2:9. See Atzmon, "לטוב. . .וַיִּשְׁנֶהָ," 113.

[85] B. Megillah 13a; see Leila Leah Bronner, *From Eve to Esther: Rabbinic Reconstructions of Biblical Women*, Gender and the Biblical Tradition (Louisville: Westminster John Knox, 1994), 178–79.

[86] See b. Avoda Zara 38a. Ancelovits' insight was shared at a conference in 2012; I am indebted to him for it.

[87] Atzmon, "וַיִּשְׁנֶהָ. . .לטוב," 117–18; on Samuel in this regard, see Elman, "Middle Persian Culture and Babylonian Sages," 174 and 192.

c. Israel earned its punishment

Most importantly, it appears that the basic theology evident in the book of Daniel determined the theology that the Rabbis found in Esther. A particularly powerful example is the question asked in a number of rabbinic texts: "Why did Israel deserve the punishment of Haman?" Let us be clear that within the book of Esther, there is no answer to this question, since there is not even the faintest suggestion that Israel did deserve the threat of Haman. Instead, the book seems to argue that genocidal threats are simply part of life, at least in the unpredictable Diaspora. This, however, was theologically unacceptable to many readers, who instead searched for an explanation for the near-catastrophe. One favored response is that the Jews earned this by enjoying the food at Xerxes' banquet, narrated in Esther 1. There are a number of variations on this theme.[88] In one text, R. Shimon b. Yohai is quoted as saying that the Jews ate food cooked by non-Jews, but that they did so because they were coerced.[89] Another midrash (in the same collection) goes out of its way to say that because "none coerced" (Esther 1:8), no one was forced to attend the banquet – and therefore the Jews could not claim that they attended against their will.[90] According to yet another text, the Jews were singled out for the banquet by Haman, just for the purpose of condemning them to their God for having participated.[91]

It should be noted that other midrashim contain other suggestions for why the Jews deserved to suffer as they did in the story, and these remove the "sin" from the book of Esther and see it as originating centuries earlier. One view relies on the phrase (Esther 4:1) describing Mordecai's reaction to Haman's decree: "he screamed a great and bitter scream (ze'aqa gedola u-mara)." The midrash points out that nearly an identical phrase is attested in Genesis, when Esau discovers that his blessing has been stolen by Jacob: "he screamed a great and bitter scream (ṣe'aqa gedola u-mara)."[92] Jacob

---

[88] A brief suggestion in midrash Panim Aherot A, p. 26a, apparently reflects this view: ומרדכי ידע את כל אשר נעשה... ידע מאיזה חטא לקר, על שאכלו בישולי גוים "Mordecai knew all that had been done ... he knew for which sin they were suffering: because they had eaten food cooked by non-Jews." See also the Aramaic poem from Byzantine Palestine published in Yahalom and Sokoloff, שירת בני מערבא, 186: "since they took part in the banquet, it was as if they were not Jews / ... but Mordecai did not eat / so the One chose him ..." The Bavli (Megillah 11a) quotes R. Elazar as saying, "Because of the laziness of Israel, who should have studied Torah but didn't, Israel (literally: 'the enemy of God') became poor."

[89] Midrash Abba Gurion, p. 5a: אמר ר' שמעון בר יוחאי, מכאן שאכלו בשולי נכרים בעל כרחם "R. Shimon b. Yohai said: from here we learn that they ate food cooked by non-Jews against their will."

[90] According to Midrash Abba Gurion, p. 16b, this was Haman's idea: ומי שירצה לבוא, יבא, ומי שלא ירצה לבוא, לא יבא, כדי שלא יהיה להם פתחון פה לומר על כרחם הביאום "whoever wants to come will come, and whoever does not want to come will not come – so that they will have no excuse to say that they were brought against their will."

[91] Esther Rabbah 7:13.   [92] Genesis 27:34.

made Esau suffer, says the midrash, and this could not go unpunished. "Where was the payback? Here."[93] The verbal allusion shows that the suffering experienced by the Jews in Esther was retribution for the suffering that Jacob inflicted on Esau in Genesis. Along similar lines, perhaps the Jews were being punished for the sin committed by their ancestors, when they sold their brother Joseph many years ago: "God said to the tribes: 'You sold your brother after eating and drinking so I will do to you!' – as it says, 'the king and Haman sat to drink' (Esther 3:15)."[94]

Going less far back in time is an interpretation found in the midrash Panim Aherot A.[95] Referring again to Esther 6:1, "On that night, the king's sleep was disturbed," R. Yohanan says that God's sleep was disturbed because he was thinking about the sin of the Jews. He called in the Patriarchs and informed them that their children deserved to be destroyed, "because they did not sanctify my name in the days of the wicked Nebuchadnezzar, and made me out like one who has no power to save." They said to him, "Master of the world, do with them as you will." The mention of the failure to sanctify God's name in the days of Nebuchadnezzar is transparently a reference to the behavior of the Jews in general in the story of Hananiah, Mishael, and Azariah in Daniel 3. In that story, Nebuchadnezzar erected an idol and ordered that everyone bow to it when particular music was played. The three Jews Hananiah, Mishael, and Azariah refused, and told the king in no uncertain terms that they would not prostrate themselves before the idol under any circumstances, but that although God might not choose to save them, it should be known that he had the power to do so if he wished. This was admirable behavior, but where were the rest of the Jews of Babylonia? Tens of thousands of Jews had been exiled there, and yet only three stood up to the king! Since the argument offered by Hananiah, Mishael, and Azariah was that God has the power to save, it must have been this very claim that the rest of the Jews doubted (or appeared to doubt). For this, the Jews would now have to pay. They were saved, according to this story, because God determined that they had violated the law out of fear only. It is tempting to think that there is a lesson in this story for the Jews of rabbinic times. True, some might be violating various laws in order to become better acculturated into Roman society, and this is not behavior to be condoned. On the other hand, the

---

[93] Bereshit Rabbah 67:4; Panim Aherot A, p. 26a; Esther Rabbah 8:1. See also Grossman, "'Dynamic Analogies,'" 399.
[94] Esther Rabbah 7:25.   [95] Panim Aherot A, p. 24a.

story reassures its readers, violations performed through fear of the empire are not deserving of a real punishment, only a real scare.

The idea that the Jews were punished for their participation in Xerxes' banquet seems to be a particularly widespread one, however, as well as a particularly powerful one. In one text, the view that the Jews were condemned for eating at the royal banquet is cited in the name of R. Shimon b. Yohai's students. They had asked their teacher this question, but he told them to suggest an answer. "Because they enjoyed the banquet of that wicked man," they suggested. R. Shimon b. Yohai objected, though: this could only condemn the Jews in Susa. What about those in the rest of the empire? The students gave up, and asked their teacher, again, for an answer. He said: "Because they bowed down to the idol."[96] Now the students objected: "Did they really mean to show devotion?" "No," said R. Shimon, "they only acted for appearances' sake, so the Holy One, blessed be He, only acted with them for appearances' sake." This is why he invited Haman to threaten the Jews, but not to actually destroy them.[97] Here the claim that the Jews "deserved" their punishment is modified somewhat. God did not actually decree the destruction of the Jews; he decreed only the *apparent* destruction of the Jews, because they *appeared* to betray him and worship an idol.[98] Near-annihilation for ostensible idolatry: façade for façade.

The claim made by R. Shimon's disciples, that the Jews' sin was their participation in the royal banquet, also contains some deep irony. Although the claim is that the sharing of the banquet led to the threat of annihilation, it is impossible not to be reminded of the rabbinic prohibition of sharing meals with Gentiles, *lest the commensality lead to intermarriage.*[99] Is the suggestion being made that the Jews' participation in Xerxes' banquet was what led to the intermarriage of Esther with the king – and that such interactions were what led to the divine decree of destruction?[100]

Most importantly, it seems clear that besides any inner-Esther considerations which may have led the Rabbis to see food violations as operative in chapter 1, the comparison with Daniel is central to this line of reasoning. In

---

[96] For some discussion of R. Shimon b. Yohai's position, and the medieval views regarding it, see Angel, "*Hadassa Hi Esther*, 82–83.

[97] B. Megillah 12a.   [98] The same claim is found later in the Midrash Leqaḥ Ṭov, p. 86.

[99] For discussion of this prohibition, see Jordan D. Rosenblum, "From their Bread to their Bed: Commensality, Intermarriage, and Idolatry in Tannaitic Literature," *JJS* 61 (2010), 18–29.

[100] There is the further irony that some midrashim (b. Megillah 13b; Panim Aherot B, p. 34b) claim that one of Haman's accusations regarding the Jews was that they wouldn't marry "our" daughters or let their daughters marry "us". This is the charge he lays when talking to the Persian king married to a Jewish woman!

Table 14.2 *Comparison of Esther and Daniel*

Daniel	Esther
Begins with food in the palace	Begins with food in the palace
Exiled Jews do not partake	[Exiled Jews do or do not partake]
God *shows* that he is protecting the Jews in exile	God *does not show* that he is protecting the Jews in exile

the introductory chapter of the book, Daniel himself, as a new member of the palace, is supposed to join in the consumption of the palace foods, but resists, and he emerges from this story, and into the rest of the book, proven pure.[101] Furthermore, the fact that he thrives despite his vegan diet assures him (and the reader) that he has divine assistance, and so the remainder of the book unfolds with little tension; the reader knows with as much certainly as Daniel himself that God will help him when he is in need.

In Esther the opposite is the case. There has been no sign of God, and there is no certainty that he will come to the Jews' aid (until the events of chapter 6 unfold as they do). Furthermore, this book, too, opens with a narrative of the food of the palace, but here there is no indication that any the Jews did not partake. The Rabbis latched onto this intertextual comparison as a way of explaining the difference in tenors between the narratives, then. The contrast can be charted as shown in Table 14.2.

The disciples (and the other Rabbis cited in the other texts) drew a reasonable conclusion: the absence of God is *the result of* the blurred boundaries in chapter 1. No distinction is drawn in that chapter between the Jews and the rest of the residents of Susa – and that is precisely the sin which led to the threat which now unfolds in the story. The contention here is, though, that the reason why the Rabbis read Jewish participation into Esther 1 is the expectation, set by Daniel 1, that Jews in the foreign environment would refrain from partaking in the royal food. When Esther 1 tells of a feast and *fails* to make it clear that the Jews did not participate, the conclusion is drawn that they did, indeed, participate.

This claim, then, has a substantial interpretive payoff: it can explain why the entire trajectory of the subsequent story differs from the stories in Daniel. Daniel's refusal to eat earned him divine assistance; the failure of the Jews in Xerxes' day to resist similarly nearly earned them divinely

---

[101] For an analysis of the use of the table in Daniel 1, see above, pp. 65–68.

sponsored annihilation. The final detail of this story emerges from a midrash elsewhere. R. Yose says that when Xerxes made the banquet, all the
Jews attended with everyone else, and ate the food of non-Jews. Only
Mordecai, out of all the Jews, did not eat with them or drink, and this is
why he was called a "Jewish man."[102]

Thus, according to the disciples of R. Shimon b. Yohai, the Jews condemned themselves by failing to emulate the impeccable behavior modeled
by Daniel and his friends.[103] Mordecai, on the other hand, is singled out for
being Daniel-like in his refusal to eat the king's food.[104] In another way,
Mordecai is being implicitly compared to Hananiah, Mishael, and Azariah:
these great individuals, unlike the masses of Jews, all stood strong in their
opposition to the king's decrees in violation of Torah law.[105]

6. Reading Purim in light of Passover

A different way in which Esther was incorporated into the rabbinic worldview was that it was assimilated into the paradigm of salvation provided by

---

[102] Midrash Panim Aherot B, p. 40a. The same interpretation is found earlier in this collection, p. 31b, in
the name of R. Isaac.

[103] A similar interpretation is found in another midrash: "the king made a banquet for the whole people
('am) – said R. Hanina b. Papa, this teaches that the leaders of the generation heard about it and fled"
(Esther Rabbah 2:5; Abba Gurion, p. 5a). This apparently relies on a binary opposition between the
'am "people" and the leaders (gedole ha-dor). The king made a feast for the whole 'am, but the leaders
were not in attendance. Thus, on this reading, all the Jewish leaders in the days of Xerxes were like
Daniel, Hananiah, Mishael, and Azariah: they, too, avoided the violations imposed on the massed by
the king. The opposite perspective is found in a different statement in the Bavli. Here Haman's
accusation that the Jews' laws are different from those of all other residents of the Persian Empire is
glossed, "they do not eat of our [food], and they do not marry our [children] or marry [theirs] to us!"
See b. Megillah 13b, along with Judith R. Baskin, "Erotic Subversion: Undermining Female Agency
in bMegillah 10b–17a," in Tal Ilan, Tamara Or, Dorothea M. Salzer, Christiane Steuer, and
Irina Wandrey (eds.), A Feminist Commentary on the Babylonian Talmud: Introduction and Studies
(Tübingen: Mohr Siebeck, 2007), 228. Thus, kashrut and the ban on intermarriage, rather than
being ignored, as in MT Esther, are scrupulously adhered to. Ironically, the observance of these
commandments here causes the ensuing troubles. This, of course, does not provide an explanation
for why the Jews were being punished in Esther's day. Indeed, an Aramaic poem from Byzantine
Palestine has Esther saying, "If our fathers sinned, what did the sons sin? . . . If the children sinned,
how did the suckling babes sin?" Yahalom and Sokoloff, שירת בני מערבא, 176. Against the editors'
note, ibid., 175, Esther does not admit sin in her own age (as this line makes explicit), and line 6 refers
to sins which caused the destruction of the First Temple, not the threat of Haman.

[104] See also the story from Esther Rabbah 7:13 cited in Chapter 15 (see p. 211). The supposition that
Mordecai alone did not partake of the banquet is also found in Panim Aherot B, p. 31b, and Targum
Rishon to 1:5.

[105] See also the Targum in T-S B 11.52 2v 2–10 (Kasher and Klein, "New Fragments of Targum to
Esther," 98), in which Haman's wife and friends tell him that there were once Jews named Hananiah,
Mishael, and Azariah, who were miraculously saved from the fiery furnace; if Mordecai is like them,
Haman cannot prevail.

the Exodus and incarnated in the festival of Passover. It is true within the narrative that the deliverance of Purim took place on Passover, and the significance of this for the political understanding of Esther was discussed above.[106] The Rabbis noted this confluence of dates, and exploited it in various ways. Some of the rabbinic comments amount to no more than the observation. Thus, one passage identifies Esther as "one who kept the commandment" because she was "busy with the commandment to get rid of leavened bread."[107] In the Targum Rishon, Esther 5:1 ("It was on the third day") is translated, "It was on the third day of Passover."[108]

Most often, it was not the deliverance on Passover that was the focus of attention, but the fact that Mordecai and the rest of the Jews were fasting for three days (Esther 4:16–17), which spanned 15 Nisan. There was no *seder* that year, and indeed the Jews were all in violation of the prohibition on fasting on a festival.[109]

Rav interprets the clause "Mordecai passed" (*va-ya'avor Mordecai* [Esther 4:17]) as a reference to this very point: "He passed (*he'evir*) the first day of Passover in fasting."[110] Many manuscripts of the Talmud read "transgressed" (*'avar 'al*) instead of "passed," thus injecting a critical note into the description of Mordecai's actions. This is paralleled in the Targum Rishon, which paraphrases this clause with "he transgressed (*'avar 'al*) the festival (*hedvat hagga*) of Passover: he declared a fast and sat on ashes."[111] Other versions of this same dialogue even have Mordecai quoting Megillat Ta'anit regarding the prohibition of fasting in the first weeks of Nisan.[112]

If some texts are critical, if only mildly, of the decision taken to fast through the first day of Passover, others are stridently defensive regarding this point. Esther berates Mordecai for his initial refusal to violate the

---

[106] See above, Chapter 8.   [107] Qohelet Rabbah §8, on Qohelet 8:5, שׁוֹמֵר מִצְוָה לֹא יֵדַע דָּבָר רָע.
[108] Grossfeld, *The First Targum to Esther*, 22.
[109] See also Michael G. Wechsler, "The Purim-Passover Connection: A Reflection of Jewish Exegetical Tradition in the Peshitta Book of Esther," *JBL* 117 (1998), 321–35, who argues for the echoes of a connection between the two festivals in the Peshitta, as well.
[110] B. Megillah 15a.
[111] Similar statements, which seem to be critical of Mordecai, are found also in Esther Rabbah 8:7 and elsewhere; see further Grossfeld, *The First Targum to Esther*, 139–40. The expression חדות חגא is relatively rare in the Targumim, but see the four-fold use in Targum Pseudo-Jonathan to Deuteronomy 16. Interestingly, the word חדות is used by the Targum Rishon later on (9:19, 22) to refer to the new holiday of Purim.
[112] Panim Aherot B, p. 36a: "Mordecai answered, saying to Esther: 'Look, you told me to declare a fast, but I cannot annul Megillat Ta'anit, in which it says, "From the first day of Nisan until the eighteenth, the Tamid is offered, one is not to eulogize and not to fast on them" – but you said to decree a fast, that the people should fast three days: the fourteenth, the day of the paschal offering, the fifteenth, which is a festival, and the sixteenth, when the *'omer* of the wave-offering is offered!'"

Passover festival when national catastrophe looms: "You are an elder of
Israel?! If there is no Israel in the world, what good are the festivals?!"[113]

Other midrashim do discuss the fact that the salvation itself is executed
on Passover; the focus is, once again, on "that very night," when the king's
sleep is disturbed. One particularly striking passage plays somewhat loose
with the chronology of the story, in an effort to make "that very night" the
"very night" of the Exodus. As we saw, Haman's decree was promulgated on
the 13th of Nisan, and the three days of fasting could have started that day or
the next day. If we assume they began that very day, the third day, on which
Esther approached the king, would have been the 15th, and the night Xerxes
could not sleep would have been the following night (the night after the
first day of Passover).[114] This does not prevent R. Ḥelbo from claiming
otherwise:

> "On that night the king's sleep was disturbed" (Esther 6:1): R. Ḥelbo says, in
> four places it says "on that night," and all four were on the evening of
> Passover; two were of [the tribes descended from] Rachel, and two were of
> [the tribes descended from Leah] ... as it says:
>   i. "It was, in the middle of the night" (Exodus 12:29): this was the evening
>   of the Passover, and miracles were done at the hand of Moses, who was
>   among the children of the children of Leah.
> ii. "It was on that very night, an angel of the Lord went out and struck in
>   the Assyrian camp" (2 Kings 19:35): that night was the evening of
>   Passover ... and this miracle was performed at the hand of Hezekiah,
>   who was among the children of the children of Leah ...
> And two by the children of Rachel:
> iii. "On that night, the Lord said to Gideon, 'Get up and go down to the
>   camp'" (Judges 7:9)[115]: it was the evening of Passover, since it is written,

---

[113] Panim Aherot B, p. 36a; see further references in Segal, *The Babylonian Esther Midrash*, vol. II, 260–
65. A parallel is found in Pirqe de-Rabbi Eliezer §49, and in Esther Rabbah 8:7; Atzmon was able to
show that Esther Rabbah B borrowed from Pirqe de-Rabbi Eliezer, and that in this case, the text of
Esther Rabbah should even be emended in light of the evidence of Pirqe de-Rabbi Eliezer. See
Arnon Atzmon, "מעשה אסתר" בפרקי דרבי אליעזר ובאסתר רבה ב: לביסוסה של זיקה בין מקבילות בספרות
חז"ל," *Tarbiz*, 75 (2006), 329–43, and, for our case, Arnon Atzmon, "שחזור נוסח המדרש על פי
מקבילות-מקורות," *JSIJ* 9 (2010), 8–10. פרדיגמה חדשה לבעיה ישנה Compare the motif of Guenevere
criticizing Lancelot for hesitating when it came to violating his code of honor in order to save her
(portrayed as a conflict between Reason and Love): Chrétien de Troyes, *Arthurian Romances*, tr.
William W. Kibler and Carleton W. Carroll (London: Penguin, 1991), 212.

[114] See above, Chapter 8, n. 5 for references.

[115] The MT reads, "the Lord said to him." Rather than seeing this as a textual variant, it is more
reasonable to assume that the midrash identifies the referent of the pronoun for the benefit of the
audience.

"Behold, there was a cake of barley bread" (Judges 7:13) – this was the *'omer* that is offered on Passover.

iv. And one in the days of Mordecai, who was among the children of the children of Leah, therefore it says, "On that night the king's sleep was disturbed."[116]

R. Ḥelbo is apparently willing to pay the price of inexactitude with regard to the dates, since the midrashic payoff is quite large: on this reading, the night of the salvation of the Jews in Egypt and the night of the salvation of the Jews in Persia are one and the same.[117] Indeed, R. Ḥelbo also claimed that there are four occurrences of the phrase "on that night" (*ba-layla ha-hu*), but the paradigmatic example, Exodus 12:29, does not actually use that phrase at all. Apparently the power of the idea convinced R. Ḥelbo that the details could be fudged somewhat if necessary.[118]

The resonance of the comparison between Purim and Passover must have been a powerful one for Jews living under Roman dominion, especially after the catastrophic failure of the Bar Koseba revolt in the early second century. Hopes for a Passover-type redemption had faded, and so Jews may naturally have asked, "is there hope for any redemption at all?" A number of the rabbinic comments on the dates comprise thoughtful reactions to the type of "redemption" represented by Esther and Purim, which includes no miracles, no prophets, no movement, and no God. The sharpest criticism of such a redemption comes from the Babylonian Amora Rava, who explains that the songs of Hallel are not sung on Purim, as opposed to Passover, because "There [on Passover] it is fine [to say Hallel], because they were slaves to God and not slaves to Pharaoh [any longer], but here [in the Purim story], is it true that they are God's slaves and not Ahauerus' slaves?! We are still Ahasuerus' slaves (*akkatei 'avdei Aḥashverosh anan*)!"[119]

The continuation of the Talmudic discussion, in the wake of Rava's comment, is also relevant to this point. A different view cited in the Talmud was that Hallel could never be recited on a miracle which took place outside the land of Israel; the Exodus was explained as exceptional since it took place

---

[116] Panim Aherot B, p. 37a.

[117] The tradition of the "four nights," all of which were the 14th of Nisan, has a long history, and appears in the Palestinian Targumim to Exodus 12:42, as Moshe Bernstein pointed out to me. In these texts, however, the story of Esther is not involved, and the four events mentioned are Creation, the announcement of Isaac's birth, the Exodus, and the messianic redemption.

[118] A similar (but more elaborate) typological reading of the date is found in Yannai's *piyyut*, *Az rov nissim* (which includes the refrain *vayhi ba-hatzi ha-layla*), as Shalom Holtz reminded me.

[119] B. 'Arakhin 10b; b. Megillah 14a. See the comments of Gottlieb, "המדרש על מגילת אסתר: "ונהפוך הוא"," 125.

prior to the Jewish entry into the land of Israel.[120] Why, then, does Rava[121] feel the need to provide a different explanation for the lack of Hallel? The Talmud suggests that there is a disupute over when "since they were exiled, the other lands reverted to their original acceptable status."[122] This is a fundamental question of the meaning of the exile: has it reversed the process of the entry into the land, or is it merely a parenthesis in the grand scheme of history?

A complex commentary on the juxtaposition of Purim and Passover is found in a rabbinic commentary on Megillat Ta'anit. The text cites two views on the relative values of the festivals. R. Joshua b. Qorḥah says that the age legislation ended with Moses: "From the day Moses died, no prophet arose and innovated commandments for Israel, except for the commandment of Purim." Still, he emphasizes, Purim is not a festival on the scale of the festivals instituted by Moses, such as Passover: "But the redemption of Egypt is celebrated for seven [days], and the redemption of Mor[decai and Esther] is celebrated for only one." Another view then quoted, on the other hand, points out that the redemption celebrated by Purim transcends that celebrated by Passover: only Haman actually tried to annihilate the entire Jewish people, "male and female, youth to elderly, children and women on the same day"![123] In Egypt only the newborn baby boys were actually to be killed; in Persia the decree was for the massacre of everyone, man, woman, and child.

One might respond that in Egypt the true redemption cannot be measured by the number of people who otherwise would have died, since the central theme of the story is the redemption from slavery, not from death. This is true, and a different comment of R. Joshua b. Qorḥah makes just that point: "If we sing praise about going from slavery to freedom, it is obvious that we must sing when we go from death to life!"[124]

Most significantly, the rabbinic halakhah mandates a connection between the celebrations of Purim and Passover. Passover is celebrated in Nisan, the first month of the year; Purim is celebrated in Adar, the year's

---

[120] Some modern historians do not accept any of the Talmudic explanations for the lack of Hallel on Purim, and argue that this merely reflects the uncertain status of Purim during the era of the Temple. See Oppenheimer, "אהבת מרדכי ושנאת המן?'," 409.

[121] The same question is asked of Rav Nahman, who claimed that the act of reading the book of Esther was tantamount to reciting Hallel.

[122] B. Megillah 14a.

[123] This is Scholion A on Megillat Ta'anit, corrected according to the 'kil'ayim' text; see Noam, מגילת תענית, 304.

[124] R. Hiyya b. Abin quotes this in the name of R. Joshua b. Qorḥah in b. Megillah 14a. See Noam, מגילת תענית, 304.

last. When the year is intercalated, it is Adar that is doubled. The mishnah raises the question of what to do if Purim is celebrated and the Megillah ritually read on the 14th of Adar, and then the year is intercalated and an extra month added. Does Purim need to be celebrated again in the second Adar? The mishnah rules that it does. The Yerushalmi quotes R. Ḥelbo – who argued above that the redemptions of Purim and Passover were both effected on the same night – with an explanation why: "so as to juxtapose redemption to redemption."[125]

It would seem that R. Ḥelbo argues that the values of Purim and Passover are most enhanced when the two are celebrated in conjunction with one another. Recall that it was R. Ḥelbo who posited that both the redemption of the Exodus and the redemption of Purim took place on the 15th of Nisan. Therefore, the festivals need to be exactly a month apart. Clearly R. Ḥelbo sees a deep and intrinsic connection between Passover and Purim. He bends the text to force them to be exactly a month apart, and insists that despite possible wrinkles in the calendar, their celebrations must always be juxtaposed.

Juxtaposing these two festivals forces the celebrant to meditate on the vastly different types of "redemption" they commemorate. One was accomplished through overt miracles, the other with none. One was directed by the greatest of all prophets, the other with only lay leaders. One was accompanied at all time by clear signs of divine involvement, and the other with only questions. One climaxed with a mass movement of people from exile to Israel, and the other with no exodus and no geographic passage, but the Jews continuing to exist in the Diaspora. R. Ḥelbo may be claiming that for the Jews post-destruction, the two need to be celebrated together, "to juxtapose redemption to redemption."[126]

---

[125] Y. Megillah 1:5 (70d).

[126] For a different view on the different values encoded in Purim and Passover – the former as an immature, vindictive response to an enemy, and the latter a mature, developed response – see Jeremy Schonfield, "Esther: Beyond Murder," *European Judaism*, 32 (1999), 11–25, esp. 14–19.

CHAPTER 15

Restoring God and Torah

1. Theodicy

The single most important, and most objectionable, point about Esther is the absence of God from the book.[1] The Sages in the Talmud ask where one can find an allusion to Esther within the Torah. They point in response to a passage from the end of Deuteronomy, in which God tells Moses, "I will indeed hide my face on that day."[2] On one level, this is merely a pun on the name Esther, which sounds very much like the Hebrew expression "I will indeed hide" (*haster astir*). On another level, however, this is a serious theological argument.[3] Where, the Rabbis ask, did the Torah ever speak of a story in which God would not be revealed? Is there license for such a narrative from the Torah? Once again, the problem the Rabbis grapple with is that Esther seems to be entirely un-biblical, different in its essence from the rest of the Hebrew Bible. Is such a story possible, in a biblical context? The answer: yes. Back in Deuteronomy, God promised that one day he would hide his face from his people. Esther shows that he kept his word.

Such an approach, while finding canonical precedent for Esther, thus solves a literary problem by creating a theological one. Can God be hidden? What does this mean, and what are the implications of this for life? For the Rabbis, God's disappearance from the text was only the tip of the iceberg: the real problem was God's disappearance from the world. After all, they lived in a post-*hurban* world, where the Temple had been destroyed, Bar Koseba's revolt had been crushed, massive numbers of Jews had been killed, Jewish autonomy had been lost, and God was nowhere to be seen. The "promise" of "I will surely hide (*haster astir*) my face" is chillingly frightening. Esther, in which God is literarily hidden, thus provides an opportunity for the Rabbis to explain where God is when he is actually hidden.

---

[1] See above, pp. 96–106.   [2] B. Hullin 139a, citing Deuteronomy 31:18.
[3] See Claude-Anne Gugenheim, "Les femmes prophétesses: À partir du traité *Meguila* 14a du Talmud de Babylone," *Pardés*, 43 (2007), 118–19.

a. The presence of God

If God was "hidden," is that to say that he was uninvolved, or simply that he was not visible? In scattered rabbinic texts, there is a willingness to entertain the possibility that God had retreated from the world.[4] Such a view has biblical roots. Psalm 44, after bitterly complaining that the people are suffering despite not "departing from your way," cries to God: "Rouse yourself! Why do you sleep, O Lord?!"[5] R. Meir is cited as following this line of thought: "R. Meir taught: He is indeed indifferent to the world. Just like a judge, in front of whose face they draw a curtain and he does not know what happens outside." The audacity of this claim raised the ire of R. Meir's colleagues: "They said to him: 'Enough, Meir!'"[6]

R. Meir's contemporary R. Shimon b. Yohai also harshly criticized God's failures of intervention: "It resembles two athletes who were standing and wrestling in front of the king. Had the king wanted, he could have separated them; since he doesn't want to separate them, one prevails over the other and kills him. [The loser] cries out and says, 'May my case appear before the king!'"[7] These bold claims struggle with the fact that God has failed to intervene on behalf of people who desperately need his help. R. Meir seems to go so far as to claim that God is oblivious to what is happening in the world; R. Shimon b. Yohai, perhaps more disturbingly, portrays God as a spectator in the violence, who – at least according to the dying athlete – will one day have to answer for the deaths of those sporting in front of him.

Once again, the book of Daniel set the standard by which later events were to be judged. An oft-told rabbinic tale of two brothers explicitly contrasts the reality known to the Rabbis – in which innocents were massacred and nothing was seen from God – with the biblical stories familiar to them:

> When Trajan killed Pappus and his brother Lulianus in Lydda, he said to them, "Aren't you from the people of Hannaniah, Mishael, and Azariah? Let your God come and save you from my hand!" They said to him, "Hannaniah, Mishael, and Azariah were worthy men, and

[4] These texts were collected and insightfully analyzed by Adiel Schremer, "'The Lord has Forsaken the Land': Radical Explanations of the Military and Political Defeat of the Jews in Tannaitic Literature," *JJS* 59 (2008), 183–200. For a discussion of this question in Second Temple literature, especially apocalyptic, see Koller, "Negotiating Empire."

[5] Psalm 44:24. For a sophisticated intertextual analysis, see Dalit Rom-Shiloni, "Psalm 44: The Powers of Protest," *CBQ* 70 (2008), 683–98, and see Schremer, "'The Lord has Forsaken the Land,'" 185.

[6] Bereshit Rabbah 36:1 (Theodor and Albeck, בראשית רבא, 334); see Schremer, "'The Lord has Forsaken the Land,'" 192.

[7] Bereshit Rabbah 22:9 (Theodor and Albeck, בראשית רבא, 216); see Schremer, "'The Lord has Forsaken the Land,'" 193.

Nebuchadnezzar suitable that a miracle would be done on his account. But you are a wicked king, and not suitable that a miracle would be done on your account, and we are liable to the death penalty from heaven [anyway], so if it's not you who kills us, God has many agents . . . On the other hand, at the end, God will demand our blood from you!"[8]

In the rabbinic readings of Esther, no text goes so far as to deny God's involvement from beginning to end. This is, fortunately, not necessary: the Jews triumph in the end of the story, and so this must certainly reveal God's involvement. Whether God was involved from the beginning or not, however, was very much debated; and if he was not, this necessitated some discussion.

There seem to be different views among the Rabbis as to where exactly he is to be seen first. Did he step in only after the situation had turned gravely dangerous, or had he orchestrated that danger to begin with? One place where this question finds expression is in a rabbinic debate about how much of the story one has to read in order to fulfill the obligation of reading the Megillah on Purim. R. Meir rules that one must read the entire book of Esther, beginning to end. R. Judah says that one must read only from the introduction of Mordecai in 2:5; the prologue about Vashti is dispensable. R. Yose rules that one must read only from the beginning of chapter 3, from the promotion of Haman and the beginning of the troubles. On his view, even the selection of Esther to be queen is not necessary for the story. Finally, R. Shimon b. Yohai goes so far as to say that one fulfills the obligation even by beginning the story in chapter 6, with Xerxes' sleepless night. All agree that to fulfill the obligation, one must reach the end of the book.[9]

Encoded in this technical legal debate is, it may be assumed, the fundamental question: what is it within the story of Esther that makes it worth reading at all? R. Shimon b. Yohai, who requires only that one read from the beginning of chapter 6, apparently sees the first five chapters as prologue: they are needed only in order to understand what preceded, but they are not the story of the salvation of Israel. R. Yose, who says that one must read at

---

[8] Sifra Emor 9:5 (Louis Finkelstein, [ed.], *Sifre on Deuteronomy* [Berlin: Gesellschaft zur Förderung der Wissenschaft des Judentums, 1939; reprinted New York: Jewish Theological Seminary, 1969], 442), and numerous parallels; see Schremer, "'The Lord has Forsaken the Land,'" 190 with n. 25, for further references.

[9] Tosefta Megillah 2:9. The same question is addressed in m. Megillah 2:3, but there R. Shimon's view is not recorded. M. B. Lerner observed that in one midrashic collection (Panim Aherot B), there are *petiḥ taot* to just four verses: 1:1, 2:5, 3:1, and 6:1. He further observed that these are "passages which represent the crucial turning points of the Esther narrative in the Bible" (Lerner, "The Works of Aggadic Midrash," 197, and see also *ibid.*, 208 regarding "Panim Aherot III").

least from the beginning of chapter 3, the ascent of Haman to power, apparently believes that understanding the threat to the Jewish people is critical to understanding their escape from that threat. R. Judah, who requires a reading beginning with the introduction of Mordecai and Esther early in chapter 2, may be arguing that in order to understand how the story unfolds, one must know the situation prior to the crisis, including the existence of a Jewish queen of Persia and the Jewish bureaucrat Mordecai. And R. Meir, who insists on nothing less than a complete reading, beginning to end, obviously believes that from the very beginning there are important details revealed in the story which clarify the subsequent events.[10]

In what follows, various views within the rabbinic texts will be discussed. These texts will be arranged conceptually, rather than chronologically; texts which minimize God's involvement, restricting his presence to the last part of the story, will come first, and we will move in order of increasing perception of divine involvement.

b. God never was involved

One solitary rabbinic text claims that God was a would-be destroyer – much like Haman – throughout the story. In this version, Israel is protected by some type of aura which God himself cannot penetrate. This assertion is so surprising that it must be quoted in full:

> R. Levi said, Haman can be compared to a bird that made its nest on the shore of the sea, and the sea rose and flooded the nest. What did the bird do? It got up and started filling its mouth with water and putting it in the sand, then filling its mouth with sand and putting it in the sea. Its friend came and said, "What are you doing, working so hard?" It said, "I am not leaving here until I make this sea into sand!" The friend said, "Fool of the world! What will you accomplish in the end?"[11]

---

[10] The debate is analyzed, in slightly different and slightly more cryptic terms, in y. Megillah 2:4. Alternatively, we may see the Rabbi disagreeing regarding the basic point of the story of Esther. According to R. Shimon b. Yohai, who requires reading only from chapter 6, the obligation is simply to read about the salvation of Israel. R. Yose, who requires reading from the moment when Haman was promoted, claims that one must read not only of the salvation, but of the initial threat. The other two Rabbis, R. Judah and R. Meir, seem to agree that one must read not only about the threat and the deliverance, but also about the background to the story. (They disagree, however, on how much background is necessary.)

[11] This is the only occurrence of the Hitpolel verb להסתופף in the databases of the *Historical Dictionary of the Hebrew Language*, http://hebrew-treasures.huji.ac.il/ (accessed February, 2012). The parallel in Esther Rabbah 7:10 reads, סוף סוף, במה את יכיל "In the end, what can you really do?"

So, too: "Haman sought to destroy all the Jews" (Esther 3:6), and God said to him, "Fool of the world! I sought to destroy the Jews, and was not able to – as it says, 'he thought to destroy them, had it not been for Moses, his chosen one' (Psalm 106:23) – and now you seek to destroy them?!" The end will be that he falls in their hands.

For Israel is compared to rocks – as it says, "for from the top, I see him as rocks" (Numbers 23:9)[12] – and idolaters are compared to pottery – as it says, "he shall break it like the breaking of a potter's vessel" (Isaiah 30:14). If a bowl falls on a domed roof, woe to the bowl; if a domed roof falls on a bowl, woe to the bowl! So, too, all who confront Israel, their honor will be taken out of their hands.[13]

This midrash, it should be emphasized, may be most in line with the theology of the book of Esther itself. The ideology of the biblical book, as voiced by Zeresh, is that the Jews are invincible once they have begun to triumph, despite the absence of God from the story.

c. God woke up

More common, but still daring, is the claim that God remained out of the story until a fairly late point in the narrative. R. Shimon b. Yohai, it will be recalled, asserted that one fulfilled the obligation even by reading only from the beginning of chapter 6, "on that night the king's sleep was disturbed." We unfortunately are not told precisely how R. Shimon read this verse.[14] In other texts, not only was the king's sleep disturbed; so was God's. The following is from an Aramaic text from the Cairo Geniza:

[12] The more obvious way of translating this passage is, "for I see him from the tops of rocks," but the midrash takes the "rocks" to be the object of the seeing.

[13] Midrash Abba Gurion p. 12a–b. The text has been emended in line with Buber's n. 64 there. See also Esther Rabbah 7:10.

[14] As we saw above (p. 121), the Greek text had explicitly seen God acting in the story at that point: "But the Lord kept sleep from the king that night." Rabbinic sources, too, see God's hand especially overtly at this moment (see Wechsler, *Strangers in the Land*, 269–70 n. 239); one midrash (Panim Aherot B, p. 37a) makes exactly the same claim as the Greek text: "What did God do? He disturbed the sleep of Xerxes." This is as opposed to the claim made by Tabory, "השפעת תרגום השבעים למגילת אסתר על הספרות הרבנית," 486–87: "This verse was read numerous ways by the midrashim, but the common denominator is that in none of them does God intervene directly in Xerxes' sleep. Besides the interpretations and midrashim which seek a naturalistic explanation for the disruption of Xerxes' sleep, we find two religious approaches. One is that it was the sleep of the King of the world which was disturbed (alone, or together with the sleep of Xerxes). The other approach, which is closer to the Greek version, is that Xerxes' sleep was disturbed through supernatural means – but not by God himself, but by an angel." R. Tanhum asserts that it was the sleep of "the king of the world" which was disturbed. He is countered by Rava, however, who insists that only the sleep of Xerxes himself was lost that night. The Rabbis embrace both positions, claiming that both heaven and earth could not sleep that night (b. Megillah 15b).

On that night sleep [deserted] the carpenters who were preparing the cross for Haman; on that night sleep deserted the smiths who were preparing nails to be set in the cross; on that night sleep deserted the King of Kings (were it not written, it would not be possible to say it!), as it is written, "Wake up, why do you sleep, O Lord?" (Psalm 44:24) – "And the Lord awoke, like one who had been sleeping" (Psalm 78:65). On that very night the Holy One blessed be He revealed himself.[15]

It should be recalled that R. Shimon b. Yohai was the one who accused God in a different context of callous indifference to suffering in the world. In the case of Esther, he is prepared to grant that although God was uninvolved for much of the time, he did step up at the critical moment: "on that night, the king's sleep was disturbed."

Other texts, too, contain the claim that God had not been involved in the story to this point, but now "awoke." One midrash locates the disturbance at precisely the end of the third hour of the night. At that moment, the cries of the Jews reached the heavens. Moses cried in front of God,

Master of the world, you know that these are not the sounds of kids and lambs, but the sound of the children of your people Israel, who are in the midst of a fast today, for three days, as they are imprisoned with collars and iron chairs around their necks, and tomorrow they will be slaughtered like kids and lambs, and their enemy's heart will rejoice over them!

With that provocation, the mercy of God took over: he shattered the seal and ripped up the letters, refuted Haman's evil plans, and effected a salvation for Israel.[16]

---

[15] Kasher and Klein, "New Fragments of Targum to Esther," 5 (text) and 15 (translation, modified here); see also Tal, "קטעי תרגום אסתר מן הגניזה והם עדות שהם מעידים," 153. A similar midrash appears elsewhere: "On that night the sleep of the king was disturbed – at that hour, Gabriel went down to Xerxes and disturbed his sleep. He hit him on the ground 366 times and said, 'Ingrate! Reward those who deserve it!'" (Midrash Abba Gurion, 19b, with a close parallel in Panim Aherot A, p. 24b, where the angel is named Michael rather than Gabriel). See also Panim Aherot B, p. 37b: "the sleep of Gabriel, who was confusing (מטרף) the heart of Xerxes because of the prayer of Mordecai." Earlier in Panim Aherot B, p. 37b, it is said only that "on that night the sleep of the ministering angels was disturbed."

[16] Abba Gurion, p. 19b. In the similar versions which appear in Esther Rabbah 9:4 and Targum Rishon on 6:1, this episode ends with God disturbing Xerxes' sleep, and thus explains בלילה ההוא נדדה שנת המלך. Similarly, Pirqe de-Rabbi Eli'ezer (§49) asserts that "the throne of the King of kings of kings, the Holy One, blessed be He, shook, and disturbed the king on the earth and he rose from his sleep." Other midrashim, obviously aware of the claims that God was sleeping, take pains to reject it. In one version, *Haman* claims that God slumbered; this is based on his words *yeshno 'am 'ehad*, glossed as "The One (*'ehad*) is sleeping (*yashen*)." On the idea that God's name is "One" – based first of all on Zechariah 14:9, ביום ההוא יהיה ה' אחד ושמו אחד "on that day the Lord will be one and his name will be 'One'"; see Cyrus H. Gordon, "His Name is 'One,'" *JNES* 29 (1970), 198–99. This is countered in the midrash (Panim Aherot A, p. 25a; also Esther Rabbah 7:12), however, by citation of Psalm 121:4:

The rejection of this claim in another text does little to dispel its power. Here, too, it is suggested that the "king" whose "sleep was disturbed" is "the King of kings of kings, the Holy One blessed be He." The midrash objects, however: "Is there sleep in heaven?!" No, of course not, but the midrash is not prepared to back away from its initial reading. Instead, it suggests, God was *pretending* to sleep, and it was therefore legitimate to say to him, "Wake, O Lord, why do you sleep?" It is only when Israel does the will of God that it can be said that "the Guardian of Israel does not slumber and does not sleep."[17] It is not certain that the final claim here, that God *as if* sleeps, was in fact the intention of the original midrashist, who does seem to have said, daringly, that God himself was roused from his slumber. Even the conclusion is not much less radical, however: if God does not literally sleep, he does withdraw to heaven and pretend to sleep (with his eyes closed?), waiting for the Jews to return to him and "wake" him up.

All of these texts, in various ways, oppose the claim that God was orchestrating events from the beginning. Instead, God was uninvolved for the first part of the story. It was only "on that night" that God "awoke," literally or figuratively, and began to fight on behalf of Israel.[18]

There are three other variations, which all claim that God began to help only in chapter 6, but which disagree on why he was unhelpful before that point. One remarkable claim is that for much of the story, God was actually unsure whose side he should take. After all, Haman leveled some serious accusations against the people, claiming that they did not fulfill their religious obligations. If he is correct, God reasoned, then the Jews in fact deserved to be annihilated. Fortunately for the Jews, the angel Michael was paying attention, and rebutted Haman's claims: "Master of the world! It is revealed and known to you that they are not accusing them of idolatry, or sexual crimes, or murder, but because they are observing your Torah!" This convinced God, and he vowed not to abandon them.[19]

A strident comment of Samuel's suggests that until a certain point in the story, God was *losing the battle*. Commenting on the verse "Mordecai knew all that had happened" (4:1), Samuel says: "He knew that the upper king

---

"Look, the Guardian of Israel does not slumber or sleep!" This midrash seems designed to undercut any claim that God was asleep, a claim which, as we have seen, other Rabbis were prepared to entertain (see also Panim Aherot B, p. 34b).

[17] Panim Aherot B, p. 37b; Esther Rabbah 10:1.

[18] This view is neatly encapsulated in a statement of Rav Nahman b. Isaac. He quoted a verse from Psalms, and applied it to the story of Esther (b. Megillah 11a, quoting Psalm 124:2): "Were it not for God, who was with us when a man rose up against us . . . !" Note the dynamic: a man rose up against Israel, without the help of God; God was with us to defeat him.

[19] Midrash Abba Gurion 14a and Esther Rabbah 7:12.

triumphed over the lower king." This is obviously a euphemism (as observed by Rashi); his claim is that Mordecai saw that at this point the "lower king," Xerxes, was triumphing over the "upper king," God.[20]

Finally, we encounter that astonishing claim that God was involved throughout the text – but rather than being on Israel's side, he was the force behind the annihilation looming in the guise of Haman. Satan takes the opportunity presented by the Jews' participation in the king's banquet[21] to convince God to repudiate Israel once and for all: "How long will you stick by this nation which so angers you? If you want, destroy this nation from the world!" In agreement with the basic point, God only asked, "But what will happen to the Torah?" Satan told him that the angels would care for it, and God made his peace with the plan to massacre the Jews. He ordered: "So bring me letters and write destruction on them!"

The Torah, however, was not prepared to lose her beloved caretakers. She dressed in mourning clothes and cried loudly. The angels, who stand to inherit Israel's position in the world, also protested: "If Israel does not extract a drop[22] of blood after eight days, what do we need the world for?!" The sun and moon donned sackcloth and screamed, as did the heaven and earth. Immediately, Elijah ran in haste to the righteous of days past, and berated them: "Heaven and earth and the hosts of the world are crying bitterly, and the entire world is gripped with pain like a woman in childbirth, and you are lying here resting?!" They said to him, "Why?" He said to them, "Because destruction was decreed for the enemies of Israel." "Why?" "Because they enjoyed the banquet of Xerxes!"

Moses leapt into action. He asked Elijah if there were any righteous person among the Jews at all. Elijah responded that there was: "There is one person, and his name is Mordecai." Moses ordered Elijah to go rouse Mordecai to prayer, in the hope that his earthly prayers, coupled with the heavenly prayers the Patriarchs would offer, would convince God to relent. Elijah resisted: "Destruction has already been written regarding your flock, and it is already sealed!" Moses explained, however, that it depended on the type of seal affixed to the decrees of annihilation: "If it is sealed with clay, our pleas for mercy will be heard, but if it was sealed with blood, what was, was."[23]

---

[20] B. Megillah 15a, and Rashi, s.v. גבר מלכא עילאה.   [21] On this motif, see above, p. 194.

[22] The text reads מעטיפים, which is apparently a phonetic equivalent (reflecting a folk etymology, or perhaps the influence of the emphatic [pharygealized?] ט) for מטיפים "cause to drip," the usual rabbinic word for the extraction of the blood of circumcision.

[23] Esther Rabbah 7:13; see also Targum Rishon to 4:1.

d. God was involved in the arrangement of it all

According to R. Judah and R. Meir, knowing only about the actions of Haman and how the Jews escaped from him is not sufficient. For R. Judah, it is necessary to see God's hand from the introductions of Mordecai and Esther, and especially in Esther's selection as queen. One midrash makes this claim explicitly, asserting that when the text says (2:4) that the idea to search for a new queen was "good in the eyes of the king,"the reference is not to Xerxes, but to God. This was a good idea, thought God, and so he put the plan into action. Then immediately: "There was a Jewish man in the fortress of Susa."[24] Once God decided on a plan, he wasted no time in executing it.[25]

Another motif of the rabbinic reading of Esther makes it clear what a reader would be missing by not reading chapter 2. Commenting on the sequence in 2:23 – 3:1, in which Mordecai saves the king's life and Haman is immediately thereafter promoted, Rava makes an important claim: Haman could not be promoted until chapter 3, because God would not allow the threat to develop until after the mechanism of salvation was in place, and this was not the case until Mordecai saved the king's life. At this point, Mordecai has stored-up credit with the king, and now God can let Haman rise to power. Rava asserts that Haman could only be promoted "after God created the cure for the ailment."[26]

---

[24] Midrash Panim Aherot, p. 31b.

[25] Other midrashic claims about Esther also seem designed to emphasize the miraculous nature of Xerxes' choice of her to be queen. R. Joshua b. Qorḥah is quoted in the Bavli as saying that Esther was "greenish" (*yeraqroqet*), in an explicit effort to emphasize the miraculous: she was chosen not for her natural beauty, but despite her odd appearance (b. Megillah 13a). Similarly (b. Megillah 15b), as Esther entered the palace (in chapter 5), Xerxes beheld her, and R. Yohanan comments, "three ministering angels appeared to help her at that moment: one lifted her neck, one drew a cord of charm around her, and one extended the scepter." Along similar lines, the Babylonian tradition – cited in the Palestinian Bereshit Rabbah (39:13), but in the name of Babylonian sages – discusses Esther's age: "Rav said she was forty years old; Samuel said she was eighty years old; the Rabbis of there [= Babylonia] said she was seventy-five." See also Targum Rishon to 2:7; Panim Aherot B, p. 32a (74 is the *gematria* [numerical value] of 'Hadassah'). Later the Bavli makes the point that Esther was "fortuitously" called to the king for the first time in the dead of winter, "the month in which a body enjoys another body" (b. Megillah 13a, and see Rashi, s.v. שהגוף נהנה מן הגוף, who explains that the cold encourages people to seek out others for body heat). Rashi understands the import of this statement: "Thus scripture testified that the Heavens desired that Esther should be beloved by her husband."

[26] B. Megillah 13b. The Talmud cites a precedent for Rava's interpretation from a general principle articulated by the third-century Palestinian sage Resh Laqish: "As Resh Laqish said: God does not strike Israel unless he has already created the cure for them, as it says, 'As I heal Israel, and [then] the sin of Ephraim is uncovered' (Hosea 7:1)." Another midrash, Panim Aherot A, p. 23a, is more explicit about what the cure is: "What cure did he create for them? What is written above this topic: "In those days, Mordecai was sitting at the gate, etc."

Now that the groundwork was laid for the Jews to be saved, God could set the wheels in motion to begin the near-annihilation of the Jews. This idea is picked up by many of the medieval commentators, who express the idea as "he creates the cure before the ailment" (*maqdim refu'a la-makka*).[27] R. Judah's view, that the reader must encounter the story from at least the introduction of Mordecai in 2:5, may result from such a reading: the story which begins to unfold in chapter 3 could, theologically speaking, begin to unfold only after the events of chapter 2 occurred.[28]

e. God is everywhere

The most extreme expression of a theological reading of Esther is attributed to R. Yohanan: "Every time it says 'King Xerxes' in the Scroll of Esther, Scripture is talking about Xerxes, but every time it says 'king' alone, Scripture is talking about the King of Kings of Kings."[29] In a series of midrashim, he then applies this to various verses in Esther, such as "the king was very wrathful" (1:12) and "the wrath of the king abated" (7:10).[30] This is a powerful claim. Now it was not Xerxes, who was "wrathful" in chapter 1, and thus led to the near-catastrophe, but God. It was also not Xerxes whose "wrath abated," and thus led to the Jews' escape and triumph; that, too, was God. In this mode of reading, R. Yohanan has made Esther into another iteration of the cycle familiar from the entire Bible: God was angry, so an enemy threatened Israel; Israel repented, so God's anger abated, and the enemy was brought low. R. Yohanan has theologically tamed Esther.

---

[27] The phrase appears in the commentaries of Salmon, Yefet, and Tanḥum ha-Yerushalmi (references and citations in Wechsler, *Strangers in the Land*, 256–57, with n. 211), and similar phrases are used by Rashi on 2:23 and Joseph Qara on 3:1 (also quoted by Wechsler, *Strangers in the Land*). In Panim Aherot C, p. 39b, we find the same idea, illustrated by examples: Noah is introduced before the Flood, Abraham was prepared to introduce God into the world, Moses was there to save the Jews from Egypt, David was there to defeat Goliath, and Mordecai was prepared to defeat Haman.

[28] See also Panim Aherot B, p. 33b. See also Panim Aherot C, p. 40a–b.

[29] Midrash Abba Gurion 7b.

[30] Esther Rabbah 3:10–15. One midrash reads this in 7:10, וַחֲמַת הַמֶּלֶךְ שָׁכָכָה "the anger of the king subsided." Picking on the geminate כ in the verb שָׁכָכָה*, the midrash asks: "Why two 'subsidings'? One of the king of the world, and the other for Xerxes" (Panim Aherot A, p. 24b; b. Megillah 16a; see also Panim Aherot B, p. 37a). The anger of *both* kings subsided. In one passage in the Targum Rishon (7:3), the two kings are combined. At the fateful moment when Esther is about to plead for her nation from the king, the Hebrew text quotes her as beginning, "If I have found favor in the eyes of your eyes, O king, and if it pleases the king." This double language, combined with the theory of double causality, gave rise to the following rendering, in which she appeals to *both* kings: "Esther lifted her eyes up to heaven and said, 'If I have found favor in your eyes, O Lofty King, and if it is pleases the earthly king of, let my own salvation be given to me at my request, and the redemption of my people from the enemy for my entreaty.'"

2. Halakhah

Before moving to the effects these subtle and sophisticated rabbinic interpretations had on their views of the book, it should be added that in a more
heavy-handed way, the Rabbis injected the central components of Jewish
life into the story of Esther. This is a tactic more reminiscent of the Greek
Additions studied above.[31] Although we said earlier that since the book was
canonical, the Rabbis could not tamper with it, they could add midrashic
stories behind and around the text, embellishing the narrative with extra-
textual tales. The import of these "additions" is self-evident, so I will little
more than mention them in the following paragraphs.

a. Prayer

According to the Targum Rishon, the first chapter of Esther is suffused with
prayer. Mordecai spends all seven days of the royal banquet immersed in
prayer.[32] The king's advisors were actually, at first, members of the tribe of
Issachar. When the king asks what to do with Vashti, they decline to pass
judgment and instead pray to God for a way out of their predicament.[33]
Another key moment of prayer in the rabbinic tellings of the story is the
three-day period that Esther decrees for "fasting" at the end of chapter 4. In
one midrash, Mordecai is said to have prayed on his way to rouse the people
to fast and pray.[34] More significantly, the midrashim in general take it for
granted that the days of fasting were also days of prayer.[35] Esther, too, prays,
during the three days and then on her way to the king.[36]

b. Niddah

Interestingly, the idea that Esther was sleeping with the king while she was
legally a menstruant particularly exercised the Rabbis.[37] This was solved by

---

[31] See above, pp. 113–23.   [32] Targum Rishon to 1:10.
[33] Targum Rishon to 1:14; Esther Rabbah 4:1.   [34] Esther Rabbah 8:7.
[35] See, e.g., Targum Rishon on 4:16.   [36] B. Megillah 15b.
[37] Ironically, this is one prohibition that Esther would not have had to worry about. Xerxes, a
Zoroastrian, would have been even more stringent regarding the status of menstruants than the
Jews were. For Zoroastrian menstrual laws and some of their effects on rabbinic Jewish law, see Shai
Secunda, "'Dashtana-Ki Derekh Nashim Li': A Study of Babylonian Rabbinic Laws of Menstruation
in Relation to Corresponding Zoroastrian Texts," unpublished Ph.D. dissertation (Yeshiva
University, 2007), and Shai Secunda, "Talmudic Text and Iranian Context: On the Development
of Two Talmudic Narratives," AJS Review, 33 (2009), 40–70. Might this be what Esther means when
she says the king has not summoned her "this thirty days"?

positing that Esther was actually meticulous in her observance of the restrictions on sexual activity while menstruating. Thus, "'Xerxes': until Esther came to him he *was* Xerxes, but after Esther came to him, he did not sleep with menstruating women."[38] Mordecai used to visit the palace daily (2:11) in order to check on her menstrual status and to inspect her menstrual stains.[39] Similarly, Esther used to send questions regarding her menstrual status to the Sages.[40]

These last two comments may have overt gender-oriented agendas, as well. It is possible that Esther threatened the Rabbis' conception of heroism for many reasons, but the bare fact of her womanhood, and of her use of her womanhood to save the Jews, would certainly have been one of them.[41] By commenting that she showed her menstrual stains to Mordecai, or to the Sages – but in any event, to male authority figures – the Rabbis were able to bring Esther back under control and restore control to the men.

c. Shabbat

Rava claims that Esther rotated through her seven maidservants (mentioned in 2:9) on a daily basis, and that this allowed her to calculate when it was the Sabbath (since, Rava apparently knows, the institution of the "week" was not operative in Achaemenid Persia).[42] Similarly, the Targum claims, "she would observe Shabbats and festivals; during her menstrual periods she would be careful; she would not eat the food or drink the wine of non-Jews, and all obligations which are incumbent upon Jewish women she would observe by listening to Mordecai."[43]

d. Sexual union

The most obvious legal difficulty in the book is the intermarriage of Esther with Xerxes. The discomfort is put into the mouth of Esther herself (in much the same way as in Addition C, seen above in Chapter 9) in a prayer that she is said to have uttered when she was about to approach the king.[44] The divine spirit leaves her just then, and she says in her own defense: "Perhaps you judge one who sins accidentally like one who sins purposely, and one who is forced to sin like one who sins willingly?!"

---

[38] Esther Rabbah 1:3. [39] Esther Rabbah 6:8. [40] B. Megillah 13b.
[41] See the discussion in Crawford, "Esther not Judith," 22–31, 45.
[42] Avi Rabinovich reminded me of this text in this context. [43] Targum Rishon to 2:20.
[44] B. Megillah 15b.

The Rabbis even ask why Esther was not obligated to martyr herself rather than engage in a sexual relationship with a non-Jew. The question, to be specific, is that since it was public knowledge that she was married to a non-Jew, it was therefore public knowledge that she was sleeping with him. Since the rule is that a Jew is obligated to martyr himself or herself rather than violate any law publicly, shouldn't Esther have resisted, even at the cost of her life? It should be emphasized that the Talmud never raises the possibility that Esther's decision may not have been correct; it is taken for granted that her behavior is beyond reproach. What is needed, then, is the legal rationale behind her actions.

The explanations given, by the fourth-century Babylonian Amoraim Abbaye and Rava, are legally innovative: "Abbaye says, Esther was like the soil of the earth. Rava says, it is different if [the coercers] intends for their own pleasure [rather than for the purpose of a Jew violating the law]."[45] Abbaye's explanation apparently has to do with a woman's passive role in sexual intercourse, although it is debated by the commentators whether he means to say that women are, legally speaking, always the passive partners, or that Esther was particularly passive.[46] Rava argues differently that the motivation of the one who is forcing a Jew to violate the law is all-important, and that if the intention is for their own pleasure – as Xerxes' manifestly was in sleeping with Esther – no martyrdom is necessary. Both of these considerations, it must be emphasized, are not found in earlier rabbinic texts, which may suggest that they were invented by the Amoraim in order to justify Esther's actions. Rava's view in particular, which depends heavily on the *intention* of the non-Jew involved in the sexual intercourse, is legally novel. It seems to be the result of his own deep and abiding belief that liability must be based on the intention of the actor.[47]

---

[45] See b. Sanhedrin 74a-b.

[46] Cf. the Tosafot *ad loc.* and esp. on b. Yoma 82a–b, s.v. מה, the comments of R. Nissim of Gerona here, and the Ritba on Ketubbot 3b.

[47] For a thorough and insightful discussion of Rava's views in this regard, see Shana Strauch-Schick, "Intention in the Babylonian Talmud," unpublished Ph.D. dissertation (Yeshiva University, 2011), 92–172. Strauch-Schick comments on the text under discussion here on pp. 112–17, where she points out that Jews in Rava's day did engage in conceptually comparable actions, providing Zoroastrians with fires which were being brought to a religious site. Thus, the Jews were contributing to idolatry, but, Rava argues, "since the intention of the *magi* in soliciting [the fires] was not aimed at having Jews violate their religion, there was no prohibition in compliance" (*ibid.*, 116).

3. Results: Torah

Crucially, and perhaps most surprisingly, some rabbinic texts assert that the book of Esther is a story of Torah. One of the best-known passages of this type comes from the Bavli in Shabbat:

> "They stood under the mountain" (Exodus 19:17): Rav Abdimi b. Hama b. Hasa said, this teaches that the Holy One blessed be He turned the mountain over on them like a tank and said to them, "If you accept the Torah – good. But if not, there will be your graves!" R. Aha b. Jacob said, "This is a powerful protest against the Torah!" Rava said, "Even so, they later accepted it [willingly] in the time of Xerxes, as it says, "the Jews upheld and accepted" (Esther 9:27) – they upheld what they had once accepted.[48]

Gottlieb observed that "the new ritual of receiving the Torah in the days of Esther reminds us of the ceremony of Torah reading and contraction of a covenant regarding the Torah in the days of Ezra (Nehemiah 8; 10:1). There is here an attempt to equate Mordecai and Ezra in their jobs as disseminators of Torah."[49] A triangle has been constructed, then, equating Moses, Ezra, and Mordecai as the sages most involved in the teaching of the Torah to the Jews.[50]

4. Holy of Holies

Subjected to this intensive onslaught of exegetical brilliance, the book of Esther surrendered. It was biblicized, and read as part of the triangular saga

---

[48] B. Shabbat 88a.

[49] Gottlieb, "ונהפוך הוא": המדרש על מגילת אסתר," 129. Gottlieb suggests (*ibid.*, n. 36) that Rava may have been relying on an equation of the verb קְיָמוּ with the Aramaic noun קימא "oath" for his midrashic reading.

[50] A passage in Esther Rabbah (6:2 and Panim Aherot D, p. 41b) makes the same claim, actually equating Mordecai with Moses on the basis of the fact that they are both called "man." In what ways were they similar? Both "stood in the breach," as a prophet is supposed to do, to protect the people of Israel. Just as Moses taught Torah to Israel, so too did Mordecai. This last point is inferred from the fact that Mordecai is said to have spoken "words of peace and truth." That the "words of peace and truth" are Torah is learned from Proverbs 23:23: "Acquire truth and do not let it go." In another variation, the Targum Rishon replaces the biblical clause "the Jews had light and happiness" (8:16) with "the Jews had the right to study Torah and to keep Shabbat and the festivals, to circumcise their uncircumcised sons, and to put *tefillin* on their arms and their heads." In the same vein, the verse at the end of the narrative, "The Jews had light (אורה), joy, rejoicing, and glory" (8:16), is glossed by Rav Judah: "*orah* is Torah." Thus the joyous ending of the book is re-read as "The Jews had Torah." Although the text explains that אורה is Torah based on a verse from Proverbs ("for a commandment is a candle, and Torah light" [6:23]), this midrash is presumably based on an equation of Hebrew אורה "light" with Aramaic אורייתא "Torah". At the end of the long story of diaspora troubles, the ultimate salvation is achieved. Although life in exile goes on, "the Jews had Torah."

of Israel-Jews-Torah. Readers no longer perceived any differences in ideology between Esther and other biblical books, only differences in tone and form. Indeed, Esther was elevated to a status normally reserved only for the Torah itself. One view even has it that Esther was "given," like the Torah, to Moses at Sinai: "Rav, R. Hanina, R. Jonathan, Bar Kappara, and R. Joshua b. Levi said: This megillah was said to Moses at Sinai, but there is no earlier and later in the Torah."[51] The phrase "there is no earlier and later in the Torah" is a familiar one in rabbinic literature, but its usual meaning has no connection to the claim being made here. Normally it is used to legitimize texts that are not narrated in chronological order.[52] In our case, the claim is that a book about the Persian period was revealed to Moses nearly a millennium earlier. It is tempting to agree with Gottlieb that the purpose of the invocation of "there is no earlier and later" is "to give a pseudo-scientific justification for the midrashic exaggeration of the claim."[53] The Rabbis knew that they are overstating their case, and teasingly defended their claims (and made it clear that they were conscious of the hyperbole) by invoking a principle not really relevant to the point.

The third century in Eretz Israel saw the rhetorical heights of Esther's reputation. In the Yerushalmi, R. Helbo quoted R. Yose, who quoted R. Elazar b. Pedat (third century, Eretz Israel) as comparing Esther to the Torah: "just as this [Torah] can be the basis for midrash, so too can this [Esther] be the basis for midrash."[54] R. Elazar b. Pedat's teacher, R. Yoḥanan, makes a shocking statement, cited in the Yerushalmi: in the future, the books of the Prophets and the Writings will be "cancelled," but the Torah will never be. His colleague R. Shimon b. Laqish, however, adds that the book of Esther (and the laws) will also never be cancelled, since the book concludes, "their remembrance will never cease from among their seed"

---

[51] Y. Megillah 1:5 (70d). For comments on this text, as well as some of the others discussed in this chapter, see Abraham Joshua Heschel, תורה מן השמים באספקלריה של הדורות, ספר שני: תורה מסיני ותורה מן השמים (London and New York: Soncino, 1965), 239–41, ed. and tr. Gordon Tucker as *Heavenly Torah: As Refracted through the Generations* (New York: Continuum, 2006), 568–71.

[52] See, e.g., Mekhilta Shirta §7, for a sampling list of such texts, glossed each time, לפי שאין מוקדם ומאוחר בתורה "for there is no earlier or later in the Torah."

[53] Gottlieb, "ונהפוך הוא": המדרש על מגילת אסתר," 126.

[54] Y. Megillah 1:2 (70a). Gottlieb, "ונהפוך הוא": המדרש על מגילת אסתר," 121, notes the paradox involved: the rule that Esther can serve as the basis for midrash is derived from a midrash which presupposes that rule! On the more mundane but equally significant level, the Rabbis rule that the form of the text of Esther has to be comparable to that of the Torah: "[the scroll of the Megillah] needs scoring like the very truth of the Torah" (b. Megillah 16b). In other words, not only the content, but the physical text of Esther is legally comparable to the book of the Torah.

(Esther 9:28).[55] Similarly, and equally surprisingly, a different text claims that "all the festivals will eventually be cancelled, but the days of Purim will never be cancelled." It is clear from the context that "all the festivals" includes the biblical festivals; thus on this view, in some messianic age, Purim will be the only festival on the Jewish calendar.[56]

Interestingly, all the sources cited in this section are from Amoraim who lived and worked in third-century Eretz Israel. It would be overly reductionist to claim that there was something about that century that led these Amoraim to focus on Esther as the "Holy of Holies," the most sacred, or at least most eternal, of the biblical books. It is worth speculating, though, that we may be witness here to a revaluation of Esther in changed political circumstances. Moshe Benovitz has argued that R. Yohanan was also responsible for the revaluation of Hanukka, and further, that this was due to the new imperial threat in the late third century: the conflicts between the Palmyrenes and the Romans in the early 270s may have cast a long shadow over the political thought of the contemporary Rabbis.[57]

5. Ambivalence

At the same time, in third-century Babylonia, the Amora Samuel was calling the sanctity of the book into question. He asserted that the book of Esther "does not defile the hands." Sacred scriptures render hands that touch them rabbinically impure.[58] Samuel, however, exempts the book of

---

[55] Y. Megillah 1:5 (70d). The translations of the verses given are meant to reflect how the midrash here reads them, not their contextual meanings. The opinion of Resh Laqish was codified by Maimonides; see his *Laws of Megillah and Hanukkah*, 2:18, and the critical comments of the Raabad there.

[56] Midrash Mishle 9:2. A contrary view holds that even Yom ha-Kippurim will not be cancelled, showing clearly that biblical festivals are very much part of the discussion.

[57] Moshe Benovitz, "נר חנוכה בארץ ישראל בימי התנאים ואמוראים," in 'עד דכליא ריגלא דתרמודאי, in David Golinkin, Moshe Benovitz, Mordechai Akiva Friedman, Menachem Schmelzer, and Daniel Sperber (eds.), *Torah Li-Shma: Essays in Jewish Studies in Honor of Professor Shamma Friedman* (Jerusalem, New York, and Ramat Gan: Mekhon Schechter, Jewish Theological Seminary of America, andBar Ilan University Press, 2007), 75–78.

[58] This rule is stated in m. Yadaim 3:5. No reason is given there, and the various explanations suggested for this rabbinically instituted impurity need not detain us here. The position that hand defilement has nothing to do with canonization was argued by Leiman, *The Canonization of Hebrew Scripture*, esp. 114–15, and more recently by Menahem Haran, האסופה המקראית: תהליכי הגיבוש עד סוף ימי בית שני ושינויי הצורה עד מוצאי ימי הביניים (Jerusalem: Bialik and Magnes, 1996–2008), vol. 1, 223–36. It is almost certain that the concept of a book defiling the hands and its connection to a book's sacred status was subject to various interpretations within rabbinic literature. Some of the comments of Goodman, *Judaism in the Roman World*, 69–78, in this regard are worthwhile, in that he raises the possibility that different views of "defiling hands" are found in various places within rabbinic literature. (Goodman's

Esther from this category.[59] Somewhat later in the same century, R. Levi b. Samuel and R. Huna b. Hiyya ruled that unlike all other sacred texts, which one must cover with a mantle out of respect, "Esther does not require a mantle."[60]

The Talmud objects to Samuel's claim by juxtaposing it to another statement of Samuel's, to wit, that Esther was composed under divine inspiration. The contradiction is resolved eventually: "it was 'said' (ne'emrah) to be read (le-hiqqarot) and not 'said' to be written (ve-lo ne'emra le-hikkatev)." The suggestion seems to be that the book's religious significance lies in its liturgical function, and not in its textual incarnation.[61] It would appear that such a view would disagree with the statements above that the book of Esther is to be compared – in its form and significance – to the Torah itself.

In support of the notion that not everyone in Babylonia was sanguine about the religious value of the book of Esther are other texts which reflect complex attitudes toward the heroes in the book. Despite all the rabbinic efforts to make the book conform to their norms, the Rabbis certainly did not paper over all of the tensions and ambivalences latent in the narrative.

a. The identity of Esther

Indeed, in the case of the Jewish identity of Esther, they seem to have magnified the tension. A number of statements seem to emphasize the amorphous nature of Esther's character. R. El'azar claims that "Esther found favor" in everyone's eyes because to each person she appeared as though from his own country. Rav said that the reason why Xerxes "loved Esther more than all the women, and she found favor in his eyes more than all the virgins," was that she was particularly adept sexually. If he wanted to "taste" a virgin, she could provide that; if he wanted to "taste" an

---

handling of some of the rabbinic texts he cites is problematic, however; in *ibid.*, 73, the word he takes to be the personal name עזרא "Ezra" is actually the noun *'ăzārāh* "courtyard," which makes the text discussed much more reasonable.)

[59] See the recent discussion of this passage in Claudine Cavalier, "La canonicité d'*Esther* dans la judaïsme rabbinique: Les documents talmudiques," *REJ* 163 (2004), 14–15. Cavalier's study does not go beyond the goals articulated in its subtitle.

[60] B. Sanhedrin 100a; see Robert Gordis, "Studies in the Esther Narrative," *JBL* 95 (1976), 49 n. 27; Oppenheimer, "המן' ושנאת מרדכי אהבת" 409, and Herman, "אסתר מגילת נכללה מתי," 333–34. One might argue that the fact that Esther is here assumed to be among the sacred books indicates that it did have a place there, but certainly these Babylonian Amoraim did not accord the book the same respect with which the other books were treated.

[61] The text is similarly understood by Goodman, *Judaism in the Roman World*, 71. A very different explanation is offered by Haran, המקראית האסופה, vo. 1, 234–36, based on the observation that for the reading of Esther – as opposed to the reading of the Torah – there is only one reader.

experienced woman, she could provide that, too.[62] Even if Esther had a well-formed identity, these statements suggest that it was hidden beneath layers of camouflage.[63]

b. Esther's polyandry

Most striking, however, is the claim that Esther was actually married to Mordecai. This may have roots in the LXX, which renders the Hebrew phrase לְקָחָהּ מָרְדֳּכַי לוֹ לְבַת ("Mordecai took her to himself as a daughter") as "he raised/educated (*epaideusen*) her to be a wife (*eis gunaika*)."[64] But in rabbinic literature this motif is much dramatized, to the extent that the claim is made that Esther was not only married to both Mordecai and Xerxes simultaneously, but also sleeping with both of them at the same time. Rabbah b. Lima makes this as explicit as possible: "Esther would rise from the lap of Xerxes, immerse in the *miqveh*, and sit in the lap of Mordecai."[65] Such a radical claim runs not only counter to the simple sense of the narrative, but also so counter to usual rabbinic mores that exegetes have struggled to make sense of it. Why would the Rabbis make such a claim, which creates innumerable legal and moral problems?

It is possible that there was no exegetical impulse behind this, and that it was merely an attempt to make the story even more dramatic (and more salacious) than it was.[66] It may be, however, that the complexity this claim introduces into the story is itself the point. The moment of highest tension in Esther is chapter 4, when Mordecai asks Esther to go to the king to plead for "her" people. At that point, Esther is faced with a stark choice, which can easily be framed in terms of her very identity: will she violate the rules of the kingdom, embodied in the person of her husband, the king, in order to save her ethnic group, or will she turn her back on her people, including the one

---

[62] B. Megillah 13a.

[63] In general, the Rabbis avoid liminal characters, and tend to either fully embrace or fully reject characters. It has been argued that this way of viewing historical characters was deeply embedded in the rabbinic worldview; see Nissan Rubin, "זמן היסטורי וזמן לימינלי – פרק בהיסטוריוסופיה של חז"ל," *Jewish History*, 2 (1988), 7–22. The treatment of Esther suggests that this may deserve further attention.

[64] For recent discussion of the Greek translation, its background, and its possible relationship to rabbinic literature, see Moshe A. Zipor, "When Midrash met Septuagint: The Case of Esther 2,7," *ZAW* 118 (2006), 82–92. For a similar case of a motif appearing in both the Hellenistic-era Greek texts and later rabbinic literature, see Noah Hacham, "Haman, Mordekhai's Slave," *ZAW* 122 (2010), 96–101.

[65] B. Megillah 13b.

[66] Barry Dov Walfish, "Kosher Adultery? The Mordecai-Esther-Ahasuerus Triangle in Midrash and Exegesis," *Prooftexts*, 22 (2002), 305–33.

Jew who most nurtured her as a youth, Mordecai, and remain loyal to her husband and his laws? In other words, if she has to choose, does she choose Mordecai or Xerxes?

The Rabbis may have found a simple way of encapsulating this tension. Let us imagine that she is married to both men. Mordecai is the husband of her youth, the man who protected her and brought her up, and who represents her childhood way of life and web of loyalties. Xerxes represents the foreigner, to whom she was married without regard for her will, and who threatens by his very presence to rend Esther from her people. Whom does she choose?

In a brilliant literary ending to this saga, the Rabbis tell that she chooses Xerxes, and thereby betrays him, or, put differently, she chooses to be loyal to Mordecai, and therefore has to leave him. Or, as the Talmud explains: every day Esther had been sleeping with Xerxes only because she was coerced, but today she was offering herself to him willingly. The Jewish law is that a married woman who has an affair is forbidden to continue her sexual relationship with her husband, but a woman who is raped is not similarly forbidden. Thus, as long as Esther was sleeping with Xerxes only under duress, her relationship with Mordecai was not (legally) threatened. Now that she is entering in to the king's throne room willingly, however, she will have to renounce her relationship with Mordecai. Therefore, she says to Mordecai: "'As I am lost, I am lost': as I have been lost to my father's house, so will I now be lost to you."[67]

Thus, in order to save the Jews, Esther has to give up her marriage to Mordecai. She has resolved her identity problem in a way which the Rabbis approve of, but has to pay the price of remaining forever married only to Xerxes as a result. Once she asserts her loyalty to the Jews, her connection to them is severed, and she becomes even more firmly ensconced in the Persian palace.

c. Mordecai: politics vs. Torah

A number of comments are comparably ambivalent about Mordecai, per-haps even more explicitly so; some overtly call his status as a hero into question. Is he, in fact, a Jewish hero? It is clear that he saved the Jews, but is he a model worthy of emulation? The book of Esther concludes by noting that he was "great among the Jews and accepted by most of his brethren."

[67] B. Megillah 15a, reading with the Vatican manuscript Ebr. 134 and the Göttingen manuscript Hebrew 3, Oriental 13.

The Talmud does not let that last phrase go by unappreciated: he was accepted by *most* of his brethren, but not of *all* of his brethren. This teaches, concludes the Talmud, that some members of the Sanhedrin separated from him.[68] Furthermore, the Talmud reports, it was not only possibly fringe members of the Sanhedrin who criticized Mordecai. Indeed, Rav Joseph observes a "downgrading" in Mordecai's biography. In Ezra 2, the list of returnees to Judea lists Mordecai fifth, but the same list when repeated in Nehemiah 7 lists him sixth. Rav Joseph therefore concludes that what Mordecai did – save the Jewish people – is not as important as learning Torah: "The study of the Torah is superior to the saving of life."[69] This is a remarkable claim. After all that Mordecai did, Rav Joseph reports, he was *demoted*, from fourth on the list to fifth, because all that time spent on politics detracted from his study of Torah.[70] One can imagine Mordecai retorting, "But if there is no Israel, of what value is the Torah?"[71] But for Rav Joseph, the answer may well be that the Torah is of transcendent value, and indeed, it is the people of Israel who have no value without the Torah.

This was very much a live issue in rabbinic times. R. Nehonia b. ha-Qanah is quoted as saying, for example, "whoever accepts the yoke of Torah is relieved of the yoke of the empire; whoever throws off the yoke of Torah has the yoke of the empire and the yoke of work placed on him."[72] On one reading, this "means that each Jew is faced with a choice: religion or politics, but not both."[73] Mordecai could naturally be invoked by those who favored opting for a life of politics, on behalf of the Jews, over one devoted entirely to Torah. Rav Joseph can be understood as offering the rebuttal: this was indeed Mordecai's choice, but this is not to be taken as a endorsement of this choice; Mordecai himself suffered the consequences.

d. Diaspora reactions

It is important to emphasize that all the sources surveyed in this section – emphasizing the ambiguous nature of Esther's character, Esther's marriage

---

[68] B. Megillah 16b.   [69] B. Megillah 16b.

[70] Another text which is far from complimentary about Mordecai is a comment of Rava's in b. Megillah 12b–13a; he suggested that the double attribution of Mordecai to both the tribe of Judah (*ish yehudi*) and the tribe of Benjamin (*ish yemini*) was due to a conflict between the tribes, in which each tried to *dis*sociate themselves from Mordecai. The Jews blamed the tribes of both Judah and Benjamin for Mordecai. First they turned to Judah and blamed them for David's failure to kill Shimei, from whom Mordecai was descended. Then they turned to Benjamin and blamed them for the failure of Saul to kill Agag, from whom Haman was descended.

[71] See Panim Aherot B, p. 36a, cited above, in Chapter 14, nn. 112–13.   [72] Mishah Avot 3:5.

[73] See De Lange, "Jewish Attitudes to the Roman Empire," 262.

to Mordecai alongside her marriage to Xerxes, criticizing Mordecai for his time spent away from Torah, and reporting that the tribes distanced themselves from Mordecai because he endangered the Jews to begin with – are all Babylonian.[74] They stand in sharp contrast to the traditions from Eretz Israel encountered in the previous section, which paint the book of Esther as the religious book par excellence.[75] The very existence of the Babylonian Esther Midrash in Bavli Megillah (see above, Chapter 13) already suggests particular Babylonian attention paid to the book; indeed, Boyarin has suggested that the Babylonian Jews "understandably seem to have adopted Purim as their special holiday," relying on the fact that it is for Esther alone, of all the books of the Bible, that we have a Babylonian midrash.[76] That the popularity of Esther extended beyond the literary elites, to the Babylonian Jewish masses, is suggested by onomastic evidence from the Jewish Aramaic magic bowls from the region: Esther is the most common female name attested in the bowls.[77]

The popularity of Esther among the Babylonian Jews does not imply a wholesale acceptance of the book, however. It is plausible that there was deep ambivalence among those Jews when studying the book. For the Jews still living in Babylonia, nearly a millennium after the reign of Xerxes, it was probably difficult to escape the sentiment so powerfully captured by Rava himself: "we are still the slaves of Xerxes!" Whereas the author of Esther may have been suggesting that the Jews of the Diaspora make their peace with a story set entirely in their homelands, the Babylonian Rabbis are uncomfortable with such a story, and work hard to transform it into one centered on the Temple, the Rabbis, and halakhah.

e. Thoroughly ambivalent

Despite all this, it is in Esther Rabbah, from Eretz Israel, that the hardest and most poignant question is asked: is Esther fundamentally a "happy" story or a "sad" story?

---

[74] In the Mishnah, the question of whether or not the Song of Songs and Qohelet defile the hands is discussed (m. Yadaim 3:5–6), but nothing there is said about Esther. It is only the Babylonian Samuel who questions the status of Esther in similar terms.

[75] Herman, "מתי נכללה מגילת אסתר בכתבי הקודש?," 322–23 and 332–33.

[76] Daniel Boyarin, "Introduction: Purim and the Cultural Poetics of Judaism – Theorizing Diaspora," *Poetics Today*, 15 (1994), 4 with n. 2. See also Orit Ramon, "'One Hundred and Twenty Seven Provinces': Political Reality, Political Thought, and Jewish Existence in Exile in Maharal's Commentary on the Book of Esther," *Judaica Bohemiae*, 46 (2011), 8.

[77] Joseph Naveh and Shaul Shaked, *Amulets and Magic Bowls: Aramaic Incantations of Late Antiquity* (Jerusalem: Magnes, 1998), 25.

"When the king's decree, which he will do in all his kingdom, will be heard – it will be great" (Esther 1:20): R. Levi and R. Isaac. R. Levi said, what is the great matter we will hear about from this one [Esther] who is going into the kingship? "There was great mourning for the Jews" (4:3). R. Isaac said, what is the great matter we will hear about from this one [Esther] who is going into the kingship? "The Jews had happiness and joy" (8:17).[78]

On R. Isaac's reading of the book, it is the happiness and joy that Esther provides to the Jews. R. Levi insists, though, that the pain and suffering that preceded the salvation must not be forgotten; prior to the happiness was much mourning.

The legacy of Esther is a complex one. A book that challenged its contemporaries at every level, it went through various incarnations and tribulations before becoming a sacred text. Even with that hard-won status, however, this short story continued to be read and re-read, interpreted and reinterpreted throughout the centuries. The different communities of readers shaped Esther in their own images, so that for the book as much as the queen, "to each person she appeared as from his own country."

---

[78] Esther Rabbah 4:10.

Bibliography

Abadie, P. "Le livre d'Esdras: Un midrash de l'Exode?," *Transeuphratène*, 14 (1998), 19–31.

Abusch, Tzvi, "The Development and Meaning of the Epic of Gilgamesh: An Interpretive Essay," *JAOS* 121 (2001), 614–22.

Alexander, Philip S. "Targum, Targumim," *ABD*, vol. VI, 320–31.

Amit, Yairah. "The Saul Polemic in the Persian Period," in Oded Lipschits and Manfred Oeming (eds.), *Judah and the Judaeans in the Persian Period* (Winona Lake, IN: Eisenbrauns, 2006), 647–61.

Angel, Hayyim. "*Hadassa Hi Esther*: Issues of Peshat and Derash in the Book of Esther," *Tradition*, 34 (2000), 79–97.

Assis, Elie. "To Build or Not to Build? A Dispute between Haggai and his People (Hag 1)," *ZAW* 119 (2007), 514–27.

"A Disputed Temple (Haggai 2,1–9)," *ZAW* 120 (2008), 582–96.

"Zechariah 8 and its Allusions to Jeremiah 30–33 and Deutero-Isaiah," *Journal of Hebrew Scriptures*, 11.1 (2011), www.jhsonline.org/Articles/article_148.pdf (accessed September, 2011).

Atzmon, Arnon. "מעשה אסתר" בפרקי דרבי אליעזר ובאסתר רבה ב: לביסוסה של זיקה" "בין"מקבילות בספרות חז"ל," *Tarbiz*, 75 (2006), 329–43.

"חלום מרדכי: מהוספה למדרש," *JSIJ* 6 (2007), 127–40

"התרגום לאסתר: התרגום המדרשי או המדרש התרגומי?," *HUCA* 80 (2009), כ–א.

"שחזור נוסח המדרש על פי מקורות מקבילות: פרדיגמה חדשה לבעיה ישנה," *JSIJ* 9 (2010), 1–15.

"וישנה...לטוב (אס' ב 9): על פרשנות וזהות במגילת אסתר" *Bet Miqra*, 57 (2012), 107–23.

Aven, Tricia M. *Three Versions of Esther: Their Relationship to Anti-Semitic and Feminist Critique of the Story* (forthcoming).

Baker, Cynthia. "A 'Jew' by Any Other Name?" *JAJ* 2 (2011), 153–80.

Bar-Asher, Moshe. "Il y avait à Suse un homme juif – איש יהודי היה בשושן הבירה," *REJ* 161 (2002), 227–31.

Barclay, John M. G. *Against Apion*, Flavius Josephus: Translation and Commentary 10 (Leiden: Brill, 2007).

Barkay, Gabriel. "חידושים בארכיאולוגיה של ירושלים" in "מבט נוסף על ירושלים בימי נחמיה, ירושלים וסביבותיה, 2 (2008), 47–54.

Bar-Kokhba, Bezalel. "על חג הפורים ועל מקצת ממנהגי הסוכות בימי הבית השני ולאחריו," *Zion*, 62 (1997), 387–407.

חג הפורים בימי הבית השני ומגילת אסתר ב"אסיה": "גישה היסטורית" ו"היסטוריה אורתודוכסית," *Sinai*, 121 (1998), 37–85.

Barnes, T. D. "Trajan and the Jews," *JRS* 40 (1989), 145–62.

Baskin, Judith R. "Erotic Subversion: Undermining Female Agency in bMegillah 10b–17a," in Tal Ilan, Tamara Or, Dorothea M. Salzer, Christiane Steuer, and Irina Wandrey (eds.), *A Feminist Commentary on the Babylonian Talmud: Introduction and Studies* (Tübingen: Mohr Siebeck, 2007), 227–44.

Baumgarten, Albert I. "Rabbinic Literature as a Source for the History of Jewish Sectarianism in the Second Temple Period," *DSD* 2 (1995), 14–57.

Beal, Timothy. *The Book of Hiding: Gender, Ethnicity, Annihilation, and Esther* (London and New York: Routledge, 1997).

Beaulieu, Paul-Alain. "The Babylonian Background of the Motif of the Fiery Furnace in Daniel 3," *JBL* 128 (2009), 273–90.

Becking, Bob. "Continuity and Community: The Belief System of the Book of Ezra," in Bob Becking and M. C. A. Korpel (eds.), *The Crisis of the Israelite Religious Traditions in Exilic and Post-Exilic Times*, Oudtestamentliche Studien 42 (Leiden: Brill, 1999), 256–75.

"'We All Returned as One!' Critical Notes on the Myth of the Mass Return," in Oded Lipschits and Manfred Oeming (eds.) *Judah and the Judaeans in the Persian Period* (Winona Lake, IN: Eisenbrauns, 2006), 3–18.

Beckwith, Roger. *The Old Testament Canon of the New Testament Church: And its Background in Early Judaism* (London: SPCK, 1985).

Bedford, Peter Ross. *Temple Restoration in Early Achaemenid Judah* (Leiden: Brill, 2001).

"Diaspora: Homeland Relations in Ezra-Nehemiah," *VT* 52 (2002), 147–65.

Beer, Moshe. "הרקע המדיני ופעילותו של רב בבבל," *Zion*, 50 (1985), 155–72, reprinted in Beer, *חכמי המשנה והתלמוד: הגותם פועלם ומנהיגותם* (Ramat Gan: Bar Ilan University Press, 2011), 10–26.

Ben-Dov, Jonathan. "A Presumed Citation of Esther in 4QDb," *DSD* 6 (1999), 282–84.

Benovitz, Moshe. "הורדוס וחנוכה," *Zion*, 68 (2003), 5–40.

"עד דכליא ריגלא דתרמודאי': נר חנוכה בארץ ישראל בימי התנאים ואמוראים" in David Golinkin, Moshe Benovitz, Mordechai Akiva Friedman, Menachem Schmelzer, and Daniel Sperber (eds.), *Torah Li-Shma: Essays in Jewish Studies in Honor of Professor Shamma Friedman* (Jerusalem, New York, and Ramat Gan: Mekhon Schechter, Jewish Theological Seminary of America, and Bar Ilan University Press, 2007), 39–78.

Berg, Sandra Beth. *The Book of Esther: Motifs, Themes, and Structure*, SBL Dissertation Series 44 (Missoula, MT: Scholars, 1979).

Berger, Yitzhak. "Esther and Benjaminite Royalty: A Study in Inner-Biblical Allusion," *JBL* 129 (2010), 625–44.

Bergey, Ronald L. "Late Linguistic Features in Esther," *JQR* 75 (1984), 66–78.

Berlin, Adele. *Esther*, JPS Bible Commentary (Philadephia: JPS, 2001).

"The Book of Esther and Ancient Storytelling," *JBL* 120 (2001), 3–14.

"The Message of Psalm 114," in Chaim Cohen, Victor Hurowitz, Avi Hurvitz, Yochanan Muffs, Baruch Schwartz, and Jeffrey Tigay (eds.),*Birkat Shalom: Studies in the Bible, Ancient Near Eastern Literature, and Postbiblical Judaism Presented to Shalom M. Paul on the Occasion of his Seventieth Birthday* (Winona Lake, IN: Eisenbrauns, 2008), 347–63.

Berman, Joshua. "Aggadah and Anti-Semitism: The Midrashim to Esther 3:8," *Judaism* 38 (1989), 185–96.

"*Hadassah bat Abihail*: The Evolution from Object to Subject in the Character of Esther," *JBL* 120 (2001), 647–69.

Bernstein, Moshe J. "Oaths and Vows in the Pentateuchal Targumim: Semantics and Exegesis," in Aharon Maman, Steven E. Fassberg, and Yochanan Breuer (eds.), *Sha'arei Lashon: Studies in Hebrew, Aramaic and Jewish Languages Presented to Moshe Bar-Asher* (Jerusalem: Bialik Institute, 2007), vol. II, 20–41.

Reading and Re-Reading Scripture at Qumran, Studies and Texts from the Judean Desert 107 (Leiden: Brill, 2013).

Bernstein, Moshe J., and Aaron Koller. "The Aramaic Texts and Hebrew and Aramaic Languages at Qumran: the North American Contributions," in Devorah Dimant with the assistance of Ingo Kottsieper (eds.), *The Dead Sea Scrolls in Scholarly Perspective: A History of its Research*,; Studies and Texts from the Judean Desert 99 (Leiden: Brill, 2012), 155–96.

Berquist, Jon L. *Judaism in Persia's Shadow: A Social and Historical Approach* (Minneapolis: Fortress, 1995).

"Constructions of Identity in Postcolonial Yehud," in Oded Lipschits and Manfred Oeming (eds.), *Judah and the Judeans in the Persian Period* (Winona Lake, IN: Eisenbrauns, 2006), 53–66.

Beyerle, Stefan. "Joseph and Daniel: Two Fathers in the Court of Foreign King," in Friedemann W. Golka and Wolfgang Weiß (eds.), *Joseph: Bibel und Literatur: Symposion Helsinki/Lathi 1999*, Oldenburgische Beiträge zu Jüdischen Studien 6 (Bibliotheks- und Informationssystem der Universität Oldenburg, 2000), 55–65.

Bhabha, Homi K. *The Location of Culture* (London and New York: Routledge, 1994).

Bickerman, Elias J. "The Colophon of the Greek Book of Esther," *JBL* 63 (1944), 339–62.

"Notes on the Greek Book of Esther," *PAAJR* 20 (1951), 101–33.

Four Strange Books of the Bible: Jonah, Daniel, Koheleth, Esther (New York: Schocken, 1967).

Bin-Nun, Yoel. "הפילוג והאחדות – כפל הטעות המרה והלם הגילוי: מפני מה לא שלח יוסף אל אביו? (שליח)," *Megadim*, 1 (1986), 20–31.

Birnbaum, Pierre. "Exile, Assimilation, and Identity: From Moses to Joseph," in Elisheva Carlebach, John M. Efron, and David M. Myers (eds.), *Jewish History and Jewish Memory: Essays in Honor of Yosef Hayim Yerushalmi*

(Hanover and London: Brandeis University Press and the University Press of New England, 1998), 249–70.

Black's Law Dictionary, 5th edn (St. Paul: West, 1983).

Blenkinsopp, Joseph. "Temple and Society in Achaemenid Judah," in Philip R. Davies (ed.), *Second Temple Studies 1: Persian Period, JSOT* Suppl. 117 (Sheffield Academic, 1991), 22–53.

"Benjamin Traditions Read in the Early Persian Period," in J. Andrew Dearman and M. Patrick Graham (eds.), *Judah and the Judeans in the Persian Period* (Winona Lake, IN: Eisenbrauns, 2011), 629–45.

Judaism, the First Phase: The Place of Ezra and Nehemiah in the Origins of Judaism (Grand Rapids, MI: Eerdmans, 2009).

Bodendorfer, Gerhard. "Der Babylonische Ester-Midrasch: Diaspora 'positiv denken', ohne sie zu verklären," *Kirche und Israel*, 18 (2003), 134–49.

"Die Diaspora, die Juden und die 'Anderen,'" in Ekkehard W. Stegemann and Klaus Wengst (eds.), *"Eine Grenze hast Du gesetzt": Edna Brocke zum 60. Geburtstag* (Stuttgart: Kohlhammer, 2003), 193–214.

Börner-Klein, Dagmar. *Eine babylonische Auslegung der Ester-Geschichte: Der Midrasch in Megilla 10b–17a*, Judentum und Umwelt 30 (Frankfurt am Main: Peter Lang, 1991).

Bowitck, James. "Characters in Stone: Royal Ideology and Yehudite Identity in the Behistun Inscription and the Book of Haggai," in Gary N. Knoppers and Kenneth A. Ristau (eds.), *Community Identity in Judean Historiography: Biblical and Comparative Perspectives* (Winona Lake, IN: Eisenbrauns, 2009), 87–117.

Boyarin, Daniel. "Introduction: Purim and the Cultural Poetics of Judaism – Theorizing Diaspora," *Poetics Today*, 15 (1994), 1–8.

"Tricksters, Martyrs, and Collaborators: Diaspora and the Gendered Politics of Resistance," in Daniel Boyarin and Jonathan Boyarin, *Powers of Diaspora: Two Essays on the Relevance of Jewish Culture* (Minneapolis: University of Minnesota Press, 2002), 35–102.

Brauner, Ronald A. "'To Grasp the Hem' and 1 Samuel 15:27," *JANES* 6 (1974), 35–38.

Braverman, Jay. *Jerome's Commentary on Daniel: A Study of Comparative Jewish and Christian Interpretations of the Hebrew Bible*, CBQMS 7 (Washington, DC: Catholic Biblical Association, 1978).

Brenner, Athalya. "Who's Afraid of Feminist Criticism? Who's Afraid of Biblical Humour? The Case of the Obtuse Foreign Ruler in the Hebrew Bible," *JSOT* 63 (1994), 38–55.

"Esther Politicised in a Personal Context: Some Remarks on Foreignness," *European Judaism*, 32 (1999), 4–10.

Brettler, Marc Zvi. "Judaism in the Hebrew Bible? The Transition from Ancient Israelite Religion to Judaism," *CBQ* 61 (1999), 429–47.

Briant, Pierre. *From Cyrus to Alexander: A History of the Persian Empire* (Winona Lake, IN: Eisenbrauns, 2002).

Bronner, Leila Leah. *From Eve to Esther: Rabbinic Reconstructions of Biblical Women*, Gender and the Biblical Tradition (Louisville: Westminster John Knox, 1994).

Burns, Joshua E. "The Special Purim and the Reception of the Book of Esther in the Hellenistic and Early Roman Eras," *JSJ* 37 (2006), 1–34.

Bush, Frederic W. *Ruth, Esther*, Word Biblical Commentaries 9 (Waco, TX: Word, 1996).

"The Book of Esther: *Opus non gratum* in the Christian Canon," *Bulletin for Biblical Research*, 8 (1998), 39–54.

Butting, Klara. "Esther: A New Interpretation of the Joseph Story in the Fight Against Anti-Semitism and Sexism," in Athalya Brenner (ed.), *Ruth and Esther*, A Feminist Companion to the Bible (Second Series) (Sheffield Academic, 1999), 239–48.

Carroll, Robert P. "The Myth of the Empty Land," *Semeia*, 59 (1992), 79–93.

Cavalier, Claudine. "La canonicité d'*Esther* dans la judaïsme rabbinique: Les documents talmudiques," *REJ* 163 (2004), 5–23.

Clines, David J. A. *The Esther Scroll: The Story of the Story*, *JSOT* Suppl. 30 (Sheffield: JSOT, 1984).

Cochran, Clarke E. "Joseph and the Politics of Memory," *Review of Politics*, 64 (Summer 2002), 421–44.

Cogan, Mordecai. "For We, Like You, Worship Your God: Three Biblical Portrayals of Samaritan Origins," *VT* 38 (1988), 286–92.

"Raising the Walls of Jerusalem (Nehemiah 3:1–32): The View from Dur-Sharrukin," *Israel Exploration Journal*, 56 (2006), 84–95.

Cohen, Abraham D. "'Hu ha-goral': The Religious Significance of the Book of Esther," *Judaism*, 23 (1974), 87–94.

Cohen, Gabriel Haim. "Introduction [to Esther]," in חמש מגילות, Da'at Miqra Commentaries (Jerusalem: Mossad ha-Rav Kook, 1990), 1–22.

Cohen, Gerson D. "Esau as Symbol in Early Medieval Thought," in Alexander Altmann (ed.), *Jewish Medieval and Renaissance Studies* (Cambridge, MA: Harvard University Press, 1967), 19–48, reprinted in Cohen, *Studies in the Variety of Rabbinic Cultures*, JPS Scholar of Distinction Series (Philadelphia: JPS, 1991), 243–69.

Cohen, Shaye J. D. "From the Bible to the Talmud: The Prohibition of Intermarriage," *HAR* 7 (1983), 23–39.

"Solomon and the Daughter of Pharaoh: Intermarriage, Conversion, and the Impurity of Women," *JANES* 16–17 (1984–85), 23–37.

Cohn Eskenazi, Tamara. "The Missions of Ezra and Nehemiah," in Oded Lipschits and Manfred Oeming (eds.), *Judah and the Judaeans in the Persian Period* (Winona Lake, IN: Eisenbrauns, 2006), 509–29.

Collins, John J. *Daniel*, Hermeneia (Minneapolis: Fortress, 1993).

"The Judaism of the Book of Tobit," in Géza G. Xeravits and József Zsengellér (eds.), *The Book of Tobit – Text, Tradition, Theology: Papers of the First International Conference on the Deuteronomical Books, Pápa, Hungary, 20–21 May, 2004*, *JSJ* Suppl. 98 (Leiden: Brill, 2005), 23–40.

Collins, Nina L. "Did Esther Fast on the 15th of Nisan? An Extended Comment on Esther 3:12," *RB* 100 (1993), 533–61.

Cook, Edward M. "Remarks on the Testament of Kohath from Qumran Cave 4," *JJS* 44 (1993), 209–10.

Cook, H. J. "The A-Text of the Greek Version of the Book of Esther," *ZAW* 81 (1969), 369–76.

Corley, Jeremy. "Septuagentalisms, Semitic Interference, and the Original Language of the Book of Judith," in Jeremy Corley and Vincent Skemp (eds.), *Studies in the Greek Bible: Essays in Honor of Francis T. Gignac, S.J.*, CBQMS 44 (Washington, DC: Catholic Biblical Association, 2008), 65–96.

Cowley, A. E. *Aramaic Papyri of the Fifth Century b.c.* (Oxford University Press, 1923).

Crawford, Sidnie White. "The Additions to Esther," in *New Interpreter's Bible*, 12 vols. (Nashville: Abingdon Press, 1994–2004), vol. III, 943–72.

"Additions to Esther," in David Noel Freedman, Allen C. Myers, and Astrid B. Beck (eds.), *Eerdman's Dictionary of the Bible* (Grand Rapids, MI: Eerdmans, 2000), 426–27.

"Esther not Judith: Why One Made it and the Other Didn't," *Bible Review*, 18.1 (2002), 22–31, 45.

"Esther and Judith: Contrasts in Character," in Sidnie White Crawford and Leonard J. Greenspoon (eds.), *The Book of Esther in Modern Research*, JSOT Suppl. 380 (London: T. & T. Clark, 2003), 61–76.

Rewriting Scripture in Second Temple Times, Studies in the Dead Sea Scrolls and Related Literature (Grand Rapids, MI: Eerdmans, 2008).

See also White, Sidnie Ann.

Cutler, Allan Harris. "Third-Century Palestinian Rabbinic Attitudes towards the Prospect of the Fall of Rome," *Jewish Social Studies*, 31 (1969), 275–85.

Dalley, Stephanie. *Esther's Revenge at Susa: From Sennacherib to Ahasuerus* (Oxford University Press, 2007).

Day, Linda. *Three Faces of a Queen: Characterization in the Books of Esther*, JSOT Suppl. 186 (Sheffield: JSOT Press, 1995).

De Lange, Nicholas R. M. "Jewish Attitudes to the Roman Empire," in P. D. A. Garnsey and C. R. Whittaker (eds.), *Imperialism in the Ancient World*, The Cambridge University Research Seminar in Ancient History (Cambridge University Press, 1978), 255–81 and 354–57.

De Troyer, Kristin. *The End of the Alpha Text of Esther: Translation and Narrative Technique in MT 8:1–17, LXX 8:1–17, and AT 7:14–41*, tr. Brian Doyle, Septuagint and Cognate Studies Series 48 (Atlanta: SBL, 2000).

"The Letter of the King and the Letter of Mordecai," *Textus*, 21 (2002), 175–207.

Rewriting the Sacred Text: What the Old Greek Texts Tell us about the Literary Growth of the Bible, SBL Text-Critical Studies 4 (Atlanta: SBL, 2003).

"Is God Absent or Present in the Book of Esther? An Old Problem Revisited," in Ingolf U. Dalferth (ed.), *The Presence and Absence of God: Claremont Studies in the Philosophy of Religion, Conference 2008* (Tübingen: Mohr Siebeck, 2009), 35–40.

de Troyes, Chrétien. *Arthurian Romances*, tr. William W. Kibler and Carleton W. Carroll (London: Penguin, 1991).

Deel'Acqua, Anna Passoni. "The Liberation Decree of 'Addition' E in Esther LXX: Some Lexical Observations Starting from a New Papyrus (POxy LXVI, 4443). New Evidence for the 'Egyptian Flavour' of this 'Addition,'" *Admantius*, 10 (2004), 72–88.

Dimant, Devorah. "The Book of Tobit and the Qumran Halakhah," in Devorah Dimant and Reinhard G. Kratz (eds.), *The Dynamics of Language and Exegesis at Qumran*, Forschungen zum Alten Testament, 2nd Series 35 (Tübingen: Mohr Siebeck, 2009), 121–43.

Donner, Herbert, and Wolfgang Röllig. *Kanaanäische und aramäische Inschriften*, 5th edn. (Wiesbaden: Harrassowitz, 2002).

Dor, Yonina. האומנם גורשו הנשים הנכריות' 'הנשים הנכריות'? שאלת ההיבדלות בימי שיבת ציון (Jerusalem: Magnes, 2006).

Douglas, Mary. "Responding to Ezra: The Priests and the Foreign Wives," *Biblical Interpretation*, 10 (2002), 1–23.

Eckhardt, Benedikt. "Reclaiming Tradition: The Book of Judith and Hasmonean Politics," *JSP* 18 (2009), 243–63.

Edelman, Diana V. "Did Saulide–Davidic Rivalry Resurface in Early Persian Yehud?" in J. Andrew Dearman and M. Patrick Graham (eds.), *The Land that I Will Show You: Essays on the History and Archaeology of the Ancient Near East in Honour of J. Maxwell Miller*, JSOT Suppl. 343 (Sheffield Academic, 2001), 69–91.

Efron, Joshua. *Studies on the Hasmonean Period*, Studies in Judaism in Late Antiquity 39 (Leiden: Brill, 1987).

Ego, Beate. *Targum Scheni zu Esther: Übersetzung, Kommentar und theologische Deutung* (Tübingen: Mohr Siebeck, 1996).

"All Kingdoms and Kings Trembled before Him: The Image of King Solomon in Targum Sheni on Megillat Esther," *Journal of the Aramaic Bible*, 3 (2001), 57–73.

"The Book of Esther: A Hellenistic Book," *JAJ* 1 (2010), 279–302.

Eisenman, Robert H., and Michael O. Wise. *The Dea Sea Scrolls Uncovered* (Shaftesbury, Dorset, and Rockport, MA: Element, 1992).

Elman, Yaakov. "How Should a Talmudic Intellectual History be Written? A Response to David Kraemer's *Responses* (Review of *Responses to Suffering in Classical Rabbinic Literature* by David Kraemer)," *JQR* 89 (1999), 361–86.

"'Up to the Ears' in Horses' Necks (B.M. 108a): On Sasanian Agricultural Policy and Private 'Eminent Domain,'" *JSIJ* 3 (2004), 95–149.

"Middle Persian Culture and Babylonian Sages: Accommodation and Resistance in the Shaping of Rabbinic Legal Tradition," in Charlotte E. Fonrobert and Martin S. Jaffee (eds.), *The Cambridge Companion to the Talmud and Rabbinic Literature* (New York: Cambridge University Press, 2007), 165–97.

Elsner, Jaś. "Cultural Resistance and the Visual Image: The Case of Dura Europos," *Classical Philology*, 96 (2001), 269–304.

Eph'al, Israel. "The Western Minorities in Babylonia in the 6th–5th Centuries BC: Maintenance and Cohesion," *Orientalia*, 47 (1978), 74–90.

"לקביעת זמנה של הגאולה בתקופת שיבת ציו," *Tarbiz*, 76 (2007), 5–16.

Epstein, J. N. מבוא לנוסח המשנה, reprint edn. (Jerusalem: Magnes, 2000 [orig. 1964]).

Eshel, Esther, and Michael E. Stone. "לשון הקודש באחרית הימים לאור קטע מקומראן," *Tarbiz*, 62 (1993), 169–77.

Eshel, Hanan. "ירושלים בימי שלטון פרס: מתאר העיר והרקע ההיסטורי," in Shmuel Ahituv and Amihai Mazar (eds.), *The History of Jerusalem: The Biblical Period* (Jerusalem: Yad Yitzhak Ben-Zvi, 2000), 327–43.

Falk, Daniel K. *The Parabiblical Texts: Strategies for Extending the Scriptures in the Dead Sea Scrolls*, T. & T. Clark Library of Biblical Studies, Companion to the Qumran Scrolls 8, Library of Second Temple Studies 63 (London and New York: T. & T. Clark, 2007).

Feldman, Louis H. "Hellenizations in Josephus' Version of Esther," *Proceedings of the American Philosophical Society*, 101 (1970), 143–70.

"Flavius Josephus Revisited: The Man, his Writings, and his Significance," *ANRW* 11.21/2 (1984), 763–862.

"Josephus' Portrait of Jacob," *JQR* 79 (1988–89), 101–51.

"Abba Kolon and the Founding of Rome," *JQR* 81 (1991), 239–66.

Judaism and Hellenism Reconsidered, JSJ Suppl. 107 (Leiden: Brill, 2006).

Finkel, Joshua. "מחבר המגילה החיצונית לבראשית הכיר את מגילת אסתר," in Yigael Yadin and Chaim Rabin (eds.), זיכרון לאליעזר ליפא סוקניק ז"ל מחקרים במגילות הגנוזות: ספר (Jerusalem: Hekhal ha-Sefer, 1961), 163–82.

Finkelstein, Israel. "Persian Period Jerusalem and Yehud: A Rejoinder," *Journal of Hebrew Scriptures*, 9 (2009), www.jhsonline.org/Articles/article_126.pdf (accessed January, 2010),

Finkelstein, Louis (ed.). *Sifre on Deuteronomy* (Berlin: Gesellschaft zur Förderung der Wissenschaft des Judentums, 1939; reprinted New York: Jewish Theological Seminary, 1969).

Fishbane, Michael. *Biblical Interpretation in Ancient Israel* (Oxford University Press, 1985).

Fitzmyer, Joseph A. *Tobit*, CEJL (Berlin and New York: De Gruyter, 2003).

The Genesis Apocryphon of Qumran Cave 1 (1Q20): A Commentary, 3rd edn., Biblica et Orientalia 18/B (Rome: Pontifical Biblical Institute, 2004).

Foster, Benjamin R. *The Epic of Gilgamesh: A New Translation, Analogues, Criticism* (New York and London: W. W. Norton, 2001).

Fox, Michael. "בייל לישני," *Lešonénu*, 41 (1976–77), 75.

"The Structure of the Book of Esther," in Alexander Rofé and Yair Zakovitch (eds.), *Isaac Leo Seeligmann Volume: Essays on the Bible and the Ancient World* (Jerusalem: Rubinstein, 1983), vol. III, 291–303.

"Three Esthers," in Sidnie White Crawford and Leonard J. Greenspoon (eds.), *The Book of Esther in Modern Research, JSOT* Suppl. 380 (London: T. & T. Clark, 2003), 50–60.

    Character and Ideology in the Book of Esther, 2nd edn. (Grand Rapids, MI: Eerdmans, 2001).

    The Redaction of the Books of Esther: On Reading Composite Texts, SBL Monograph Series 40 (Atlanta: Scholars, 1991).

Frei, Peter. "Persian Imperial Authorization: A Summary," in J. W. Watts (ed.), *Persia and Torah: The Theory of Imperial Authorization of the Pentateuch*, SBL Symposium Series 17 (Atlanta: SBL, 2001), 5–40.

Freidenreich, David Moshe. *"Foreign Food: A Comparatively-Enriched Analysis of Jewish, Christian, and Islamic Law,"* unpublished Ph.D. dissertation (Columbia University, 2006).

Fried, Lisbeth S. "Towards the *Ur*-Text of Esther," *JSOT* 88 (2000), 49–57.

    "Cyrus the Messiah? The Historical Background to Isaiah 45:1," *HTR* 95 (2002), 373–93.

    "The House of God Who Dwells in Jerusalem," *JAOS* 126 (2006), 89–102.

Friedman, Richard Elliott. *The Disappearance of God: A Divine Mystery* (Boston: Little, Brown, 1995).

Frisch, Amos. "בין מגילת אסתר לספר מלכים," *Mehqerei Hag*, 3 (1992), 25–35.

Fröhlich, Ida. "'Mamzer' in Qumran Texts: The Problem of Mixed Marriages from Ezra's Time – Law, Literature and Practice," *Transeuphratène*, 29 (2005), 103–15.

Frolov, Serge. "Two Eunuchs, Two Conspiracies, and One Loyal Jew: The Narrative of Botched Regicide in Esther as Text- and Redaction-Critical Test Case," *VT* 52 (2002), 304–25.

Gan, Moshe. "מגילת אסתר באספקלריית קורות יוסף במצרים," *Tarbiz*, 31 (1962), 144–49.

Gardner, Anne E. "The Relationship of the Additions to the Book of Esther to the Maccabean Crisis," *JSJ* 15 (1984), 1–8.

Gaster, Moses. *The Chronicles of Jerahmeel, or The Hebrew Bible historiale*, Oriental Translation Fund, New Series 4 (London: Royal Asiatic Society, 1899).

Geller, M. J. "Alexander Jannaeus and the Pharisee Rift," *JJS* 30 (1979), 202–11.

Gerleman, Gillis. *Esther*, Biblischer Kommentar: Altes Testament 21 (Neukirchen-Vluyn: Neukirchener, 1973).

Ginsberg, H. L. *Five Megilloth and Jonah: A New Translation* (Philadelphia: JPS, 1969).

Ginzberg, Louis. *The Legends of the Jews,*, tr. Henrietta Szold, 7 vols. (Philadelphia: JPS of America, 1909–38).

Glatzer, Nahum N. "The Attitude toward Rome in Third-Century Judaism," in Alois Dempf, Hannah Arendt, and Friedrich Engel-Janosi (eds.), *Politische Ordnung und menschliche Existenz: Festgabe für Eric Vögelin zum 60. Geburtstag* (Munich: Beck, 1962), 243–67, reprinted in Glatzer, *Essays in Jewish Thought*, Judaic Studies Series 8 (University, AL: University of Alabama Press, 1978), 1–14.

    "The Attitude to Rome in the Amoraic Period," *Proceedings of the Sixth World Congress of Jewish Thought* (Jerusalem: World Union of Jewish Studies, 1975), vol. II, 9–19.

Gnuse, Robert. "The Jewish Dream Interpreter in a Foreign Court: The Recurring Use of a Theme in Jewish Literature," *JSP* 7 (1990), 29–53.

Goitein, Shlomo Dov. עיונים במקרא: בחינתו הספרותית והחברתית (Tel Aviv: Yavneh, 1967).

Goldingay, John E. *Daniel*, Word Biblical Commentary 30 (Dallas: Word, 1989).

Goldman, Bernard. "A Dura-Europos Dipinto and Syrian Frontality," *Oriens Antiquus*, 24 (1985), 279–300.

Goldstein, Jonathan. *II Maccabees*, AB 41A (Garden City, NY: Doubleday, 1983).

"The Message of 'Aristeas to Philokrates' in the Second Century B.C.E.: Obey the Torah, Venerate the Temple of Jerusalem, but Speak Greek, and Put your Hopes in the Ptolemaic Dynasty," in Menachem Mor (ed.),*Eretz Israel, Israel, and the Jewish Diaspora: Mutual Relations – Proceedings of the First Annual Symposium of the Philip M. and Ethel Klutznick Chair in Jewish Civilization, Held on Sunday–Monday, October 9–10, 1988*, Studies in Jewish Civilization 1 Lanham, MD, and Omaha, NE: University Press of America and the Center for the Study of Religion and Society, Creighton University, 1991), 1–23.

Goodman, Martin. "Diaspora Reactions to the Destruction of the Temple," in James D. G. Dunn (ed.), *Jews and Christians: The Parting of the Ways, A.D. 70 to 135* (Tübingen: J. C. B. Mohr (P. Siebeck), 1992), 27–38.

"Trajan and the Origins of Roman Hostility to the Jews," *Past & Present*, 182 (2004), 3–29.

Judaism in the Roman World: Collected Essays, Arbeiten zur Geschichte des antiken Judentums und des Urchristentums 66 (Leiden: Brill, 2007).

Gordis, Robert. "Studies in the Esther Narrative," *JBL* 95 (1976), 43–58.

"Religion, Wisdom and History in the Book of Esther: A New Solution to an Ancient Crux," *JBL* 100 (1981), 359–88.

Gordon, Cyrus H. "His Name is 'One,'" *JNES* 29 (1970), 198–99.

Gottlieb, Isaac Boaz. "ונהפוך הוא": המדרש על מגילת אסתר," in Shmuel Vargon, Amos Frisch, and Moshe Rahimi (eds.), מנחות כרך ח: עיוני מקרא ופרשנות, ידידות והוקרה לאלעזר טויטו (Ramat Gan and Elkanah: Bar Ilan University Press and Mikhlelet Orot, 2008), 119–37.

Grabbe, Lester L. "Biblical Historiography in the Persian Period: Or, How the Jews Took Over the Empire," in Steven W. Holloway (ed.), *Orientalism, Assyriology and the Bible*, Hebrew Bible Monographs 10 (Sheffield Phoenix Press, 2006), 400–14.

Green, Alexander. "Power, Deception, and Comedy: The Politics of Exile in the Book of Esther," *Jewish Political Studies Review*, 23 (2011), 61–78.

Greenberg, Moshe. "A House of Prayer for All Peoples," in Alviero Niccacci (ed.), *Jerusalem – House of Prayer for All Peoples in the Three Monotheistic Religions* (Jerusalem: Franciscan Printing Press, 2001), 31–37.

Greenstein, Edward L. "'To Grasp the Hem' in Ugaritic Literature," *VT* 32 (1982), 217–18.

"A Jewish Reading of Esther," in Jacob Neusner, Baruch A. Levine, and Ernest S. Frerichs (eds.), *Judaic Perspectives on Ancient Israel* (Philadelphia: Fortress, 1987), 225–43.

Grintz, Jehoshua. ספר יהודית: תחזורת הנוסח הנוסח המקורי (Jeruslem: Bialik, 1957).

Grossfeld, Bernard. *The First Targum to Esther: According to the MS Paris Hebrew 110 of the Bibliotheque Nationale* (New York: Sepher-Hermon, 1983).

The Two Targums of Esther: Translated, with Apparatus and Notes, Aramaic Bible 18 (Collegeville, MN: Liturgical Press, 1991).

The Targum Sheni to the Book of Esther: A Critical Edition Based on MS Sassoon 282 with Critical Apparatus (New York: Sepher-Hermon, 1994).

Grossman, Jonathan. "'Dynamic Analogies' in the Book of Esther," *VT* 59 (2009), 394–414.

Esther: The Outer Narrative and the Hidden Reading, Siphrut 6 (Winona Lake, IN: Eisenbrauns, 2011).

"The Vanishing Character in Biblical Narrative: The Role of Hathach in Esther 4," *VT* 62 (2012), 561–71.

Gruen, Erich S. *Heritage and Hellenism: The Reinvention of Jewish Tradition*, Hellenistic Culture and Society 30 (Berkeley: University of California Press, 1998).

Diaspora: Jews amidst Greeks and Romans (Cambridge, MA: Harvard University Press, 2002).

"Persia through the Jewish Looking Glass," in Tessa Rajak, Sarah Pearce, James Aitken, and Jennifer Dines (eds.), *Jewish Perspectives on Hellenistic Rulers* (Berkeley: University of California Press, 2007), 53–75.

Gugenheim, Claude-Anne. "Les femmes prophétesses: À partir du traité *Meguila* 14a du Talmud de Babylone," *Pardés*, 43 (2007), 103–21.

Gutmann, Joseph. "Early Synagogue and Jewish Catacomb Art and its Relation to Christian Art," *ANRW* II.21/2 (1984), 1315–28.

"Introduction," in Joseph Gutmann (ed.), *The Dura-Europos Synagogue: A Reevaluation (1932–1992)*, South Florida Studies in the History of Judaism 25 (Atlanta: Scholars, 1992), ix–xl.

Review of Kurt Weitzman and Herbert Kessler, *The Frescoes of the Dura Synagogue and Christian Art*, *Speculum*, 67 (1992), 502–04.

Hacham, Noah. "3 Maccabees – An Anti-Dionysian Polemic," in Jo-Ann A. Brant, Charles W. Hedrick, and Chris Shea (eds.), *Ancient Fiction: The Matrix of Early Christian and Jewish Narrative*, SBL Symposium Series 32 (Atlanta: SBL, 2005), 167–83.

"3 Maccabees and Esther: Parallels, Intertextuality, and Diaspora Identity," *JBL* 126 (2007), 765–85.

"Haman, Mordekhai's Slave," *ZAW* 122 (2010), 96–101.

"*Bigthan* and *Teresh* and the Reason Gentiles Hate Jews," *VT* 62 (2012), 318–56.

Hachlili, Rachel. *Ancient Jewish Art and Archaeology in the Diaspora*, Handbuch der Orientalistik, part 1: Der Nahe und Mittlere Osten 35 (Leiden: Brill, 1998).

"The Dura-Europos Synagogue Wall Paintings: A Question of Origin and Interpretation," in Zeev Weiss, Oded Irshai, Jodi Magness, and Seth Schwartz (eds.), *"Follow the Wise": Studies in Jewish History and Culture in Honor of Lee I. Levine* (Winona Lake, IN: Eisenbrauns, for the Jewish Theological Seminary of America and the Hebrew University, 2010), 403–20.

Hadas-Lebel, Mireille. "Jacob et Esaü, ou Israël et Rome dans le Talmud et le Midrash," *Revue de l'histoire des religions*, 201 (1984), 369–92.

Hagedorn, Anselm C. "The Absent Presence: Cultural Responses to Persian Presence in the Eastern Mediterranean," in Oded Lipschits and Gary N. Knoppers (eds.), *Judah and the Judeans in the Achaemenid Period: Negotiating Identity in an International Context* (Winona Lake, IN: Eisenbrauns, 2011), 39–66.

Halbertal, Moshe. *People of the Book* (Cambridge, MA: Harvard University Press, 1997).

Halvorson-Taylor, Martien A. "Secrets and Lies: Secrecy Notices (Esther 2:10, 20) and Diasporic Identity in the Book of Esther," *JBL* 131 (2012), 467–85.

Hamilton, Mark W. "Who Was a Jew? Jewish Ethnicity during the Persian Period," *Restoration Quarterly*, 37 (1995), 102–17.

Hanisch, Carol. "The Personal is Political," reprinted in Shulamith Firestone and Anne Koedt (eds.), *Notes from the Second Year: Women's Liberation* (New York: Radical Feminist, 1970), 76–78.

Haran, Menahem. האסופה המקראית: תהליכי הגיבוש עד סוף ימי בית שני ושינויי הצורה עד ימי הביניים מוצאי (Jerusalem: Bialik and Magnes, 1996–2008).

Harvey, Charles D. *Finding Morality in the Diaspora? Moral Ambiguity and Transformed Morality in the Books of Esther*, BZAW 328 (New York and Berlin: De Gruyter, 2003).

Hayes, Christine. "Intermarriage and Impurity in Ancient Jewish Sources," *HTR* 92 (1999), 3–36.

Hayward, Robert. "Profile Targum Esther Sheni, Excerpt From: *Database of Anonymous and Pseudepigraphic Jewish Literature of Antiquity, c. 200 BCE to c. 700 CE*, ed. A. Samely, R. Bernasconi, P. Alexander, and R. Hayward," *Aramaic Studies*, 9 (2011), 65–82.

"Targum a Misnomer for Midrash? Towards a Typology for the Targum Sheni of Esther," *Aramaic Studies*, 9 (2011), 47–63.

"Mules, Rome, and a Catalogue of Names: Genesis 36 and its Aramaic Targumim," in Geoffrey Khan and Diana Lipton (eds.), *Studies on the Text and Versions of the Hebrew Bible in Honour of Robert Gordon*, VT Suppl. 149 (Leiden: Brill, 2012), 295–314.

Hazony, Yoram. *The Dawn: Political Teachings of the Book of Esther*, revised edn. (Jerusalem: Shalem Press, 2000 [orig. 1995]).

Heinemann, Joseph. אגדות ותולדותיהן: עיונים בהשתלשלותן של מסורות (Jerusalem: Keter, 1974).

Herman, Dov. "מתי נכללה מגילת אסתר בכתבי הקדש?," *Beit Mikra*, 48 (2003), 321–34.

Herman, Geoffrey. "Ahasuerus, the Former Stable-Master of Belshazzar, and the Wicked Alexander of Macedon: Two Parallels between the Babylonian Talmud and Persian Sources," *AJS Review*, 29 (2005), 283–97.

Herr, Moshe David. "Pirkei de-Rabbi Eliezer," in Fred Skolnik (ed.), *Encyclopaedia Judaica*, 2nd edn., (Detroit: Macmillan Reference USA in association with the Keter Publishing House, 2007), vol. XVI, 182–83.

Heschel, Abraham Joshua. תורה מן השמים באספקלריה של הדורות, ספר שני: תורה מסיני: ותורה מן השמים (London and New York: Soncino, 1965), ed. and tr. Gordon Tucker as Heavenly Torah: As Refracted through the Generations (New York: Continuum, 2006).

Hieke, Thomas. "Endogamy in the Book of Tobit, Genesis, and Ezra-Nehemiah," in Géza G. Xeravits and József Zsengellér (eds.), *The Book of Tobit – Text, Tradition, Theology; Papers of the First International Conference on the Deuteronomical Books, Pápa, Hungary, 20–21 May, 2004, JSJ* Suppl. 98 (Leiden: Brill, 2005), 103–20.

Himmelfarb, Martha. "Levi, Phinehas, and the Problem of Intermarriage at the Time of the Maccabean Revolt," *JSQ* 6 (1999), 1–24.

Hintze, Almut. "The Greek and Hebrew Versions of the Book of Esther and its Iranian Background," *Irano-Judaica*, 3 (1994), 34–39.

Historical Dictionary of the Hebrew Language, http://hebrew-treasures.huji.ac.il/ (accessed February, 2012).

Hoglund, Kenneth. "The Achaemenid Context," in Philip R. Davies (ed.), *Second Temple Studies 1: Persian Period, JSOT* Suppl. 117 (Sheffield Academic, 1991), 54–72.

Honigman, Sylvie. "The Birth of a Diaspora: The Emergence of a Jewish Self-Definition in Ptolemaic Egypt in the Light of Onomastics," in Shaye J. D. Cohen and Ernest S. Frerichs (eds.), *Diasporas in Antiquity*, Brown Judaic Studies 288 (Atlanta: Scholars, 1993), 94–95.

Horbury, William. "The Beginnings of the Jewish Revolt under Trajan," in Peter Schäfer (ed.), *Geschichte – Tradition – Reflexion: Festschrift für Martin Hengel zum 70. Geburtstag* (Tübingen: J. C. B. Mohr (Paul Siebeck), 1996), vol. 1, 283–304.

Horowitz, Elliott. *Reckless Rites: Purim and the Legacy of Jewish Violence* (Princeton University Press, 2006).

Humphreys, W. Lee. "A Lifestyle for the Diaspora: A Study of the Tales of Esther and Daniel," *JBL* 92 (1973), 211–23.

Hurvitz, Avi. "The Date of the Prose-Tale of Job Linguistically Reconsidered," *HTR* 67 (1974), 17–34.

Hutton, Jeremy M. "Isaiah 51:9–11 and the Rhetorical Appropriation and Subversion of Hostile Theologies," *JBL* 126 (2007), 271–303.

Idestrom, Rebecca G. S. "Echoes of the Book of Exodus in Ezekiel," *JSOT* 33 (2009), 489–510.

Ilan, Tal. *Integrating Women into Second Temple History*, TSAJ 76 (Tübingen: Mohr Siebeck, 1999).

Jaffee, Martin S. "The Hermeneutical Model of Midrashic Studies: What it Reveals and What it Conceals," *Prooftexts*, 11 (1991), 67–76.

Janzen, David. *Witch Hunts, Purity, and Social Boundaries: The Expulsion of the Foreign Women in Ezra 9–10, JSOT* Suppl. 350 (Sheffield Academic, 2002).
"Scholars, Witches, Ideologues, and What the Text Said: Ezra 9–10 and its Interpretation," in Jon L. Berquist (ed.), *Approaching Yehud: New Approaches*

to the Study of the Persian Period, Semeia Studies 50 (Atlanta: SBL, 2007), 49–69.

Japhet, Sara. "Sheshbazzar and Zerubbabel against the Background of the Historical and Religious Tendencies of Ezra-Nehemiah: Part 1," *ZAW* 94 (1982), 66–98, reprinted in Sara Japhet, *From the Rivers of Babylon to the Highlands of Judah: Collected Studies on the Restoration Period* (Winona Lake, IN: Eisenbrauns,2006), 53–84.

"People and Land in the Restoration Period," in Georg Strecker (ed.), *Das Land Israel in biblischer Zeit* (Göttingen: Vandenhoeck & Ruprecht, 1983), 103–25, reprinted in Sara Japhet, *From the Rivers of Babylon to the Highlands of Judah: Collected Studies on the Restoration Period* (Winona Lake, IN: Eisenbrauns, 2006), 96–116.

גירוש הנשים הנכריות (עזרא ט'-י'): המסגרת המשפטית התקדימים וההשלכות על קביעת" "הזהות היהודית," in Moshe Bar-Asher, Noah Ḥakham, and Yosef Ofer (eds.), *Teshurah le-Amos: Asupat Meḥkarim be-farshanut ha-mikra mugeshet le-Amos Ḥakham* (Alon Shvut: Tevunot, 2007), 379–401.

Joannès, F., and André Lemaire. "Trois tablettes cunéiformes à onomastique ouest-sémitique (collection Sh. Moussaïeff) (Pls. I–II)," *Transeuphratène*, 17 (1999), 17–34.

Jobes, Karen H. *The Alpha-Text of Esther: Its Character and Relationship to the Masoretic Text*, SBL Dissertation Series 153 (Atlanta: Scholars, 1996).

Johnson, Sara R. *Historical Fictions and Hellenistic Jewish Identity: Third Maccabees in its Cultural Context* (Berkeley: University of California Press, 2004).

"Novelistic Elements in Esther: Persian or Hellenistic, Jewish or Greek?" *CBQ* 67 (2005), 571–89.

Joosten, Jan. "The Original Language and Historical Milieu of the Book of Judith," *Meghillot*, 5–6 (2008), *159–*176.

Kalimi, Isaac. "The Place of the Book of Esther in Judaism and Jewish Theology," *Theologische Zeitschrift*, 59 (2003), 193–204.

"The Book of Esther and the Dead Sea Scrolls' Community," *Theologische Zeitschrift*, 60 (2004), 101–06.

"Fear of Annihilation and Eternal Covenant: The Book of Esther in Judaism and Jewish Theology," in Isaac Kalimi (ed.), *Jewish Bible Theology: Perspectives and Case Studies* (Winona Lake, IN: Eisenbrauns, 2012), 231–47.

Kasher, Rimon, and Michael L. Klein. "New Fragments of Targum to Esther from the Cairo Geniza," *HUCA* 61 (1990), 89–124.

Kass, Leon. Review of Aaron Wildavsky, *Assimilation versus Separation: Joseph the Administrator and the Politics of Administration in Biblical Israel*, *Commentary*, 96.3 (September, 1993), 58–61.

Katzenelenbogen, M. L. תורת חיים: מגילת אסתר (Jerusalem: Mossad ha-Rav Kook, 2009).

Katzin, David. "The Time of Testing: The Use of Hebrew Scriptures in 4Q171's Pesher of Psalm 37," *Hebrew Studies*, 45 (2004), 121–62.

Kessler, John. "Building the Second Temple: Questions of Time, Text, and History in Haggai 1.1–15," *JSOT* 27 (2002), 243–56.

"Diaspora and Homeland in the Early Achaemenid Period: Community, Geography and Demography in Zechariah 1–8," in Jon L. Berquist (ed.), *Approaching Yehud: New Approaches to the Study of the Persian Period*, Semeia Studies 50 (Atlanta: SBL, 2007), 137–66.

"The Diaspora in Zechariah 1–8 and Ezra-Nehemiah: The Role of History, Social Location, and Tradition in the Formulation of Identity," in Gary N. Knoppers and Kenneth A. Ristau (eds.), *Community Identity in Judean Historiography: Biblical and Comparative Perspectives* (Winona Lake, IN: Eisenbrauns, 2009), 119–45.

Klingbeil, Gerald A. "'Not So Happily Ever After . . .': Cross-Cultural Marriages in the Time of Ezra-Nehemiah," *Maarav*, 14 (2007), 39–75.

Knoppers, Gary N. "Intermarriage, Social Complexity, and Ethnic Diversity in the Genealogy of Judah," *JBL* 120 (2001), 15–30.

"Beyond Jerusalem and Judah: The Mission of Ezra in the Province of Transeuphrates," *Eretz-Israel*, 29 (2009), 78–87.

"Ethnicity, Genealogy, Geography, and Change: The Judean Community of Babylon and Jerusalem in the Story of Ezra," in Gary N. Knoppers and Kenneth A. Ristau (eds.), *Community Identity in Judean Historiography: Biblical and Comparative Perspectives* (Winona Lake, IN: Eisenbrauns, 2009), 147–71.

Knowles, Melody D. "Pilgrimage Imagery in the Returns in Ezra," *JBL* 123 (2004), 57–74.

Centrality Practiced: Jerusalem in the Religious Practice of Yehud and the Diaspora during the Persian Period, Archaeology and Biblical Studies 16 (Atlanta: SBL, 2006).

"Pilgrimage to Jerusalem in the Persian Period," in Jon L. Berquist (ed.), *Approaching Yehud: New Approaches to the Study of the Persian Period* (Leiden: Brill, 2008), 7–24.

Koch, Klaus. "Ezra and the Origins of Judaism," *Journal of Semitic Studies*, 19 (1974), 173–97.

Koller, Aaron. "The Exile of Kish: Syntax and History in Esther 2:5–6," *JSOT* 37 (2012), 45–56.

"The Kos in the Levant: Thoughts on its Distribution, Function, and Spread from the Late Bronze through the Iron Age II," in Gershon Galil, Ayelet Gilboa, Aren M. Maeir, and Dan'el Kahn (eds.), *The Ancient Near East in the 12th–10th Centuries BCE, Culture and History: Proceedings of the International Conference Held in the University of Haifa, 2–5 May 2010*, Alter Orient und Altes Testament (Münster: Ugarit-Verlag, 2012), 269–90.

Review of Stephanie Dalley, *Esther's Revenge at Susa: From Sennacherib*, *Review of Biblical Literature*, www.bookreviews.org/pdf/6731_7297.pdf (accessed June 19, 2013).

"Negotiating Empire: Living Jewishly under the Achaemenids in Persia and Palestine," in Daniel Tsadik (ed.), *Israel and Iran: From Cyrus the Great to the Islamic Republic* (Leiden: Brill, forthcoming).

Kugel, James L. *In Potiphar's House: The Interpretive Life of Biblical Texts* (San Francisco: HarperSanFrancisco, 1990).

Kuhrt, Amélie. "The Cyrus Cylinder and Achaemenid Imperial Policy," *JSOT* 25 (1983), 83–97.

Lacocque, André. *The Feminine Unconventional: Four Subversive Figures in Israel's Tradition* (Minneapolis: Fortress, 1990).

"The Different Versions of Esther," *Biblical Interpretation*, 7 (1999), 301–22.

Esther Regina: A Bakhtinian Reading, Rethinking Theory (Evanston, IL: Northwestern University Press, 2008).

Lambert, W. G. "A Document from a Community of Exiles in Babylonia," in Meir Lubetski (ed.), *New Seals and Inscriptions: Hebrew, Idumean, and Cuneiform* (Sheffield: Phoenix, 2007), 201–05.

Lange, Armin. "'The Law, the Prophets, and the Other Books of the Fathers (Sir, Prologue): Canonical Lists in Ben Sira and Elsewhere?," in Géza G. Xeravits and József Zsengellér (eds.), *Studies in the Book of Ben Sira: Papers of the Third International Conference on the Deuterocanonical Books, Shime'on Centre, Pápa, Hungary, 18–20 May, 2006, JSJ* Suppl. 127 (Leiden and Boston: Brill, 2008), 55–80.

"Your Daughters do not Give to their Sons and their Daughters do not Take for your Sons (Ezra 9:12): Intermarriage in Ezra 9–10 and in the Pre-Maccabean Dead Sea Scrolls," *BN* 137 (2008), 17–39, and 139 (2008), 79–98.

"The Significance of the Pre-Maccabean Literature from the Qumran Library for the Understanding of the Hebrew Bible: Intermarriage in Ezra/Nehemiah – Satan in 1 Chr 21:1 – the Date of Psalm 119," in André Lemaire (ed.), *Congress Volume Ljubljana 2007, VT* Suppl. 133 (Leiden: Brill, 2010), 171–218.

Laniak, Timothy S. *Shame and Honor in the Book of Esther*, SBL Dissertation Series 165 (Atlanta: Scholars, 1998).

Lau, Binyamin. במגילה קריאה – אסתר (Tel Aviv: Yedi'ot Aharonot and Sifre Hemed, 2011).

Lee, Kyong-Jin. *The Authority and Authorization of Torah in the Persian Period*, Contributions to Biblical Exegesis and Theology (Leuven: Peeters, 2011).

Lefkovitz, Lori Hope. *In Scripture: The First Stories of Jewish Sexual Identities* (Lanham: Rowman and Littlefield, 2010).

Leibtag, Menachem. "Megillat Esther: Its 'Hidden' Message," www.tanach.org/special/purim.txt (accessed September, 2011).

Leiman, Shnayer Z. *The Canonization of Hebrew Scripture: The Talmudic and Midrashic Evidence*, Transactions of the Connecticut Academy of Arts and Sciences 47 (Hamden, CT: Published for the Academy by Archon Books, 1976).

"Josephus and the Canon of the Bible," in Louis H. Feldman and Gohei Hata (eds.), *Josephus, the Bible, and History* (Detroit: Wayne State University Press, 1989), 50–58.

Lemaire, André, and Hélène Lozachmeur. "Bīrāh/Birtā' en Araméen," *Syria*, 64 (1987), 261–66.

Lerner, Myron Bialik. "The Works of Aggadic Midrash and the Esther Midrashim," in Shmuel Safrai, Zeev Safrai, Joshua Schwartz, and Peter J. Tomson (eds.), *The Literature of the Sages, Second Part: Midrash and Targum, Liturgy, Poetry, Mysticism, Contracts, Inscriptions, Ancient Science, and the Languages of Rabbinic Literature* (Assen and Minneapolis: Van Gorcum and Fortress, 2006), 133–229.

Leuchter, Mark. "Jeremiah's 70-Year Prophecy and the קמ'/ששך לב *Atbash* Codes," *Biblica*, 85 (2004), 503–22.

Levenson, Jon D. "The Scroll of Esther in Ecumenical Perspective," *Journal of Ecumenical Studies*, 13 (1976), 440–51.

   Esther: A Commentary, Old Testament Library (Louisville and London: Westminster John Knox, 1997).

Levi, Israel. "Les sources talmudiques de l'histoire juive: I. Alexandre Jannee et Simon ben Schetah; II. La rupture de Jannee avec les Pharisiens," *REJ* 35 (1897), 213–23.

Levine, Baruch A. "הוי, אשור שבט אפי' (יש' י, טו): אמונת הייחוד המקראית באספקלריה מדינת בינלאומית," *Eretz Israel*, 27 (2003), 136–42.

   "Assyrian Ideology and Israelite Monotheism," *Iraq*, 67 (2005), 411–27.

Levine, Lee I. *The Ancient Synagogue: The First Thousand Years*, 2nd edn. (New Haven: Yale University Press, 2005).

Levinson, Bernard M. *Deuteronomy and the Hermeneutics of Legal Innovation* (New York and Oxford: Oxford University Press, 1997).

Lévi-Strauss, Claude. *Introduction to a Science of Mythology*, vol. 1: *The Raw and the Cooked*, tr. John and Doreen Weightman (New York: Harper & Row, 1969 [French orig. 1964]).

Levit-Tawil, Dalia. "The Enthroned King Ahasuerus at Dura in Light of the Iconography of Kingship in Iran," *Bulletin of the American Sschools of Oriental Research*, 250 (1983), 57–78.

   "Queen Esther at Dura: Her Imagery in Light of Third-Century c.e. Oriental Syncretism," *Irano-Judaica*,4 (1999), 274–97.

Levitt Kohn, Risa. *A New Heart and a New Soul: Ezekiel, the Exile and the Torah*, *JSOT* Suppl. 358 (London: Sheffield Academic, 2002).

Lieberman, Saul. תוספתא כפשוטה: באור ארוך לתוספתא (New York: Jewish Theological Seminary, 1955–88).

Lipiński, E. "Recherches sur le livre de Zacharie," *VT* 20 (1970), 25–55, 494–95.

Lipschits, Oded. "Achaemenid Imperial Policy, Settlement Processes in Palestine, and the Status of Jerusalem in the Middle of the Fifth Century b.c.e.," in Oded Lipschits and Manfred Oeming (eds.), *Judah and the Judaeans in the Persian Period* (Winona Lake, IN: Eisenbrauns, 2006), 19–52.

Loader, J. A. "Esther as a Novel with Different Levels of Meaning," *ZAW* 90 (1978), 417–21.

Loewenstamm, Samuel E. "Esther 9:29–32: The Genesis of a Late Addition," *HUCA* 42 (1971), 117–24.

Luchner, Katharina. "4443. LXX, Esther E.16 – 9.3," in M. W. Haslam, A. Jones, F. Maltomini, and M. L. West (eds.),*Oxyrhynchus Papyri 65*, Graeco-Roman

Memoirs 85 (London: Egypt Exploration Society for the British Academy, 1998), 4–8.

Lust, Johan. "Exodus 6,2–8 and Ezekiel," in Marc Vervenne (ed.), *Studies in the Book of Exodus: Redaction, Reception, Interpretation* (Leuven: Leuven University Press and Peeters, 1996), 209–24.

Macchi, Jean-Daniel. "The Book of Esther: A Persian Story in Greek Style," in Ehud Ben Zvi, Diana V. Edelman, and Frank Polak (eds.), *A Palimpsest: Rhetoric, Ideology, Stylistics, and Language Relating to Persian Israel*, Perspectives on Hebrew Scriptures and its Contexts 5 (Piscataway, NJ: Gorgias, 2009), 109–27, also published as "Le livre d'Esther: Regard hellénistique sur le pouvoir et le monde perses," *Transeuphratène*, 30 (2005), 97–135.

Macdonald, Nathan. "Food and Drink in Tobit and Other 'Diaspora Novellas,'" in (Mark Bredin (ed.), *Studies in the Book of Tobit: A Multidisciplinary Approach* (London: T. & T. Clark, 2006), 165–78.

Not Bread Alone: The Uses of Food in the Old Testament (Oxford University Press, 2008).

Magliano-Tromp, Johannes. "The Relations between Egyptian Judaism and Jerusalem in Light of 3 Maccabees and the Greek Book of Esther," in C. M. Tuckett (ed.), *Feasts and Fasts*, Contributions to Biblical Exegesis and Theology 53 (Leiden: Peeters, 2009), 57–76.

Magness, Jodi. "The Arch of Titus at Rome and the Fate of the God of Israel," *JJS* 59 (2008), 201–217.

Mandel, Paul. "'ל"חז בספרות כמונה אדריכלי 'בירה','" *Tarbiz*, 61 (1992), 195–217.

Maraqten, Mohammed. *Die semitischen Personennamen in den alt- und reichsaramäischen Inschriften aus Vorderasien* (Hildesheim and New York: G. Olms, 1988).

Marshall, Anthony J. "Flaccus and the Jews of Asia (Cicero 'Pro Flacco' 28:67–69)," *Phoenix*, 29 (1975), 139–54.

Martens, Karen. "'With a Strong Hand and an Outstretched Arm': The Meaning of the Expression נטויה ובזרוע חזקה ביד," *Scandinavian Journal of the Old Testament*, 15 (2001), 123–41.

Martin, R. A. "Syntax Criticism of the LXX Additions to the Book of Esther," *JBL* 94 (1975), 65–72.

Marx, Karl, and Friedrich Engels. *The German Ideology, Part One: With Selections from Parts Two and Three, Together with Marx's "Introduction to a Critique of Political Economy"*, ed. and intro. C. J. Arthur (New York: International Publishers, 1970).

Mason, Steve. "Josephus and his Twenty-Two Book Canon," in Lee Martin McDonald and James A. Sanders (eds.), *The Canon Debate* (Peabody, MA: Hendrickson Publishers, 2002), 110–27.

Mathys, Hans-Peter. "Der Achämenidenhof im Alten Testament," in Bruno Jacob and Robert Rollinger (eds.), *Der Achämenidenhof/The Achaemenid Court: Akten des 2. Internationalen Kolloquiums zum Thema "Vorderasien im Spannungsfeld klassischer und altorientalischer Überlieferungen," Landgut*

Castelen bei Basel, 23.–25. Mai 2007, Classica et Orientalia 2 (Wiesbaden: Harrassowitz, 2010), 231–308.

Mazar, Eilat. "The Wall that Nehemiah Built," *Biblical Archaeology Review*, 35.2 (2009), 24–33, 66.

McGeough, Kevin. "Esther the Hero: Going beyond 'Wisdom' in Heroic Narratives," *CBQ* 70 (2008), 44–65.

McKane, William. "A Note on Esther ix and I Samuel xv," *JTS* 12 (1961), 260–61.

Meyers, Carol L., and Eric Meyers. *Haggai, Zechariah 1–8*, AB 25B (Garden City, NY: Doubleday, 1987).

"The Future Fortunes of the House of David: The Evidence of Second Zechariah," in Astrid B. Beck, Andrew H. Bartelt, Paul R. Raabe, and Chris A. Franke (eds.), *Fortunate the Eyes that See: Essays in Honor of David Noel Freedman in Celebration of his Seventieth Birthday* (Grand Rapids, MI: Eerdmans, 1995), 207–22.

Middlemas, Jill. "The Greek Esthers and the Search for History: Some Preliminary Observations," in Bob Becking and Lester L. Grabbe (eds.), *Between Evidence and Ideology: Essays on the History of Ancient Israel Read at the Joint Meeting of the Society for Old Testament Study and the Oud Testamentisch Werkgezelschap, Lincoln, July 2009*, Oudtestamentische Studiën 59 (Leiden: Brill, 2011), 145–63.

Mílik, J. T. "Le patrie de Tobie" *RB* 73 (1966), 522–30.

Milikowsky, Chaim. "*Seder 'Olam* and Jewish Chronography in the Hellenistic and Roman Periods," *PAAJR* 52 (1985), 115–39.

"Josephus Between Rabbinic Culture and Hellenistic Historiography," in James L. Kugel (ed.), *Shem in the Tents of Japhet: Essays on the Encounter of Judaism and Hellenism* (Leiden: Brill, 2002), 159–200.

"Notions of Exile, Subjugation and Return in Rabbinic Literature," in James M. Scott (ed.), *Exile: Old Testament, Jewish, and Christian Conceptions* (Leiden: Brill, 1997), 265–96.

Mills, Mary E. *Biblical Morality: Moral Perspectives in Old Testament Narratives*, Heythrop Studies in Contemporary Philosophy, Religion, & Theology (Aldershot: Ashgate, 2001).

"Household and Table: Diasporic Boundaries in Daniel and Esther," *CBQ* 68 (2006), 408–20.

Mokhtarian, Jason Sion. "Rabbinic Depictions of the Achaemenid King Cyrus the Great: The 'Babylonian Esther Midrash' (bMeg. 10b–17a) in its Iranian Context," in Carol Bakhos and M. Rahim Shayegan (eds.), *The Talmud in its Iranian Context*, TSAJ 135 (Tübingen: Mohr Siebeck, 2010), 112–39.

"Empire and Authority in Sasanian Babylonia: The Rabbis and King Shapur in Dialogue," *JSQ* 19 (2012), 148–80.

Moore, Carey A. "A Greek Witness to a Different Hebrew Text of Esther," *ZAW* 79 (1967), 351–58.

"On the Origins of the LXX Additions to the Book of Esther," *JBL* 92 (1973), 382–93.

"Archaeology and the Book of Esther," *Biblical Archaeologist*, 38 (1975), 62–79.

Daniel, Esther, and Jeremiah: The Additions, AB 44 (Garden City, NY: Doubleday, 1977).

"Esther Revisited Again: A Further Examination of Certain Esther Studies of the Past Ten Years," *HAR* 7 (1983), 169–86.

Moran, William. "The Gilgamesh Epic: A Masterpiece from Ancient Mesopotamia," in Jack M. Sasson (ed.), *Civilizations of the Ancient Near East* (New York: Scribner, 1995), vol. IV, 2327–36.

Morgenstern, Mira. *Conceiving a Nation: The Development of Political Discourse in the Hebrew Bible* (University Park, PA: Pennsylvania State University Press, 2009).

Motzo, R. B. "Il rifacimento Greco di Ester e il III Maccabei," in *Saggi di storia e letteratura giudeo-ellenistica*, Contributi alla scienza dell' Antichità 5 (Florence: Le Monnier, 1924), 272–90.

Narkiss, Bezalel. "סיפורי מגילת אסתר בבית הכנסת של דורא אירופוס," in I. S. Recanati (ed.), הגות, אמנות, עיצוב, קובץ מאמרים מגילה ככתבה: חמש המגילות – (Jerusalem: Ministry of Education Department of Publications, 2008), 51–69.

Naveh, Joseph, and Shaul Shaked. *Amulets and Magic Bowls: Aramaic Incantations of Late Antiquity* (Jerusalem: Magnes, 1998).

Neher, André. *The Exile of the Word* (Philadephia: JPS, 1980).

Neusner, Jacob. "Esther in Esther Rabbah," in Jacob Neusner and Alan J. Avery-Peck (eds.), and William Scott Green and Günter Stemberger (consulting eds.), *Encyclopaedia of Midrash: Biblical Interpretation in Formative Judaism* (Leiden: Brill, 2005), vol. I, 59–74.

Nickelsburg, George W. E. *Jewish Literature between the Bible and the Mishnah: A Historical and Literary Introduction*, 2nd edn. (Minneapolis: Fortress, 2005).

Niditch, Susan. *Underdogs and Tricksters: A Prelude to Biblical Folklore* (San Francisco: Harper & Row, 1987).

Noam, Vered. מגילת תענית: הנוסחים, פרשם, ותולדותיהם בצירוף מהדורה ביקורתית (Jerusalem: Yad Ben-Zvi, 2003).

"The Story of King Jannaeus (b. Qiddushin 66a): A Pharisaic Reply to Sectarian Polemic," *Harvard Theological Review* (forthcoming, 2013).

Novick, Tzvi. "Law and Loss: Response to Catastrophe in Numbers 15," *HTR* 101 (2008), 1–14.

"Charity and Reciprocity: Structures of Benevolence in Rabbinic Literature," *HTR* 105 (2012), 33–52.

Oded, Bustenay. "Exile–Homeland Relations during the Exilic Period and Restoration," in Michael Heltzer and Meir Malul (eds.), *Tᵉshûrôt LaAvishur: Studies in the Bible and the Ancient Near East, in Hebrew and Semitic Languages – Festschrift Presented to Prof. Yitzhak Avishur on the Occasion of his 65th Birthday* (Tel Aviv and Jaffa: Archaeological Center Publications, 2004), 153*–160*.

"The Judean Exiles in Babylonia: Survival Strategy of an Ethnic Minority," in Menahem Mor, Jack Pastor, Israel Ronen, and Yakov Ashenazi (eds.), *For Uriel: Studies in the History of Israel in Antiquity Presented to Professor Uriel*

Rappaport (Jerusalem: Zalman Shazar Center for Jewish History, 2005), 53*–76*.

Oeming, Manfred. "'See, We Are Serving Today' (Nehemiah 9:36): Nehemiah 9 as a Theological Interpretation of the Persian Period," in Oded Lipschits and Manfred Oeming (eds.), *Judah and the Judaeans in the Persian Period* (Winona Lake, IN: Eisenbrauns, 2006), 571–88.

Olley, John W. "Ezekiel LXX and Exodus Comparisons," *VT* 59 (2009), 116–19.

Olyan, Saul M. "Purity Ideology in Ezra-Nehemiah as a Tool to Reconstitute the Community," *JSJ* 35 (2004), 1–16.

Oppenheimer, Aharon. "אהבת מרדכי ושנאת המן'? פורים בימי הבית השני ולאחריו'," *Zion*, 62 (1997), 408–18.

Pace, Sharon. "Diaspora Dangers, Diaspora Dreams," in Peter W. Flint, Emanuel Tov, and James C. VanderKam (eds.), *Studies in the Hebrew Bible, Qumran, and the Septuagint Presented to Eugene Ulrich*, *VT* Suppl. 102 (Leiden: Brill, 2006), 21–59.

Paton, L. B. *A Critical and Exegetical Commentary on the Book of Esther* (Edinburgh: T. & T. Clark, 1908).

Paul, Shalom M. "Gleanings from the Biblical and Talmudic Lexica in Light of Akkadian," in Marc Brettler and Michael Fishbane (eds.), *Minhah le-Nahum: Biblical and Other Studies Presented to Nahum M. Sarna*, *JSOT* Suppl. 154 (Sheffield: JSOT Press, 1993), 242–56, reprinted in Shalom M. Paul, *Divrei Shalom: Collected Studies of Shalom M. Paul on the Bible and the Ancient Near East, 1967–2005*, Culture and History of the Ancient Near East 23 (Leiden: Brill, 2005), 182–86.

Pearce, Laurie. "New Evidence for Judaeans in Babylonia," in Oded Lipschits and Manfred Oeming (eds.), *Judah and the Judaeans in the Persian Period* (Winona Lake, IN: Eisenbrauns, 2006), 399–411.

Perrot, Jean. "'Shoshan ha-Birah,'" *Eretz Israel*, 20 (1989), 155*–160*.

Petersen, David L. "The Temple in Persian Period Prophetic Texts," in Philip R. Davies (ed.), *Second Temple Studies 1: Persian Period*, *JSOT* Suppl. 117 (Sheffield Academic, 1991), 125–44.

Petterson, Anthony R. *Behold your King: The Hope for the House of David in the Book of Zechariah*, Library of Hebrew Bible/Old Testament Studies 513 (New York and London: T. & T. Clark, 2009).

Pietersma, Albert, and Benjamin G. Wright (eds.). *A New English Translation of the Septuagint and the Other Greek Translations Traditionally Included under that Title* (New York: Oxford University Press, 2007).

Polaski, Donald C. "*Mene, Mene, Tekel, Parsin*: Writing and Resistance in Daniel 5 and 6," *JBL* 123 (2004), 649–69.

Porten, Bezalel. "The Structure and Orientation of the Jewish Temple at Elephantine: A Revised Plan of the Jewish District," *JAOS* 81 (1961), 38–42.

　Archives from Elephantine: The Life of an Ancient Jewish Military Colony (Berkeley: University of California Press, 1968).

　"The Revised Draft of the Letter of Jedaniah to Bagavahya (TAD A4.8 = Cowley 31)," in Meir Lubetski, Claire Gottlieb, and Sharon Keller (eds.), *Boundaries of the Ancient World: A Tribute to Cyrus H. Gordon, JSOT* Suppl. 273 (Sheffield Academic, 1998), 230–42.

Price, Jonathan J. "Josephus and the Dialogue on the Destruction of the Temple," in Christfried Böttrich and Jens Herzer (eds.), *Josephus und das Neue Testament: Wechselseitige Wahrnehmungen. II. Internationales Symposium zum Corpus Judaeo-Hellenisticum, Mai 2006, Greifswald*, Wissenschaftliche Untersuchungen zum Neuen Testament 209 (Tübingen: Mohr Siebeck, 2007), 181–94.

"Some Aspects of Josephus' Theological Interpretation of the Jewish War," in Mauro Perani (ed.), *"The Words of a Wise Man's Mouth are Gracious" (Qoh 10,12): Festschrift for Günter Stemberger on the Occasion of his 65th Birthday*, Studia Judaica 32 (Berlin: De Gruyter, 2005), 109–19.

Qimron, Elisha, and John Strugnell. *Qumran Cave 4, V: Miqṣat Ma'aśe ha-Torah*, Discoveries in the Judean Desert 10 (Oxford: Clarendon, 1994).

Qimron, Elisha, John Strugnell, and Raphael Nir. פרקים בתולדות הלשון העברית (Tel Aviv: Open University, 2004).

Rabin, Chaim. "The Historical Background of Qumran Hebrew," in Chaim Rabin and Yigael Yadin (eds.), *Aspects of the Dead Sea Scrolls*, Scripta Hierosolymitana 4 (Jerusalem: Magnes, 1958), 144–61.

Rajak, Tessa. "The Angry Tyrant," in Tessa Rajak, Sarah Pearce, James Aitken, and Jennifer Dines (eds.), *Jewish Perspectives on Hellenistic Rulers* (Berkeley: University of California Press, 2007), 110–27.

Translation and Survival: The Greek Bible of the Ancient Jewish Diaspora (Oxford University Press, 2009).

Ramon, Orit. "'One Hundred and Twenty Seven Provinces': Political Reality, Political Thought, and Jewish Existence in Exile in Maharal's Commentary on the Book of Esther," *Judaica Bohemiae*, 46 (2011), 5–32.

Rappaport, Uriel. "3 Maccabees and the Jews of Egypt," *JQR* 99 (2009), 551–57.

Ratzaby, Yehuda. "מפירוש ר' סעדיה למגילת אסתר" in Shaul Yisraeli, Norman Lamm, and Isaac Rafael (eds.), ספר יובל לכבוד מורנו הגאון רבי יוסף דוב הלוי סולובייצ'יק (Jerusalem and New York: Mossad ha-Rav Kook and Yeshiva University, 1984), 1153–78.

"שרידים מפירוש ר' סעדיה למגילת אסתר," *Sinai*, 104 (1989), 193–214.

Raviv, Rivkah. "השפעתו של ספר דניאל על פרשנות המקרא של חז"ל," in Shmuel Vargon, Amos Frisch, and Moshe Rahimi (eds.), עיוני מקרא ופרשנות ח מנחת ידידות והוקרה לאלעזר טויטו (Ramat Gan and Elkanah: Bar Ilan University Press and Mikhlelet Orot, 2008), 97–118.

Reade, Julian. *Assyrian Sculpture* (Cambridge, MA: Harvard University Press, 1983).

Regev, Eyal. "Hanukkah and the Temple of the Maccabees: Ritual and Ideology from Judas Maccabeus to Simon," *JSQ* 15 (2008), 87–114.

"Herod's Jewish Ideology Facing Romanization: On Intermarriage, Ritual Baths, and Speeches," *JQR* 100 (2010), 202–06.

Retsö, Jan. *The Arabs in Antiquity: Their History from the Assyrians to the Umayyads* (New York: RoutledgeCurzon, 2003).

Rezetko, Robert. "Dating Biblical Hebrew: Evidence from Samuel-Kings and Chronicles," in Ian Young (ed.), *Biblical Hebrew: Studies in Chronology and Typology* (London: T. & T. Clark International, 2003), 215–50.

Richardson, Peter. *Herod: King of the Jews and Friend of the Romans* (Minneapolis: Fortress, 1999).

Rindge, Matthew. "Jewish Identity under Foreign Rule: Daniel 2 as a Reconfiguration of Genesis 41," *JBL* 129 (2010), 85–104.

Roitman, Adolpho, and Amnon Shapira. "ספר יהודית כסיפור-בבואה "מתקן" של מגילת אסתר," *Beit Mikra*, 49 (2004), 127–43.

Rom-Shiloni, Dalit. "Ezekiel as the Voice of the Exiles and Constructor of Exilic Ideology," *HUCA* 76 (2005), 1–45.

"Facing Destruction and Exile: Inner-Biblical Exegesis in Jeremiah and Ezekiel," *ZAW* 117 (2005), 189–205.

"Psalm 44: The Powers of Protest," *CBQ* 70 (2008), 683–98

"Deuteronomic Concepts of Exile Interpreted in Jeremiah and Ezekiel,"in Chaim Cohen, Victor Hurowitz, Avi Hurvitz, Yochanan Muffs, Baruch Schwartz, and Jeffrey Tigay (eds.), *Birkat Shalom: Studies in the Bible, Ancient Near Eastern Literature, and Postbiblical Judaism Presented to Shalom M. Paul on the Occasion of his Seventieth Birthday* (Winona Lake, IN: Eisenbrauns, 2008), 101–23.

אלהים בעידן של חורבן וגלויות: תיאולוגיה תנ"כית (Jerusalem: Magnes, 2009).

Rose, W. H. *Zemah and Zerubbabel: Messianic Expectations in the Early Postexilic Period, JSOT* Suppl. 304 (Sheffield Academic, 2000).

Rosenblum, Jordan D. "From their Bread to their Bed: Commensality, Intermarriage, and Idolatry in Tannaitic Literature," *JJS* 61 (2010), 18–29.

Food and Identity in Early Rabbinic Judaism (Cambridge University Press, 2010).

Rosenthal, L. A. "Die Josephgeschichte, mit den Büchern Ester und Daniel verglichen," *ZAW* 15 (1895), 278–84.

"Nochmals der Vergleich Ester, Joseph – Daniel," *ZAW* 17 (1897), 125–28.

Rubenstein, Jeffrey L. *Talmudic Stories: Narrative Art, Composition, and Culture* (Baltimore: Johns Hopkins University Press, 1999).

Rubin, Nissan. "זמן היסטורי וזמן לימינלי – פרק בהיסטוריוסופיה של חז"ל," *Jewish History*, 2 (1988), 7–22.

Rudman, Dominic. "Zechariah 8:20–22 & Isaiah 2:2–4/Micah 4:23: A Study in Intertextuality," *BN* 107–08 (2001), 50–54.

Sabar, Shalom. "The Purim Panel at Dura: A Socio-Historical Interpretation," in Lee I. Levine and Zeev Weiss (eds.), *From Dura to Sepphoris: Studies in Jewish Art and Society in Late Antiquity JRS* Suppl. 40 (Portsmouth, RI: Journal of Roman Studies, 2000), 154–63.

Safrai, Shmuel. "Relations between the Diaspora and the Land of Israel," in Shmuel Safrai and Menachem Stern in co-operation with David Flusser and W. C. van Unnik (eds.), *The Jewish People in the First Century: Historical Geography, Political History, Social, Cultural and Religious Life and Institutions,* CRINT 1.1 (Philadelphia: Fortress, 1974), 184–215.

Said, Edward. "Reflections on Exile," in *Reflections on Exile and Other Essays* (Cambridge, MA: Harvard University Press, 2002), 173–86.

Sanders, James A. "Canon: Old Testament," *ABD*, vol. 1, 838–52.

Schaper, Joachim. "Hebrew and its Study in the Persian Period," in William Horbury (ed.), *Hebrew and its Study from Ezra to Ben-Yehuda* (Edinburgh: T. & T. Clark, 1999), 15–26.

"The Pharisees," in William Horbury, W. D. Davies, and John Sturdy (eds.), *The Cambridge History of Judaism*, vol. III: *The Early Roman Period* (Cambridge University Press, 1999), 402–27.

Schellekens, Jona. "Accession Days and Holidays: The Origins of the Jewish Festival of Purim," *JBL* 128 (2009), 115–34.

Schiffman, Lawrence H. *Who Was a Jew? Rabbinic and Halakhic Perspectives on the Jewish–Christian Schism* (Hoboken, NJ: Ktav, 1985).

"Prohibited Marriages in the Dead Sea Scrolls and Rabbinic Literature," in Steven D. Fraade, Aharon Shemesh, and Ruth A. Clements (eds.), *Rabbinic Perspectives: Rabbinic Literature and the Dead Sea Scrolls*, STDJ 62 (Leiden: Brill, 2006), 113–25.

"Temple, Sacrifice and Priesthood in the Epistle to the Hebrews and the Dead Sea Scrolls," in Florentino García Martínez (ed.), *Echoes from the Caves: Qumran and the New Testament* (Leiden: Brill, 2009), 165–76.

Schmid, Herbert. "Die 'Juden' im Alten Testament," in Brigitta Benzing, Otto Böcher, and Günter Maye (eds.), *Wort und Wirklichkeit:Studien zur Afrikanistik und Orientalistik, Eugen Ludwig Rapp zum 70. Geburtstag*, vol. 1: Geschichte und Religionswissenschaft – Bibliographie (Meisenheim am Glan: Anton Hain, 1976), 17–29.

Schmitt, Rüdiger, "Artaxerxes," in *Encyclopædia Iranica*, www.iranicaonline.org/articles/artaxerxes-throne-name-of-several-persian-kings-of-the-achaemenid-dynasty (accessed May, 2012).

"Dāta," in *Encyclopædia Iranica*, www.iranicaonline.org/articles/data (accessed February, 2013).

Schniedewind, William M. "'Are We His People or Not?' Biblical Interpretation during Crisis," *Biblica*, 76 (1995), 540–50.

Schonfield, Jeremy. "Esther: Beyond Murder," *European Judaism*, 32 (1999), 11–25.

Schremer, Adiel. "'The Lord has Forsaken the Land': Radical Explanations of the Military and Political Defeat of the Jews in Tannaitic Literature," *JJS* 59 (2008), 183–200.

Schwartz, Baruch J. "Ezekiel's Dim View of Israel's Restoration," in Maragret S. Odell and John T. Strong (eds.), *The Book of Ezekiel: Theological and Anthropological Perspectives*, SBL Symposium Series 9 (Atlanta: SBL, 2000), 43–67.

Schwartz, Daniel R. *Studies in the Jewish Background of Christianity*, Wissenschaftliche Untersuchungen zum Neuen Testament 60 (Tübingen: J. C. B. Mohr (P. Siebeck), 1992).

"How at Home were the Jews of the Hellenistic Diaspora?," *Classical Philology*, 95 (2000), 349–57.

2 Maccabees, CEJL (Berlin: De Gruyter, 2008).

ספר מקבים ב : מבוא, תרגום, ופירוש (Jerusalem: Yad Yitzhak Ben Zvi, 2004).

Schwartz, Seth. "Israel and the Nations Roundabout: 1 Maccabees and the Hasmonean Expansion," *JJS* 42 (1991), 16–38.

"Language, Power and Identity in Ancient Palestine," *Past & Present*, 148 (1995), 3–47.

Schwartzmann, Julia. "The Book of Esther – A Case Study of Ideological Interpretation," *Shofar*, 29 (2011), 124–47.

Secunda, Shai. "'Dashtana-Ki Derekh Nashim Li': A Study of Babylonian Rabbinic Laws of Menstruation in Relation to Corresponding Zoroastrian Texts," unpublished Ph.D. dissertation (Yeshiva University, 2007).

"Talmudic Text and Iranian Context: On the Development of Two Talmudic Narratives," *AJS Review*, 33 (2009), 40–70.

Seeman, Chris. "Enter the Dragon: Mordecai as Agonistic Combatant in Greek Esther," *Biblical Theology Bulletin*, 41 (2011), 3–15.

Segal, Eliezer. "'The Same from Beginning to End': On the Development of a Midrashic Homily," *JJS* 32 (1981), 158–65.

The Babylonian Esther Midrash: A Critical Commentary, 3 vols., Brown Judaic Studies 291–93 (Atlanta: Scholars, 1994).

From Sermon to Commentary: Expounding the Bible in Talmudic Babylonia, Études sur le christianisme et le judaïsme 17 (Waterloo, Ontario: Wilfrid Laurier University Press for the Canadian Corporation for Studies in Religion, 2005).

Segal, M. H. *Grammar of Mishnaic Hebrew* (Oxford: Clarendon, 1927).

Segal, Michael. "From Joseph to Daniel: The Literary Development of the Narrative in Daniel 2," *VT* 59 (2009), 123–49.

"The Chronological Conception of the Persian Period in Daniel 9," *JAJ* 2 (2011), 283–303.

Sharp, Carolyn B. *Irony and Meaning in the Hebrew Bible*, Indiana Studies in Biblical Literature (Bloomington: Indiana University Press, 2009).

Sherman, Miriam. "Do Not Interpretations Belong to God? A Narrative Assessment of Genesis 40 as it Elucidates the Persona of Joseph," in *Milk and Honey: Essays on Ancient Israel and the Bible in Appreciation of the Judaic Studies Program at the University of California, San Diego* (Winona Lake, IN: Eisenbrauns, 2007), 37–49.

Shupak, Nili. "A Fresh Look at the Dreams of the Officials and of Pharaoh in the Story of Joseph (Genesis 40–41) in the Light of Egyptian Dreams," *JANES* 30 (2006), 103–38.

Silverstein, Adam. "The Book of Esther and the Enūma elish," *Bulletin of the School of Oriental and African Studies*, 69 (2006), 209–23.

Simkovitch, Malka Zeiger. "Greek Influence on the Composition of 2 Maccabees," *JSJ* 42 (2011), 293–310.

Slivniak, Dmitri M. "The Book of Esther: The Making and Unmaking of Jewish Identity," in Yvonne Sherwood (ed.), *Derrida's Bible (Reading a Page of*

Scripture with a Little Help from Derrida) (New York: Palgrave Macmillan, 2004), 135–48.

Smith, Mark S. *The Origins and Development of the Waw-Consecutive: Northwest Semitic Evidence from Ugarit to Qumran*, HSS 39 (Atlanta: Scholars, 1991).

Smith, Morton. *Palestinian Parties and Politics that Shaped the Old Testament* (New York: Columbia University Press, 1971).

Smith-Christopher, Daniel L. "The Politics of Ezra: Sociological Indicators of Postexilic Judaean Society," in Philip R. Davies (ed.), *Second Temple Studies 1: Persian Period, JSOT* Suppl. 117 (Sheffield Academic, 1991), 73–97.

"The Mixed Marriage Crisis in Ezra 9–10 and Nehemiah 13: A Study of the Sociology of Post-Exilic Judaean Community," in Tamara C. Eskenazi and Kent H. Richards (eds.), *Second Temple Studies 2: Temple Community in the Persian Period, JSOT* Suppl. 175 (Sheffield Academic, 1994), 243–95.

"Reassessing the Historical and Sociological Impact of the Babylonian Exile (597/587–539 BCE)," in James M. Scott (ed.), *Exile: Old Testament, Jewish, and Christian Conceptions, JSJ* Suppl. 56 (Leiden: Brill, 1997), 7–36.

"Prayers and Dreams: Power and Diaspora Identities in the Social Setting of the Daniel Tales," in John J. Collins and Peter W. Flint (eds.), *The Book of Daniel: Composition and Reception, VT* Suppl. 83.1 (Leiden: Brill, 2001), 266–90.

Solvang, Elna K. "The First Orientalist? Fantasy and Foreignness in the Book of Esther," in Steven Holloway, JoAnn Scurlock, and Richard Beal (eds.), *In the Wake of Tikva Frymer-Kensky*, Gorgias Précis Portfolios 4 (Piscataway, NJ: Gorgias, 2009), 199–213.

Southwood, Katherine E. "'And They Could Not Understand Jewish Speech': Language, Ethnicity, and Nehemiah's Intermarriage Crisis," *JTS* 62 (2011), 1–19.

Spencer, Richard A. "The Book of Tobit in Modern Research," *Currents in Research: Biblical Studies*, 7 (1999), 147–80.

Steiner, Richard C. "*The mbqr* at Qumran, the *Episkopos* in the Athenian Empire, and the Meaning of *lbqr'* in Ezra 7:14: On the Relation of Ezra's Mission to the Persian Legal Project," *JBL* 120 (2001), 623–46.

"Bishlam's Archival Search Report in Nehemiah's Archive: Multiple Introductions and Reverse Chronological Order as Clues to the Origin of the Aramaic Letters in Ezra 4–6," *JBL* 125 (2006), 641–85.

"Why Bishlam (Ezra 4:7) cannot Rest 'in Peace': On the Aramaic and Hebrew Sound Changes that Conspired to Blot out the Remembrance of Bel-Shalam the Archivist," *JBL* 126 (2007), 390–401.

Early Northwest Semitic Serpent Spells in the Pyramid Texts, HSS 61 (Winona Lake, IN: Eisenbrauns, 2011).

Stemberger, Günter. "Midrasch in Babylonien, am Beispiel von Sota 9b–14a," *Henoch*, 10 (1988), 183–203.

Stern, Elsie R. "Esther and the Politics of Diaspora," *JQR* 100 (2010), 25–53.

Stern, Menachem. "The Jewish Diaspora," in Shmuel Safrai and Menachem Stern in co-operation with David Flusser and W. C. van Unnik (eds.), *The Jewish People in the First Century: Historical Geography, Political History, Social,*

Cultural and Religious Life and Institutions, CRINT 1.1 (Philadelphia: Fortress, 1974), 17–83.

Stern, Sacha. "Attribution and Authorship in the Babylonian Talmud," *JJS* 45 (1994), 28–51.

Strauch-Schick, Shana. "Intention in the Babylonian Talmud," unpublished Ph.D. dissertation (Yeshiva University, 2011).

Sweeney, Marvin A. "The Critique of Solomon in the Josianic Edition of the Deuteronomistic History," *JBL* 114 (1995), 607–22.

Tabory, Joseph. "התקופה הפרסית בעיני חז"ל," *Millēt*, 2 (1984), 65–77. מועדי ישראל בתקופת המשנה והתלמוד (Jerusalem: Magnes, 1995).

"פתיחות רב ושמואל למדרש 'מגילת אסתר'," in David Golinkin, Moshe Benovitz, Mordechai Akiva Friedman, Menachem Schmelzer, and Daniel Sperber (eds.), *Torah Li-Shma: Essays in Jewish Studies in Honor of Professor Shamma Friedman* (Jerusalem: Bar Ilan University Press, Jewish Theological Seminary of America, and Mekhon Schechter, 2008), 481–99.

"השפעת תרגום השבעים למגילת אסתר על הספרות הרבנית," *Sidra*, 24–25 (2010), 485–502.

Tadmor, Hayim. "The Aramaization of Assyria: Aspects of Western Impact," in H.-J. Nissen and J. Renger (eds.), *Mesopotamien und seine Nachbarn: Politische und kulturelle Wechselbeziehungen im alten Vorderasien vom 4. bis 1. Jt. v. Chr.* (Berlin: Dietrich Reimer, 1987), 449–70.

"On the Role of Aramaic in the Assyrian Empire," in Masao Mori, Hideo Ogawa, Mamoru Yoshikawa (eds.), *Near Eastern Studies Dedicated to H.I.H. Prince Takahito Mikasa on the Occasion of his Seventy-Fifth Birthday* (Wiesbaden: O. Harrassowitz, 1991), 419–35.

"'The Appointed Time has not yet Arrived': The Historical Background of Haggai 1:2," in Robert Chazan, William W. Hallo, and Lawrence H. Schiffman (eds.), *Ki Baruch Hu: Ancient Near Eastern, Biblical, and Judaic Studies in Honor of Baruch A. Levine* (Winona Lake, IN: Eisenbrauns, 1999), 401–08.

Tal, Avraham. "קטעי תרגום אסתר מן הגניזה והעדות שהם מעידים," in Moshe Bar-Asher and Hayyim E. Cohen (eds.), *Mas'at Ahron: Studies Presented to Ahron Dotan* (Jerusalem: Bialik, 2010), 139–71.

Talmon, Shemaryahu. "Wisdom in the Book of Esther," *VT* 13 (1963), 419–55. "שיבת ציון – השלכותיה לעתיד," *Cathedra*, 4 (1977), 26–30.

"Was the Book of Esther Known at Qumran?," *DSD* 2 (1995), 249–67.

Tawil, Dalia. "The Purim Panel in Dura in the Light of Parthian and Sasanian Art," *JNES* 38 (1979), 93–109.

Tawil, Hayim. "Hebrew נָפַץ יַד = Akkadian *qāta napāṣu*: A Term of Non-Allegiance," *JAOS* 122 (2002), 79–82.

Testen, David. "Semitic Terms for 'Myrtle': A Study in Covert Cognates," *JNES* 57 (1998), 281–90.

Theodor, Julius, and Hanokh Albeck. מדרש בראשית רבא: על פי כתבי יד ועל'י דפוסי..י דפוסי המדרש הראשונים הראשונים, 3 vols. (Berlin: Itskovski, 1912–29, reprinted Jerusalem: Wahrmann, 1965).

Torrey, C. C. Review of A. E. Brooke, Norman McLean, and H. St. John Thackeray (eds.), *The Old Testament in Greek*, *JBL* 61 (1942), 130–36.

"The Older Book of Esther," *HTR* 37 (1944), 1–40.

Tov, Emanuel. "The 'Lucianic' Text of the Canonical and the Apocryphal Sections of Esther: A Rewritten Biblical Book," *Textus*, 10 (1982), 1–25, revised in Emanuel Tov, *The Greek and Hebrew Bible: Collected Essays on the Septuagint*, *VT* Suppl. 72 (Leiden: Brill, 1999), vol. 1, 535–48.

"The LXX Translation of Esther: A Paraphrastic Translation of MT or a Free Translation of a Rewritten Version?," in Alberdina Houtman, Albert de Jong, and Magda Misset-van de Weg (eds.), *Empsychoi Logoi – Religious Innovations in Antiquity: Studies in Honour of Pieter Willem van der Horst* (Leiden: Brill, 2008), 507–26.

"Three Strange Books of the LXX: 1 Kings, Esther, and Daniel Compared with Similar Rewritten Compositions from Qumran and Elsewhere," in Martin Karrer and Wolfgang Kraus; (eds.), *Die Septuaginta – Texte, Kontexte, Lebenswelten: Internationale Fachtagung veranstaltet von Septuaginta Deutsch (LXX.D), Wuppertal 20.–23. Juli 2006* (Tübingen: Mohr Siebeck, 2008), 369–93.

Tuell, Steven S. "The Priesthood of the 'Foreigner': Evidence of Competing Polities in Ezekiel 44:1–14 and Isaiah 56:1–8," in John T. Strong and Steven S. Tuell (eds.), *Constituting the Community: Studies on the Polity of Ancient Israel in Honor of S. Dean McBride Jr.* (Winona Lake, IN: Eisenbrauns, 2005), 183–204.

Ulrich, Eugene C. "The Notion and Definition of Canon," in Lee Martin McDonald and James A. Sanders (eds.), *The Canon Debate* (Peabody, MA: Hendrickson Publishers, 2002), 21–35.

"Qumran and the Canon of the Old Testament," in J.-M. Auwers and H. J. de Jonge (eds.), *The Biblical Canons*, Bibliotheca Ephemeridum theologicarum Lovaniensium 163 (Leuven: Leuven University Press and Peeters, 2003), 57–80.

VanderKam, James C. "Authoritative Literature in the Dead Sea Scrolls," *DSD* 5 (1998), 382–402.

van der Walt, C. P. "The Prayers of Esther (LXX) and Judith Against their Social Backgrounds – Evidence of a Possible Common *Grundlage*," *Journal for Semitics* = *Tydskrif vir Semitistiek*, 17 (2008), 194–206.

van Henten, Jan Willem. *The Maccabean Martyrs as Saviours of the Jewish People*, *JSJ* Suppl. 57 (Leiden: Brill, 1997).

Van Seters, John. "The Joseph Story – Some Basic Observations," in J.-M. Auwers and H. J. de Jonge (eds.), *Egypt, Israel, and the Mediterranean World: Studies in Honor of Donald B. Redford* (Leiden: Brill, 2004), 361–88.

"The Pharisees and the Dead Sea Scrolls," in Jacob Neusner and Bruce D. Chilton (eds.), *In Quest of the Historical Pharisees* (Waco, TX: Baylor University Press, 2007), 225–36.

von Weissenberg, Hanne. "'Canon' and Identity at Qumran: An Overview and Challenges for Future Research," in Anssi Voitila and Jutta Jokiranta (eds.), *Scripture in Transition: Essays on Septuagint, Hebrew Bible, and Dead Sea*

Scrolls in Honour of Raija Sollamamo, JSJ Suppl. 126 (Leiden and Boston: Brill, 2008), 629–40.

Wahl, Harald Martin. "'Jahwe, wo bist Du?' Gott, Glaube, und Gemeinde in Esther," *JJS* 31 (2000), 1–22.

Wahl, Harald Martin. "Die Sprache des hebräischen Esterbuches, mit Anmerkungen zu seinem historischen und traditionsgeschichtlichen Referenzrahmen," *Zeitschrift für Althebraistik*, 12 (1999), 21–47.

Walfish, Barry Dov. "Kosher Adultery? The Mordecai-Esther-Ahasuerus Triangle in Midrash and Exegesis," *Prooftexts*, 22 (2002), 305–33.

Wechsler, Michael G. "Shadow and Fulfillment in the Book of Esther," *Bibliotheca sacra*, 154 (1997), 275–84.

"The Purim-Passover Connection: A Reflection of Jewish Exegetical Tradition in the Peshitta Book of Esther," *JBL* 117 (1998), 321–35.

"The Appelation BOUGAIOS and Ethnic Contextualization in the Greek Text of Esther," *VT* 51 (2001), 109–14.

"An Early Karaite Commentary on the Book of Esther," *HUCA* 72 (2001), 101–37.

Strangers in the Land: The Judaeo-Arabic Exegesis of Tanhum ha-Yerushalmi on the Books of Ruth and Esther (Jerusalem: Magnes, 2010).

Weiss, Avraham. על היצירה הספרותית של האמוראים (New York: 'Horev' Yeshiva University, 1962).

Weitzman, Steven. "Forced Circumcision and the Shifting Role of Gentiles in Hasmonean Ideology," *HTR* 92 (1999), 37–59.

Surviving Sacrilege: Cultural Persistence in Jewish Antiquity (Cambridge, MA: Harvard University Press, 2005).

Werman, Cana. "Epochs and End-Time: The 490 Year Scheme in Second Temple Literature," *DSD* 13 (2006), 229–55.

Wetter, Anne-Marie. "How Jewish is Esther? Or: How is Esther Jewish? Tracing Ethnic and Religious Identity in a Diaspora Narrative," *ZAW* 123 (2011), 596–603.

Wharton, Annabel Jane. "Good and Bad Images from the Synagogue of Dura Europos: Contexts, Subtexts, Intertexts," *Art History*, 17 (1994), 1–25.

Refiguring the Post Classical City: Dura Europos, Jerash, Jerusalem and Ravenna (Cambridge University Press, 1995).

Whedbee, William. *The Bible and the Comic Vision* (Cambridge University Press, 2008).

White, Sidnie Ann. "Esther, a Feminine Model for Jewish Diaspora," in Peggy L. Day (ed.), *Gender and Difference in Ancient Israel* (Minneapolis: Fortress, 1989), 161–77.

See also Crawford, Sidnie White.

Whitters, Mark W. "Martyrdom as Cultic Death in the Books of Maccabees: Antecedents and Later Developments," in Jeremy Corley and Vincent Skemp (eds.), *Studies in the Greek Bible: Essays in Honor of Francis T. Gignac, S.J.*, CBQMS 44 (Washington, DC: Catholic Biblical Association, 2008), 97–119.

Wildavsky, Aaron. *Assimilation versus Separation: Joseph the Administrator and the Politics of Administration in Biblical Israel* (New Brunswick and London: Transaction, 1993).

Willi-Plein, Ina. "Problems of Intermarriage in Postexilic Times," in Moshe Bar-Asher, Dalit Rom-Shiloni, Emanuel Tov, and Nili Wazana (eds.), *Shai le-Sara Japhet: Studies in the Bible, its Exegesis and its Language* (Jerusalem: Bialik, 2007), 177–89.

Willis, Joyce, Andrew Pleffer, and Steven Llewelyn. "Conversation in the Succession Narrative of Solomon," *VT* 61 (2011), 133–47.

Wills, Lawrence M. *The Jew in the Court of the Foreign King: Ancient Jewish Court Legends*, Harvard Dissertations in Religion 26 (Minneapolis: Fortress, 1990).

Winitzer, Abraham. "The Reversal of Fortune Theme in Esther: Israelite Historiography in its Ancient Near Eastern Context," *Journal of Ancient Near Eastern Religions,* 11 (2011), 170–218.

Wrangham, Richard W. *Catching Fire: How Cooking Made us Human* (New York: Basic, 2009).

James Holland Jones, Greg Laden, David Pilbeam, and NancyLou Conklin-Brittain. "The Raw and the Stolen: Cooking and the Ecology of Human Origins," *Current Anthropology*, 40 (1999), 567–77.

Wright, Jacob L. *Rebuilding Identity: The Nehemiah-Memoir and its Earliest Readers*, BZAW 348 (Berlin: De Gruyter, 2004).

Yahalom, Joseph, and Michael Sokoloff. שירת בני מערבא: שירים ארמיים של יהודי ארץ ישראל בתקופה הביזנטית (Jerusalem: Israel Academy of Sciences and Humanities, 1999).

Young, Ian. "Is the Prose Tale of Job in Late Biblical Hebrew?" *VT* 59 (2009), 606–29.

Zadok, Ran. "Notes on Esther," *ZAW* 98 (1986), 105–10.

The Earliest Diaspora: Israelites and Judeans in Pre-Hellenistic Mesopotamia, Publications of the Diaspora Research Institute 151 (Tel Aviv: Diaspora Research Institute of Tel Aviv University, 2002).

Zalcman, Lawrence. "The Eternal City: Rome or Jerusalem?," *JJS* 48 (1997), 312–13

Zevit, Ziony. "Dating Ruth: Legal, Linguistic, and Historical Observations," *ZAW* 117 (2005), 588–89.

"Is there an Archaeological Case for Phantom Settlements in the Persian Period?," *Palestine Exploration Quarterly,* 141 (2009), 124–37.

Zipor, Moshe A. "When Midrash met Septuagint: The Case of Esther 2,7," *ZAW* 118 (2006), 82–92.

תלמוד ירושלמי: יוצא לאור על פי כתב יד סקליגר 3 שבספריית האוניברסיטה של ליידן עם השלמות ותיקונים," *Bet Miqra*, 56 (2011), 58–70.

Zlotnick-Sivan, Hagith. "The Silent Women of Yehud: Notes on Ezra 9–10," *JJS* 51 (2000), 3–18.

תלמוד ירושלמי: יוצא לאור על פי כתב יד סקליגר שבספריית האוניברסיטה של ליידן עם השלמות ותיקונים , introduction by Yaakov Sussmann (Jerusalem: Academy for the Hebrew Language, 2001).

Index